THE KEY
STUDENT STUDY GUIDE

11 Functions and Applications
...ity/College Preparation (MCF3M)

THE KEY student study guide is designed to help students achieve success in school. The content in each study guide is 100% curriculum aligned and serves as an excellent source of material for review and practice. To create this book, teachers, curriculum specialists, and assessment experts have worked closely to develop the instructional pieces that explain each of the key concepts for the course. The practice questions and sample tests have detailed solutions that show problem-solving methods, highlight concepts that are likely to be tested, and point out potential sources of errors. **THE KEY** is a complete guide to be used by students throughout the school year for reviewing and understanding course content, and to prepare for assessments.

Rao, Gautam, 1961 –
THE KEY –Math 11 – Functions and Applications
　　　　Ontario

　　1.　Mathematics – Juvenile Literature. I. Title

Published by
Castle Rock Research Corp.
2340 Manulife Place
10180 – 101 Street
Edmonton, AB T5J 3S4

　　5　6　7　FP　13　12　11

Publisher
Gautam Rao

Contributors
Jasmin Benavides
Monica Dhamrait
Bob Frizzell
Katie Pallos-Haden
Ted Whyte
Rob Zukowski

Dedicated to the memory of Dr. V. S. Rao

THE KEY – Math 11
Functions and Applications

THE KEY consists of the following sections:

KEY Tips for Being Successful at School gives examples of study and review strategies. It includes information about learning styles, study schedules, and note taking for test preparation.

Class Focus includes a unit on each area of the curriculum. Units are divided into sections, each focusing on one of the specific expectations, or main ideas, that students must learn about in that unit. Examples, definitions, and visuals help to explain each main idea. Practice questions on the main ideas are also included. At the end of each unit is a test on the important ideas covered. The practice questions and unit tests help students identify areas they know and those they need to study more. They can also be used as preparation for tests and quizzes. Most questions are of average difficulty, though some are easy and some are hard—the harder questions are called *Challenger Questions*. Each unit is prefaced by a **Table of Correlations**, which correlates questions in the unit (and in the practice tests at the end of the book) to the specific curriculum expectations. Answers and solutions are found at the end of each unit.

KEY Strategies for Success on Tests helps students get ready for tests. It shows students different types of questions they might see, word clues to look for when reading them, and hints for answering them.

Practice Tests includes one to three tests based on the entire course. They are very similar to the format and level of difficulty that students may encounter on final tests. In some regions, these tests may be reprinted versions of official tests, or reflect the same difficulty levels and formats as official versions. This gives students the chance to practice using real-world examples. Answers and complete solutions are provided at the end of the section.

For the complete curriculum document (including specific expectations along with examples and sample problems), visit www.edu.gov.on.ca/eng/curriculum/secondary).

THE KEY *Study Guides* are available for many courses.
Check www.castlerockresearch.com for a complete listing of books available for your area.

For information about any of our resources or services, please call Castle Rock Research at 905.625.3332 or visit our website at http://www.castlerockresearch.com.

At Castle Rock Research, we strive to produce an error-free resource. If you should find an error, please contact us so that future editions can be corrected.

CONTENTS

KEY Tips for Being Successful at School

KEY FACTORS CONTRIBUTING TO SCHOOL SUCCESS

In addition to learning the contents of your courses, there are some other things that you can do to help you do your best at school. Some of these strategies are listed below.

- **ATTEND SCHOOL REGULARLY** so you do not miss any classes, notes, or important activities that will help you learn.

- **KEEP A POSITIVE ATTITUDE.** Always reflect on what you can already do and what you already know.

- **BE PREPARED TO LEARN.** Have the necessary materials (pencils, pens, notebooks, and other required materials) with you in class.

- **COMPLETE ALL OF YOUR ASSIGNMENTS.** Do your best to finish all of your assignments. Even if you know the material well, practice will reinforce your knowledge. If an assignment or question is difficult for you, work through it as far as you can so your teacher can see exactly where you are having difficulty.

- **SET SMALL GOALS** for yourself when you are learning new material. For example, when learning formulas, do not try to learn everything in one night. Work on only one formula each study session. When you understand one particular formula and have memorized it, move on to another one. Continue this process until you have learned and memorized all of the required formulas.

- **REVIEW YOUR CLASSROOM WORK** regularly at home to be sure you understand the material you learned in class.

- **ASK YOUR TEACHER FOR HELP** when you do not understand something or when you are having difficulty completing your assignments.

- **GET PLENTY OF REST AND EXERCISE.** Concentrating in class is hard work. It is important to be well-rested and have time to relax and socialize with your friends. This helps you to keep a positive attitude about your school work.

- **EAT HEALTHY MEALS.** A balanced diet keeps you healthy and gives you the energy you need for studying at school and at home.

HOW TO FIND YOUR LEARNING STYLE

Every student has a certain manner in which it seems easier for him or her to learn. The manner in which you learn best is called your learning style. By knowing your learning style, you can increase your success at school. Most students use a combination of learning styles.

Do you know what type of learner you are? Read the following descriptions. Which of these common learning styles do you use most often?

- **Do you need to say things out loud?** You may learn best by saying, hearing, and seeing words. You are probably really good at memorizing dates, places, names, and facts. To learn the steps in a process, a formula, or the actions that lead up to a significant event, you may need **to write them and then read them out loud**.

- **Do you need to read or see things?** You may learn best by looking at and working with pictures. You are probably really good at puzzles, imagining things, and reading maps and charts. You may need to use strategies like **mind mapping and webbing** to organize your information and study notes.

- **Do you need to draw or write things down?** You may learn best by touching, moving, and figuring things out using manipulatives. You are probably really good at physical activities and learning through movement. You may need to **draw your finger over a diagram** to remember it, *tap out* **the steps** needed to solve a problem, or *feel* **yourself writing** or typing a formula.

SCHEDULING STUDY TIME

You should review your class notes regularly to be sure you have a clear understanding of all the new material you learned. Reviewing your lessons on a regular basis helps you to learn and remember ideas and concepts. It also reduces the quantity of material you need to study prior to a test. Creating a study schedule will help you to make the best use of your time.

Regardless of the type of study schedule you use, you may want to consider the following strategies for making the most of your study time and effort:

- Organize your work so you begin with the most challenging material first.
- Divide the subject content into small, manageable chunks.
- Alternate regularly between your different subjects and types of study activities in order to maintain your interest and motivation.
- Make a daily list with the headings *must do*, *should do*, and *could do*.
- Begin each study session by quickly reviewing what you studied the day before.
- Maintain your usual routine of eating, sleeping, and exercising to help you concentrate better for extended periods of time.

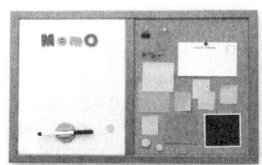

CREATING STUDY NOTES

MIND-MAPPING OR WEBBING

- Use the key words, ideas, or concepts from your class notes to create a *mind map* or *mind web*, which is a diagram or visual representation of the given information. A mind map or web is sometimes referred to as a *knowledge map*.

- Write the key word, concept, theory, or formula in the centre of your page.

- Write down related facts, ideas, events, and information and then link them to the central concept.

- The following examples of a Frayer Model illustrate how this technique can be used to study mathematical vocabulary.

Definition – Perimeter is the distance around a polygon	**Characteristics** – Measured in linear units (e.g., metres, centimetres)	**Definition** A cube is a solid 3-D object that has – 6 square faces, all equal in size – 8 vertices – 12 equal edges	**Visual Presentation**
Perimeter		**Cube**	
Examples – Fence around a yard – Distance around a circle (circumference)	**Non-examples** – Grass covering a yard – Area of rug covering a floor	**Characteristics or Properties** – 6 square faces – 8 vertices – 12 edges – 6 flat faces	**Examples**

INDEX CARDS

To use index cards while studying, follow these steps:

• Write a key word or question on one side of an index card.

• On the other side, write the definition of the word, answer to the question, or any other important information you want to remember.

> **What is a prime number?**

> **What is a prime number?**
>
> A prime number is a number that has exactly 2 factors. A prime number can be divided evenly only by itself and one. E.g., 2, 3, 5, 7, 17, 19. The number 1 is not a prime number.

SYMBOLS AND STICKY NOTES—IDENTIFYING IMPORTANT INFORMATION

• Use symbols to mark your class notes. For example, an exclamation mark (!) might be used to point out something that must be learned well because it is a very important idea. A question mark (?) may highlight something you are not certain about, and a diamond (◊) or asterisk (*) could mark interesting information you want to remember.

• Use sticky notes to mark a page in a book that contains an important diagram, formula, or explanation.

KEY Strategies for Reviewing

Reviewing textbook material, class notes, and handouts should be an ongoing activity. Spending time reviewing becomes more critical when you are preparing for tests. You may find some of the following review strategies useful when studying during your scheduled study time.

- Before reviewing a unit, note the headings, charts, graphs, and chapter questions.
- Highlight mathematical key concepts, vocabulary, definitions, and formulas.
- Carefully read over each step in a procedure.
- Draw a picture or diagram to help make the concept clearer.

KEY Strategies for Success—A Checklist

Review, review, review: that is a huge part of doing well at school and preparing for tests. Below is a checklist for you to keep track of how many suggested strategies for success you use. Read each question and then put a check mark (✓) in the correct column. Look at the questions for which you have checked the *No* column. Think about how you might try using some of these strategies to help you do your best at school.

KEY Strategies for Success	Yes	No
Do you attend school regularly?		
Do you know your personal learning style—how you learn best?		
Do you spend 15 to 30 minutes each day reviewing your notes?		
Do you study in a quiet place at home?		
Do you clearly mark the most important ideas in your study notes?		
Do you use sticky notes to mark texts and research books?		
Do you practice answering multiple-choice and written-response questions?		
Do you ask your teacher for help when you need it?		
Do you maintain a healthy diet and sleep routine?		
Do you participate in regular physical activity?		

Quadratic Functions

Quadratic Functions

Table of Correlations

Specific Expectation	Practice Questions	Unit Test Questions
QF1.0 Solving Quadratic Equations		
QF1.1 *pose problems involving quadratic relations arising from real-world applications and represented by tables of values and graphs, and solve these and other such problems*	1, 2	1a, 1b
QF1.2 *represent situations using quadratic expressions in one variable, and expand and simplify quadratic expressions in one variable*	3a, 3b, 4, 5	2, 3
QF1.3 *factor quadratic expressions in one variable, including those for which $a \neq 1$, differences of squares, and perfect square trinomials, by selecting and applying an appropriate strategy*	6, 7	4, 5
QF1.4 *solve quadratic equations by selecting and applying a factoring strategy*	8, 9	6, 7
QF1.5 *determine, through investigation, and describe the connection between the factors used in solving a quadratic equation and the x-intercepts of the graph of the corresponding quadratic relation*	10, 11	8, 9a, 9b, 9c
QF1.6 *explore the algebraic development of the quadratic formula and apply the formula to solve quadratic equations, using technology*	12, 13	10, 11
QF1.7 *relate the real roots of a quadratic equation to the x-intercepts of the corresponding graph, and connect the number of real roots to the value of the discriminant*	14, 15	12
QF1.8 *determine the real roots of a variety of quadratic equations and describe the advantages and disadvantages of each strategy (i.e., graphing; factoring; using the quadratic formula)*	16, 17	13, 14, 15
QF2.0 Connecting Graphs and Equations of Quadratic Functions		
QF2.1 *explain the meaning of the term function, and distinguish a function from a relation that is not a function, through investigation of linear and quadratic relations using a variety of representations (i.e., tables of values, mapping diagrams, graphs, function machines, equations) and strategies*	18a, 18b	16, 17
QF2.2 *substitute into and evaluate linear and quadratic functions represented using function notation, including functions arising from real-world applications*	19a, 19b	18a, 18b
QF2.3 *explain the meanings of the terms domain and range, through investigation using numeric, graphical, and algebraic representations of linear and quadratic functions, and describe the domain and range of a function appropriately*	20, 21	19, 20
QF2.4 *explain any restrictions on the domain and the range of a quadratic function in contexts arising from real-world applications*	22a, 22b	21a, 21b
QF2.5 *determine, through investigation using technology, the roles of a, h, and k in quadratic functions of the form $f(x) = a(x - h)^2 + k$, and describe these roles in terms of transformations on the graph of $f(x) = x^2$ (i.e., translations; reflections in the x-axis; vertical stretches and compressions to and from the x-axis)*	23, 24	22, 23
QF2.6 *sketch graphs of $g(x) = a(x - h)^2 + k$, by applying one or more transformations to the graph of $f(x) = x^2$*	25, 26	24a, 24b
QF2.7 *express the equation of a quadratic function in the standard form $f(x) = ax^2 + bx + c$, given the vertex form $f(x) = a(x - h)^2 + k$, and verify, using graphing technology, that these forms are equivalent representations*	27, 28	25, 26

	Specific Expectation	Practice Questions	Unit Test Questions
QF2.8	*express the equation of a quadratic function in the vertex form $f(x) = a(x - h)^2 + k$, given the standard form $f(x) = ax^2 + bx + c$, by completing the square, including cases where $\frac{b}{a}$ is a simple rational number, and verify, using graphing technology, that these forms are equivalent representations*	29, 30	27, 28a, 28b, 28c
QF2.9	*sketch graphs of quadratic functions in the factored form $f(x) = a(x - r)(x - s)$ by using the x-intercepts to determine the vertex*	31, 32	29, 30
QF2.10	*describe the information that can be obtained by inspecting the standard form $f(x) = ax^2 + bx + c$, the vertex form $f(x) = a(x - h)^2 + k$, and the factored form $f(x) = a(x - r)(x - s)$ of a quadratic function*	33, 34	31, 32
QF2.11	*sketch the graph of a quadratic function whose equation is given in the standard form $f(x) = ax^2 + bx + c$ by using a suitable strategy, and identify the key features of the graph*	35, 36a, 36b	33a, 33b
QF3.0	Solving Problems Involving Quadratic Functions		
QF3.1	*collect data that can be modelled as a quadratic function, through investigation with and without technology, from primary sources, using a variety of tools, or from secondary sources, and graph the data*	37a, 37b, 37c, 37d	34a, 34b, 34c, 34d
QF3.2	*determine, through investigation using a variety of strategies, the equation of the quadratic function that best models a suitable data set graphed on a scatter plot, and compare this equation to the equation of a curve of best fit generated with technology*		
QF3.3	*solve problems arising from real-world applications, given the algebraic representation of a quadratic function*	38a, 38b, 38c	35

QF1.1 *pose problems involving quadratic relations arising from real-world applications and represented by tables of values and graphs, and solve these and other such problems*

SOLVING REAL-WORLD QUADRATIC RELATIONS

A quadratic relation of the form $y = ax^2 + bx + c$, $a \neq 0$, will produce a graph that has the shape of a parabola (a U-shaped graph that opens upward or downward). It can be represented with a table of values, where the second differences are constant.

:Example

The trajectory of the flight of an arrow shot upward is represented by the table of values and graph shown below:

x	y
Time (s)	**Height (m)**
0	0
1	34.3
2	58.8
3	73.5
4	78.4
5	73.5
6	58.8
7	34.3
8	0

Height of Arrow Over Time

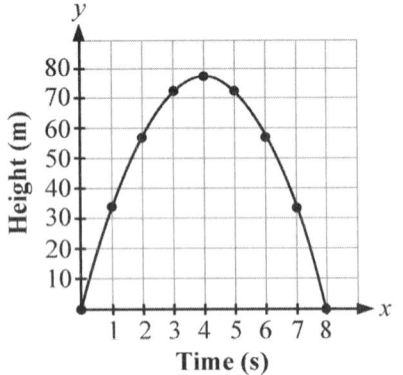

a. Find the second differences to prove that the data in the table of values represents a quadratic relation.
   Solution

x	y	1st differences	2nd differences
0	0		
		34.3	
1	34.3		−9.8
		24.5	
2	58.8		−9.8
		14.7	
3	73.5		−9.8
		4.9	
4	78.4		−9.8
		−4.9	
5	73.5		−9.8
		−14.7	
6	58.8		−9.8
		−24.5	
7	34.3		−9.8
		−34.3	
8	0		

Since the second differences for the data in the table of values is constant at −9.8, this scenario represents a quadratic relation.

b. From the graph, what is the maximum height of the arrow, and when does it occur?
   Solution
   The parabola opens downward. Its peak point indicates that the maximum height of the arrow is 78.4 m (y-coordinate) and occurs at a time of 4 s (x-coordinate) after being shot upward.

c. How many seconds does the arrow stay in the air?
   Solution
   From the table of values, the arrow hits the ground after 8 s, since the height (y-coordinate) is 0 m at that time. From the graph, the arrow hits the ground after 8 s, since the point has a y-coordinate of 0, representing a height of 0 m.

 Practice

Numerical Response

Use the following information to answer the next question.

Josie wanted to make a rectangular garden along the side of her house. She bought 28 feet of border to enclose the garden with a width, w, and length, l, in feet, as shown.

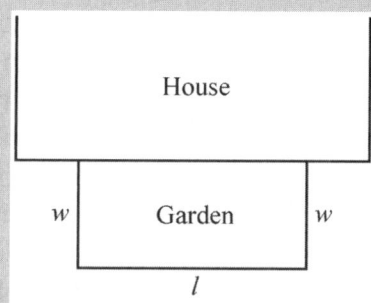

Josie wanted to enclose the garden so it would have the maximum area.
To determine this, she recorded some values of possible widths, w, lengths, l, and areas, A, in the table below.

w (ft)	4	5	6
l (ft)	$28 - 2(4)$ $= 20$	$28 - 2(5)$ $= 18$	$28 - 2(6)$ $= 16$
A (ft^2)	4×20 $= 80$	5×18 $= 90$	
w (ft)	7	8	9
l (ft)	$28 - 2(7)$ $= 14$	$28 - 2(8)$ $= 12$	$28 - 2(9)$ $= 10$
A (ft^2)			

1. If all the values of A in the table are calculated and the relation between area, A, and width, w, is quadratic, then the maximum possible area of the garden is ____ ft^2.

Open Response

Use the following information to answer the next question.

Emily posed the following problem:

Is the relationship between the width, x, and the area, y, of rectangles (whose length is twice the width) a quadratic relation? To solve the problem, she drew rectangles that had widths of $x = 1, 2, 3, 4, 5, 6, 7$, and whose corresponding lengths were twice as much. Some of these rectangles are shown below.

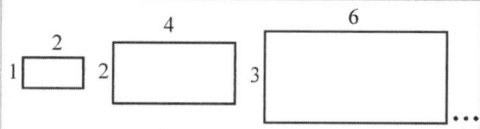

Emily then calculated the areas, y, of the rectangles and portrayed her data in the table below.

x	1	2	3	4	5	6	7
y	2	8	18	32	50	72	98

2. Find the second differences of the areas, y, and then state whether the relationship between x and y is quadratic.

QF1.2 *represent situations using quadratic expressions in one variable, and expand and simplify quadratic expressions in one variable*

EXPANDING AND SIMPLIFYING QUADRATIC EXPRESSIONS

Some problems can be represented by quadratic expressions that can be expanded and simplified using a variety of methods.

Example

A 2×3 picture is to be framed with a matte of width x, in a frame of length l, and width w, as illustrated below. Assume that all the measures are in centimetres.

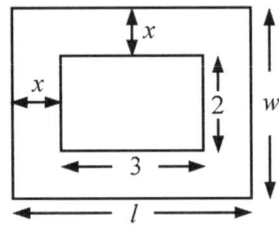

a. Determine the algebraic expression in terms of x that represents the area of the picture frame.
   Solution
   The length, l, can be expressed as $x + 3 + x = 2x + 3$, and the width, w, can be expressed as $x + 2 + x = 2x + 2$. Since the area of the frame is $A = (l)(w)$, the expression for the area is
   $A = (l)(w)$
   $= (2x + 3)(2x + 2)$

b. Simplify the expression for the area of the picture frame.
   Solution
   Method 1: Using Algebra Tiles
   Recall that positive x^2-, x-, and unit tiles are shaded, and negative x^2-, x-, and unit tiles are unshaded. To represent the product $(2x + 3)(2x + 2)$, make a rectangle that is two x-tiles and 3 unit tiles long and two x-tiles and 2 unit tiles wide. Then examine the resulting rectangular array in the middle.

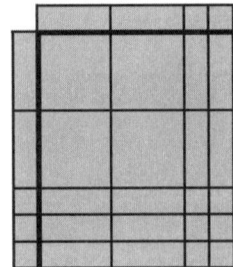

Since the array has four x^2-tiles, ten x-tiles, and six unit tiles, the resulting product is
$4x^2 + 10x + 6$.

Method 2: Using an Algebraic Approach
Recall the mathematical processes used when expanding and simplifying quadratic expressions.

- Distributive property: $ax(x + b) = ax^2 + abx$
- FOIL method:
  $(x + a)(x + b) = x^2 + ax + bx + ab$
  $\qquad\qquad\qquad = x^2 + (a + b)x + ab$
  $(x + a)^2 = (x + a)(x + a) = x^2 + 2ax + a^2$
- Collect like terms and simplify.

Therefore,

$(2x + 3)(2x + 2) = (2x)(2x) + (2)(2x) + (3)(2x) + (3)(2)$

$= 4x^2 + 4x + 6x + 6$
$= 4x^2 + 10x + 6$

The simplified expression representing the area of the picture frame is $4x^2 + 10x + 6$.

Example

Expand and simplify $4x(-x + 3) - 2(x - 3)^2$.

Solution

$4x(-x + 3) - 2(x - 3)^2$
$= 4x(-x) + 4x(3) - 2(x - 3)(x - 3)$

$= -4x^2 + 12x - 2(x^2 - 3x - 3x + 9)$
$= -4x^2 + 12x - 2(x^2) - 2(-3x) - 2(-3x) - 2(9)$
$= -4x^2 + 12x - 2x^2 + 6x + 6x - 18$
$= -6x^2 + 24x - 18$

Practice

Use the following information to answer the next multipart question.

3. A rectangular net is shown with labelled expressions for all side lengths and areas.

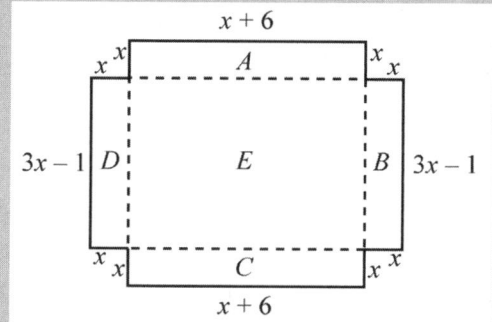

The total area of the rectangular net can be expressed as:

$$A_{total} = \text{Area } A + \text{Area } B$$
$$+ \text{Area } C + \text{Area } D + \text{Area } E$$

Part A

Open Response

Write algebraic expressions, in terms of the side dimensions, to describe each rectangular area A, B, C, D, and E.

Part B

Open Response

Expand and simplify each area expression. Then, combine all terms to produce a simplified expression representing the total area.

Use the following information to answer the next question.

Josh wanted to expand and simplify the quadratic expression $(-2x + 3)(3x - 4)$. To find all terms in the multiplication process he used a rectangular grid as shown.

	$-2x$	3
$3x$	$-6x^2$	A
-4	B	-12

4. When the terms represented by A and B are combined, the resulting term is

A. x B. $-x$

C. $12x$ D. $17x$

5. When the algebraic expression $5x(2 - x) - (x + 3)^2$ is expanded and simplified, the resulting expression is

A. $-6x^2 + 16x + 9$

B. $-6x^2 + 10x - 9$

C. $-6x^2 - 4x + 9$

D. $-6x^2 + 4x - 9$

QF1.3 *factor quadratic expressions in one variable, including those for which a ≠ 1, differences of squares, and perfect square trinomials, by selecting and applying an appropriate strategy*

FACTORING QUADRATIC EXPRESSIONS

A quadratic expression can be factored by writing it as a product of two linear expressions. A variety of strategies can be used to factor binomial and trinomial quadratic expressions.

FACTORING A BINOMIAL OF THE FORM $ax^2 + bx$

To factor a binomial of the form $ax^2 + bx$, find the greatest common factor (largest factor common to both terms), and divide it out of each term of the binomial.

Example

Factor $12x^2 - 8x$.

Solution
The greatest common factor is $4x$, since 4 is the largest numerical factor and x is the largest variable common to $12x^2$ and $-8x$.
$$12x^2 - 8x = 4x(3x - 2)$$

FACTORING A BINOMIAL OF THE FORM $ax^2 - c$

If a and c are perfect squares (e.g., 1, 4, 9, 16…) so that $\sqrt{a}$ and $\sqrt{c}$ are natural numbers, then $ax^2 - c$ is called a *difference of squares* and can be factored as follows:
$$ax^2 - c = (\sqrt{a}x + \sqrt{c})(\sqrt{a}x - \sqrt{c})$$

Example

Factor $4x^2 - 81$.

Solution
The values 4 and 81 are perfect squares, since $\sqrt{4} = 2$ and $\sqrt{81} = 9$. Therefore, the binomial quadratic expression can be factored as:
$$4x^2 - 81 = (\sqrt{4}x + \sqrt{81})(\sqrt{4}x - \sqrt{81})$$
$$= (2x + 9)(2x - 9)$$

FACTORING A TRINOMIAL OF THE FORM $x^2 + bx + c$

To factor a quadratic trinomial $x^2 + bx + c$, you need to find two integers d and e that have a **product** of $d \times e = c$ and a **sum** of $d + e = b$. Then, the trinomial will factor as follows:
$$x^2 + bx + c = (x + d)(x + e).$$

Example

Factor $x^2 + 5x + 6$.

Solution
Look for two numbers that have a product of 6 and a sum of 5. The two numbers are 3 and 2, since $3 \times 2 = 6$ and $3 + 2 = 5$. Therefore, the trinomial will factor as follows:
$$x^2 + 5x + 6 = (x + 3)(x + 2).$$

Note: This factoring process can also be illustrated using algebra tiles. Arrange the algebra tiles representing x^2, x, and units into a rectangular array, and then add algebra tiles to the outside of the rectangular array. The tiles representing $x^2 + 5x + 6$ can be arranged into the following rectangular array:

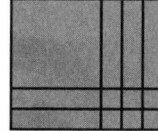

Now add algebra tiles to the left and upper sides of the rectangular array to form the two factors $(x + 2)$ and $(x + 3)$.

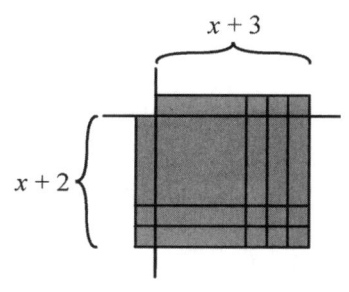

FACTORING A TRINOMIAL OF THE FORM $ax^2 + bx + c$

One commonly used procedure for factoring quadratic trinomials of the form $ax^2 + bx + c$, is called **decomposition**. Decomposition splits the term bx into two separate terms and then factors the four terms by grouping. This process is clarified in the factoring of the following example.

Example

Factor $2x^2 - 5x - 3$

Solution

1. Find two numbers that have a product equal to $a \times c$ and a sum of b. These two numbers are -6 and 1, since the product $(-6) \times (1)$ is equal to $a \times c = -6$ and the sum $(-6) + (1)$ is equal to $b = -5$.

2. Split the middle term bx into two terms of x that contain the two numbers found in step 1.

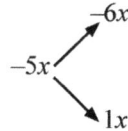

3. Group the four terms and factor out the greatest common factor from each pair of two terms.
$$(2x^2 - 6x) + (1x - 3)$$
$$2x(x - 3) + 1(x - 3)$$

4. Factor out the common binomial.
$$2x(x - 3) + 1(x - 3)$$
$$(2x + 1)(x - 3)$$
Therefore,
$$2x^2 - 5x - 3 = (2x + 1)(x - 3).$$

Note: If the value of a is a perfect square and c is a perfect square then the expression $ax^2 + bx + c$, is called a perfect square trinomial, and is factored as follows:

$ax^2 + bx + c = (\sqrt{a}x + \sqrt{c})(\sqrt{a}x + \sqrt{c})$, if $b > 0$ or
$ax^2 + bx + c = (\sqrt{a}x - \sqrt{c})(\sqrt{a}x - \sqrt{c})$, if $b < 0$

:Example

Factor $8x^2 - 40x + 50$

Solution

Note: If there is a greatest common factor in a binomial or trinomial, it **must** be factored out first before applying the factoring strategies mentioned earlier. Since 2 is common to all terms,
$8x^2 - 40x + 50 = 2(4x^2 - 20x + 25)$.
The trinomial formed after 2 was factored out is a perfect square trinomial, since $\sqrt{a} = \sqrt{4} = 2$ and $\sqrt{c} = \sqrt{25} = 5$. Since $b < 0$, the trinomial factors to
$2(4x^2 - 20x + 25)$
$= 2(\sqrt{4}x - \sqrt{25})(\sqrt{4}x - \sqrt{25})$
$= 2(2x - 5)(2x - 5)$ or
$= 2(2x - 5)^2$

:Practice

6. One of the factors of $2x^2 + x - 15$ is
   A. $x - 3$ B. $x - 5$
   C. $2x - 3$ D. $2x - 5$

   Open Response

7. When the two quadratic expressions given by, $18x^2 - 8$ and $6x^2 - 11x - 10$ are factored, what common factor do they share?

QF1.4 *solve quadratic equations by selecting and applying a factoring strategy*

SOLVING QUADRATIC EQUATIONS BY FACTORING

A quadratic **equation** is a quadratic expression set equal to zero, resulting in $ax^2 + bx + c = 0$. Many of these equations can be solved by using the factoring strategies explained in the previous section. Once the two factors are found, you can find the value(s) of the variable (usually x) that satisfy the given equation. These solutions are called the **roots** of the equation, since they make the equation equal to zero.

:Example

Solve the quadratic equation $2x^2 - 7x = -5$.
Solution

1. Set the quadratic equation equal to zero.
   $2x^2 - 7x + 5 = -5 + 5$
   $2x^2 - 7x + 5 = 0$

2. Factor the quadratic expression (decomposition).
   $2x^2 - 7x + 5 = 0$
   $2x^2 - 2x - 5x + 5 = 0$
   $2x(x - 1) - 5(x - 1) = 0$
   $(2x - 5)(x - 1) = 0$

3. Set each factor equal to zero, and solve for x.

   $2x - 5 = 0$
   $2x = 5$ and $x - 1 = 0$
   $x = \dfrac{5}{2}$ $x = 1$

Note: You can verify that these are the solutions of the equation $2x^2 - 7x + 5 = 0$ by substituting the values for x.

$x = \dfrac{5}{2}$	$x = 1$
$2\left(\dfrac{5}{2}\right)^2 - 7\left(\dfrac{5}{2}\right) + 5 = 0$ $2\left(\dfrac{25}{4}\right) - \dfrac{35}{2} + 5 = 0$ $\dfrac{50}{4} - \dfrac{70}{4} + \dfrac{20}{4} = 0$ $\dfrac{0}{4} = 0$ $0 = 0$	$2(1)^2 - 7(1) + 5 = 0$ $2 - 7 + 5 = 0$ $0 = 0$

Since the values $\frac{5}{2}$ and 1 make the equation equal to zero, these values are the roots or solutions of the equation.

***

Practice

8. Which of the following quadratic equations has the solutions of $x = -1$ and $x = 3$?

    A. $x^2 - 4x + 3 = 0$

    B. $x^2 + 4x + 3 = 0$

    C. $x^2 - 2x - 3 = 0$

    D. $x^2 + 2x - 3 = 0$

Numerical Response

CHALLENGER QUESTION

9. If one of the roots of the quadratic equation $-2x^2 + kx + 24 = 0$ is -3, then the value of k must be ____.

QF1.5 *determine, through investigation, and describe the connection between the factors used in solving a quadratic equation and the x-intercepts of the graph of the corresponding quadratic relation*

RELATIONSHIP BETWEEN FACTORS AND x-INTERCEPTS

Recall:
*   The x-intercept of the graph of a relation is the x-coordinate of the point where the graph touches or crosses the x-axis.
*   The roots or solutions of a factored quadratic equation are the values of x that make each factor equal to zero.

Through investigation you can determine the connection between the x-intercepts of the graph of a quadratic relation $y = ax^2 + bx + c$ and the factors of the corresponding quadratic equation $0 = ax^2 + bx + c$.

Example

The path of a dolphin during its jump out of the water in a training pool can be represented by the quadratic relation $y = -2x^2 + 20x - 42$, where y is the height of the dolphin, in metres, above the surface of the water and x is the horizontal distance, in metres, of the dolphin from the trainer at the edge of the pool. The corresponding graph of this relation is represented by the parabola shown below.

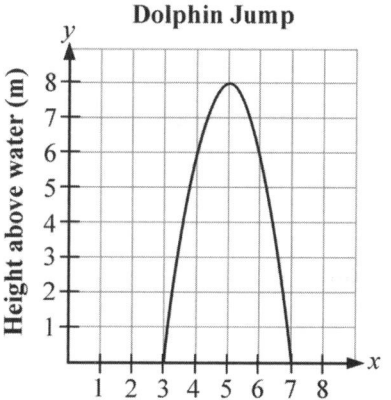

a. Determine the x-intercepts of the graph of $y = -2x^2 + 20x - 42$, and explain what they describe in the context of this scenario.

Solution

The x-intercepts of the graph are located at the points $(3, 0)$ and $(7, 0)$, since these are the points where the graph touches the x-axis.

The x-intercepts of 3 m and 7 m describe the horizontal locations of the dolphin from the trainer when the dolphin left and reentered the water during its jump into the air.

b. Factor the corresponding quadratic equation $0 = -2x^2 + 20x - 42$.

Solution

Factor out the greatest common factor of -2 from all terms of the equation.

$$-2x^2 + 20x - 42 = 0$$
$$-2\left(x^2 - 10x + 21\right) = 0$$

Factor the trinomial $x^2 - 10x + 21$.

$$-2\left(x^2 - 10x + 21\right) = 0$$
$$-2(x - 3)(x - 7) = 0$$

c. What are the roots or solutions of x of the factored quadratic equation?

Solution

$$\begin{array}{ccc} x - 3 = 0 & & x - 7 = 0 \\ x = 3 & \text{and} & x = 7 \end{array}$$

d. What is the relationship between the factors of the quadratic equation and the corresponding graph of the quadratic relation describing the dolphin's path?

Solution

The x-intercepts of 3 m and 7 m of the graph of the quadratic relation $y = -2x^2 + 20x - 42$ describing the dolphin's jump are the same as the roots or solutions of the factors of the corresponding quadratic equation $-2x^2 + 20x - 42 = 0 \Rightarrow -2(x - 3)(x - 7) = 0$.

Practice

10. A quadratic equation $0 = ax^2 + bx + c$ was factored as $0 = (5x + 3)(4x - 7)$. If the corresponding quadratic function $y = ax^2 + bx + c$ was graphed, the x-intercepts would be

A. $-\dfrac{3}{5}$ and $\dfrac{7}{4}$

B. $\dfrac{3}{5}$ and $-\dfrac{7}{4}$

C. $-\dfrac{5}{3}$ and $\dfrac{4}{7}$

D. $\dfrac{5}{3}$ and $-\dfrac{4}{7}$

Open Response

11. Rene correctly factored the quadratic equation $0 = -x^2 + 4$ to $0 = -(x + 2)(x - 2)$. Explain how you know what the x-intercepts should be for the corresponding graph of the function $y = -x^2 + 4$.

QF1.6 *explore the algebraic development of the quadratic formula and apply the formula to solve quadratic equations, using technology*

THE QUADRATIC FORMULA

Not all quadratic equations can be factored. This is evident when technology is used to find the x-intercepts of their corresponding functions. The values are only approximate, and not exact. In order to obtain the exact roots of such equations, a formula, called the quadratic formula, can be used. This formula can be developed by completing the square of the general form $ax^2 + bx + c = 0$.

DEVELOPING THE QUADRATIC FORMULA

Isolating x in the equation $ax^2 + bx + c = 0$ is accomplished by completing the square.

$$ax^2 + bx + c = 0$$

$$a\left(x^2 + \frac{b}{a}x\right) + c = 0$$

$$a\left(x^2 + \frac{b}{a}x + \frac{b^2}{4a^2} - \frac{b^2}{4a^2}\right) + c = 0$$

$$a\left(x + \frac{b}{2a}\right)^2 - \frac{b^2}{4a} + c = 0$$

$$a\left(x + \frac{b}{2a}\right)^2 = \frac{b^2}{4a} - c$$

$$\left(x + \frac{b}{2a}\right)^2 = \frac{b^2}{4a^2} - \frac{c}{a}$$

$$\left(x + \frac{b}{2a}\right)^2 = \frac{b^2}{4a^2} - \frac{4ac}{4a^2}$$

$$\left(x + \frac{b}{2a}\right)^2 = \frac{b^2 - 4ac}{4a^2}$$

$$\sqrt{\left(x + \frac{b}{2a}\right)^2} = \pm\sqrt{\frac{b^2 - 4ac}{4a^2}}$$

$$x + \frac{b}{2a} = \pm\frac{\sqrt{b^2 - 4ac}}{2a}$$

$$x = -\frac{b}{2a} \pm \frac{\sqrt{b^2 - 4ac}}{2a}$$

$$x = \frac{-b \pm \sqrt{b^2 - 4ac}}{2a}$$

The roots of the quadratic equation $ax^2 + bx + c = 0$, where $a \neq 0$, can be expressed in terms of a, b, and c by using the quadratic formula:

$$x = \frac{-b \pm \sqrt{b^2 - 4ac}}{2a}$$

Example

Find the exact roots to the quadratic equation $0 = x^2 - 8x + 5$ by applying the quadratic formula.

Solution

Step 1: Identify the values of a, b, and c in the equation.

$$0 = \underset{\underset{a=1}{\downarrow}}{1x^2} \underset{\underset{b=-8}{\downarrow}}{-8x} \underset{\underset{c=5}{\downarrow}}{+5}$$

Step 2: Substitute these values into the quadratic formula.

$$x = \frac{-b \pm \sqrt{b^2 - 4ac}}{2a}$$

$$= \frac{-(-8) \pm \sqrt{(-8)^2 - 4(1)(5)}}{2(1)}$$

$$= \frac{8 \pm \sqrt{64 - 20}}{2}$$

$$= \frac{8 \pm \sqrt{44}}{2}$$

$$= \frac{8 \pm \sqrt{4 \times 11}}{2}$$

$$= \frac{8 \pm 2\sqrt{11}}{2}$$

$$= \frac{2(4 \pm \sqrt{11})}{2}$$

$$= 4 \pm \sqrt{11}$$

The exact roots of the given equation are $4 + \sqrt{11}$ and $4 - \sqrt{11}$.

Note: You can find the approximate roots by using your graphing calculator. Enter your values of a, b, and c into the quadratic formula as follows, and press ENTER each time.

```
(-(-8)+√((-8)²-4
*1*5))/(2*1)
          7.31662479
(-(-8)-√((-8)²-4
*1*5))/(2*1)
          .6833752096
```

Practice

Use the following information to answer the next question.

Matt used the quadratic formula to solve the quadratic equation $2x^2 - 5x - 1 = 0$. His steps used to arrive at a solution are shown.

Step 1: $x = \dfrac{-5 \pm \sqrt{(-5)^2 - 4(2)(-1)}}{2(2)}$

Step 2: $x = \dfrac{-5 \pm \sqrt{25 + 8}}{4}$

Step 3: $x = \dfrac{-5 \pm \sqrt{33}}{4}$

Step 4: $x = 0.186, -2.686$

12. Matt's first error occurred in

A. Step 1   B. Step 2

C. Step 3   D. Step 4

13. When using a graphing calculator to solve the equation $5x^2 - 11x = 3$ by applying the quadratic formula, one of the roots to the nearest tenth is

A. 0.2   B. 1.9   C. 2.4   D. 5.6

QF1.7 *relate the real roots of a quadratic equation to the x-intercepts of the corresponding graph, and connect the number of real roots to the value of the discriminant*

USING THE DISCRIMINANT TO DETERMINE THE ROOTS OF A QUADRATIC EQUATION

As discussed in an earlier section, the real roots of a quadratic equation are the same as the x-intercepts of the graph of the corresponding quadratic function. The roots of any quadratic equation $ax^2 + bx + c = 0$, $a \neq 0$ can be found using the quadratic formula:

$$x = \frac{-b \pm \sqrt{b^2 - 4ac}}{2a}$$

The quantity under the radical sign, $b^2 - 4ac$, is called the **discriminant** (D) of the quadratic equation. Its value determines the type of real roots of the equation and also predicts the number of real x-intercepts of the graph of the corresponding function. There are three different outcomes for the discriminant: $D > 0$, $D = 0$, and $D < 0$.

Example

For the three equations $0 = x^2 - 4x + 3$, $0 = x^2 - 4x + 4$, and $0 = x^2 - 4x + 5$, determine the discriminants and roots. Connect these values to the type of real roots and number and values of the x-intercepts of the graph of their corresponding functions.

Solution

i.   Equation: $x^2 - 4x + 3 = 0$

Formula	Discriminant
$x = \dfrac{-b \pm \sqrt{D}}{2a}$	$\begin{aligned} D &= b^2 - 4ac \\ &= (-4)^2 - 4(1)(3) \\ &= 16 - 12 \\ &= 4 \end{aligned}$
$= \dfrac{-(-4) \pm \sqrt{4}}{2(1)}$	$\downarrow$
$= \dfrac{4+2}{2}$ and $\dfrac{4-2}{2}$	$D > 0$
$= 3$ and 1	$\downarrow$

Roots: $x = 3$ and 1 **Type**: Two different and real

Function: $y = x^2 - 4x + 3 = 0$

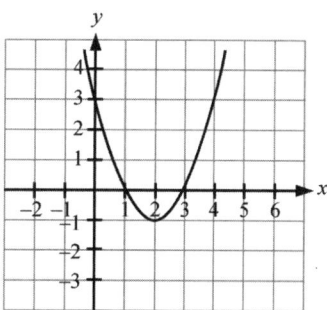

Conclusion: The values of the roots are the same as the x-intercepts, and since there are two different, real roots, there are two x-intercepts.

ii.   Equation: $x^2 - 4x + 4$

Formula	Discriminant
$x = \dfrac{-b \pm \sqrt{D}}{2a}$	$\begin{aligned} D &= b^2 - 4ac \\ &= (-4)^2 - 4(1)(4) \\ &= 16 - 16 \\ &= 0 \end{aligned}$
$= \dfrac{-(-4) \pm \sqrt{0}}{2(1)}$	$\downarrow$
$= \dfrac{4+0}{2}$ and $\dfrac{4-0}{2}$	$D = 0$
$= 2$ and 2	$\downarrow$

Roots: $x = 2$ and 2 **Type**: Two equal and real

Function: $y = x^2 - 4x + 4$

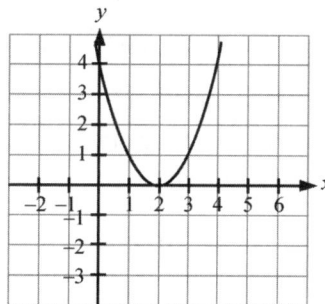

Conclusion: The values of the roots are the same as the x-intercept, and since there are two equal, real roots, there is one x-intercept.

iii. Equation: $x^2 - 4x + 5 = 0$

Formula   **Discriminant**

$$x = \frac{-b \pm \sqrt{D}}{2a}$$ $D = b^2 - 4ac$

$$= \frac{-(-4) \pm \sqrt{-4}}{2(1)}$$ $= (-4)^2 - 4(1)(5)$

          $= 16 - 20$

$= $ undefined $= -4$

                    $\downarrow$

                    $D < 0$

                    $\downarrow$

Roots: Not defined   **Type:** Non-real

Function: $y = x^2 - 4x + 5$

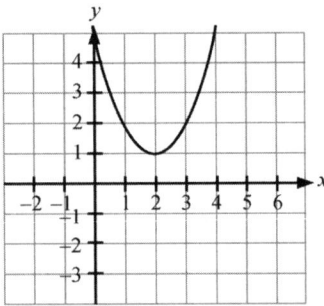

Conclusion: The values of the roots are undefined, producing no x-intercepts. Since the roots are non-real, there are zero x-intercepts.

 **Practice**

CHALLENGER QUESTION

14. For the quadratic equation

$0 = -2x^2 + 6x + k$ to have two equal, real roots, the value of k must be

A. $-\dfrac{9}{2}$ B. -3

C. 3 D. $\dfrac{9}{2}$

Open Response

15. For the quadratic equation $2x^2 - 8x - 7 = 0$, determine the discriminant (D), and describe the type of roots.

QF1.8 *determine the real roots of a variety of quadratic equations and describe the advantages and disadvantages of each strategy (i.e., graphing; factoring; using the quadratic formula)*

STRATEGIES USED TO DETERMINE ROOTS FOR QUADRATIC EQUATIONS

When solving a quadratic equation for its roots, you could factor it or use the quadratic formula. You could also graph the corresponding quadratic function and find its x-intercept(s). When choosing a strategy, consider the possible advantages and disadvantages.

FACTORING

Factoring is a useful method if the values of a, b, and c in the equation $ax^2 + bx + c = 0$ are small and do not require much time thinking about the possible factors (i.e., $x^2 - 7x + 12 = 0$, $4x^2 - 49 = 0$, $2x^2 - 5x + 3 = 0$). However, there are many equations that cannot be factored or are too complex.

QUADRATIC FORMULA

Using the quadratic formula has several advantages. The quadratic formula can find the exact values of the real roots of any quadratic equation. However, it does not provide a contextual understanding of the roots in a real-life application, especially if the roots are non-real.

GRAPHING

Graphing is useful in providing contextual understanding of the x-intercepts of the graph of a quadratic function (e.g., find the time when the ball hits the ground given that $h(t) = -4.9t^2 - 19.6t + 1)$. However, the graphing method is not useful when the x-intercepts are extremely close together (i.e., $x = 1.246$ and 1.284) or when exact values are required.

⋮Example

Use factoring, the quadratic formula, and graphing to solve the quadratic equation $1000x^2 - 1050x + 275 = 0$, and find the x-intercepts of the graph of $y = 1000x^2 - 1050x + 275$. Then, decide which strategy is most advantageous.

Solution
Factoring
$$1000x^2 - 1050x + 275 = 0$$
$$25(40x^2 - 42x + 11) = 0$$
Find two numbers that have a product of $(40)(11)$ and a sum of -42, namely -20 and -22.
Then, use decomposition to factor.
$$25(40x^2 - 20x - 22x + 11) = 0$$
$$25[20x(2x - 1) - 11(2x - 1)] = 0$$
$$25(20x - 11)(2x - 1) = 0$$
$$x = \frac{11}{20} \text{ and } \frac{1}{2}$$

Quadratic Formula
$$1000x^2 - 1050x + 275 = 0$$
$$x = \frac{1050 \pm \sqrt{(-1050)^2 - 4(1000)(275)}}{2(1000)}$$
$$x = \frac{1050 \pm \sqrt{1\,102\,500 - 1\,100\,000}}{2000}$$
$$x = \frac{1050 \pm 50}{2000}$$
$$x = \frac{1050 + 50}{2000} \text{ and } \frac{1050 - 50}{2000}$$
$$x = \frac{11}{20} \text{ and } \frac{1}{2}$$

Graphing

Enter the function $y = 1000x^2 - 1050x + 275$ into $[Y_1 =]$, and observe that there is almost nothing visible in the standard window setting.
After several ZOOM IN processes to a WINDOW setting of $[x: 0.45, 0.58, 1]$ and $[y: -0.05, 0.05, 1]$, you can use the 2nd TRACE ZERO buttons to determine x-intercepts of $x = 0.5$ and $x = 0.55$.

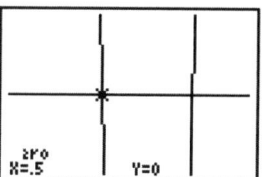

Conclusion: The quadratic formula is the most advantageous method, since the solutions are quick and easy to calculate. The factoring method is quite slow and tedious, and is quite complex when decomposing the trinomial. The graphing method is also quite involved in that a lot of zooming into the x-intercepts is required before finding the two x-intercepts.

⋮Practice

CHALLENGER QUESTION

16. When solving for the **exact** roots of the quadratic equation $4x^2 + 8x + 2 = 0$ or the exact x-intercepts of the graph of the corresponding quadratic function $y = 4x^2 + 8x + 2$, which of the following strategies should be used?

   A. Factoring

   B. Graphing

   C. Finding the discriminant

   D. Using the quadratic formula

Numerical Response

17. The largest root of the quadratic equation $15x^2 + 105x - 66\,150 = 0$, to the nearest whole number, is ____.

QF2.1 *explain the meaning of the term function, and distinguish a function from a relation that is not a function, through investigation of linear and quadratic relations using a variety of representations (i.e., tables of values, mapping diagrams, graphs, function machines, equations) and strategies*

FUNCTIONS

A **relation** is a set of ordered pairs (x, y), where x is the input element and y is the corresponding output element. A **function** is a special relation. It is a set of ordered pairs (x, y) in which for every x-value, there is only one corresponding y-value. In other words, a function is a rule that assigns only one output element for each input element.

Relations and functions can be represented as ordered pairs, tables of values, mapping diagrams, function machines, graphs, and equations. To test whether a relation is or is not a function, you can do the following:

- examine numeric representations to see if any x-value has only one or more corresponding y-values. If it has more than one y-value, it is a relation, but **not** a function.
- examine the graphical representation, and use the **vertical-line test**, which states: "If any vertical line drawn through a relation intersects the graph at more than one point, the relation is not a function."

Example

Represent the linear relation $y = 2x + 1$ and the quadratic relation $x = y^2$ in various ways, and determine whether they are functions.

Solution

$$y = 2x + 1$$

x	y
−2	−3
−1	−1
0	1
1	3
2	5

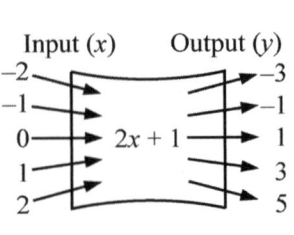

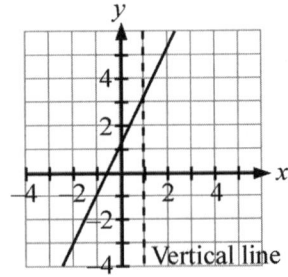

The relation $y = 2x + 1$ is a function, since

- every x-value (input) value has only one y-value (output) value.
- any vertical line drawn through the graph only passes through one point.

$$x = y^2 \text{ or } y = \pm\sqrt{x}$$

x	y
4	2
4	−2
1	1
1	−1
0	0

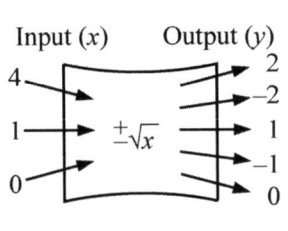

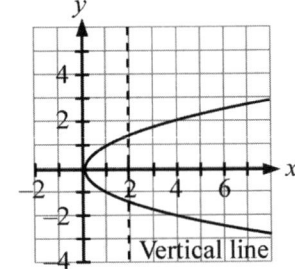

The relation $x = y^2$ is **not** a function, since there is at least one

- x-value (input) value that has more than one y-value (output) value.
- vertical line that passes through more than one point on the graph.

:Practice

CHALLENGER QUESTION

Use the following information to answer the next multipart question.

18. A student examined the four mappings representing linear and quadratic relations.

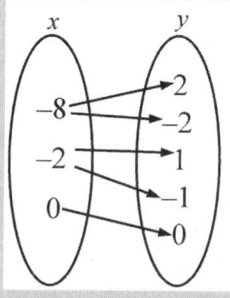
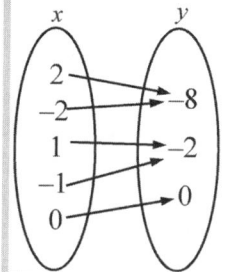

Mapping A   *Mapping B*

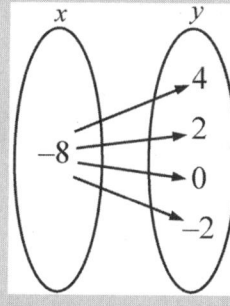
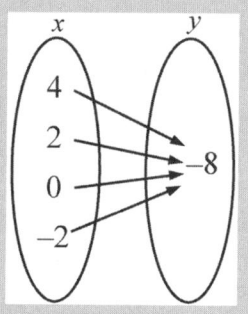

Mapping C   *Mapping D*

Part A

How many of the relations represented are quadratic?

A. 4   **B.** 3   **C.** 2   **D.** 1

Part B

How many of the relations represented are also functions?

A. 3   **B.** 2   **C.** 1   **D.** 0

QF2.2 *substitute into and evaluate linear and quadratic functions represented using function notation, including functions arising from real-world applications*

EVALUATING LINEAR AND QUADRATIC FUNCTIONS

The ordered pairs (x, y) that satisfy the equations $y = 2x + 3$ and $y = 2x^2 - 3x + 1$ form two functions. An equation that is a function can be named using **function notation**.

Equation
$y = 2x + 3$
$y = 2x^2 - 3x + 1$

Function Notation
$f(x) = 2x + 3$
$f(x) = 2x^2 - 3x + 1$

The symbol $f(x)$ is read as "the value of f at x" or "f of x." Function notation describes the output $f(x)$ as a result of an input of x into a function machine f.

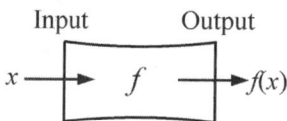

For example, $f(5)$ means substitute the input value of 5 into the function machine defined by f to produce the resulting output value $f(5)$.

Input (5)	Function (f)	Output $[f(5)]$
5→	$2x + 3 = 2(5) + 3$→	13
5→	$2x^2 - 3x + 1$ $= 2(5)^2 - 3(5) + 1$→	36

Example

If the function $h(t) = -4.9t^2 + 19.6t + 6$ describes the relationship between the height, $h(t)$, in metres, of a stone above the ground as a function of its time, t, in seconds, in the air, then evaluate $h(3)$, and explain its meaning.

Solution
To find $h(3)$, substitute the value 3 for t in $h(t) = -4.9t^2 + 19.6t + 6$, and solve for the output value.

$$h(3) = -4.9(3)^2 + 19.6(3) + 6$$
$$= -44.1 + 58.8 + 6$$
$$= 20.7$$

The value $h(3)$ describes the height of the stone at 20.7 m above the ground after 3 seconds.

Practice

Use the following information to answer the next multipart question.

19. The percentage, $P(t)$, of information memorized by Bridget is a function of the time, t, in minutes, of the length of a lecture.

$$P(t) = \frac{12}{5}t - \frac{1}{50}t^2$$

Bridget's friend wanted to determine the percentage memorized at various times and evaluated the four values: $P(40)$, $P(50)$, $P(60)$, $P(70)$.

Part A

Numerical Response

The percentage of a 40-minute lecture memorized by Bridget is ____%.

Part B

During what length of a lecture did Bridget memorize the most information?

A. 40 min   B. 50 min

C. 60 min   D. 70 min

QF2.3 *explain the meanings of the terms domain and range, through investigation using numeric, graphical, and algebraic representations of linear and quadratic functions, and describe the domain and range of a function appropriately*

DOMAIN AND RANGE

The **domain** of a function is the set of all input elements (x-values) for which the function is defined. The **range** of a function is the set of all output elements, $f(x)$ or y-values, which are defined by all input elements (x-values) of the domain.

Example

Find the domain and range of the two functions $y = x^2 - 3$ and $y = x - 2$.

Solution
You can graph or provide a table of values to help you visualize the domain and range of both functions.

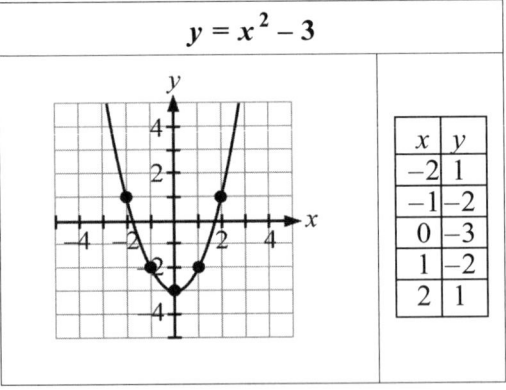

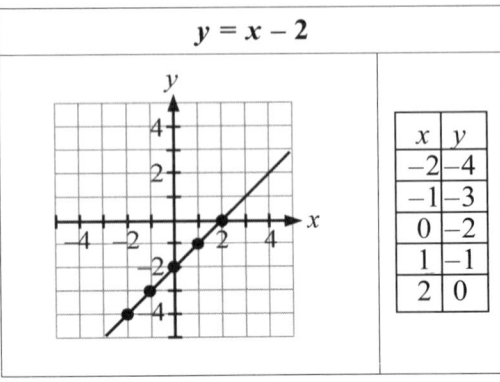

Both graphs of the functions show that the graph continues infinitely to the right and left for all positive and negative real input elements or x-values. Therefore, the domain is the set of real numbers. It is written as $x \in \mathbb{R}$, which reads as "x is defined by or belongs to the real numbers." The sample input values (x) of both tables imply this reasoning as well.

The graph of the function $y = x^2 - 3$ and sample output values $f(x)$ in the table show that the function's y-values do not go lower than -3 but increase infinitely for all real numbers above and including -3. This description of the range is written as $y \geq -3$.

The graph of the function $y = x - 2$ and sample output values (y) in the table show that the graph continues infinitely upward and downward for all positive and negative real numbers. Therefore, the range of this function is the set of all real numbers, $y \in \mathbb{R}$.

 **Practice**

Use the following information to answer the next question.

The graph of the function $f(x) = 0x + 3$ is shown.

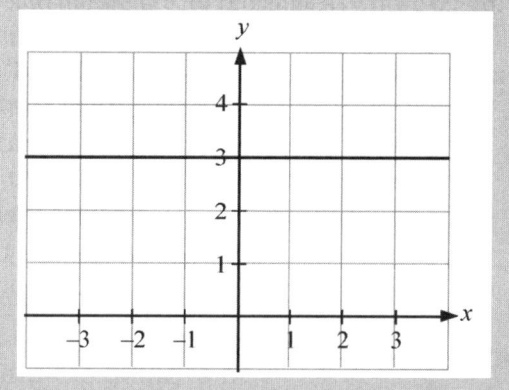

20. The domain (D) and range (R) of this linear function, respectively, are

A. $D: x \in \mathbb{R}$
$R: y \in \mathbb{R}$

B. $D: x = 3$
$R: y \in \mathbb{R}$

C. $D: x \in \mathbb{R}$
$R: y = 3$

D. $D: x \geq -4$
$R: y = 3$

Open Response

21. Complete the table of values for the

quadratic function $y = -\dfrac{1}{2}x^2 + 3$, and

explain why the range is $y \le 3$.

x	y
−3	
−2	
−1	
0	
1	
2	
3	

QF2.4 *explain any restrictions on the domain and the range of a quadratic function in contexts arising from real-world applications*

RESTRICTIONS ON DOMAIN AND RANGE

The domain and range of quadratic functions that describe real-life contexts are restricted or limited by certain factors pertaining to the context.

:Example

The revenue, R, in dollars, earned by a company selling T-shirts is related to the cost, c, in dollars, of each T-shirt. The function describing this relation is given by $R = -48c^2 + 2400c$.

a. What is the least possible T-shirt cost and revenue possible?

Solution

You cannot have a negative T-shirt cost, so the lowest possible T-shirt cost is $0 or $c = 0$. When $c = 0$ is substituted into the equation, the resulting lowest possible revenue is $0, or $R = 0$.

$R = -48(0)^2 + 2400(0) = 0$

This is logical. You cannot make any revenue if you do not sell any T-shirts.

b. Is it possible for this company to make a T-shirt that costs so much that no one would buy it, making the revenue, $R = 0$?

Solution

Set $R = 0$, and solve the equation for the cost, c, using the quadratic formula.

$0 = -48c^2 + 2400c$

$c = \dfrac{-2400 \pm \sqrt{(2400)^2 - 4(-48)(0)}}{2(-48)}$

$c = \dfrac{-2400 \pm 2400}{-96}$

$c = 0$ or 50

When the cost of the T-shirt is increased to $50, there is no revenue, $R = 0$.

c. Determine the maximum possible revenue, R, that the company can make.

Solution

Substitute different values of c between 0 and 50 into the equation to find corresponding values of R.

$c = 10 \Rightarrow R = -48(10)^2 + 2400(10) = 19\ 200$
$c = 15 \Rightarrow R = -48(15)^2 + 2400(15) = 25\ 200$
$c = 20 \Rightarrow R = -48(20)^2 + 2400(20) = 28\ 800$
$c = 25 \Rightarrow R = -48(25)^2 + 2400(25) = 30\ 000$
$c = 30 \Rightarrow R = -48(30)^2 + 2400(30) = 28\ 800$
$c = 35 \Rightarrow R = -48(35)^2 + 2400(35) = 25\ 200$
$c = 40 \Rightarrow R = -48(40)^2 + 2400(40) = 19\ 200$

This process shows that the maximum revenue of \$30 000 occurs when the price of the T-shirt is \$25.

d. What is the domain and range of this real-life application?

Solution

The domain is related to the limits or restrictions on c, the cost of the T-shirt. The lowest value is \$0, and the highest value is \$50. Therefore, you can write:

Domain: $0 \le c \le 50$

The range is related to the limits or restrictions on R, the revenue made. The lowest value is \$0, and the maximum is at \$30 000. Therefore, you can write:

Range: $0 \le R \le 30\ 000$

e. What change could affect the upper limit of the range in this context?

Solution

The upper limit of the range, which is the revenue made, R, would **increase** if more T-shirts were sold at the given prices. The upper limit of the range, R, would **decrease** if fewer T-shirts were sold at the given prices.

Practice

Use the following information to answer the next multipart question.

22. A world-class athlete threw a javelin during a competition so that its flight can be represented by the quadratic function $h = -0.008x^2 + 0.72x + 1.5$, where h is the height of the javelin above the ground and x is the horizontal distance travelled by the javelin, in metres.

Part A

Open Response

What physical outcome determines the restrictions of the domain (x-values) of this function, and how would this restriction change if the athlete had thrown the javelin with less force? Give reasons for your answer.

Part B

Numerical Response

The **maximum** limit on the domain, x, occurs when $h = 0$. By solving the corresponding quadratic equation $0 = -0.008x^2 + 0.72x + 1.5$, this maximum limit value, to the nearest tenth metre, is ____ m.

QF2.5 *determine, through investigation using technology, the roles of a, h, and k in quadratic functions of the form*
$f(x) = a(x - h)^2 + k$, *and describe these roles in terms of transformations on the graph of* $f(x) = x^2$ *(i.e., translations; reflections in the x-axis; vertical stretches and compressions to and from the x-axis)*

EFFECTS OF a, h, AND k ON QUADRATIC FUNCTIONS

When the graph of the quadratic function $f(x) = x^2$ is transformed to the graph of $f(x) = a(x - h)^2 + k$, the parameters a, h, and k have specific roles in these transformations. They also determine the new characteristics of the transformed graph.

THE ROLE AND EFFECT OF h

When $f(x) = x^2$ is transformed to $f(x) = (x - h)^2$, the value of h causes a **horizontal translation**. When $h < 0$, the whole graph shifts left h units, and when $h > 0$, the whole graph shifts right h units. In particular, the vertex moves from $(0, 0)$ to $(h, 0)$, and the equation of the axis of symmetry moves from $x = 0$ to $x = h$.

Example

The graph of $f(x) = x^2$ has been transformed to produce two new graphs. What is the new vertex and the equation of the axis of symmetry of each new graph?

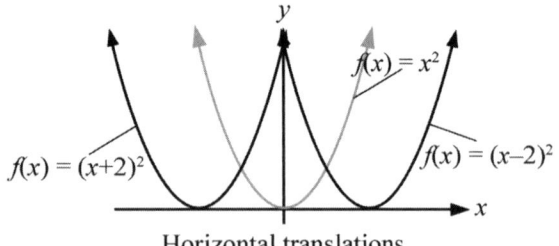

Horizontal translations

Solution

In $f(x) = (x - 2)^2$, the graph of $f(x) = x^2$ has been horizontally translated to the right 2 units, creating a new vertex at $(2, 0)$ and an equation of the axis of symmetry defined by $x = 2$. In $f(x) = (x + 2)^2$, the graph of $f(x) = x^2$ has been horizontally translated to the left 2 units, creating a new vertex of $(-2, 0)$ and an equation of the axis of symmetry defined by $x = -2$.

THE ROLE AND EFFECT OF k

When $f(x) = x^2$ is transformed to $f(x) = x^2 + k$, the value of k causes a **vertical translation**. When $k < 0$, the whole graph shifts down k units, and when $k > 0$, the whole graph shifts up k units. In particular, the vertex moves from $(0, 0)$ to $(0, k)$, the range is $y \geq k$, and the minimum value is k.

Example

The graph of $f(x) = x^2$ has been transformed to produce two new graphs. What is the new vertex, range, and minimum value of each new graph?

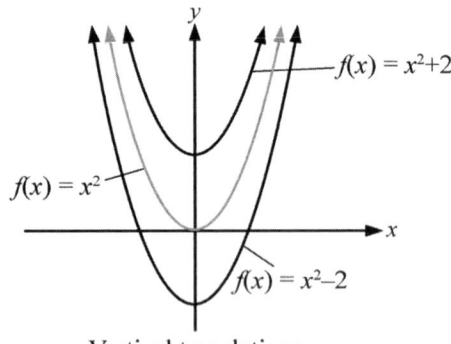

Vertical translations

Solution

In $f(x) = x^2 - 2$, the graph of $f(x) = x^2$ has been vertically translated down 2 units, creating a new vertex at $(0, -2)$, a range of $y \geq -2$, and a minimum of -2. In $f(x) = x^2 + 2$, the graph of $f(x) = x^2$ has been vertically translated up 2 units, creating a new vertex of $(0, 2)$, a range of $y \geq 2$, and a minimum of 2.

THE ROLE AND EFFECT OF a

When $f(x) = x^2$ is transformed to $f(x) = ax^2$, the value of a causes a **vertical stretch** by a factor of a about the x-axis when $|a| > 1$, a **vertical compression** by a factor of a about the x-axis when $0 < |a| < 1$, and a **reflection** about the x-axis when $a < 0$. Other features of the graph are affected when:

- $a > 0$, the graph opens upward, has a minimum of k, and a range of $y \geq k$.
- $a < 0$, the graph opens downward, has a maximum of k, and a range of $y \leq k$.

Example

The graph of $f(x) = x^2$ has been transformed to produce three new graphs. Identify the transformations that were applied to $f(x) = x^2$ to produce the new graphs.

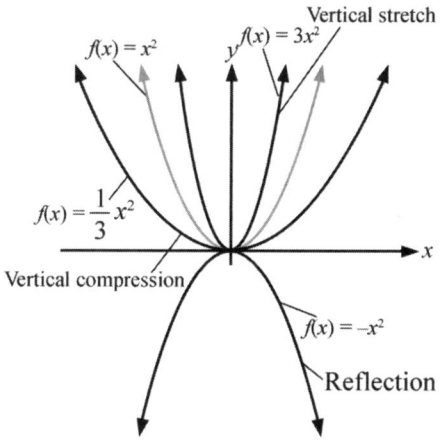

Solution

In $f(x) = \frac{1}{3}x^2$, the graph of $f(x) = x^2$ is compressed vertically about the x-axis by a factor of $\frac{1}{3}$, with all other features staying the same as $f(x) = x^2$.

In $f(x) = 3x^2$, the graph of $f(x) = x^2$ is stretched vertically about the x-axis by a factor of 3, with all other features staying the same as $f(x) = x^2$.

In $f(x) = -x^2$, the graph of $f(x) = x^2$ is reflected in the x-axis, causing the graph to open downward, have a maximum of 0, and a new range of $y \leq 0$.

Example

For the quadratic function $f(x) = -2(x + 3)^2 + 5$, describe the transformations on the graph of $f(x) = x^2$ to produce the function, and describe its new features. Verify these changes by examining the graph on your graphing calculator.

Solution

- The value of $a = -2$ means that the graph of $f(x) = x^2$ is stretched vertically by a factor of 2 and reflected in the x-axis $(a < 0)$.
- The value of $h = (-3)$ means that the graph of $f(x) = x^2$ is translated horizontally to the left by 3 units.
- The value of $k = 5$ means that the graph of $f(x) = x^2$ is translated vertically up 5 units.

The new features of the graph are as follows:

$$\text{Vertex } (h, k) \Rightarrow (-3, 5)$$
$$\text{Axis of symmetry } \Rightarrow x = -3$$
$$\text{Maximum } (k) \Rightarrow 5$$
$$\text{Range } (y \leq k) \Rightarrow y \leq 5$$
$$\text{Direction } \Rightarrow \text{ downward}$$

Note: The domain for any quadratic function is always $x \in \mathbb{R}$.

Examine the graph of $Y_1 = -2(x + 3)^2 + 5$ on your graphing calculator to see these new features.

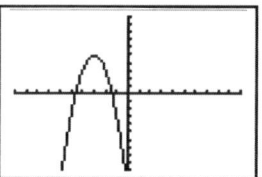

:**Practice**

CHALLENGER QUESTION

23. When the graph of the quadratic function
$f(x) = x^2$ is transformed so that the axis of
symmetry becomes $x = -3$ and the range
become $y \leq 2$, then the graph of the
transformed function
$f(x) = a(x - h)^2 + k$ will have

A. no x-intercepts and opens downward

B. two x-intercepts and a vertex in
quadrant II

C. no x-intercepts and a minimum value
of 2

D. a maximum value of 2 and a vertex in
quadrant III

*Use the following information to
answer the next question.*

The partial graph of a quadratic function of
the form $f(x) = a(x - h)^2 + k$ is shown.

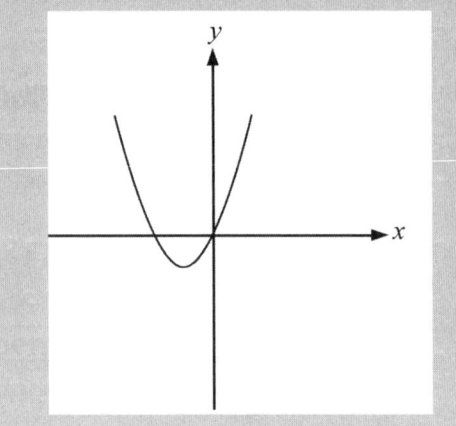

24. Which of the following conditions with
respect to the variables a, h, and k is
correct?

A. $a > 0$, $h > 0$, and $k < 0$

B. $a > 0$, $h < 0$, and $k < 0$

C. $a < 0$, $h > 0$, and $k > 0$

D. $a < 0$, $h < 0$, and $k > 0$

QF2.6 *sketch graphs of*
$g(x) = a(x - h)^2 + k$, *by applying one or
more transformations to the
graph of* $f(x) = x^2$

SKETCHING GRAPHS OF TRANSFORMED FUNCTIONS

The letters g, h… can also be used to describe a
function (i.e., $f(x)$, $g(x)$, $h(x)$, $k(x)$…). To sketch
the graph of a transformed function
$g(x) = a(x - h)^2 + k$, begin by examining the base
graph of $f(x) = x^2$, where $a = 1$, $h = 0$, and $k = 0$.

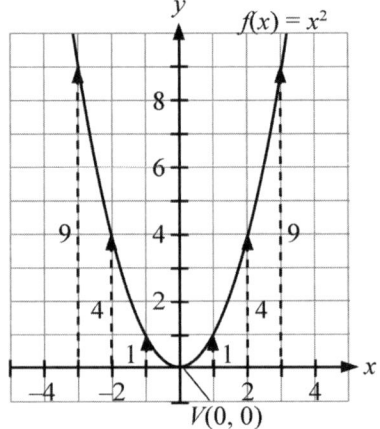

- Place the vertex at $(0, 0)$, since $h = 0$ and $k = 0$.
- The value of a affects the vertical steps to the
  graph. As you move 1 unit at a time to the left or
  right of the vertex, you move up as follows:
  $(1 \to 1, 1 \to 4, 1 \to 9, 1 \to 16, …)$

Sketch the graph of $g(x) = -\frac{1}{2}(x-2)^2 + 4$.

Solution

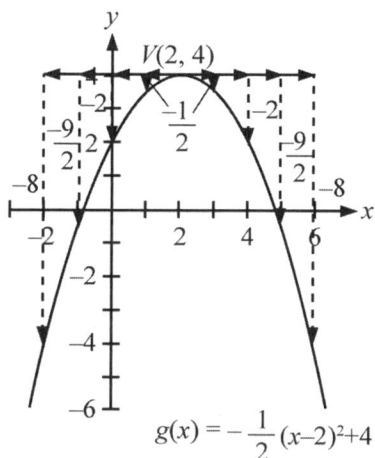

$$g(x) = -\frac{1}{2}(x-2)^2 + 4$$

- Place the vertex at $(2, 4)$, since $h = 2$ and $k = 4$.
- The value of $a = -\frac{1}{2}$, means that all vertical steps will be divided by -2 and be moved downward (since $a < 0$)
As you move 1 unit to the right and left of the vertex, you move down as follows:
$$\left(1 \rightarrow -\frac{1}{2},\ 1 \rightarrow \frac{-4}{2} = -2,\ 1 \rightarrow \frac{-9}{2},\right.$$
$$\left. 1 \rightarrow \frac{-16}{2} = -8...\right)$$

Use the following information to answer the next question.

Jasmine drew a partial sketch of the transformed function
$h(x) = a(x-h)^2 + k$, as shown.

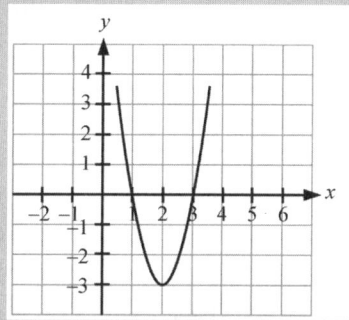

She drew her vertex at $(2, -3)$. Then, she stretched her graph vertically so that the graph passed through the x-axis at $(1, 0)$ and $(3, 0)$.

25. The function that she drew was

A. $h(x) = 2(x-2)^2 - 3$

B. $h(x) = 3(x-2)^2 - 3$

C. $h(x) = 2(x+2)^2 - 3$

D. $h(x) = 3(x+2)^2 - 3$

Use the following information to answer the next question.

A student applied transformations to the graph of $f(x) = x^2$ to sketch the graph of $g(x) = a(x - h)^2 + k$, as shown.

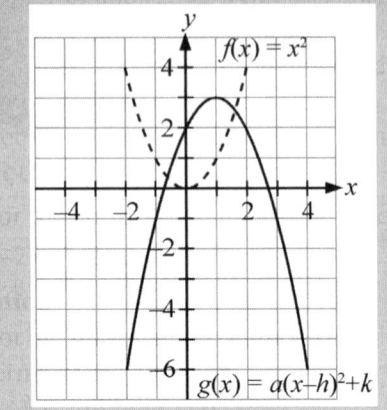

26. Which of the following steps shows the correct transformations made by the student?

A. Reflection in the x-axis, translated right 1 unit, and translated up 3 units

B. Reflection in the x-axis, compressed vertically by a factor of $\frac{1}{2}$ about the x-axis, and translated up 3 units

C. Reflection in the x-axis, stretched vertically by a factor of 3 about the x-axis, and translated right 1 unit

D. Reflection in the x-axis, stretched vertically by a factor of 2 about the x-axis, translated right 1 unit, and translated up 3 units

QF2.7 *express the equation of a quadratic function in the standard form* $f(x) = ax^2 + bx + c$, *given the vertex form* $f(x) = a(x - h)^2 + k$, *and verify, using graphing technology, that these forms are equivalent representations*

CONVERTING EQUATIONS FROM VERTEX FORM TO STANDARD FORM

When a quadratic function is written as $f(x) = a(x - h)^2 + k$, it is called the **vertex form**, since you can easily identify the vertex as (h, k). The expanded form $f(x) = ax^2 + bx + c$ is called the **standard form**, where all terms with different exponents of x (2, 1, and 0) are separated in the function.

Example

Convert the function $f(x) = -2(x + 1)^2 + 9$ in vertex form to standard form $f(x) = ax^2 + bx + c$, and verify that they represent the same graph using your graphing calculator.

Solution
Expand the quadratic function by using the following steps:
$f(x) = -2(x + 1)^2 + 9$

Rewrite $(x + 1)^2$ as $(x + 1)(x + 1)$.
$f(x) = -2(x + 1)(x + 1) + 9$

Expand the two binomials using FOIL.
$f(x) = -2(x^2 + 1x + 1x + 1) + 9$

Multiply each term in the brackets by -2.
$f(x) = -2x^2 - 2x - 2x - 2 + 9$

Collect like terms.
$f(x) = -2x^2 - 4x + 7$

Verify that the two forms of the function represent the same graph by entering one form in $\left[Y_1 = \right]$ and the other in $\left[Y_2 = \right]$ in your graphing calculator:
$Y_1 = -2(x + 1)^2 + 9$
$Y_2 = -2x^2 - 4x + 7$

Set your WINDOW to ZOOM 6, and analyze the graph of both functions by pressing GRAPH.

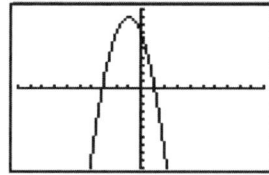

Since there is only one graph on the screen, both $f(x) = -2(x + 1)^2 + 9$ and $f(x) = -2x^2 - 4x + 7$ represent the same quadratic function, with a vertex at $(-1, 9)$ and a y-intercept at 7.

Practice

Use the following information to answer the next question.

Zeke expanded the quadratic function $g(x) = -3(x - 2)^2 + 5$ into standard form using the following steps:

$$g(x) = -3(x - 2)^2 + 5$$
Step 1: $g(x) = -3(x - 2)(x - 2) + 5$
Step 2: $g(x) = (-3x + 6)(-3x + 6) + 5$
Step 3: $g(x) = 9x^2 - 18x - 18x + 36 + 5$
Step 4: $g(x) = 9x^2 - 36x + 41$

27. In which step did Zeke make his first error?

A. Step 1   B. Step 2

C. Step 3   D. Step 4

Open Response

28. Convert the quadratic function

$$f(x) = -\frac{1}{2}(x + 4)^2 - 3 \text{ into standard form,}$$

$$f(x) = ax^2 + bx + c.$$

Show your work.

QF2.8 *express the equation of a quadratic function in the vertex form*

$$f(x) = a(x - h)^2 + k, \text{ given the standard}$$

form $f(x) = ax^2 + bx + c$, by completing

the square, including cases where $\dfrac{b}{a}$ is a

simple rational number, and verify, using graphing technology, that these forms are equivalent representations

COMPLETING THE SQUARE

Completing the square is the mathematical process used to change the form of a quadratic function from the standard form $y = ax^2 + bx + c$ to the vertex form $y = a(x - h)^2 + k$. You can complete the square by using algebra tiles or algebraically.

USING ALGEBRA TILES

When using algebra tiles to complete the square, the focus needs to be on creating a figure that represents a perfect square trinomial.

Example

Using algebra tiles, create a perfect square trinomial for $x^2 + 6x + c = (x + ?)^2$.

Solution
Step 1: Create a partial square with algebra tiles to represent $x^2 + 6x$. Start with the x^2-tile, and arrange the x-tiles around x^2 to create a square.

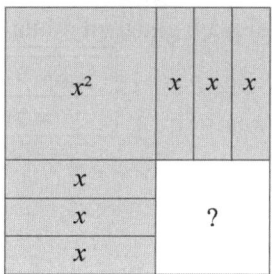

Step 2: Determine how many unit tiles are needed to complete the square.

x^2	x	x	x
x	1	1	1
x	1	1	1
x	1	1	1

In this case, 9 unit tiles are needed to completely fill this square.

Step 3: Determine the dimensions of the completed square.

x^2	x	x	x
x	1	1	1
x	1	1	1
x	1	1	1

$x + 3$

$x + 3$

Therefore, $(x + 3)(x + 3) = (x + 3)^2 = x^2 + 6x + 9$

USING ALGEBRA

The following example shows the steps for algebraically completing the square.

Example

Complete the square for $y = 2x^2 + 5x - 3$.

Solution

Step 1: Identify and remove the common factor of a from the x^2- and x-terms of the expression. In this example, the common factor is 2.

$y = 2(x^2 + 2.5x) - 3$

Step 2: Identify the coefficient of the x-term to be 2.5, divide this value by 2, and square it.

$y = 2(x^2 + \boxed{2.5}x) - 3$ $\left(\dfrac{2.5}{2}\right)^2 = 1.5625$

Step 3: Both add and subtract this value of 1.5625 inside the brackets in order to keep the algebraic expression unchanged.

$y = 2(x^2 + 2.5x + 1.5625 - 1.5625) - 3$

Step 4: Move the negative value -1.5625 out of the brackets by multiplying it by the leading coefficient.

$y = 2(x^2 + 2.5x + 1.5625 - 1.5625)) - 3$

$y = 2(x^2 + 2.5x + 1.5625) - 3.125 - 3$

Step 5: Factor the perfect square trinomial inside the brackets, and collect the constant terms outside the brackets.

$y = 2(x + 1.25)^2 - 6.125$

Note: The numerical part of the binomial in the final bracket is always $\dfrac{1}{2}$ of the coefficient on the x-term of the perfect square trinomial $\left(\text{i.e.,} + 1.25 = \dfrac{+2.5}{2}\right)$.

You can verify that the two forms of the quadratic function represent the same graph on your graphing calculator by following the same steps as mentioned in the previous section.

Enter:
$Y_1 = 2x^2 + 5x - 3$
$Y_2 = 2(x + 1.25)^2 - 6.125$
WINDOW ZOOM 6 ENTER GRAPH:

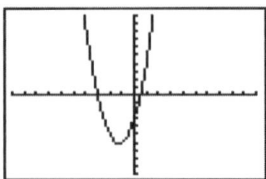

Use the following information to answer the next question.

Mark was going to convert the quadratic function $g(x) = -3x^2 + 4x - 5$ to the form $g(x) = a(x - h)^2 + k$ by completing the square.

$$g(x) = -3x^2 + 4x - 5$$

Step 1: $g(x) = -3\left(x^2 - \dfrac{4}{3}x\right) - 5$

Step 2: $g(x) = -3\left(x^2 - \dfrac{4}{3}x + m - m\right) - 5$

Step 3: $g(x) = -3\left(x - \dfrac{2}{3}\right)^2 + n$

29. If Mark completed the square correctly, what would the values be for m and n?

A. $m = \dfrac{16}{9}, n = \dfrac{1}{3}$

B. $m = \dfrac{4}{9}, n = -\dfrac{57}{9}$

C. $m = \dfrac{64}{9}, n = \dfrac{49}{3}$

D. $m = \dfrac{4}{9}, n = -\dfrac{11}{3}$

Open Response

CHALLENGER QUESTION

30. Complete the square for $f(x) = -\dfrac{1}{5}x^2 + 3x - 14$. Show all of your steps to convert the function into the vertex form $f(x) = a(x - h)^2 + k$.

QF2.9 sketch graphs of quadratic functions in the factored form $f(x) = a(x - r)(x - s)$ by using the x-intercepts to determine the vertex

SKETCHING GRAPHS FROM FACTORED FORM

When the graph of a quadratic function has two distinct x-intercepts r and s, the axis of symmetry lies *halfway* between these x-intercepts. Therefore, the equation of the axis of symmetry, which is defined by the vertex (h, k), is

$x = h = \dfrac{r + s}{2}$, and the vertex, with respect to

the x-intercept, is $\left(\dfrac{r + s}{2}, k\right)$.

Using this understanding, you can sketch the graph of a quadratic function in factored form $f(x) = a(x - r)(x - s)$, where r and s are distinct x-intercepts.

Example

Sketch the graph of $f(x) = -2(x - 3)(x + 1)$ by using the x-intercepts and vertex defined by this function.

Solution

Step 1: The x-intercepts are zeros of the factors of the function.

$$x - 3 = 0 \qquad \text{and} \qquad x + 1 = 0$$
$$x = 3 \qquad\qquad\qquad x = -1$$

Therefore, the x-intercepts are 3 and -1.

Step 2: Find the equation of the axis of symmetry, which is located halfway between the x-intercepts.

$$x = h = \frac{3 + (-1)}{2}$$
$$x = 1$$

Step 3: Find the vertex (h, k) by substituting the value of h, corresponding to the equation of the axis of symmetry $x = 1$, into the function to determine the y-coordinate k.

$$f(x) = -2(x - 3)(x + 1)$$
$$k = -2(1 - 3)(1 + 1)$$
$$k = -2(-2)(2)$$
$$k = 8$$

The vertex is $(1, 8)$.

Step 4: Sketch the graph of the function using the x-intercepts $(3, 0)$ and $(-1, 0)$ and the vertex $(1, 8)$.

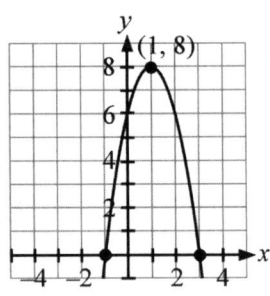

Practice

Use the following information to answer the next question.

Brad is attempting to sketch the graph of the quadratic function $f(x) = -2(x + 4)(x + 2)$. He makes the following four statements:

Statement I: The x-intercepts of the graph are -4 and -2.

Statement II: The equation of the axis of symmetry of the graph is $x = -3$.

Statement III: The vertex of the graph is $(-3, 8)$.

Statement IV: The graph opens downward.

31. Which of the statements is **incorrect**?

    A. I   **B.** II   **C.** III   **D.** IV

32. For the graph of the quadratic function $f(x) = 8(x + 4)(x - 5)$, the respective values of the equation of the axis of symmetry and vertex, V, are

    A. $x = 0.5, V(0.5, -162)$

    B. $x = 0.5, V(0.5, -198)$

    C. $x = -0.5, V(-0.5, -160)$

    D. $x = -0.5, V(-0.5, -154)$

QF2.10 *describe the information that can be obtained by inspecting the standard form* $f(x) = ax^2 + bx + c$, *the vertex form* $f(x) = a(x - h)^2 + k$, *and the factored form* $f(x) = a(x - r)(x - s)$ *of a quadratic function*

GATHERING INFORMATION FROM QUADRATIC FUNCTIONS

As mentioned in section 2.5, there are many features of the graph that can be recognized from the vertex form $f(x) = a(x - h)^2 + k$.

- The vertex is (h, k).
- The equation of the axis of symmetry is $x = h$.
- When $a > 0$, the minimum value is k, and the range is $y \geq k$.
- When $a < 0$, the maximum value is k, and the range is $y \leq k$.

The x-intercepts of the graph are easily recognizable from the factored form $f(x) = a(x - r)(x - s)$. The x-intercepts are r and s.

From the standard form $f(x) = ax^2 + bx + c$, the y-intercept of the graph is easily recognizable. The y-intercept is c (when $x = 0$, $y = a(0)^2 + b(0) + c \Rightarrow y = c$).

Note: The value of a in all forms determines the direction of the parabola.

- When $a < 0$, the graph opens downward.
- When $a > 0$, the graph opens upward.

Practice

Use the following information to answer the next question.

Natalie examined two forms of the same quadratic function and identified the following features of the corresponding graph by inspection.

$$g(x) = -\frac{1}{2}(x + 3)^2 + \frac{9}{2}$$

$$g(x) = -\frac{1}{2}x^2 - 3x$$

Observation I: The vertex is $\left(-3, \frac{9}{2}\right)$.

Observation II: The y-intercept is the origin.

Observation III: The graph opens downward.

Observation IV: The minimum value of the graph is 4.5.

33. Which of the given observations made about the graph of the function is **incorrect**?

A. I   B. II   C. III   D. IV

CHALLENGER QUESTION

34. If the quadratic function written in factored form $f(x) = a(x - r)(x + s)$ was written in the standard form of $f(x) = ax^2 + bx + c$, what would the value of c be in terms of the values a, r, and s?

A. ars

B. $-ars$

C. $-rs$

D. rs

QF2.11 *sketch the graph of a quadratic function whose equation is given in the standard form* $f(x) = ax^2 + bx + c$ *by using a suitable strategy, and identify the key features of the graph*

SKETCHING GRAPHS OF QUADRATIC FUNCTIONS

In the previous section you learned that each form of a quadratic function provides key features about its graph by inspection.

:Example

Given the following two quadratic functions in standard form, determine the…

- vertex
- axis of symmetry
- x- and y-intercepts
- the intervals where the function is positive and/or negative
- the intervals where the function is increasing and decreasing
- and sketch the graph

Function 1: $f(x) = x^2 + 6x + 5$

Function 2: $g(x) = -x^2 + 4x + 2$

Solution

Function 1:

- The y-intercept by inspection is 5 or $(0, 5)$.
- The function is easy to factor (factorable), so convert it to the $f(x) = a(x - r)(x - s)$ form.
  $f(x) = (x + 5)(x + 1)$
- By inspection, the x-intercepts are -5 and -1.
- To determine the equation of the axis of symmetry and the vertex, you could use the "halfway method" or complete the square as described in previous sections.
  Halfway Method: The axis of symmetry is located halfway between the x-intercepts.
  Equation of axis of symmetry:
  $$x = \frac{-5 + (-1)}{2} = -3$$
  Vertex: $[-3, \underbrace{(-3 + 5)(-3 + 1)}_{\text{substitution}}] = (-3, -4)$
- Sketch the graph using these key features.

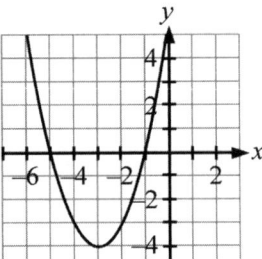

Function 2:

- The y-intercept by inspection is 2 or $(0, 2)$.
- Since the function cannot be factored, convert it to the $g(x) = a(x - h)^2 + k$ form by completing the square.
$$g(x) = -1(x^2 - 4x) + 2$$
$$= -1(x^2 - 4x + 4 - 4) + 2$$
$$= -1(x - 2)^2 + 6$$
By inspection, the vertex is $(2, 6)$, and the equation of the axis of symmetry is $x = 2$.
- To find the x-intercepts, set the function equal to zero $(0 = -x^2 + 4x + 2)$ and use the quadratic formula.
$$x = \frac{-b \pm \sqrt{b^2 - 4ac}}{2a}$$
$$= \frac{-4 \pm \sqrt{(4)^2 - 4(-1)(2)}}{2(-1)}$$
$$= \frac{-4 \pm \sqrt{24}}{-2} = \frac{-4 \pm 2\sqrt{6}}{-2} = 2 \pm \sqrt{6}$$
The x-intercepts are approximately 4.45 and -0.45.
- Sketch the graph using these key features.

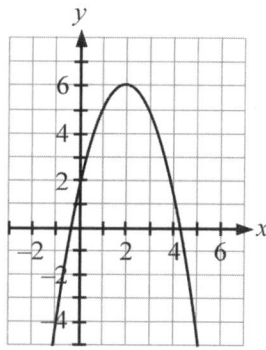

Note: The interval of x, where each function's y-values increase and decrease, is related to the vertex (h, k).

For Function 1:

- The y-values *increase* for x-values moving from the vertex to the right, over the interval $x \geq h \Rightarrow x \geq -3$.
- The y-values *decrease* for x-values moving from the left toward the vertex, over the interval $x \leq h \Rightarrow x \leq -3$.

For Function 2:

- The y-values *decrease* for x-values moving from the vertex to the right, over the interval $x \geq h \Rightarrow x \geq 2$.
- The y-values *increase* for x-values moving from the left toward the vertex, over the interval $x \leq h \Rightarrow x \leq 2$.

Note: The interval of x, where each function's y-values are positive and negative, is related to the x-intercepts. For the x-interval where the graph is *above* the x-axis, the function is positive, and for the x-interval where the graph is *below* the x-axis, the function is negative.

For Function 1:

- The y-values are positive (above the x-axis) over the x-intervals of $x < -5$ and $x > -1$.
- The y-values are negative (below the x-axis) over the x-interval of $-5 < x < -1$.

For Function 2:

- The y-values are positive (above the x-axis) over the x-interval of $-0.45 < x < 4.45$.
- The y-values are negative (below the x-axis) over the x-intervals of $x < -0.45$ and $x > 4.45$.

Practice

CHALLENGER QUESTION

Use the following information to answer the next question.

By looking at the sketch of her graph, Teresa realized that the graph was increasing over the interval of $x \geq -5$ and was positive over the interval $x > -2.5$ and $x < -7.5$.

35. Based on this information alone, what key features of the graph are known?

A. Vertex, x-intercepts, y-intercept, range
B. Vertex, x-intercepts, y-intercept
C. Only the x-intercepts
D. Vertex, x-intercepts

Use the following information to answer the next multipart question.

36. A quadratic function is given as $f(x) = 2x^2 - x - 6$.

Part A

Open Response

Convert the function to the factored form $f(x) = a(x - r)(x - s)$, and state the x-intercepts.

Part B

Open Response

Without sketching the graph, determine the x-interval where the graph of the function is positive. Support your answer by communicating your reasoning.

QF3.1 *collect data that can be modelled as a quadratic function, through investigation with and without technology, from primary sources, using a variety of tools, or from secondary sources, and graph the data*

QF3.2 *determine, through investigation using a variety of strategies, the equation of the quadratic function that best models a suitable data set graphed on a scatter plot, and compare this equation to the equation of a curve of best fit generated with technology*

DATA COLLECTION

Quadratic functions can model certain types of motion, structures, populations, and other numerical data collected from various sources.

There are several methods in which data can be collected for mathematical analysis. These include the following:

- Conducting experiments in class involving motion and concrete materials.
- Conducting experiments using technology such as graphing calculators and the CBR™. Note that when collecting data by conducting experiments, several trials should be done to ensure more realistic results.
- Using a secondary source such as the Internet or Statistics Canada.

GRAPHING THE DATA

After data is collected, it can be represented by a set of points on a Cartesian plane and may generate a pattern that can be represented by drawing a single curve. This curve is called the **curve of best fit** and can be drawn either by hand or by using technology.

FINDING THE EQUATION

The equation of the quadratic function representing the set of points or curve of best fit can be found as follows:

- Find the vertex (h, k) of the curve by locating the highest or lowest point of the parabola.
  Then choose another point from the graph (e.g., y-intercept, x-intercept, etc.), substitute the values of x, y, h and k into the equation $y = a(x - h)^2 + k$, and determine the stretch factor a. Finally, write the equation in the form $y = a(x - h)^2 + k$. You could also follow a similar process by selecting the two x-intercepts and another point to write the equation in the form $y = a(x - r)(x - s)$.
- You could enter the data as lists in your graphing calculator and perform a quadratic regression to find the equation of the curve of best fit.

 **Example**

Number of Registered Apprentices in Building Construction Trades in Canada, from 1991 to 2003

Year	Year (Number)	Number (thousands)
1991	1	46 925
1992	2	43 703
1993	3	40 996
1994	4	36 679
1995	5	34 786
1996	6	33 394
1997	7	32 957
1998	8	33 395
1999	9	36 496
2000	10	39 090
2001	11	42 109
2002	12	47 545
2003	13	53 606

Source: Statistics Canada, Registered Apprenticeship Information System.

Draw, by hand as well as by using technology, the curve of best fit that represents the data. Then, find the equation of the quadratic function representing this curve.

Solution

Method 1: Plot the points on graph paper, and sketch a curve by hand that best represents the points, as illustrated on the diagram.

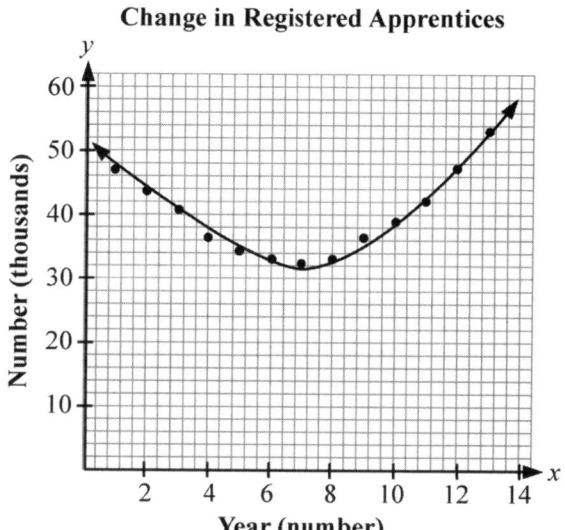

Change in Registered Apprentices

Find the vertex (h, k) by identifying the lowest point on the curve, which is approximately at (7, 31 500). Then, choose another point that the curve passes through. For example, the curve passes through the y-intercept (0, 52 000).

Finally, determine the equation in the form $y = a(x - h)^2 + k$ using the following steps:

Substitute the value of the vertex into h and k, and the values of the y-intercept in for x and y. Then, solve for a.

$$y = a(x - h)^2 + k$$
$$52\ 000 = a(0 - 7)^2 + 31\ 500$$
$$52\ 000 = a(-7)^2 + 31\ 500$$
$$52\ 000 - 31\ 500 = 49a$$
$$20\ 500 = 49a$$
$$a = \frac{20\ 500}{49}$$

Therefore, the equation modelling the curve is
$$y = \frac{20\ 500}{49}(x - 7)^2 + 31\ 500.$$

Method 2: Use a TI-83 Plus graphing calculator to enter the data, graph the points, and perform a quadratic regression to draw the curve of best fit as well as the representative equation.

1. Enter the lists into the list editor.

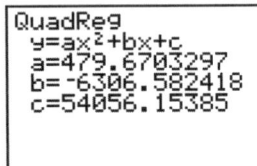

2. Perform a quadratic regression by using STAT CALC to produce the equation.

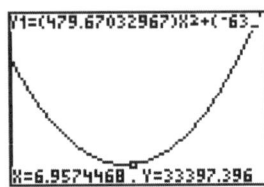

Rounding each value to two decimal places, the quadratic equation representing the data is

$y = 479.67x^2 - 6306.58x + 54\,056.15$

3. Enter the resulting equation in $\left[Y_1 = \right]$ to plot the curve of best fit.

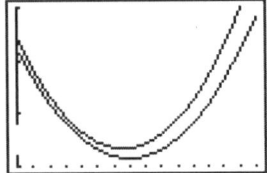

Note: When both equations are graphed on the graphing calculator, they are quite similar over $x = 0$ to $x = 9$, but then diverge slightly for $9 \le x \le 14$. These differences would have been decreased if more data points were plotted.

:Practice

Use the following information to answer the next multipart question.

37.

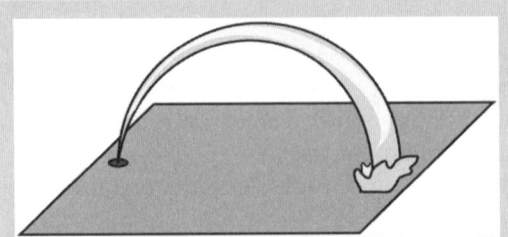

A group of students went to a waterpark and noticed that a waterjet followed a parabolic curve. With a metre stick, they measured the horizontal distance, x, in metres, and the height, y, in metres, of the waterjet at several different positions. Their data is shown.

x (m)	0	0.4	0.6	1.0	1.4
y (m)	0	0.8	1.15	1.60	1.80
x (m)	1.6	2.0	2.4	2.8	3.0
y (m)	1.80	1.60	1.14	0.45	0

Part A

Open Response

Plot the data values as points on the grid, and draw a curve of best fit through these points.

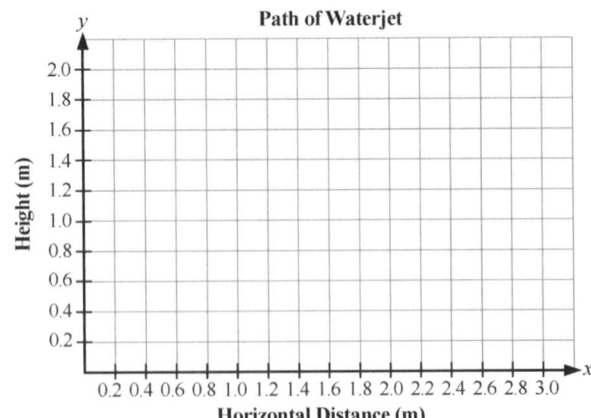

Part B

Numerical Response

When the data values are entered as lists on your graphing calculator and the quadratic regression equation is determined in the form $y = ax^2 + bx + c$, then what is the value of b ____? (Round your answer to two decimal places).

Part C

When the quadratic regression equation $y = ax^2 + bx + c$, where a, b, and c are three decimals, is entered into the graphing calculator and graphed, the maximum height of the waterjet is

A. 1.50 m   **B.** 1.60 m

C. 1.80 m   **D.** 1.82 m

Part D

If you use the x-intercepts of the graph drawn in Part A and the point (2.0, 1.6), then the equation representing the graph of the waterjet path in factored form is

A. $y = -0.8(x - 0)(x - 3)$

B. $y = -1.6(x - 0)(x - 3)$

C. $y = -2(x - 0)(x - 3)$

D. $y = -0.6(x - 0)(x - 3)$

QF3.3 *solve problems arising from real-world applications, given the algebraic representation of a quadratic function*

SOLVING REAL-WORLD PROBLEMS INVOLVING QUADRATIC FUNCTIONS

Quadratic functions can be used to describe real-world situations, and problems related to the equation can be solved.

Example

A city's population can fluctuate. A small Ontario city that has a declining population is expecting the population to begin increasing in the near future because of the introduction of several industrial development initiatives. The city planners predict that the city's population can be modelled by the quadratic function.

$P = 150t^2 - 1200t + 14\,900$, $t \geq 0$, where t is the time in years since January 1st, 2006 and P is the population. Use algebra and technology to answer the following three questions.

a. What was the city's population on January 1st, 2008?
   Solution
   On January 1st, 2008, exactly 2 years will have passed since January 1st, 2006.
   Therefore, substitute the value of 2 for t, and solve for P.

   $P = 150t^2 - 1200t + 14\,900$
   $\quad = 150(2)^2 - 1200(2) + 14\,900$
   $\quad = 600 - 2400 + 14\,900$
   $\quad = 13\,100$

   The population on January 1st, 2008 was 13 100.

b. At the beginning of what year will the city's population be the lowest?

Solution

Method 1: Algebra

The minimum can be found when the function is rewritten in the vertex form,

$f(x) = a(x - h)^2 + k$, by completing the square.

$$
\begin{aligned}
P &= 150t^2 - 1200t + 14\ 900 \\
&= 150(t^2 - 8t) + 14\ 900 \\
&= 150(t^2 - 8t + 16 - 16) + 14\ 900 \\
&= 150(t - 4)^2 + 12\ 500
\end{aligned}
$$

The minimum population of 12 500 occurs when $t = 4$, since the vertex is (4, 12 500).

Therefore, the city's population will be at its lowest at the beginning of $2006 + 4 = 2010$.

Method 2: Graphing calculator TI-83 Plus

Enter the equation $P = 150t^2 - 1200t + 14\ 900$ into $\left[Y_1 = \right]$ as follows:

$Y_1 = 150x^2 - 1200x + 14\ 900$

Then, use the MINIMUM feature of your calculator and a WINDOW setting such as:
$x: [-5, 12, 2]\ y: [7500, 20\ 000, 2500]$

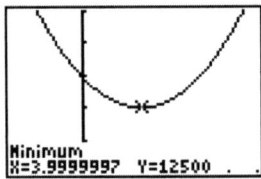

Since the graphing calculator's cursor is at $x = 4$, the minimum population occurs at the beginning of $t = 4$ or $2006 + 4 = 2010$.

c. What is the first year that the city's population will be more than 24 000?

Solution

Method 1: Algebra

Substitute the value 24 000 for P and solve for t using the quadratic formula.

$$
\begin{aligned}
P &= 150t^2 - 1200t + 14\ 900 \\
24\ 000 &= 150t^2 - 1200t + 14\ 900 \\
0 &= 150t^2 - 1200t - 9100
\end{aligned}
$$

$$
\begin{aligned}
t &= \frac{-b \pm \sqrt{b^2 - 4ac}}{2a} \\
&= \frac{1200 \pm \sqrt{(-1200)^2 - 4(150)(-9100)}}{2(150)} \\
&= \frac{1200 \pm 2626.785\ 107}{300} \\
&\approx 12.76 \text{ or } -4.76
\end{aligned}
$$

Since -4.76 refers to a time in the past (before 2006), the value $t = 12.76$ is the solution to this question. The first year that the population will be more than 24 000 is $2006 + 12.76 = 2018.76$ or 2019.

Method 2: Graphing calculator TI-83 Plus

Enter the line referring to the population of 24 000 in $\left[Y_2 = \right]$ as follows:

$Y_2 = 24\ 000$

Then, use the INTERSECTION feature of your calculator to find the first positive intersection point between this line and the quadratic function,

$Y_1 = 150x^2 - 1200x + 14\ 900$

The first positive intersection point occurs when $x = 12.76$ as shown below:

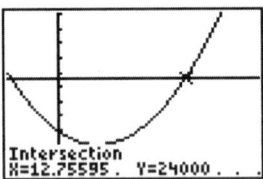

Therefore, the first year that the population will be more than 24 000 is $2006 + 12.76 = 2018.76$ or 2019.

Use the following information to
answer the next multipart question.

38. The field goal kicker for the Toronto
Argonauts attempts a 50-yard field goal.
If he succeeds, his team wins the football
game. A diagram portraying the flight of
the ball is shown.

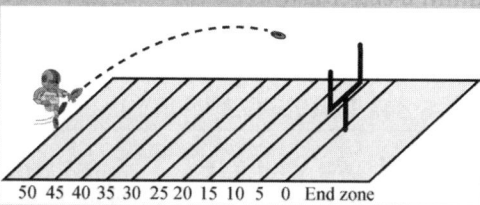

50 45 40 35 30 25 20 15 10 5 0 End zone

The quadratic function representing the
parabolic flight of the ball is given by
$h(x) = -0.019x^2 + 1.026x + 0.049$, where
$h(x)$ is the height of the ball, in yards,
and x is the horizontal distance covered by
the ball, in yards. (Use your graphing
calculator to answer the following
questions.)

Part A

The maximum height of the ball during its
flight is

A. 27.0 yards   B. 18.8 yards

C. 13.9 yards   D. 11.6 yards

Part B

Open Response

What is the total horizontal distance the
ball travelled before it hit the ground?
Describe how you found this result.

Part C

Open Response

If the height of the crossbar of the uprights
is exactly 3 yards above the ground at the
goal line (0 yard line), does he make the
field goal and win the game? Give reasons
for your answer.

SOLUTIONS–QUADRATIC FUNCTIONS

1. 98	10. A	19. Part A- **64**	27. B	Part B- **OR**
2. OR	11. OR	Part B- C	28. OR	37. Part A- **OR**
3. Part A- **OR**	12. A	20. C	29. D	Part B- **2.41**
Part B- **OR**	13. C	21. OR	30. OR	Part C- C
4. D	14. A	22. Part A- **OR**	31. C	Part D- A
5. D	15. OR	Part B- **92.0**	32. A	38. Part A- C
6. D	16. D	23. B	33. D	Part B- **OR**
7. OR	17. 63	24. B	34. B	Part C- **OR**
8. C	18. Part A- C	25. B	35. C	
9. 2	Part B- B	26. A	36. Part A- **OR**	

1. 98

The completed table of values is given as:

w (ft)	4	5	6
l (ft)	20	18	16
A (ft²)	80	90	6 × 16 = 96
w (ft)	7	8	9
l (ft)	14	12	10
A (ft²)	7 × 14 = 98	8 × 12 = 96	9 × 10 = 90

According to the table of values, 98 is the maximum value. Therefore, when the width is 7 ft and the length is 14 ft, the maximum possible area, A, for the garden is 98 ft^2.

2. Open Response

Determine the first and second differences of y by subtracting consecutive y-values, as shown below.

x	y	1st differences	2nd differences
1	2		
		} 6	
2	8		} 4
		} 10	
3	18		} 4
		} 14	
4	32		} 4
		} 18	
5	50		} 4
		} 22	
6	72		} 4
		} 26	
7	98		

Since the second differences of the areas, y, are constant at 4 for every increase of 1 in the x-values, this data represents a quadratic relation.

3. Part A – Open Response

Each area, A, is the result of multiplying the length, l, by the width, w. $A = (l)(w)$.
Area A: $(x)(x + 6)$
Area B: $(x)(3x - 1)$
Area C: $(x)(x + 6)$
Area D: $(x)(3x - 1)$
Area E: $(x + 6)(3x - 1)$

Part B – Open Response

To expand and simplify each area expression, use the distributive property on areas A, B, C, and D, and use the FOIL method on Area E.

Area A: $(x)(x + 6) = x^2 + 6x$

Area B: $(x)(3x - 1) = 3x^2 - x$

Area C: $(x)(x + 6) = x^2 + 6x$

Area D: $(x)(3x - 1) = 3x^2 - x$

Area E: $(x + 6)(3x - 1) = 3x^2 - 1x + 18x - 6$
$= 3x^2 + 17x - 6$

Now, take all the area expressions, and add them to find the total area.

Total area = Area A + Area B + Area C + Area D + Area E
$= x^2 + 6x + 3x^2 - x + x^2 +$
$6x + 3x^2 - x + 3x^2 + 17x - 6$
$= (x^2 + 3x^2 + x^2 + 3x^2 + 3x^2) +$
$(6x - x + 6x - x + 17x) - 6$
$= 11x^2 + 27x - 6$

The simplified expression for the total area of the rectangular net is $11x^2 + 27x - 6$.

4. D

To find the term represented by A, you need to multiply $(3)(3x) = 9x$. Similarly, to find the term represented by B, you need to multiply $(-4)(-2x) = 8x$. When the two terms are combined or added, the result is $17x$.

5. D

To expand and simplify the algebraic expression
$5x(2-x)-(x+3)^2$, use the distributive property and FOIL method, as shown below.

$5x(2-x)-(x+3)^2$

$= 5x(2-x)-(x+3)(x+3)$

$= (5x)(2)+(5x)(-x)-[(x)(x)+(3)(x)+3(x)+(3)(3)]$

$= 10x-5x^2-(x^2+3x+3x+9)$

$= 10x-5x^2-x^2-3x-3x-9$

Collect like terms.

$= (-5x^2-x^2)+(10x-3x-3x)-9$

$= -6x^2+4x-9$

6. D

To factor $2x^2+x-15$ use the procedure of decomposition.

1. Find two numbers that have a product of $(2)(-15)=-30$ and a sum of 1. Those two numbers are 6 and -5.

2. Split the middle term into two terms of x that contain the two numbers 6 and -5.

$$2x^2+x-15$$
$$2x^2+6x-5x-15$$

3. Group the four terms, and factor the greatest common factor out of each pair of two terms.

$(2x^2+6x)+(-5x-15)$
$2x(x+3)-5(x+3)$

4. Factor out the common binomial.

$$2x(x+3)-5(x+3)$$
$$(2x-5)(x+3)$$

Looking at both factors, one of the correct factors is $2x-5$.

7. Open Response

Factor each expression, the first one as a binomial with differences of squares, and the second one as a trinomial using decomposition.

Expression 1

• Factor out the GCF of 2 out of each term.
$18x^2-8=2(9x^2-4)$

• Since 9 and 4 are perfect squares the expression factors to
$2(\sqrt{9}x-\sqrt{4})(\sqrt{9}x+\sqrt{4})=2(3x-2)(3x+2)$

Expression 2

• Find two numbers that multiply to give $(6)(-10)=-60$, and that have a sum of -11. The two numbers are -15 and 4. Split the middle term.
$$= 6x^2-11x-10$$
$$= 6x^2+4x-15x-10$$

• Group the four terms and factor the GCF of each pair.
$(6x^2+4x)+(-15x-10)$
$2x(3x+2)-5(3x+2)$

• Factor out the common binomial.
$(2x-5)(3x+2)$

Examining the factored form of each expression, the common factor is $(3x+2)$.

8. C

Solve each quadratic equation by factoring the quadratic expression and then setting each factor to zero to solve for x.

Choice A—trinomial, where $a=1$

$x^2-4x+3=0$
$(x-3)(x-1)=0$

$$\begin{array}{ccc} x-3=0 & & x-1=0 \\ x=3 & \text{and} & x=1 \end{array}$$

This choice does not have the solutions of $x=-1$ and $x=3$.

Choice B—trinomial, where $a=1$

$x^2+4x+3=0$
$(x+3)(x+1)=0$

$$\begin{array}{ccc} x+3=0 & & x+1=0 \\ x=-3 & \text{and} & x=-1 \end{array}$$

This choice does not have the solutions of $x=-1$ and $x=3$.

Choice C—trinomial, $a=1$

$x^2-2x-3=0$
$(x-3)(x+1)=0$

$$\begin{array}{ccc} x-3=0 & & x+1=0 \\ x=3 & \text{and} & x=-1 \end{array}$$

This is the correct choice since the solutions are $x=-1$ and $x=3$.

Choice D—trinomial, $a=1$

$x^2+2x-3=0$
$(x+3)(x-1)=0$

$$\begin{array}{ccc} x+3=0 & & x-1=0 \\ x=-3 & \text{and} & x=1 \end{array}$$

This choice does not have the solutions of $x=-1$ and $x=3$.

9. 2

A root is a solution of a quadratic equation. Since the root of -3 is a solution of the quadratic equation $-2x^2 + kx + 24 = 0$, you can substitute -3 in for x and solve for k.

$$-2(-3)^2 + k(-3) + 24 = 0$$
$$-2(9) - 3k + 24 = 0$$
$$-18 - 3k + 24 = 0$$
$$-3k + 6 = 0$$
$$-3k = -6$$
$$k = 2$$

The value of k must be 2 in order for -3 to be a root of the quadratic equation.

10. A

To determine the roots (or solutions), set each factor to zero and solve for x.
$$0 = (5x + 3)(4x - 7)$$

$$
\begin{array}{ccc}
5x + 3 = 0 & & 4x - 7 = 0 \\
5x = -3 & \text{and} & 4x = 7 \\
x = -\dfrac{3}{5} & & x = \dfrac{7}{4}
\end{array}
$$

The roots of the factored equation are $-\dfrac{3}{5}$ and $\dfrac{7}{4}$.

Since the roots of a quadratic equation are identical to the x-intercepts of its corresponding function, the x-intercepts are $-\dfrac{3}{5}$ and $\dfrac{7}{4}$. This can be verified using your graphing calculator to examine the graph.

Step 1: Rewrite the equation in expanded form
$$0 = ax^2 + bx + c$$
$$0 = (5x + 3)(4x - 7)$$
$$= 20x^2 - 35x + 12x - 21$$
$$= 20x^2 - 23x - 21$$

Step 2: Enter the corresponding quadratic function into $\left[Y_1 = \right]$ of your graphing calculator.

$$Y_1 = 20x^2 - 23x - 21$$

Step 3: Set your WINDOW to $x:[-5, 5, 1]$, $y:[-30, 10, 2]$, and then press GRAPH.

Step 4: Find the two x-intercepts using the 2nd TRACE ZERO buttons.

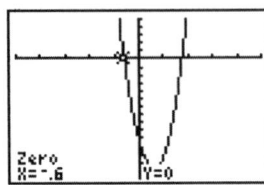 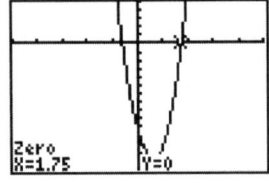

The x-intercepts of the graph of the quadratic function $y = 20x^2 - 23x - 21$ are -0.6 or $-\dfrac{3}{5}$ and 1.75 or $\dfrac{7}{4}$.

11. Open Response

The x-intercepts of the quadratic function $y = -x^2 + 4$ are the same as the roots of its corresponding quadratic equation $0 = -x^2 + 4$ or $0 = -(x + 2)(x - 2)$. To find the roots of the equation in factored form, set each factor to zero, and solve for x.

$$0 = -(x + 2)(x - 2)$$

$$
\begin{array}{ccc}
x + 2 = 0 & & x - 2 = 0 \\
x = -2 & \text{and} & x = 2
\end{array}
$$

The roots of the equation are -2 and 2.
Therefore, the x-intercepts of the corresponding quadratic function must also be -2 and 2.

12. A

The correct steps for solving the quadratic equation $2x^2 - 5x - 1 = 0$ using the quadratic formula are given below.

$$
\begin{array}{ccccccc}
2x^2 & - & 5x & - & 1 & = & 0 \\
\downarrow & & \downarrow & & \downarrow & & \\
a = 2 & & b = -5 & & c = -1 & &
\end{array}
$$

$$x = \frac{-b \pm \sqrt{b^2 - 4ac}}{2a}$$
$$= \frac{-(-5) \pm \sqrt{(-5)^2 - 4(2)(-1)}}{2(2)}$$
$$= \frac{5 \pm \sqrt{25 + 8}}{4}$$
$$= \frac{5 \pm \sqrt{33}}{4}$$
$$\approx 2.686, \ -0.186$$

The first error Matt made was in step 1, where he forgot to put a negative sign in front of his b-value in the first part of the formula.

$$x = \frac{\overset{\substack{missing \\ \downarrow}}{-} (-5) \pm \sqrt{(-5)^2 - 4(2)(-1)}}{2(2)}$$

13. C

Rewrite the equation $5x^2 - 11x = 3$ as $5x^2 - 11x - 3 = 0$. Identify the values of a, b, and c in this equation: $a = 5$, $b = -11$, and $c = -3$. Now, enter these values of a, b, and c into the quadratic formula, $x = \dfrac{-b \pm \sqrt{b^2 - 4ac}}{2a}$, as follows on your graphing calculator to find the solutions for x.

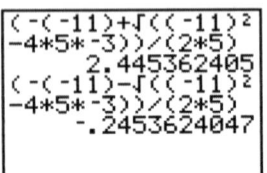

The values of x, to the nearest tenth, are 2.4 and -0.2. Therefore, one of the roots of the quadratic equation $5x^2 - 11x = 3$ is 2.4.

14. A

A quadratic equation has two equal, real roots when the discriminant $D = 0$.

Step 1: Find the values of a, b, and c in the quadratic equation.

$$0 = \underset{\downarrow}{-2x^2} + \underset{\downarrow}{6x} + \underset{\downarrow}{k}$$
$$a = -2 \quad b = 6 \quad c = k$$

Step 2: Set the discriminant equal to zero, and substitute the values of a, b, and c, and solve for k.

$$D = 0$$
$$b^2 - 4ac = 0$$
$$(6)^2 - 4(-2)(k) = 0$$
$$36 + 8k = 0$$
$$8k = -36$$
$$k = -\frac{36}{8}$$
$$k = -\frac{9}{2}$$

The value of k must be $-\frac{9}{2}$ in order for the quadratic equation to have two equal, real roots.

15. Open Response

To determine the discriminant (D), identify the values of a, b, and c in the equation.

$$\underset{\downarrow}{2x^2} - \underset{\downarrow}{8x} - \underset{\downarrow}{7} = 0$$
$$a = 2 \quad b = -8 \quad c = -7$$

Now, calculate the discriminant $D = b^2 - 4ac$.

$$D = b^2 - 4ac$$
$$= (-8)^2 - 4(2)(-7)$$
$$= 64 + 56$$
$$= 120$$

Since $D > 0$, the quadratic equation has two distinct, (different) real roots.

16. D

Finding the discriminant will help you find the type of roots but not the actual values of the roots. Therefore, this method does not apply to this question.

Method 1: Factoring

Determine if the equation $4x^2 + 8x + 2 = 0$ can be factored by taking out the GCF of 2 and examining the resulting trinomial, $a \neq 1$.

$$4x^2 + 8x + 2 = 0$$
$$2\left(2x^2 + 4x + 1\right) = 0$$

There are no two numbers that multiply to give $(a)(c) = (2)(1) = 2$ and have a sum of $b = 4$. Therefore, this method will not work.

Method 2: Quadratic formula

The exact roots of the quadratic equation $4x^2 + 8x + 2 = 0$ can be found easily, assuming that the roots are real.

$$x = \frac{-b \pm \sqrt{b^2 - 4ac}}{2a}, \text{ where } a = 4, b = 8, c = 2$$
$$= \frac{-8 \pm \sqrt{(8)^2 - 4(4)(2)}}{2(4)}$$
$$= \frac{-8 \pm \sqrt{64 - 32}}{8}$$
$$= \frac{-8 \pm \sqrt{32}}{8}$$
$$= \frac{-8 \pm \sqrt{16 \times 2}}{8}$$
$$= \frac{-8 \pm 4\sqrt{2}}{8}$$
$$= \frac{4(-2 \pm \sqrt{2})}{8}$$
$$= \frac{-2 \pm \sqrt{2}}{2}$$
$$= -1 + \frac{\sqrt{2}}{2} \text{ and } -1 - \frac{\sqrt{2}}{2}$$

Since the roots are real, this method enables you to find the exact roots.

Method 3: Graphing

Since the exact roots are not rational, graphing the function $y = 4x^2 + 8x + 2$ will only give you approximate x-intercepts. Therefore, this method also will not solve the problem.

The only method that answers the question is to use the quadratic formula.

17. 63

This problem is too complicated to use the factoring method. Therefore, either the graphing method or the quadratic formula seem to be the only viable choices.

Method 1: Quadratic formula—find the values of a, b, and c in the quadratic equation, and solve for x.

$$\underset{\downarrow}{15x^2} + \underset{\downarrow}{105x} - \underset{\downarrow}{66\,150} = 0$$
$$a = 15 \quad b = 105 \quad c = -66\,150$$
$$x = \frac{-b \pm \sqrt{b^2 - 4ac}}{2a}$$
$$= \frac{-105 \pm \sqrt{(105)^2 - 4(15)(-66\,150)}}{2(15)}$$
$$= \frac{-105 \pm \sqrt{11\,025 + 3\,969\,000}}{30}$$
$$= \frac{-105 \pm 1995}{30}$$
$$x = 63 \text{ or } -70$$

The largest root of the equation is 63.

Method 2: Graphing—enter the function into your graphing calculator, choose an appropriate WINDOW, and use the 2nd TRACE ZERO feature to solve for the largest x-intercept.

$Y_1 = 15x^2 + 105x - 66\ 150$

WINDOW: $x: [-75, 75, 10]$,
$y: [-70\ 000, 25\ 000, 10\ 000]$

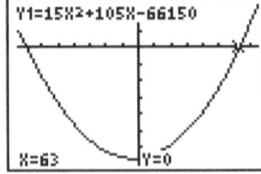

The largest x-intercept is $x = 63$.

Therefore, the largest root of the equation

$15x^2 + 105x - 66\ 150 = 0$, to the nearest whole number, is 63.

18. Part A –C

A quadratic relation is one where a particular variable squared relates directly to the other variable. Also, for a particular x-value, there are usually two y-values, or for a particular y-value, there are usually two x-values.

This means that mappings C and D cannot be quadratic, since they map one x-value to more than two y-values or map four x-values to one y-value.

Mapping A seems to be quadratic. Square the y-variable, and multiply by -2 to get the x-value.

$-2y^2 = x$
$y = \ \ \ 2 \Rightarrow x = -2(2)^2 \ \ = -8$
$y = -2 \Rightarrow x = -2(-2)^2 = -8$
$y = \ \ \ 1 \Rightarrow x = -2(1)^2 \ \ = -2$
$y = -1 \Rightarrow x = -2(-1)^2 = -2$
$y = \ \ \ 0 \Rightarrow x = -2(0)^2 \ \ = 0$

Mapping B also seems to be quadratic. Square the x-variable, and multiply by -2 to get the y-value.

$-2x^2 = y$
$x = \ \ \ 2 \Rightarrow y = -2(2)^2 \ \ = -8$
$x = -2 \Rightarrow y = -2(-2)^2 = -8$
$x = \ \ \ 1 \Rightarrow y = -2(1)^2 \ \ = -2$
$x = -1 \Rightarrow y = -2(-1)^2 = -2$
$x = \ \ \ 0 \Rightarrow y = -2(0)^2 \ \ = 0$

Therefore, mappings A and B represent quadratic relations, which means that there are two relations.

Part B –B

To be a function, any x-value cannot have more than one corresponding y-value.

In mapping A, the value $x = -8$, for example, has two output values of -2 and 2. This does not represent a function.

In mapping B, the value of $x = 2$, for example, only has a single output value of -8. This does represent a function.

In mapping C, the value $x = -8$ has four output values of $4, 2, 0$ and -2. This does not represent a function.

In mapping D, the values of $x = 4$ or $x = 2$, for example, only have a single output value of 8. This does represent a function. Therefore, there are two relations that represent functions.

19. Part A – 64

To evaluate the percentage of a 40-minute lecture that is memorized by Bridget, evaluate $P(40)$ by substituting 40 for t and solving for the output value $P(40)$.

$$P(40) = \frac{12}{5}(40) - \frac{1}{50}(40)^2$$
$$= 96 - \frac{1}{50}(1600)$$
$$= 96 - 32$$
$$= 64$$

Bridget memorizes 64% of a 40-minute lecture.

Part B –C

Evaluate $P(40)$, $P(50)$, $P(60)$, and $P(70)$

$$P(40) = \frac{12}{5}(40) - \frac{1}{50}(40)^2$$
$$= 96 - \frac{1}{50}(1600)$$
$$= 96 - 32$$
$$= 64$$
$$P(50) = \frac{12}{5}(50) - \frac{1}{50}(50)^2$$
$$= 120 - \frac{1}{50}(2500)$$
$$= 120 - 50$$
$$= 70$$
$$P(60) = \frac{12}{5}(60) - \frac{1}{50}(60)^2$$
$$= 144 - \frac{1}{50}(3600)$$
$$= 144 - 72$$
$$= 72$$
$$P(70) = \frac{12}{5}(70) - \frac{1}{50}(70)^2$$
$$= 168 - \frac{1}{50}(4900)$$
$$= 168 - 98$$
$$= 70$$

If you compare all four values, you will see that $P(60) = 72$ is the largest value. Therefore, when $t = 60$ minutes of the lecture, Bridget is able to memorize the most at 72%.

20. C

Any linear function, except for $x = a$, has a domain that is $x \in \mathbb{R}$. Thus, the function $f(x) = 0x + 3$ has a domain of $x \in \mathbb{R}$. This is shown in the graph that extends left and right infinitely due to the fact that all real numbers can be substituted for x to give a corresponding y-value. For all values of x, the corresponding y-values are always 3 (e.g., $f(1) = 0(1) + 3 = 3$, $f(-3) = 0(-3) + 3 = 3$). Therefore, the range of this function is $y = 3$.

21. Open Response

Substitute the x-values in the table of values into the function $y = -\frac{1}{2}x^2 + 3$ to determine the corresponding y-values.

x	y
-3	$-\frac{1}{2}(-3)^2 + 3 = -1.5$
-2	$-\frac{1}{2}(-2)^2 + 3 = 1$
-1	$-\frac{1}{2}(-1)^2 + 3 = 2.5$
0	$-\frac{1}{2}(0)^2 + 3 = 3$
1	$-\frac{1}{2}(1)^2 + 3 = 2.5$
2	$-\frac{1}{2}(2)^2 + 3 = 1$
3	$-\frac{1}{2}(3)^2 + 3 = -1.5$

The table of values shows that the y-values increase the same amount up to the value of 3 as they decrease after this point.

As a result of this symmetrical pattern, all y-values are below and equal to 3. Thus, the range of $y = -\frac{1}{2}x^2 + 3$ is $y \leq 3$.

22. Part A – Open Response

The domain is restricted by the horizontal distance, x, that the javelin covers from the moment it is thrown ($x = 0$) to the moment it hits the ground ($x = a$). Therefore, the restriction on the domain could be written as $0 \leq x \leq a$. If the javelin is thrown with less force, the javelin will not travel as far, and will hit the ground at a value of $x = b$, where $b < a$. Therefore, the new domain is $0 \leq x \leq b$.

Part B – 92.0

Solve the quadratic equation for x by identifying the values of a, b, and c in the equation $0 = -0.008x^2 + 0.72x + 1.5$, and then use the quadratic formula.

$$0 = \underset{\downarrow}{-0.008x^2} + \underset{\downarrow}{0.72x} + \underset{\downarrow}{1.5}$$
$$a = -0.008 \quad b = 0.72 \quad c = 1.5$$

$$x = \frac{-b \pm \sqrt{b^2 - 4ac}}{2a}$$
$$= \frac{-0.72 \pm \sqrt{(0.72)^2 - 4(-0.008)(1.5)}}{2(-0.008)}$$
$$= \frac{-0.72 \pm \sqrt{0.5664}}{-0.016}$$
$$\approx \frac{-0.72 \pm 0.752\,595\,5089}{-0.016}$$

$x \approx -2.037\,219\,306$ and $92.037\,219\,31$

Based on these two values, the maximum limit on the domain, x, when $h = 0$ occurs when the javelin hits the ground at $x = 92.0$ m.

23. B

In order for the transformed graph of the function $f(x) = a(x - h)^2 + k$ to have an axis of symmetry of $x = -3$, the value of $h = -3$. For the range to be $y \leq 2$, the value of $k = 2$ and the value of $a < 0$. This ensures that the graph opens downward with a maximum value of 2. The vertex is $(-3, 2)$, which is located in quadrant II. An example of the graph of a function such as $f(x) = -2(x - (-3))^2 + 2$ is shown.

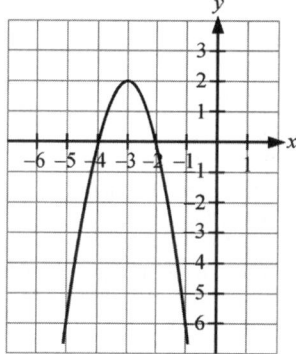

This example shows that no matter what the value of a is, the graph will also have two x-intercepts.

Therefore, the graph of $f(x) = a(x - h)^2 + k$ will have two x-intercepts and a vertex in quadrant II.

24. B

For the graph to open upward, $a > 0$. Since the vertex (h, k) is located in quadrant III, $h < 0$ (to translate the graph of $f(x) = x^2$ to the left) and $k < 0$ (to translate the graph of $f(x) = x^2$ downward).

25. B

Since the vertex is $(2, -3)$, $h = 2$ and $k = -3$ in the function $h(x) = a(x - h)^2 + k$.

For Jasmine to draw points at the x-intercepts of $(1, 0)$ and $(3, 0)$, she needed to apply a vertical stretch about the x-axis by a factor of 3 from the vertex. This is shown in the diagram below.

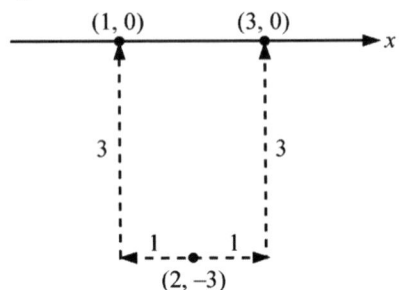

Therefore, the function that Jasmine drew is $h(x) = 3(x - 2)^2 - 3$.

26. A

For the graph of $g(x) = a(x - h)^2 + k$ to have a vertex of $(1, 3)$, the graph of $f(x) = x^2$ has to be translated right 1 unit and up 3 units. Since the transformed graph opens downward, the graph of $f(x) = x^2$ has been reflected in the x-axis.

27. B

The correct steps to expand $g(x) = -3(x - 2)^2 + 5$ into standard form are given below:

Step 1: Rewrite $(x - 2)^2$ as the product of the binomials $(x - 2)(x - 2)$.
$$g(x) = -3(x - 2)^2 + 5$$
$$= -3(x - 2)(x - 2) + 5$$
Step 2: FOIL the binomials $(x - 2)(x - 2)$, or distribute -3 to each term of the first binomial.
$$g(x) = -3(x - 2)(x - 2) + 5$$
$$= (-3x + 6)(x - 2) + 5$$
Step 3: In this case, FOIL the binomials.
$$g(x) = (-3x + 6)(x - 2) + 5$$
$$= -3x^2 + 6x + 6x - 12 + 5$$
Step 4: Collect like terms.
$$g(x) = -3x^2 + 6x + 6x - 12 + 5$$
$$= -3x^2 + 12x - 7$$
Upon analysis of Zeke's process of expansion, with respect to the above correct steps, you can see that his first error is made in step 2.

28. Open Response

To convert $f(x) = -\frac{1}{2}(x + 4)^2 - 3$ into standard form, use the following steps:
$$f(x) = -\frac{1}{2}(x + 4)^2 - 3$$
Rewrite $(x + 4)^2$ to $(x + 4)(x + 4)$, and FOIL.
$$= -\frac{1}{2}(x + 4)(x + 4) - 3$$
$$= -\frac{1}{2}\left(x^2 + 4x + 4x + 16\right) - 3$$
Distribute the value of $-\frac{1}{2}$ to each term in the brackets.
$$= -\frac{1}{2}x^2 - 2x - 2x - 8 - 3$$
Collect like terms.
$$= -\frac{1}{2}x^2 - 4x - 11$$

29. D

To find the value of m in step 2, you need to take the coefficient of x, namely $-\frac{4}{3}$, divide it by 2 and then square it.
Divide by 2.
$$-\frac{4}{3} \div 2 = -\frac{4}{3} \times \frac{1}{2} = -\frac{4}{6}$$
Square $-\frac{4}{6}$.
$$\left(-\frac{4}{6}\right)^2 = \frac{16}{36} \text{ or } \frac{4}{9}$$
Therefore, the value of $m = \frac{4}{9}$ in step 2.
$$g(x) = -3\left(x^2 - \frac{4}{3}x + \frac{4}{9} - \frac{4}{9}\right) - 5$$
To complete step 3, you need to move the value $-\frac{4}{9}$ out of the brackets by multiplying it by the leading coefficient -3 and then factoring the trinomial left in the brackets.

$$g(x) = -3\ (x^2 - \frac{4}{3}x + \frac{4}{9} - \frac{4}{9}) - 5$$
$$= -3\left(x^2 - \frac{4}{3}x + \frac{4}{9}\right) - 3\left(-\frac{4}{9}\right) - 5$$
$$= -3\left(x - \frac{2}{3}\right)^2 + \frac{12}{9} - 5$$
$$= -3\left(x - \frac{2}{3}\right)^2 - \frac{11}{3}$$

Therefore, the value of n in step 3 should be $-\frac{11}{3}$.

30. Open Response

To convert the function $f(x) = -\frac{1}{5}x^2 + 3x - 14$ to the vertex form, complete the square as follows:

Step 1: Remove the common factor $-\frac{1}{5}$ out of the first two terms.

$$f(x) = -\frac{1}{5}\left(x^2 - 15x\right) - 14$$

Step 2: Divide the coefficient of x, namely -15, by 2, and square it. Then, add and subtract this value inside the brackets.

$$f(x) = -\frac{1}{5}\left(x^2 - 15x + \frac{225}{4} - \frac{225}{4}\right) - 14$$

Step 3: Move the value $-\frac{225}{4}$ out of the brackets by multiplying it to the leading coefficient $-\frac{1}{5}$.

$$f(x) = -\frac{1}{5}\left(x^2 - 15x + \frac{225}{4}\right) - \frac{1}{5}\left(-\frac{225}{4}\right) - 14$$

Step 4: Factor the perfect square trinomial inside the brackets $\left(\frac{1}{2}$ of the coefficient of $x\right)$, and collect the constant terms outside the brackets.

$$f(x) = -\frac{1}{5}\left(x - \frac{15}{2}\right)^2 + \frac{45}{4} - 14$$

$$f(x) = -\frac{1}{5}\left(x - \frac{15}{2}\right)^2 - \frac{11}{4}$$

The vertex form of the quadratic function is

$$f(x) = -\frac{1}{5}\left(x - \frac{15}{2}\right)^2 - \frac{11}{4}.$$

31. C

For the quadratic function given in the factored form $f(x) = -2(x + 4)(x + 2)$, determine the following features of its graph:

- The x-intercepts are -4 and -2, since these values make each factor equal 0.

$$x + 4 = 0 \qquad \text{and} \qquad x + 2 = 0$$
$$x = -4 \qquad\qquad\qquad x = -2$$

- The equation of the axis of symmetry is located halfway between the x-intercepts:
$$x = h = \frac{r + s}{2} = \frac{-4 + (-2)}{2} = -3$$

- The graph of the function opens downward since the numerical coefficient $a < 0$.

- The vertex of the graph (h, k) can be found, since it lies on the axis of symmetry ($x = -3$). Substitute $x = -3$, and solve for k in the function.
$$f(x) = -2(x + 4)(x + 2)$$
$$k = -2(-3 + 4)(-3 + 2)$$
$$= -2(1)(-1)$$
$$= 2$$

The vertex is $(-3, 2)$.

In statement III, Brad incorrectly states that the vertex of the graph is $(-3, 8)$.

32. A

The x-intercepts of the function in factored form $f(x) = 8(x + 4)(x - 5)$ are $x = -4$ and 5.

The axis of symmetry is located halfway between the x-intercepts, so its equation is
$$x = h = \frac{r + s}{2} = \frac{-4 + 5}{2} = 0.5$$

The equation of the axis of symmetry is $x = 0.5$.

Since the vertex (h, k) lies on the axis of symmetry, substitute $x = 0.5$ into the function, and solve for the y-value k.
$$f(x) = 8(x + 4)(x - 5)$$
$$k = 8(0.5 + 4)(0.5 - 5)$$
$$= 8(4.5)(-4.5)$$
$$= -162$$

The vertex of the graph is $(0.5, -162)$.

33. D

The following features of the graph in the vertex form $g(x) = -\frac{1}{2}(x + 3)^2 + \frac{9}{2}$ can be obtained by inspection:

- Vertex $\left(-3, \frac{9}{2}\right)$

- Maximum is $\frac{9}{2}$ or 4.5

- Opens downward ($a < 0$)

- Range: $y \leq \frac{9}{2}$

- Axis of symmetry: $x = -3$

The following features of the graph in the standard form of $g(x) = -\frac{1}{2}x^2 - 3x$ can be obtained by inspection:

- The y-intercept is 0 (since $c = 0$) or the origin.
- The graph opens downward ($a < 0$).

Therefore, observation IV is incorrect since the graph has a maximum at 4.5.

34. B

To convert the factored form to the standard form, carry out the following steps:

FOIL the binomials.

Distribute the value of a to each term in the brackets.

Collect like terms.
$$f(x) = a(x - r)(x + s)$$
$$= a\left(x^2 + sx - rx - rs\right)$$
$$= ax^2 + asx - arx - ars$$
$$= ax^2 + (as - ar)x - ars$$

The final function is written in standard form
$$f(x) = ax^2 + bx + c, \text{ where } a = a, b = as - ar, \text{ and } c = -ars.$$

35. C

The interval where the graph increases or decreases is linked to the vertex (h, k). Therefore, since the graph is increasing over the interval of $x \geq -5$, the x-value of the vertex is -5. However, the interval does not provide the y-value. The vertex and the range are unknown.

The intervals where the graph is positive or negative is linked to the x-intercepts. Since the function is positive over the intervals $x > -2.5$ and $x < -7.5$, you know that the x-intercepts of the graph are -2.5 and -7.5. Therefore, the only information about the graph that you can derive from the interval statements are the x-intercepts.

36. Part A – Open Response

To convert $f(x) = 2x^2 - x - 6$ into factored form, use decomposition to factor the trinomial $2x^2 - x - 6$.

Step 1: Split $-1x$ into two terms, finding the two numbers -4 and 3 that have a product of $(2)(-6) = -12$ and a sum of -1.

$$2x^2 - x - 6$$
$$2x^2 - 4x + 3x - 6$$

Step 2: Factor out the GCF of each pair, and then factor out the common binomial.
$2x(x - 2) + 3(x - 2)$
$(2x + 3)(x - 2)$

Step 3: Factor out 2 from the first binomial so that the final function is in the form $f(x) = a(x - r)(x - s)$.
$f(x) = (2x + 3)(x - 2)$
$\quad = 2\left(x + \dfrac{3}{2}\right)(x - 2)$

By inspecting the factored form of the function, the x-intercepts are $-\dfrac{3}{2}$ and 2.

Part B – Open Response

The graph of the function opens upward, since $a > 0$ (namely $a = 2$ in both forms). Since the graph opens upward and has x-intercepts of $-\dfrac{3}{2}$ and 2, the vertex must be located below the x-axis. Therefore, the function is negative for x-intervals between the two x-intercepts, namely $-\dfrac{3}{2} < x < 2$.

The function is therefore positive for all other values of x to the left of the x-intercept $-\dfrac{3}{2}$ and to the right of the x-intercept 2. Therefore, the function is positive over the intervals $x < -\dfrac{3}{2}$ and $x > 2$.

37. Part A – Open Response

The plotted points and curve of best fit are shown in the graph below.

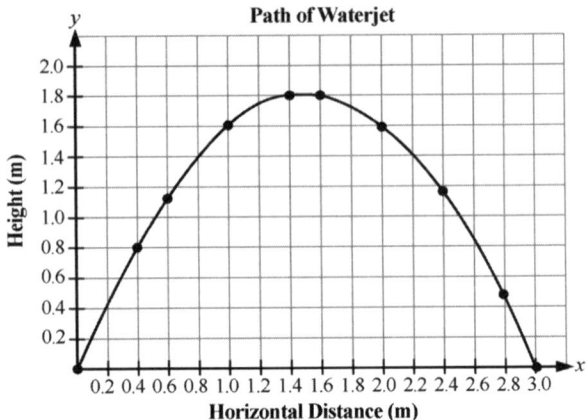

Part B – 2.41

Enter the data in the table of values in the lists L_1 and L_2 of your graphing calculator.

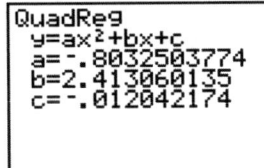

Then, perform the quadratic regression by pressing STAT CALC 5 ENTER. The resulting information will appear on your screen.

```
QuadReg
 y=ax²+bx+c
 a=⁻.8032503774
 b=2.413060135
 c=⁻.012042174
```

According to the quadratic regression given, the value of b in $y = ax^2 + bx + c$, to two decimals, is 2.41.

Part C –C

Enter the quadratic regression equation, developed in the previous question, into [Y =]. Round the values a, b, and c to three decimal places.

$Y_1 = -0.803x^2 + 2.413x - 0.012$

Set your WINDOW to x:[−2, 4, 1], y:[−2, 4, 1], and then press GRAPH. To find the maximum y-value of the graph (which represents the maximum height of the waterjet), press 2nd TRACE MAXIMUM to find the maximum y-value of 1.796 2503 at an x-value of 1.500 621, as shown on the screen below.

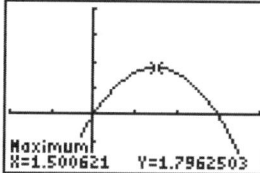

The maximum height of the waterjet, to the nearest hundredth, is 1.80 m.

Part D –A

The x-intercepts of the graph drawn in Part A are 0 and 3.0. To find the equation describing the factored form $y = a(x - r)(x - s)$, substitute the x-intercepts for r and s and substitute the other point,(2.0, 1.6), in for x and y. Then, solve for a.

$y = a(x - r)(x - s)$
$1.6 = a(2.0 - 0)(2.0 - 3.0)$
$1.6 = a(2)(-1)$
$1.6 = -2a$
$a = -0.8$

Therefore, the equation in factored form representing the graph of the waterjet path is
$y = -0.8(x - 0)(x - 3)$

38. Part A –C

Enter the quadratic equation

$h(x) = -0.019x^2 + 1.026x + 0.049$ into $\left[Y_1 = \right]$ of your graphing calculator.

$Y_1 = -0.019x^2 + 1.026x + 0.049$

Set your WINDOW to
x: [−10, 70, 10], y: [−10, 20, 10], and press GRAPH. To find the maximum y-value of the graph (which represents the maximum height of the football), press 2nd TRACE MAXIMUM to find the maximum y-value of 13.9 at an x-value of 27.0, as shown in the screen below.

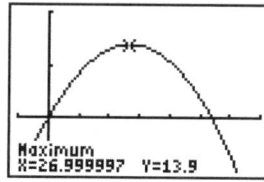

The maximum height of the ball during its flight is 13.9 yards.

Part B – Open Response

To find the total horizontal distance the ball travelled, find the second x-intercept of the graph, which represents the point where the ball hit the ground. To find this x-intercept of the graph, press 2nd TRACE ZERO.

The second x-intercept is $x = 54.047\ 716$, as shown on the screen below.

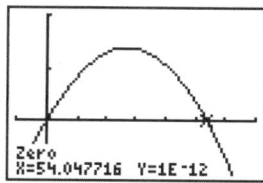

Therefore, the total horizontal distance travelled is 54 yards.

Note: Assume that the ball was kicked at an x-value of $x = 0$ on the given graph.

Part C – Open Response

The crossbar is located at the 0 yard line, which is 50 yards from where the ball was kicked. Therefore, to find the height of the ball at a horizontal distance of 50, press 2nd TRACE VALUE, and enter $x = 50$ to find the corresponding y-value of $y = 3.849$, as shown in the screen below.

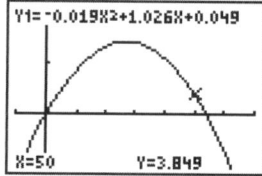

The height of the ball from the ground is 3.849 yards. Since the height of the crossbar is 3 yards, the ball clears the crossbar by a vertical distance of $3.849 - 3 = 0.849$ yards. Since it clears the crossbar, the field goal is made, and the Toronto Argonauts win the game.

Use the following information to answer the next multipart question.

1. A ball is thrown off a 25 m cliff, and its flight can be represented by the parabola shown in the graph.

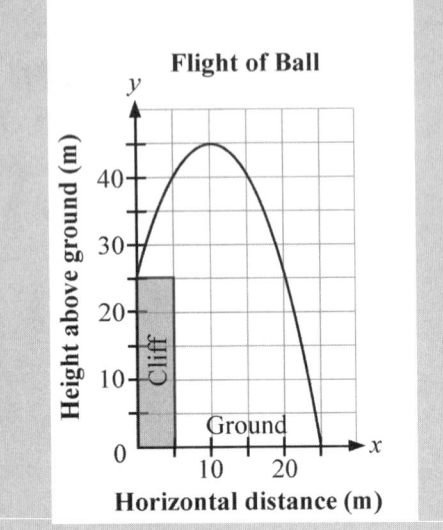

Part A

Numerical Response

When the ball strikes the ground it is located ____ m from the base of the cliff.

Part B

The total vertical distance travelled by the ball during its flight from the cliff to the ground is

A. 20 m   **B.** 45 m

C. 65 m   **D.** 90 m

CHALLENGER QUESTION

Use the following information to answer the next question.

The design of the side view of a specialized cement staircase is shown, with expressions for all side lengths.

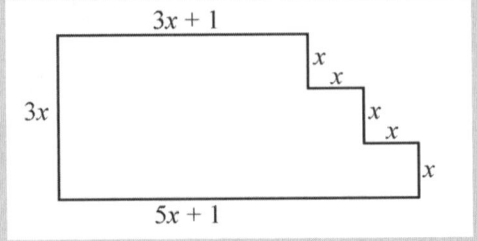

2. Which of the following simplified expressions describes the area of the side view of the staircase?

A. $6x^2$ **B.** $15x^2$

C. $12x^2 + 3x$ **D.** $13x^2 + 3x$

Open Response

CHALLENGER QUESTION

3. Determine the values of A and B so that $Ax^2 - (x + 3)^2 + (4x + 2)(3x - 5) + Bx$ simplifies to the expression $6x^2 + 8x - 19$. Show your work.

Use the following information to answer the next question.

A student factored four quadratic expressions as shown.

I. $x^2 - 19x + 60 = (x - 15)(x - 4)$

II. $3x^3 - 75x = 3x(x - 5)(x + 5)$

III. $-9x^2 + 12x - 4$
$= (3x + 2)(3x + 2)$

IV. $4x^2 + 6x + 2 = 2(x + 1)(2x + 1)$

4. The quadratic expression that the student factored **incorrectly** is

A. quadratic I   B. quadratic II

C. quadratic III   D. quadratic IV

Open Response

CHALLENGER QUESTION

5. A student was asked to factor a quadratic expression in the form $ax^2 + bx + c$ by means of decomposition. Part of this process is shown. Complete the decomposition by filling in the missing terms.

Step 1 → $6x^2 - 3x + 4x - \boxed{}$

Step 2 → $3x(\underline{}) + \boxed{} (\underline{})$

Step 3 → $(\underline{})(\underline{})$

6. If a quadratic equation is factored so that $(2x + a)(3x - b) = 0$, then the roots of the equation can be expressed as

A. $x = -\dfrac{a}{2}, \dfrac{b}{3}$

B. $x = \dfrac{a}{2}, -\dfrac{b}{3}$

C. $x = a, b$

D. $x = -a, b$

Numerical Response

7. The solutions for the quadratic equation $2x^2 - 72 = 0$ are $x = -6$ and $x = \underline{}$.

Use the following information to answer the next question.

The graph of a quadratic function $y = f(x)$ is shown below.

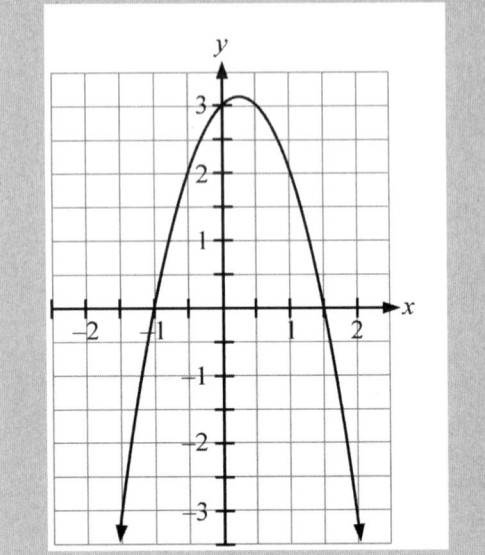

8. According to the x-intercepts of the graph, what are the factors of the corresponding quadratic equation $0 = f(x)$?

   A. $(x - 1)$ and $(2x + 3)$

   B. $(x + 1)$ and $(2x - 3)$

   C. $(x - 1)$ and $(3x + 2)$

   D. $(x + 1)$ and $(3x - 2)$

Use the following information to answer the next multipart question.

9. At a waterpark, a particular waterjet followed a parabolic path. The relationship between the height, y, in metres, and the horizontal distance from the edge of the park, x, in metres, of the waterjet is given by the quadratic function $y = -x^2 + 10x - 16$. A table of values shows some data corresponding to this function.

x	y
2	0
3	5
4	8
5	9
6	8
7	5
8	0

Part A

Open Response

Plot the points corresponding to the table of values on the grid, and draw a smooth curve through the points.

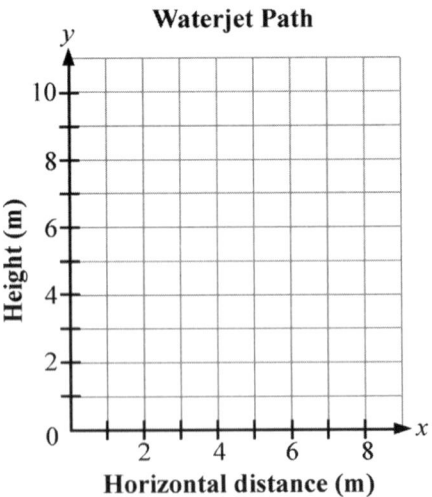

Waterjet Path

Part B

Open Response

Identify the x-intercepts of the graph.

Part C

Open Response

Factor the corresponding quadratic equation $0 = -x^2 + 10x - 16$, and explain how the roots of the factors are related to the x-intercepts of the graph of the function.

Use the following information to answer the next question.

> A student used the quadratic formula to a solve a quadratic equation in the form $ax^2 + bx + c = 0$. Her first step of entering the values of a, b, and c into the formula are shown.
>
> $$x = \frac{-2 \pm \sqrt{2^2 - 4(-1)(3)}}{2(-1)}$$

10. Which of the following quadratic equations was she trying to solve?

A. $-x^2 - 2x = 3$

B. $-x^2 + 2x = 3$

C. $-x^2 - 2x = -3$

D. $-x^2 + 2x = -3$

11. By applying the quadratic formula in solving the quadratic equation $-x^2 - 6x + 4 = 0$, one of the exact roots is

A. $6 - 2\sqrt{13}$ **B.** $-6 - 2\sqrt{13}$

C. $3 + \sqrt{13}$ **D.** $-3 + \sqrt{13}$

Use the following information to answer the next question.

> Four students examined the quadratic equation $0 = x^2 - 120$ and made the following statements:
>
> **Student 1:** The discriminant $D < 0$, and there are no real roots.
> **Student 2:** The discriminant $D > 0$, and there are two equal, real roots.
> **Student 3:** The discriminant $D = 0$, and there are two equal, real roots.
> **Student 4:** The discriminant $D > 0$, and there are two distinct, real roots.

12. Which student made the correct statement about the quadratic equation?

A. student 1   **B.** student 2

C. student 3   **D.** student 4

Use the following information to answer the next question.

Some of the steps taken by four students in solving the equation $x^2 - 2x - 3 = 0$ are shown below:

Amanda—Graphing

1. $Y_1 = x^2 - 2x - 3$ GRAPH
2. Zoom 4
3. 2nd Trace 2
4. ◄ ◄ ◄ ◄ ENTER
5. ► ► ► ► ENTER
6. and so on

Cody—Completing the square

1. $1(x^2 - 2x) - 3 = 0$
2. $1(x^2 - 2x + 1) - 1 - 3 = 0$
3. $1(x - 1)^2 - 4 = 0$
4. and so on

Dustin—Factoring

1. Find two numbers with a product of -3 and a sum of -2.
2. The two numbers are -3 and 1.
3. and so on

Danielle—Quadratic formula

1. $a = 1, b = -2, c = -3$
2. $x = \dfrac{-(-2) \pm \sqrt{(-2)^2 - 4(1)(3)}}{2(1)}$
3. and so on

13. If each student completed his or her steps, which is the **quickest** strategy to solve the equation?

   A. Graphing

   B. Factoring

   C. Quadratic formula

   D. Completing the square

Numerical Response

14. When the quadratic equation $x^2 = 6x + 8$ is solved, the exact real roots are $3 \pm \sqrt{k}$. The value of k is ____.

Numerical Response

CHALLENGER QUESTION

Use the following information to answer the next question.

Warren decided that it was most advantageous to find the roots of $2x^2 + 3x - 44 = 0$ by factoring.

His factored form of the equation was $(x - 4)(ax + b) = 0$.

15. What is the value of $a + b$? ____

Use the following information to answer the next question.

Four graphs are drawn that represent linear and quadratic relations.

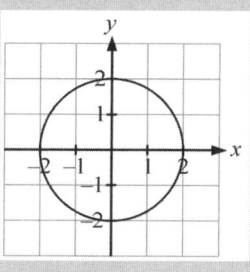

Graph 1

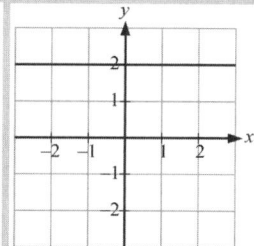

Graph 2

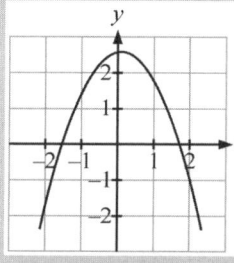

Graph 3

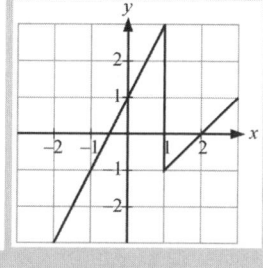

Graph 4

16. Which of the graphs do **not** represent functions?

   A. Graph 1

   B. Graph 4

   C. Graphs 1, and 4

   D. Graphs 1, 2, and 4

CHALLENGER QUESTION

17. Which of the following quadratic relations is also a quadratic function?

   A. $y^2 - 2x = 0$

   B. $y - \sqrt{2}x^2 = 0$

   C. $x - 2y^2 = 0$

   D. $(y - 2)^2 - x = 0$

Use the following information to answer the next multipart question.

18. A linear function is given by
$f(x) = -2(x + 3) + 5$

Part A

Numerical Response

The value of $f(-6)$ is ____.

Part B

If $f(x) = 21$, then the input value of x has to be

   A. -43 B. -11

   C. -5 D. 6.5

19. Which of the following quadratic functions has a range of $y \geq 4$?

   A. $y = 4x^2$

   B. $y = -x^2 + 4$

   C. $y = x^2 + 4$

   D. $y = x^2 + 2x + 1$

Open Response

20. If you graphed the quadratic function $y = x^2 - 2x - 3$ on your graphing calculator, explain how you would determine the range of this function.

Use the following information to answer the next multipart question.

21. Aerial skiers realize that the vertical and horizontal distances they achieve will depend on the angle of trajectory they have when they leave the ramp. The given graphs represent the paths of an aerial skier for two jumps at different angles of trajectory.

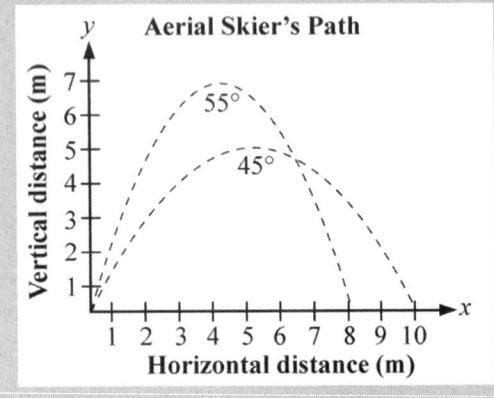

Aerial Skier's Path

Part A

Open Response

Predict the changes to the domain and range if the angle of the aerial skier's trajectory was 75°.

Part B

Numerical Response

If the range of the 45° trajectory is $0 \leq y \leq a$ and the range of the 55° trajectory is $0 \leq y \leq b$, then the difference between b and a is _____ m

CHALLENGER QUESTION

22. The value of a in a particular quadratic function changes its sign and value. Two of the effects on the transformed graph are that the

   A. range and the axis of symmetry change

   B. domain and the vertical stretch factor change

   C. vertex and the direction that the parabola opens change

   D. vertical stretch factor and the direction that the parabola opens change

Use the following information to answer the next question.

The graph of the quadratic function $f(x) = x^2$ is vertically compressed by a factor of $\frac{1}{4}$ about the x-axis, and is translated left 5 units and 3 units up.

23. If the transformed function is written in the form of $g(x) = \frac{1}{a}(x - h)^2 + k$, then the respective values of a, h, and k, are

   A. 4, –5, 3

   B. $\frac{1}{4}$, –5, –3

   C. 4, 5, 3

   D. $\frac{1}{4}$, 5, 3

Use the following information to answer the next multipart question.

24. Tina sketched the transformed quadratic function $q(x) = a(x - h)^2 + k$. By looking at the values of h and k, she labelled her vertex V. Then she used her understanding of the vertical changes to the graph, a, that cause the graph to stretch one unit each time to the left and right from the vertex, V.

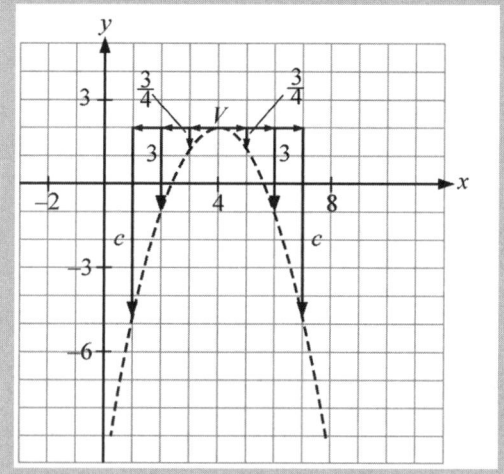

Part A

According to the value of a of the function $q(x) = a(x - h)^2 + k$, what vertical drop did she make that is labelled c on the graph?

A. $\dfrac{9}{4}$ **B.** 6

C. $\dfrac{13}{2}$ **D.** $\dfrac{27}{4}$

Part B

The quadratic function that she sketched was

A. $q(x) = \dfrac{3}{4}(x - 4)^2 + 2$

B. $q(x) = -\dfrac{3}{4}(x - 4)^2 + 2$

C. $q(x) = \dfrac{3}{4}(x + 4)^2 + 2$

D. $q(x) = -\dfrac{3}{4}(x + 4)^2 + 2$

25. When the quadratic function given as $f(x) = a(x - 2)^2 + 1$ is expanded to the form $f(x) = ax^2 + bx + c$, the value of b in terms of a is

A. $-4a$ **B.** $-2a$

C. $2a$ **D.** $4a$

Open Response

26. Verify that the quadratic function in the forms $f(x) = 3(x + 1)^2 - 4$ and $f(x) = 3x^2 + 6x - 1$ represent the same graph by showing algebraically that the vertex of the first form satisfies the function written in the second form.

Show your work.

27. The vertex form of the quadratic function

$f(x) = -\frac{1}{2}x^2 + 4x + c$ is

A. $f(x) = -\frac{1}{2}(x-1)^2 + \left(c + \frac{1}{2}\right)$

B. $f(x) = -\frac{1}{2}(x-1)^2 + (c+1)$

C. $f(x) = -\frac{1}{2}(x-4)^2 + (c+8)$

D. $f(x) = -\frac{1}{2}(x-4)^2 + (c+16)$

Use the following information to answer the next multipart question.

28. A quadratic function is given as
$f(x) = x^2 - 5x - 3.$

Part A

Open Response

Complete the square and express this function in the vertex form
$f(x) = a(x-h)^2 + k.$

Part B

Open Response

Identify the vertex from the vertex form of the quadratic function.

Part C

Open Response

Verify that the two forms of the function represent the same graph by showing that $f(2)$, $f(-3)$, and $f(6)$ are the same values in both forms.

29. Which of the following graphs correctly represents the graph of the quadratic function $f(x) = (x + 1)(x - 5)$?

A.

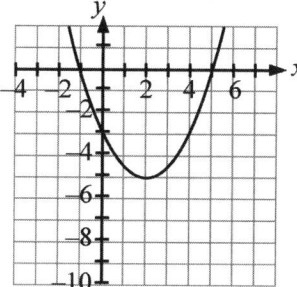

B.

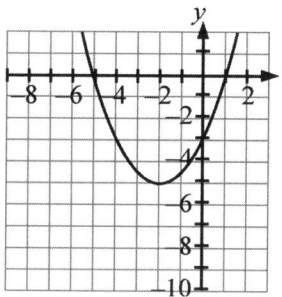

C.

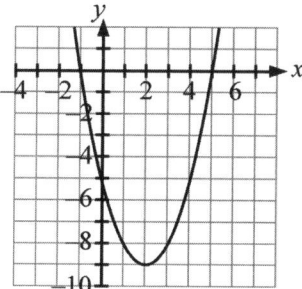

D.

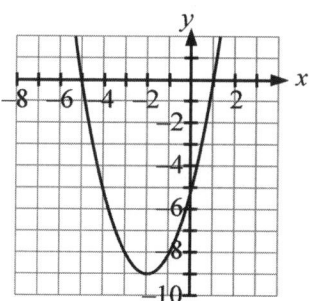

CHALLENGER QUESTION

30. If the graph of a quadratic function, given in the form $f(x) = a(x - r)(x - s)$, has an x-intercept of $r = 12.5$ and a vertex $V(6, -5)$, then the other x-intercept is

A. $s = -0.5$ **B.** $s = 0.5$

C. $s = 3.25$ **D.** $s = 9.25$

Use the following information to answer the next question.

Four different forms of the same quadratic function are shown.

Form I: $y = 2x^2 - 3x - 9$

Form II: $y = (x - 3)(2x + 3)$

Form III: $y = 2x\left(x - \dfrac{3}{2}\right) - 9$

Form IV: $y = 2\left(x - \dfrac{3}{4}\right)^2 - \dfrac{27}{2}$

31. Which form allows for the range to be identified by inspection?

A. I   **B.** II   **C.** III   **D.** IV

32. Which of the following features is **not** easily identifiable by inspection from the quadratic function in the form of

$$f(x) = -\frac{1}{3}(x + 2)^2 + 7?$$

A. Vertex

B. x-intercepts

C. Maximum value

D. Equation of the axis of symmetry

Use the following information to answer the next multipart question.

33. Devan sketched the graph of the quadratic function $f(x) = x^2 + 4x + 1$ using various strategies to find its key features.

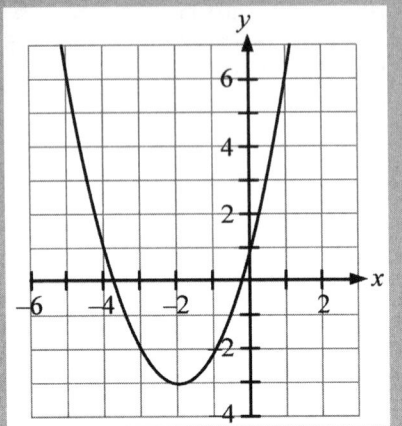

Part A

Which form did she convert the function to in order to find the vertex of the graph?

A. $f(x) = a(x - r)(x - s) \Rightarrow V(-2, -3)$

B. $f(x) = a(x - r)(x - s) \Rightarrow V(-3, -2)$

C. $f(x) = a(x - h)^2 + k \Rightarrow V(-2, -3)$

D. $f(x) = a(x - h)^2 + k \Rightarrow V(-3, -2)$

Part B

The function increases over the x-interval __i__ and is negative over the x-interval __ii__.

The row that correctly completes the statements is

A.

i	$x \geq -2$
ii	$-3.73 < x < -0.27$

B.

i	$x \leq -2$
ii	$-3.73 < x < -0.27$

C.

i	$x \geq -2$
ii	$x < -3.73$ and $x > -0.27$

D.

i	$x \leq -2$
ii	$x < -3.73$ and $x > -0.27$

Use the following information to answer the next multipart question.

34. Keri and her friends went outside to collect data related to the dimensions of one section of a chain link fence. The chain was connected between two posts and hung so that its shape represented a parabola or quadratic function. The measurements they recorded were horizontal distances from one post to the other (x), and vertical heights of the chain (y) above the ground, in metres.

x(m)	y(m)
0	1.00
0.2	0.86
0.4	0.74
0.6	0.66
0.8	0.62
1.0	0.60
1.2	0.62
1.4	0.66
1.6	0.74
1.8	0.86
2.0	1.00

Part A

Open Response

Plot these points on the grid below, and draw a curve of best fit through the points.

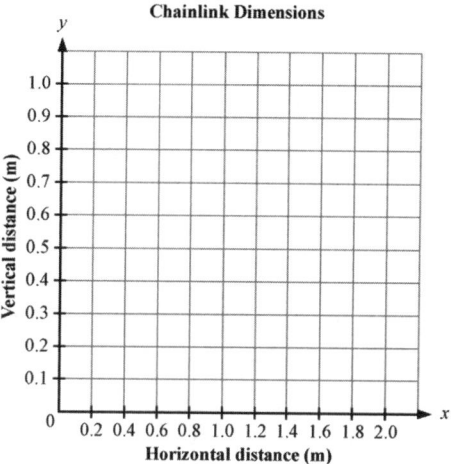

Part B

Numerical Response

According to the data and points on the graph, the minimum height of the chain, to the nearest tenth, is ____ m.

Part C

Written in vertex form, the equation representing the curve of best fit is

A. $y = 0.4(x - 1.0)^2 + 0.6$

B. $y = 0.4(x - 0.6)^2 + 1.0$

C. $y = 0.6(x - 1.0)^2 + 0.4$

D. $y = 0.6(x - 0.4)^2 + 1.0$

Part D

If the data was entered as lists on your graphing calculator, and the quadratic regression equation was determined in the form $y = ax^2 + bx + c$, then the value of b to three decimal places is

A. −0.802   **B.** −0.401

C. 0.401   **D.** 0.802

CHALLENGER QUESTION

Use the following information to answer the next question.

The approximate shape of the top ridge of a Parasaurolophus dinosaur skull can be represented by the quadratic function shown, where x is the horizontal length from the nose, in centimetres, and y is the height, in centimetres.

Parasaurolophus Skull Dimensions

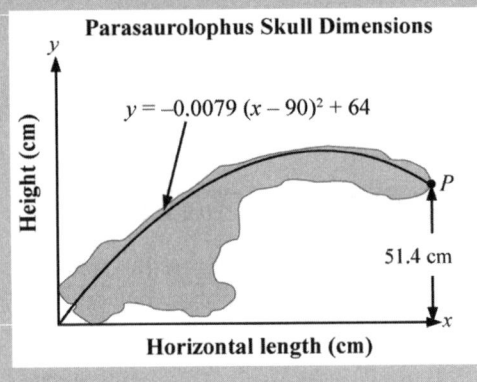

$y = -0.0079\,(x - 90)^2 + 64$

51.4 cm

Horizontal length (cm)

35. If the height of the end of the skull at point P is 51.4 cm, then what is the horizontal length of the whole skull, to the nearest centimetre?

   A. 125 cm   **B.** 130 cm

   C. 142 cm   **D.** 152 cm

SOLUTIONS

1. Part A- **20**		Part B- **OR**	18. Part A- **11**	25. **A**		33. Part A- **C**	
Part B- **C**		Part C- **OR**	Part B- **B**	26. **OR**		Part B- **A**	
2. **C**	10. **D**		19. **C**	27. **C**		34. Part A- **OR**	
3. **OR**	11. **D**		20. **OR**	28. Part A- **OR**		Part B- **0.6**	
4. **C**	12. **D**		21. Part A- **OR**	Part B- **OR**		Part C- **A**	
5. **OR**	13. **B**		Part B- **2**	Part C- **OR**		Part D- **A**	
6. **A**	14. **17**		22. **D**	29. **C**		35. **B**	
7. **6**	15. **13**		23. **A**	30. **A**			
8. **B**	16. **C**		24. Part A- **D**	31. **D**			
9. Part A- **OR**	17. **B**		Part B- **B**	32. **B**			

1. Part A – 20

The ball strikes the ground when the height is 0 m. This is represented by the x-intercept of the graph, which is 25. Therefore, the horizontal distance travelled by the ball from the time it was tossed from the cliff to the time it hit the ground is 25 m. Since the base of the cliff is located at a horizontal distance of 5 m, the ball strikes the ground at a distance of $25 - 5 = 20$ m from the cliff.

Part B –C

There are two vertical phases the thrown ball experiences. The first phase is the upward path of the ball. The upward vertical flight is from 25 m (location on the top of the cliff) to the maximum height of 45 m. Thus, the vertical distance travelled is $45 - 25 = 20$ m.

The second phase is the downward path of the ball. This flight begins at the maximum height of 45 m and ends when the ball hits the ground at a height of 0 m. Thus, the vertical distance travelled during this phase is $45 - 0 = 45$ m.

Therefore, the total vertical distance travelled over both phases is $20 + 45 = 65$ m.

2. C

Method 1: Multiply $3x(5x + 1)$ to find the total rectangular area and then subtract three squares represented by $(x)(x)$.

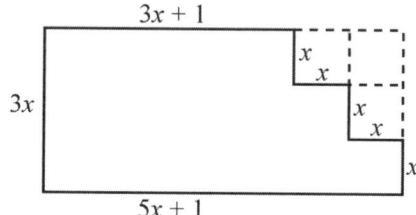

$$A_{rectangle} = 3x(5x + 1)$$
$$= 15x^2 + 3x$$
$$A_{square} = (x)(x) = x^2$$
$$A_{3\ squares} = 3(x^2) = 3x^2$$
$$A_{staircase} = A_{rectangle} - A_{3\ squares}$$
$$= 15x^2 + 3x - 3x^2$$
$$= 12x^2 + 3x$$

Method 2: Multiply three horizontal strips (A, B, and C), making up the stair as shown below.

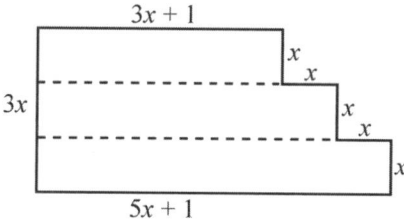

$$Area_A = (x)(3x + 1)$$
$$Area_B = (x)(3x + 1 + x)$$
$$Area_C = (x)(5x + 1)$$
$$Area_{staircase} = Area_A + Area_B + Area_C$$
$$= (x)(3x + 1) + (x)(4x + 1) + (x)(5x + 1)$$
$$= 3x^2 + x + 4x^2 + x + 5x^2 + x$$
$$= 12x^2 + 3x$$

The simplified expression describing the area of the staircase is $12x^2 + 3x$.

3. Open Response

To determine A and B you need to expand out the middle expressions using the FOIL method, and collect like terms.

$Ax^2 - (x+3)^2 + (4x+2)(3x-5) + Bx$

$= Ax^2 - (x+3)(x+3) + (4x+2)(3x-5) + Bx$

$= Ax^2 - [(x)(x) + (3)(x) + (3)(x) + (3)(3)] + [(4x)(3x)$
$+ (-5)(4x) + (2)(3x) + (2)(-5)] + Bx$

$= Ax^2 - (x^2 + 3x + 3x + 9)$
$+ (12x^2 - 20x + 6x - 10) + Bx$

$= Ax^2 - x^2 - 3x - 3x - 9 + 12x^2 - 20x + 6x - 10 + Bx$

$= Ax^2 + (12x^2 - x^2) + (-3x - 3x - 20x + 6x)$
$+ (-9 - 10) + Bx$

$= Ax^2 + 11x^2 - 20x - 19 + Bx$

Now for this expression to simplify to $6x^2 + 8x - 19$, the sum of the x^2 terms must equal $6x^2$, and the sum of the x terms must equal $8x$. Therefore,

$Ax^2 + 11x^2 = 6x^2$

$\quad Ax^2 = 6x^2 - 11x^2$

$\quad Ax^2 = -5x^2$

$Bx - 20x = 8x$

$\quad Bx = 8x + 20x$

$\quad Bx = 28x$

Thus, for the expression to simplify to $6x^2 + 8x - 19$ the values of $A = -5$ and $B = 28$.

4. C

Quadratic I: trinomial, where $a = 1$, $x^2 - 19x + 60$

Find two integers whose product is 60 and whose sum is -19. The two numbers are -15 and -4. Then, split the trinomial into two binomial factors, one with -15 and the other with -4.

$x^2 - 19x + 60 = (x - 15)(x - 4)$

This expression is factored correctly.

Quadratic II: binomial, with differences of squares:

$3x^3 - 75x$

Factor out the GCF of $3x$.

$3x^3 - 75x = 3x(1x^2 - 25)$

Since 1 and 25 are perfect squares, the expression factors to $3x(\sqrt{1}x - \sqrt{25})(\sqrt{1}x + \sqrt{25}) = 3x(x - 5)(x + 5)$

This expression is also factored correctly

Quadratic III: trinomial, where $a \neq 1$, $-9x^2 + 12x - 4$

Find two numbers that multiply to give $(-9)(-4) = 36$ and that have a sum of 12. The two numbers are 6 and 6. Split the middle term.

$$-9x^2 + 12x - 4$$
$$-9x^2 + 6x + 6x - 4$$

Group the four terms, factor out the GCF of each pair, and then factor out the common binomial.

$(-9x^2 + 6x) + (6x - 4)$
$-3x(3x - 2) + 2(3x - 2)$
$(-3x + 2)(3x - 2)$

This expression is factored incorrectly.

Quadratic IV: trinomial, where $a \neq 1$, $4x^2 + 6x + 2$

First, factor out the GCF of 2.

$2(2x^2 + 3x + 1)$

Find two numbers that multiply to give $(2)(1) = 2$ and have a sum of 3. The two numbers are 2 and 1. Split the middle term.

$$2(2x^2 + 3x + 1)$$
$$2(2x^2 + 2x + 1x + 1)$$

Group the four terms, factor out the GCF of each pair, and then factor out the common binomial.

$2[(2x^2 + 2x) + (1x + 1)]$
$2[2x(x + 1) + 1(x + 1)]$
$2(x + 1)(2x + 1)$

This expression is factored correctly.

Therefore, quadratic III is factored incorrectly.

5. Open Response

Step 1: The student shows the splitting of the middle term bx into two terms.

$bx = -3x + 4x$
$\quad = 1x$

Therefore, $b = 1$ in the original expression.

The two numbers -3 and 4 also need to multiply to produce the product of $(a)(c)$ in the original expression

$ax^2 + bx + c$, that is $(a)(c) = (-3)(4)$.

$ac = -12$, and since $a = 6$

$6c = -12$

$\quad c = -2$ or $-(2)$

Therefore, the completed first step

should be $6x^2 - 3x + 4x - \boxed{2}$

Step 2: The four terms are grouped, and the GCF is factored out of each binomial.

$(6x^2 - 3x) + (4x - 2)$
$3x(2x - 1) + 2(2x - 1)$

Therefore, the completed second step

should be $3x(\underline{2x - 1}) + \boxed{2}(2x - 1)$

Step 3: Factor out the common binomial. Therefore the completed third step should be $(\underline{3x + 2})(\underline{2x - 1})$ or $(\underline{2x - 1})(\underline{3x + 2})$.

6. A

The roots, or solutions, of a factored quadratic equation are found by setting each factor to zero and then solving for x.

$$2x + a = 0 \qquad \text{and} \qquad 3x - b = 0$$
$$2x = -a \qquad\qquad\qquad 3x = b$$
$$x = -\frac{a}{2} \qquad\qquad\qquad x = \frac{b}{3}$$

The two roots of the quadratic equation

$(2x + a)(3x - b) = 0$ can be expressed as $x = -\dfrac{a}{2}, \dfrac{b}{3}$

7. 6

To find the solutions of a quadratic equation, factor the quadratic expression, set each factor to zero, and solve for x.

$$2x^2 - 72 = 0$$
$$2\left(x^2 - 36\right) = 0$$
$$2(x - 6)(x + 6) = 0$$

$$\begin{array}{ccc} x - 6 = 0 & & x + 6 = 0 \\ x = 6 & \text{and} & x = -6 \end{array}$$

Therefore, the solutions to the quadratic equation are $x = -6$ and $x = 6$.

8. B

When you examine the graph of the quadratic function $y = f(x)$, the x-intercepts are -1 and 1.5. These are the places where the graph crosses the x-axis.
The x-intercepts of the graph of the function $y = f(x)$ are equal to the roots of the corresponding equation $0 = f(x)$. The factors of this equation, which are related to the roots of -1 and 1.5, are:

$(x + 1)(x - 1.5)$ or $(x + 1)\left(x - \dfrac{3}{2}\right) = 0$

This can be verified by setting each factor to zero.

$$\begin{array}{ccc} x + 1 = 0 & & x - \dfrac{3}{2} = 0 \\ x = -1 \checkmark & \text{and} & \\ & & x = \dfrac{3}{2} \checkmark \end{array}$$

The factor $\left(x - \dfrac{3}{2}\right)$ can be rewritten by multiplying each term by 2.

$$2\left(x - \frac{3}{2}\right) = (2x - 3)$$

Therefore, the factors of the equation $0 = f(x)$ are $(x + 1)$ and $(2x - 3)$.

9. Part A – Open Response

The plotted points and smooth parabolic curve through these points are shown below.

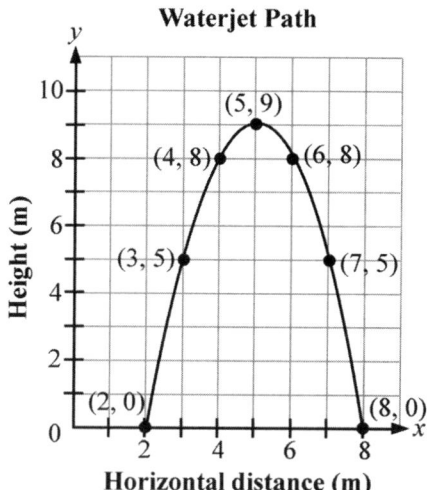

Waterjet Path

Part B – Open Response

The x-intercepts of the graph are 2 and 8, or $(2, 0)$ and $(8, 0)$.

Part C – Open Response

To factor the equation $0 = -x^2 + 10x - 16$, take out the GCF of -1, and then factor the trinomial, where $a = 1$, as follows:

$$\begin{aligned} 0 &= -x^2 + 10x - 16 \\ &= -1\left(x^2 - 10x + 16\right) \\ &= -1(x - 8)(x - 2) \end{aligned}$$

The roots of the equation can be found by setting each factor to zero.

$$\begin{array}{ccc} x - 8 = 0 & & x - 2 = 0 \\ x = 8 & \text{and} & x = 2 \end{array}$$

The roots of the factors 2 and 8 are identical to the x-intercepts of the graph of the function.

10. D

To determine the values of a, b, and c in her quadratic equation $ax^2 + bx + c = 0$, you need to examine these values in the quadratic formula, $\dfrac{-b \pm \sqrt{b^2 - 4ac}}{2a}$.

Her values are evident when you look at the entries under the square root sign of the quadratic formula,

$$\frac{-2 \pm \sqrt{(2)^2 - 4(-1)(3)}}{2(-1)}$$

The values are $b = 2$, $a = -1$, and $c = 3$.
Therefore, the equation the student was trying to solve was $-1x^2 + 2x + 3 = 0$ or $-x^2 + 2x = -3$.

11. D

Identify the values of a, b, and c in the quadratic equation.

$$-x^2 \quad - \quad 6x \quad + \quad 4 \quad = 0$$
$$\downarrow \qquad\qquad \downarrow \qquad\qquad \downarrow$$
$$a = -1 \qquad b = -6 \qquad c = 4$$

Substitute these values into the quadratic formula.

$$x = \frac{-b \pm \sqrt{b^2 - 4ac}}{2a}$$
$$= \frac{-(-6) \pm \sqrt{(-6)^2 - 4(-1)(4)}}{2(-1)}$$
$$= \frac{6 \pm \sqrt{36 + 16}}{-2}$$
$$= \frac{6 \pm \sqrt{52}}{-2}$$
$$= \frac{6 \pm \sqrt{4 \times 13}}{-2}$$
$$= \frac{6 \pm 2\sqrt{13}}{-2}$$
$$= \frac{2(3 \pm \sqrt{13})}{-2}$$
$$= -3 \pm \sqrt{13}$$

One of the exact roots is $-3 + \sqrt{13}$.

12. D

Identify the values of a, b, and c in the quadratic equation.

$$0 = \quad x^2 \quad + 0x \quad - 120$$
$$\downarrow \qquad \downarrow \qquad \downarrow$$
$$a = 1 \quad b = 0 \quad c = -120$$

Determine the discriminant $D = b^2 - 4ac$

$$D = b^2 - 4ac$$
$$= (0)^2 - 4(1)(-120)$$
$$= 0 + 480$$
$$= 480$$

When $D > 0$, then the quadratic equation has two distinct real roots. Therefore, student 4 made the correct statement.

13. B

All four methods could be used to find the solutions to the equation $x^2 - 2x - 3 = 0$. Since the equation can be factored quickly and easily, then Dustin's method is the quickest strategy, as shown below.

Find two numbers with a product of -3 and a sum of -2. The two numbers are -3 and 1.

Therefore,
$$(x - 3)(x + 1) = 0$$
$$x = 3 \text{ and } -1$$

14. 17

Since there are exact roots (which are not rational) for the quadratic equation, the best method to use is the quadratic formula.

Step 1: Rewrite the equation by setting it equal to zero, and identify a, b, and c.

$$x^2 = 6x + 8$$
$$x^2 \quad - \quad 6x \quad - \quad 8 \quad = 0$$
$$\downarrow \qquad\quad \downarrow \qquad\quad \downarrow$$
$$a = 1 \qquad b = -6 \qquad c = -8$$

Step 2: Substitute the values a, b, and c into the quadratic formula, and solve for x.

$$x = \frac{-b \pm \sqrt{b^2 - 4ac}}{2a}$$
$$= \frac{-(-6) \pm \sqrt{(-6)^2 - 4(1)(-8)}}{2(1)}$$
$$= \frac{6 \pm \sqrt{36 + 32}}{2}$$
$$= \frac{6 \pm \sqrt{68}}{2}$$
$$= \frac{6 \pm \sqrt{4 \times 17}}{2}$$
$$= \frac{6 \pm 2\sqrt{17}}{2}$$
$$= \frac{2(3 \pm \sqrt{17})}{2}$$
$$= 3 \pm \sqrt{17}$$

Since the exact roots are $3 \pm \sqrt{17}$, the value of k is 17.

15. 13

Since this is a trinomial, where $a \neq 1$, use decomposition to factor it.

Step 1: Find two numbers that have a product of $(a)(c) = (2)(-44) = -88$, and have a sum of 3. The two numbers are 11 and -8.

Step 2: Split the middle term, factor the GCF out of each pair of terms, and finally factor out the common binomial.

$$2x^2 + 3x - 44 = 0$$
$$2x^2 - 8x + 11x - 44 = 0$$
$$2x(x - 4) + 11(x - 4) = 0$$
$$(2x + 11)(x - 4) = 0$$
$$a = 2 \qquad b = 11$$

Therefore, the sum of $a + b$ is $2 + 11 = 13$.

16. C

When you examine all four graphs, you see that there are two relations that are not functions, since they fail the vertical line test.

In graph 1, if you draw a vertical line through a particular x-value (where $-2 < x < 2$), it intersects the graph in more than one place, namely, two points.

In graph 4, it seems that for most x-values of the graph, there is only one corresponding y-value. However, at $x = 1$, a vertical line would intersect the graph at infinite points. Therefore, graphs 1 and 4 do not represent functions.

17. B

If each relation is isolated for y you would get the following results.

Choice A: $y^2 - 2x = 0 \rightarrow y^2 = 2x \rightarrow y = \pm\sqrt{2x}$

Choice B: $y - \sqrt{2}x^2 = 0 \rightarrow y = \sqrt{2}x^2$

Choice C: $x - 2y^2 = 0 \rightarrow -2y^2 = -x \rightarrow y = \pm\sqrt{\dfrac{x}{2}}$

Choice D: $(y - 2)^2 - x = 0 \rightarrow (y - 2)^2 = x \rightarrow$
$y - 2 = \pm\sqrt{x} \rightarrow y = 2 \pm \sqrt{x}$

To determine which of these quadratic relations is also a function, use a mapping diagram or function machine for a given x-value.

Choice A

For $x = 2$, $\begin{aligned} y &= +\sqrt{(2)(2)} = 2 \\ y &= -\sqrt{(2)(2)} = -2 \end{aligned}$

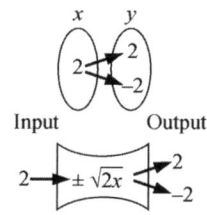

Choice B

For $x = 1$, $y = \sqrt{2}(1)^2 = \sqrt{2}$

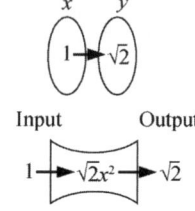

Choice C

For $x = 2$, $\begin{aligned} y &= +\sqrt{\dfrac{2}{2}} = 1 \\ y &= -\sqrt{\dfrac{2}{2}} = -1 \end{aligned}$

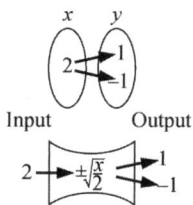

Choice D

For $x = 1$, $\begin{aligned} y &= 2 + \sqrt{1} = 3 \\ y &= 2 - \sqrt{1} = 1 \end{aligned}$

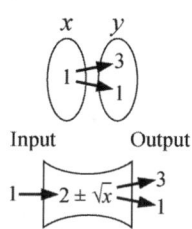

Look at all four mapping diagrams and function machines. Choices A, C, and D have two output y-values for a single x-value, whereas choice B has one output value for the single x-value. This shows that only choice B represents a quadratic function.

18. Part A – 11

To find the value of $f(-6)$, substitute the value of -6 for x in the function $f(x) = -2(x + 3) + 5$, and evaluate.
$$\begin{aligned} f(-6) &= -2(-6 + 3) + 5 \\ &= -2(-3) + 5 \\ &= 6 + 5 \\ &= 11 \end{aligned}$$

Part B – B

To find the input value of x, resulting in the output value of $f(x) = 21$, substitute $f(x)$ with 21, and solve for x.
$$\begin{aligned} f(x) &= -2(x + 3) + 5 \\ 21 &= -2(x + 3) + 5 \\ 16 &= -2(x + 3) \\ -8 &= x + 3 \\ -11 &= x \\ x &= -11 \end{aligned}$$

19. C

To determine which quadratic function has a range of $y \geq 4$ (all values of y are greater or equal to 4), examine the table of values and graph of each function.

Choice A

x	y
-2	16
-1	4
0	0
1	4
2	16

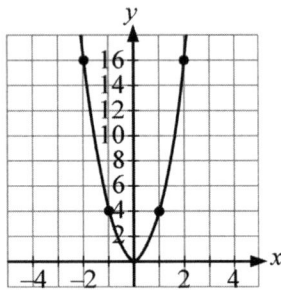

Choice B

x	y
-2	0
-1	3
0	4
1	3
2	0

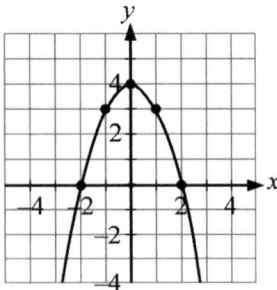

Choice C

x	y
-2	8
-1	5
0	4
1	5
2	8

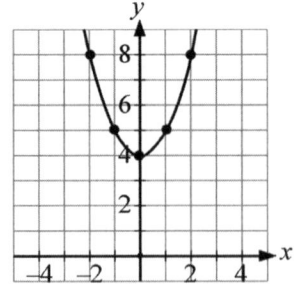

Choice D

x	y
-2	1
-1	0
0	1
1	4
2	9

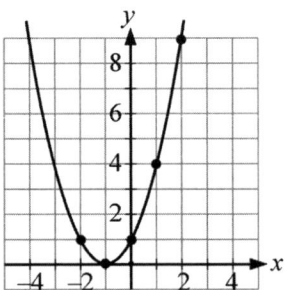

The table of values and the corresponding graphs show that the function $y = x^2 + 4$ has y-values greater or equal to 4 or a range of $y \geq 4$.

20. Open Response

To graph $y = x^2 - 2x - 3$ on your graphing calculator, enter it in $\left[Y_1 = \right]$, set the WINDOW to $x: \left[-10, 10, 1 \right]$, $y: \left[-10, 10, 1 \right]$, and then press GRAPH. Since the graph of this quadratic function opens upward infinitely, you need to find the minimum y-value of the graph by pressing 2nd TRACE MINIMUM.

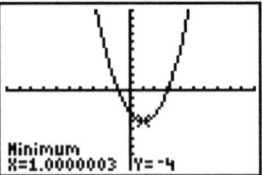

At an x-value of 1, the minimum y-value is -4. Therefore, the range of the graph is $y \geq -4$.

21. Part A – Open Response

Based on the given graph of the aerial skier's flight path for 45° and 55°, the following observations can be made by examining the x-intercepts and maximum points:

45° trajectory	Domain: $0 \leq x \leq 10$
	Range: $0 \leq y \leq 5$
55° trajectory	Domain: $0 \leq x \leq 8$
	Range: $0 \leq y \leq 7$

When the trajectory increases from an angle of 45° to 55°, the upper limit of the domain decreases, but the upper limit of the range increases. Therefore, if the trajectory of the aerial skier's flight increases to an angle of 75°, you could predict that the lower limit of both the domain and range would remain the same ($x = 0$, $y = 0$), but the upper limit of the domain would decrease (be less then $x = 8$) and the upper limit of the range would increase (be more than $y = 7$).

Part B – 2

The upper limit, a, of the range of the 45° trajectory is 5 m. The upper limit of the range, b, of the range of the 55° trajectory is 7 m. Therefore, the difference between b and a is $b - a = 7 - 5 = 2$.

22. D

When the value of a changes its sign in a quadratic function, the graph changes the direction that the parabola opens and its range.

For example:
- If $a < 0$ changes to $a > 0$, the original graph that opened downward would now open upward, and the range goes from $y \leq 0$ to $y \geq 0$.
- If $a > 0$ changes to $a < 0$, the original graph that opened upward would now open downward, and the range goes from $y \geq 0$ to $y \leq 0$.

Also, when the value of a changes (e.g., $a = 2 \rightarrow a = 3$, $a = -\frac{1}{2} \rightarrow a = -\frac{3}{4}$), the original graph would change its vertical stretch factor about the x-axis.

Note: Features of the graph that would not be affected if only the parameter a would change are the following:
- Vertex → there are no translations.
- Axis of symmetry → there is no horizontal translation.
- Domain → never changes, is always $x \in \mathbb{R}$.

23. A

When $f(x) = x^2$, is compressed by a factor $\frac{1}{4}$ about the x-axis, the value of $\frac{1}{4}$ in the transformed function $g(x) = \frac{1}{a}(x - h)^2 + k$ must be $\frac{1}{4}$, which means that $a = 4$.

When $f(x) = x^2$ is translated left 5 units and 3 units up, the value of $h = -5$ and $k = 3$ in the transformed function $g(x) = \frac{1}{a}(x - h)^2 + k$. These three changes would transform the function to $g(x) = \frac{1}{4}(x - (-5))^2 + 3$ or $g(x) = \frac{1}{4}(x + 5)^2 + 3$.

24. Part A –D

Analyze Tina's sketch. The vertical drop downward is $\frac{3}{4}$ units, when moving horizontally left 1 unit and right 1 unit from the vertex.

For the function $f(x) = x^2$, the vertical shifts for each horizontal change of 1 unit from the vertex is as follows:
$$x \rightarrow 1 \Rightarrow y = 1$$
$$x \rightarrow 1 \rightarrow 1 \Rightarrow y = 4$$
$$x \rightarrow 1 \rightarrow 1 \rightarrow 1 \Rightarrow y = 9$$

Since Tina's first vertical shift is $\frac{3}{4}$ units for the first horizontal change of 1 unit from the vertex, simply multiply $\frac{3}{4}$ to the above shifts for $f(x) = x^2$.

$$x \rightarrow 1 \Rightarrow y = 1\left(\frac{3}{4}\right) = \frac{3}{4}$$
$$x \rightarrow 1 \rightarrow 1 \Rightarrow y = 4\left(\frac{3}{4}\right) = 3$$
$$x \rightarrow 1 \rightarrow 1 \rightarrow 1 \Rightarrow y = 9\left(\frac{3}{4}\right) = \frac{27}{4}$$

Therefore, Tina's vertical drop after 3 units of horizontal change from the vertex must be $c = \frac{27}{4}$.

Part B –B

The value of a in $q(x) = a(x - h)^2 + k$ must be $a = -\frac{3}{4}$.

When you move horizontally 1 unit left and right from the vertex, the graph moves vertically downward ($a < 0$) by $\frac{3}{4}$ units. The vertex is (4, 2), which means that $h = 4$ and $k = 2$ in the function $q(x) = a(x - h)^2 + k$.

Therefore, the quadratic function that Tina sketched is $q(x) = -\frac{3}{4}(x - 4)^2 + 2$.

25. A

To expand the quadratic function $f(x) = a(x - 2)^2 + 1$ to the form $f(x) = ax^2 + bx + c$, carry out the following steps:

Rewrite $(x - 2)^2$ as the product $(x - 2)(x - 2)$, and FOIL.

$f(x) = a(x - 2)^2 + 1$

$f(x) = a(x - 2)(x - 2) + 1$

$f(x) = a(x^2 - 2x - 2x + 4) + 1$

Distribute the a-value to all terms in the brackets, and collect like terms.

$f(x) = ax^2 - 2ax - 2ax + 4a + 1$

$f(x) = ax^2 - 4ax + (4a + 1)$

The value of b, which is the coefficient of the x-term is $b = -4a$.

26. Open Response

When the function is written in the form of $f(x) = a(x - h)^2 + k$, the vertex is (h, k). Therefore, for the quadratic function $f(x) = 3(x + 1)^2 - 4$, the vertex is $(-1, -4)$.

If the x-value of the vertex $x = -1$ is substituted into the second form $f(x) = 3x^2 + 6x - 1$, the value of $f(-1)$ must be -4 to correlate to the y-value of the vertex.

$f(-1) = 3(-1)^2 + 6(-1) - 1$

$\qquad = 3 - 6 - 1$

$\qquad = -4$

Since $f(-1) = -4$ is indeed the correct output y-value and the vertex $(-1, -4)$ is the same, both forms of the quadratic function represent the same graph.

27. C

Convert $f(x) = -\dfrac{1}{2}x^2 + 4x + c$ into the vertex form

$f(x) = a(x - h)^2 + k$ as follows:

Factor out $-\dfrac{1}{2}$.

$f(x) = -\dfrac{1}{2}x^2 + 4x + c$

$f(x) = -\dfrac{1}{2}\left(x^2 - 8x\right) + c$

Find the perfect square value, and put this as both a negative and a positive value in the brackets.

$f(x) = -\dfrac{1}{2}\left(x^2 - 8x + 16 - 16\right) + c$

Multiply -16 by $-\dfrac{1}{2}$ and bring this value outside the brackets.

$f(x) = -\dfrac{1}{2}\left(x^2 - 8x + 16\right) + 8 + c$

Factor the perfect square trinomial, and combine the constant terms.

$f(x) = -\dfrac{1}{2}(x - 4)^2 + (8 + c)$

The vertex form of the function is

$f(x) = -\dfrac{1}{2}(x - 4)^2 + (c + 8)$.

28. Part A – Open Response

Complete the square of $f(x) = x^2 - 5x - 3$ by following these steps:

Step 1: Factor 1 out of the first two terms.

$f(x) = 1\left(x^2 - 5x\right) - 3$

Step 2: Divide the coefficient of x, namely, -5 by 2, and then square the product. Add and subtract this value in the brackets.

$f(x) = 1\left(x^2 - 5x + \dfrac{25}{4} - \dfrac{25}{4}\right) - 3$

Step 3: Move the value $\dfrac{-25}{4}$ out of the brackets by multiplying it by the leading coefficient 1.

$f(x) = 1\left(x^2 - 5x + \dfrac{25}{4}\right) - \dfrac{25}{4} - 3$

Step 4: Factor the perfect square trinomial inside the brackets, and collect the constant terms outside the brackets

$f(x) = 1\left(x - \dfrac{5}{2}\right)^2 - \dfrac{37}{4}$

Part B – Open Response

The vertex of the form $f(x) = a(x - h)^2 + k$ is (h, k).

Therefore, for $f(x) = 1\left(x - \dfrac{5}{2}\right)^2 - \dfrac{37}{4}$, the vertex is $\left(\dfrac{5}{2}, \dfrac{-37}{4}\right)$.

Part C – Open Response

To verify that the two forms of the quadratic function represent the same graph, determine the values of $f(2)$, $f(-3)$, and $f(6)$. Then, compare the output values.

$$f(x) = x^2 - 5x - 3$$
$$f(2) = (2)^2 - 5(2) - 3$$
$$= 4 - 10 - 3$$
$$= -9 \checkmark$$
$$f(-3) = (-3)^2 - 5(-3) - 3$$
$$= 9 + 15 - 3$$
$$= 21 \checkmark$$
$$f(6) = (6)^2 - 5(6) - 3$$
$$= 36 - 30 - 3$$
$$= 3 \checkmark$$

$$f(x) = 1\left(x - \frac{5}{2}\right)^2 - \frac{37}{4}$$
$$f(2) = 1\left(2 - \frac{5}{2}\right)^2 - \frac{37}{4}$$
$$= 1\left(-\frac{1}{2}\right)^2 - \frac{37}{4}$$
$$= \frac{-36}{4} = -9 \checkmark$$
$$f(-3) = 1\left(-3 - \frac{5}{2}\right)^2 - \frac{37}{4}$$
$$= 1\left(\frac{-11}{2}\right)^2 - \frac{37}{4}$$
$$= \frac{84}{4} = 21 \checkmark$$
$$f(6) = 1\left(6 - \frac{5}{2}\right)^2 - \frac{37}{4}$$
$$= 1\left(\frac{7}{2}\right)^2 - \frac{37}{4}$$
$$= \frac{12}{4} = 3 \checkmark$$

Since the output values of $f(2)$, $f(-3)$, and $f(6)$ are the same in both forms, these two functions represent the same quadratic graph.

29. C

The x-intercepts of the quadratic function written in the factored form $f(x) = (x + 1)(x - 5)$ are found by setting each factor to zero.

$$x + 1 = 0 \qquad \text{and} \qquad x - 5 = 0$$
$$x = -1 \qquad\qquad\qquad x = 5$$

The equation of the axis of symmetry is located halfway between the x-intercepts, so it would be defined as
$$x = \frac{-1 + 5}{2} = \frac{4}{2} = 2$$

To find the vertex $(2, k)$, substitute the x-value into the function, and solve for k.
$$f(x) = (x + 1)(x - 5)$$
$$k = (2 + 1)(2 - 5)$$
$$k = (3)(-3)$$
$$k = -9$$

The vertex of the graph is $(2, -9)$. The graph with x-intercepts of -1 and 5 and with the correct vertex is given in choice C.

30. A

The vertex $V(6, -5)$ lies on the axis of symmetry defined by $x = 6$. The two x-intercepts of the factored function $f(x) = a(x - r)(x - s)$ are r and s, and are located so that the equation of the axis of symmetry is halfway between r and s.

$$x = 6 = \frac{r + s}{2}$$

Substitute the value of $r = 12.5$, and solve for s.

$$6 = \frac{12.5 + s}{2}$$
$$12 = 12.5 + s$$
$$s = -0.5$$

The other x-intercept is $s = -0.5$.

31. D

The only form of a quadratic function that allows you to determine the range by inspection is the vertex form $f(x) = a(x - h)^2 + k$, since the range is defined as $y \leq k$, when $a < 0$, and $y \geq k$, when $a > 0$. This form of the function is given in Form IV: $y = 2\left(x - \frac{3}{4}\right)^2 - \frac{27}{2}$, where the range is $y \geq -\frac{27}{2}$.

32. B

When a quadratic function is written in the vertex form $f(x) = -\frac{1}{3}(x + 2)^2 + 7$ you can identify the following features of its graph easily by inspection only:

- Vertex: $(-2, 7)$
- Maximum: 7 (since $a < 0$)
- Range: $y \leq 7$ (since $a < 0$)
- Opens downward ($a < 0$)
- Axis of symmetry: $x = -2$

The x-intercepts are not identifiable by inspection.

33. Part A –C

The function $f(x) = x^2 + 4x + 1$ cannot be factored, so it is not possible to convert it to the factored form $f(x) = a(x - r)(x - s)$.

The function $f(x) = x^2 + 4x + 1$ can be converted to the vertex form quite easily.

$$f(x) = x^2 + 4x + 1$$
$$= 1\left(x^2 + 4x\right) + 1$$
$$= 1\left(x^2 + 4x + 4 - 4\right) + 1$$
$$= 1\left(x^2 + 4x + 4\right) - 4 + 1$$
$$= 1(x + 2)^2 - 3$$

The vertex is $(-2, -3)$, which can be found by examining the function or the graph.

Part B –A

The function $f(x) = x^2 + 4x + 1$ increases to the right of the vertex (as observed on the graph) over the x-interval $x \geq -2$.

The graph of the function is negative below the x-axis, between the two x-intercepts. One x-intercept is just to the right of -4 and just to the left of 0, by inspecting the graph. Thus, the interval where the graph is negative is about $-3.8 < x < -0.3$. This interval and the interval when the graph increases is given in choice A.

Note: More exact x-intercepts could be determined by using the quadratic formula for $f(x) = x^2 + 4x + 1$. If the formula is used, $x = -3.73$ and -0.27, which is close to the estimated values taken from the graph.

34. Part A – Open Response

The plotted points and curve of best fit is shown in the graph below.

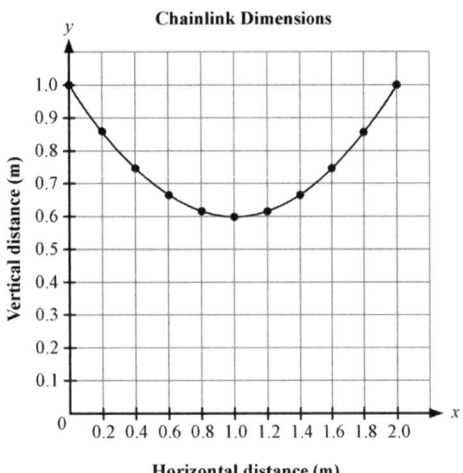

Part B – 0.6

According to the graph or table of values, the minimum height occurs at $x = 1.0$. At this point, the y-value or minimum height of the chain, to the nearest tenth is, 0.6 m.

Part C –A

To find the equation of the curve of best fit in vertex form, $y = a(x - h)^2 + k$, you need to know the vertex and one other point.

From the graph, the vertex is $(1.0, 0.60)$.

Although there are several possible points to choose from, an appropriate point is the y-intercept of $(0, 1.0)$.

Substitute the vertex for h and k and the y-intercept for x and y in $y = a(x - h)^2 + k$. Solve for a.

$$y = a(x - h)^2 + k$$
$$1.0 = a(0 - 1.0)^2 + 0.60$$
$$1.0 = a(1) + 0.60$$
$$0.40 = a$$

Therefore, the equation representing the graph of the quadratic function is $y = 0.4(x - 1.0)^2 + 0.6$.

Part D –A

Enter the data in the table of values in the Lists L_1 and L_2 of your graphing calculator.

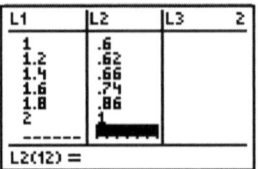

Then, perform a quadratic regression by pressing STAT CALC 5 ENTER. The resulting information will appear on your screen.

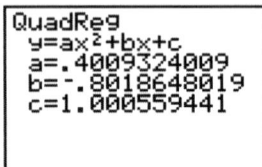

According to the quadratic regression equation given, the value of b in $y = ax^2 + bx + c$, to three decimal places, is -0.802.

35. B

The height at point P is 51.4 cm. Substitute this value into y of the equation, and solve for the x-value (the horizontal length).

$$y = -0.0079(x - 90)^2 + 64$$
$$51.4 = -0.0079(x - 90)^2 + 64$$

Expand the right side of the equation, and then rewrite it as a quadratic equation in the form $0 = ax^2 + bx + c$.

$$51.4 = -0.0079(x - 90)(x - 90) + 64$$
$$51.4 = -0.0079(x^2 - 90x - 90x + 8100) + 64$$
$$51.4 = -0.0079x^2 + 0.711x + 0.711x - 63.99 + 64$$
$$0 = -0.0079x^2 + 1.422x - 51.39$$

Now, solve for x using the quadratic formula.

$$x = \frac{-b \pm \sqrt{b^2 - 4ac}}{2a}$$
$$x = \frac{-1.422 \pm \sqrt{(1.422)^2 - 4(-0.0079)(-51.39)}}{2(-0.0079)}$$
$$x = \frac{-1.422 \pm \sqrt{2.022\,084 - 1.623\,924}}{-0.0158}$$
$$x = \frac{-1.422 \pm 0.630\,999\,2076}{-0.0158}$$
$$x = 50.063\,341\,29 \text{ or } 129.936\,6587$$

According to the graph of the skull, the value of $x = 50.1$ occurs at a point before the maximum; therefore, it is the value of $x = 129.9$, or 130, that represents the point P. Thus, the horizontal length of the whole skull is 130 cm.

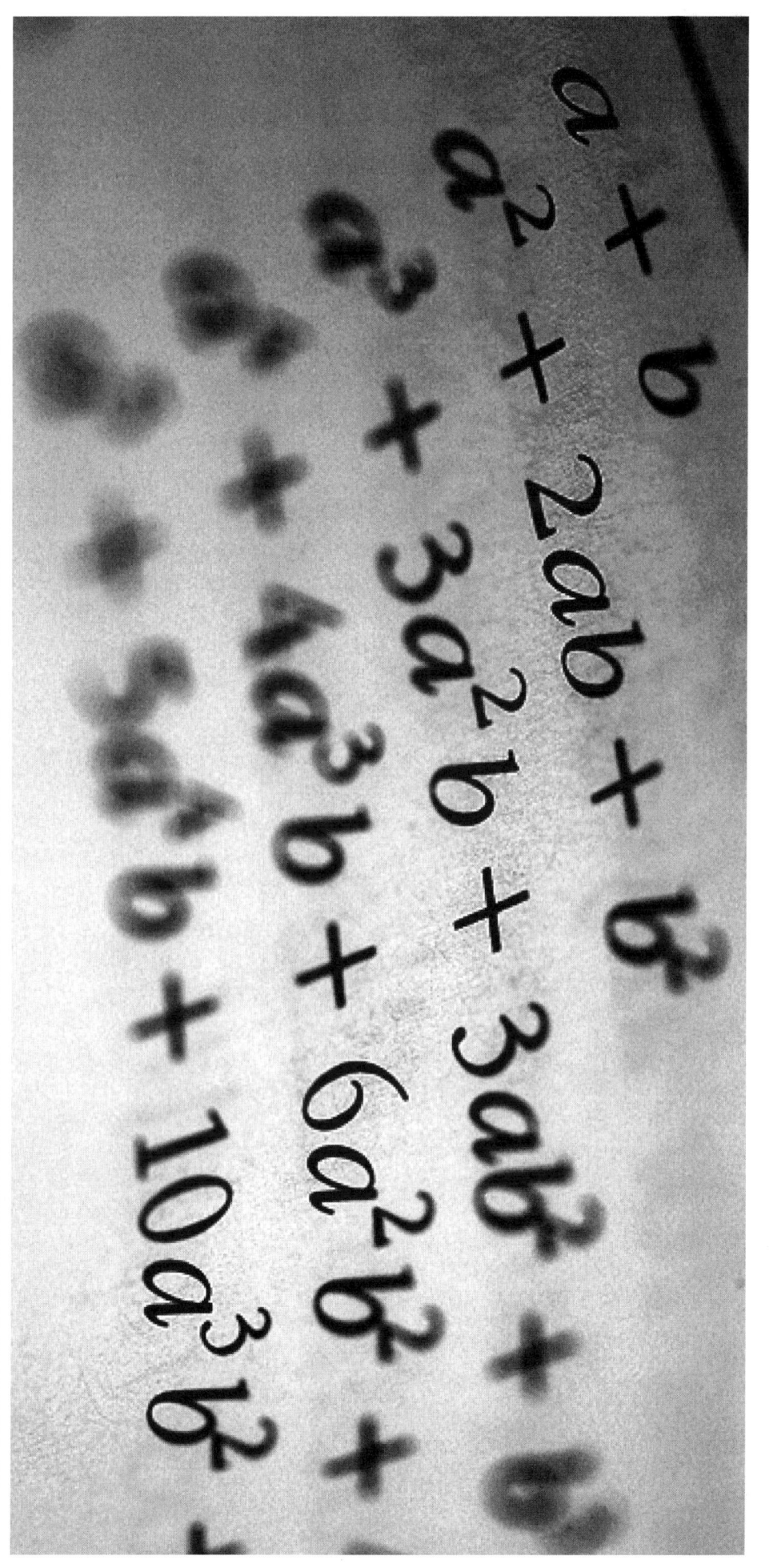

$a + b$

$a^2 + 2ab + b^2$

$a^3 + 3a^2b + 3ab^2 + b^3$

$a^4 + 4a^3b + 6a^2b^2 + $

$a^5 + 5a^4b + 10a^3b^2 + $

Exponential Functions

Table of Correlations

Specific Expectation		Practice Questions	Unit Test Questions
EF1.0	Connecting Graphs and Equations of Exponential Functions		
EF1.1	determine, through investigation using a variety of tools and strategies, the value of a power with a rational exponent (i.e., $x^{\frac{m}{n}}$, where $x > 0$ and m and n are integers)	1, 2	1, 2
EF1.2	evaluate, with and without technology, numerical expressions containing integer and rational exponents and rational bases	3, 4	3, 4
EF1.3	graph, with and without technology, an exponential relation, given its equation in the form $a^x (a > 0, a \neq 1)$, define this relation as the function $f(x) = a^x$, and explain why it is a function	5a, 5b	5a, 5b
EF1.4	determine, through investigation, and describe key properties relating to domain and range, intercepts, increasing/decreasing intervals, and asymptotes for exponential functions represented in a variety of ways	6, 7, 8a, 8b	6, 7
EF1.5	determine, through investigation, the exponent rules for multiplying and dividing numeric expressions involving exponents, and the exponent rule for simplifying numerical expressions involving a power of a power, and use the rules to simplify numerical expressions containing integer exponents	9, 10	8, 9
EF1.6	distinguish exponential functions from linear and quadratic functions by making comparisons in a variety of ways, within the same context when possible	11, 12a, 12b	10, 11a, 11b, 11c
EF2.0	Solving Problems Involving Exponential Functions		
EF2.1	collect data that can be modelled as an exponential function, through investigation with and without technology, from primary sources, using a variety of tools, or from secondary sources	13a, 13b	12a, 12b
EF2.2	identify exponential functions, including those that arise from real-world applications involving growth and decay, given various representations (i.e., tables of values, graphs, equations), and explain any restrictions that the context places on the domain and range	14a, 14b	13a, 13b
EF2.3	solve problems using given graphs or equations of exponential functions arising from a variety of real-world applications by interpreting the graphs or by substituting values for the exponent into the equations	15, 16a, 16b, 16c	14a, 14b, 15
EF3.0	Solving Financial Problems Involving Exponential Functions		
EF3.1	compare, using a table of values and graphs, the simple and compound interest earned for a given principal (i.e., investment) and a fixed interest rate over time	17a, 17b	16a, 16b
EF3.2	solve problems, using a scientific calculator, that involve the calculation of the amount, A (also referred to as future value, FV), and the principal, P (also referred to as present value, PV), using the compound interest formula in the form $A = P(1 + i)^n$ [or $FV = PV(1 + i)^n$]	18, 19	17, 18
EF3.3	determine, through investigation, that compound interest is an example of exponential growth	20a, 20b	19, 20
EF3.4	solve problems, using a TVM Solver on a graphing calculator or on a website, that involve the calculation of the interest rate per compounding period, i, or the number of compounding periods, n, in the compound interest formula $A = P(1 + i)$ or $FV = PV(1 + i)^n$	21, 22	21, 22
EF3.5	explain the meaning of the term annuity, through investigation of numeric and graphical representations using technology	23	23

	Specific Expectation	**Practice Questions**	**Unit Test Questions**
EF3.6	*determine, through investigation using technology, the effects of changing the conditions (i.e., the payments, the frequency of the payments, the interest rate, the compounding period) of ordinary simple annuities (i.e., annuities in which payments are made at the end of each period, and the compounding period and the payment period are the same)*	24a, 24b	24, 25
EF3.7	*solve problems, using technology, that involve the amount, the present value, and the regular payment of an ordinary simple annuity*	25, 26a, 26b, 26c	26a, 26b, 27a, 27b, 27c

EF1.1 *determine, through investigation using a variety of tools and strategies, the value of a power with a rational exponent*

(i.e., $x^{\frac{m}{n}}$, where $x > 0$ and m and n are integers)

POWERS WITH RATIONAL EXPONENTS

If a power with a positive base $(x > 0)$ has a rational exponent, you can use the product rule $x^m \times x^n = x^{m+n}$ to understand and evaluate it.

:Example

Evaluate the expression $4^{\frac{1}{2}}$.

Solution

$$4^{\frac{1}{2}} \times 4^{\frac{1}{2}} = 4^{\frac{1}{2}+\frac{1}{2}} = 4^1$$

Let $x = 4^{\frac{1}{2}}$

Then

$(x)(x) = 4^1$

$\quad x^2 = 4$

$\quad\quad x = \pm\sqrt{(4)^1}$

Note: Dismiss $-\sqrt{4}$, since the base > 0.

Since $x = 4^{\frac{1}{2}}$, $4^{\frac{1}{2}} = \sqrt{(4)^1} = 2$.

:Example

Evaluate the expression $27^{-\frac{1}{3}}$.

Solution

$$27^{-\frac{1}{3}} \times 27^{-\frac{1}{3}} \times 27^{-\frac{1}{3}} = 27^{-\frac{3}{3}} = 27^{-1}$$

Let $x = 27^{-1}$

$$= 27^{-1} \text{ or } \frac{1}{(27)^1}$$

Then $(x)(x)(x)x^3 = \dfrac{1}{(27)^1}$

$$x = \sqrt[3]{\frac{1}{(27)^1}} \text{ or } \frac{1}{\sqrt[3]{(27)^1}}$$

Since $x = 27^{-\frac{1}{3}}$, $27^{-\frac{1}{3}} = \dfrac{1}{\sqrt[3]{(27)^1}} = \dfrac{1}{3}$.

:Example

Evaluate the expression $125^{\frac{2}{3}}$.

Solution

$$125^{\frac{2}{3}} \times 125^{\frac{2}{3}} \times 125^{\frac{2}{3}} = 125^{\frac{6}{3}} = 125^2$$

Let $x = 125^{\frac{2}{3}}$

Then

$(x)(x)(x) = 125^2$

$\quad x^3 = 125^2$

$\quad\quad x = \sqrt[3]{(125)^2}$

Since $x = 125^{\frac{2}{3}}$, $125^{\frac{2}{3}} = \sqrt[3]{(125)^2} = 25$.

:Example

Evaluate the expression $16^{-\frac{3}{4}}$.

Solution

$16^{-\frac{3}{4}} \times 16^{-\frac{3}{4}} \times 16^{-\frac{3}{4}} \times 16^{-\frac{3}{4}} = 16^{-\frac{12}{4}} = 16^{-3}$

Let $x = 16^{-\frac{3}{4}}$

Then $(x)(x)(x)(x)$

$\quad = 16^{-3}$ or $\dfrac{1}{(16)^3}$

$x^4 = \dfrac{1}{(16)^3}$

$\quad x = \sqrt[4]{\dfrac{1}{(16)^3}}$ or $\dfrac{1}{\sqrt[4]{(16)^3}}$

Since $x = 16^{-\frac{3}{4}}$, $16^{-\frac{3}{4}} = \dfrac{1}{\sqrt[4]{(16)^3}} = \dfrac{1}{8}$.

Note: To enter $\sqrt[4]{(16)^3}$ on your graphing calculator, press 4 MATH 5:$\sqrt[x]{}$ to evaluate the expression $\dfrac{1}{\sqrt[4]{(16)^3}}$ as shown below.

```
1/4*√(16)^3
              .125
Ans▶Frac
              1/8
```

These examples show that a power with a rational exponent can be written and evaluated as a radical.

$x^{\frac{m}{n}} = \sqrt[n]{(x)^m}$ and $x^{-\frac{m}{n}} = \dfrac{1}{\sqrt[n]{(x)^m}}$

:Practice

CHALLENGER QUESTION

1. For $8^r \times 8^r \times 8^r = \dfrac{1}{64}$, the value of r must be

    A. $\dfrac{3}{2}$ **B.** $\dfrac{2}{3}$

    C. $-\dfrac{2}{3}$ **D.** $-\dfrac{3}{2}$

Open Response

Use the following information to answer the next question.

May used the graph of $y = 16^x$ to discover the pattern of y-values related to $16^{\frac{1}{4}}$, $16^{\frac{2}{4}}$, $16^{\frac{3}{4}}$, $16^{\frac{4}{4}} \ldots 16^{\frac{m}{4}}$.

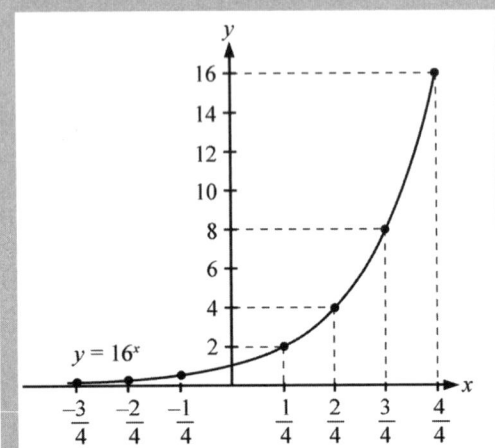

She read the following y-values for each of the following:

$16^{\frac{1}{4}} = 2$, $16^{\frac{2}{4}} = 4$, $16^{\frac{3}{4}} = 8$, $16^{\frac{4}{4}} = 16$

2. May realized that for every increase of $\frac{1}{4}$ for x-values, the y-values increased by a ratio of 2. Using this understanding, what y-values on the graph should correspond to $x = -\frac{3}{4}$ (or $16^{-\frac{3}{4}}$) and to $x = \frac{9}{4}$ (or $16^{\frac{9}{4}}$)?

Describe how you determine these values, and validate them graphically.

EF1.2 *evaluate, with and without technology, numerical expressions containing integer and rational exponents and rational bases*

EVALUATING EXPRESSIONS WITH RATIONAL EXPONENTS

Using the law of exponents or a graphing calculator, you can evaluate a power.

Example

Evaluate the following powers using the law of exponents.

Solution

- $\left(\dfrac{1}{6}\right)^{-3} = 6^3 = 6 \times 6 \times 6 = 216$

- $(-8)^4 = (-8)(-8)(-8)(-8) = 4096$

- $(64)^{-\frac{1}{2}} = \left(\dfrac{1}{64}\right)^{\frac{1}{2}} = \dfrac{1}{\sqrt{64}} = \dfrac{1}{8}$

Example

Evaluate the following powers using your graphing calculator, to the nearest hundredth.

Solution

- $(1.05)^{40} = 7.039\,988\,712 \doteq 7.04$

- $\left(\dfrac{5}{9}\right)^{-5} = 18.895\,68 \doteq 18.90$

- $\left(\dfrac{125}{64}\right)^{\frac{4}{3}} = 2.441\,406\,25 \doteq 2.44$

Note: When the power has a fraction as an exponent, make sure you put it in brackets on your calculator.

$\left(\dfrac{125}{64}\right)^{\frac{4}{3}} \Rightarrow \left(\dfrac{125}{64}\right)^{\wedge}\left(\dfrac{4}{3}\right)$

:Practice

CHALLENGER QUESTION

3. If the exponential expression $\left(\frac{1}{4}\right)^k$ is equivalent to $(2)(2)(2)$, then the value of k is

A. $\frac{3}{2}$ B. $\frac{2}{3}$

C. $-\frac{1}{2}$ D. $-\frac{3}{2}$

Numerical Response

4. To the nearest hundredth, the value of $\left(\frac{5}{4}\right)^{\frac{7}{20}}$ is ____.

EF1.3 *graph, with and without technology, an exponential relation, given its equation in the form $a^x(a > 0,\ a \neq 1)$, define this relation as the function $f(x) = a^x$, and explain why it is a function*

GRAPHING EXPONENTIAL RELATIONS AND DEFINING THEM AS FUNCTIONS

An exponential relation is given as $y = a^x$, where $a > 0$ and $a \neq 1$. These relations can be graphed for different base values, a, by hand or with the use of a graphing calculator.

:Example

Draw a sketch of the relation $y = 2^x$, and examine the graph on your graphing calculator.

Solution

To sketch $y = 2^x$, substitute values for x to define values of y in a table of values.

x	-2	-1	0	1	2
y	$\frac{1}{4}$	$\frac{1}{2}$	1	2	4

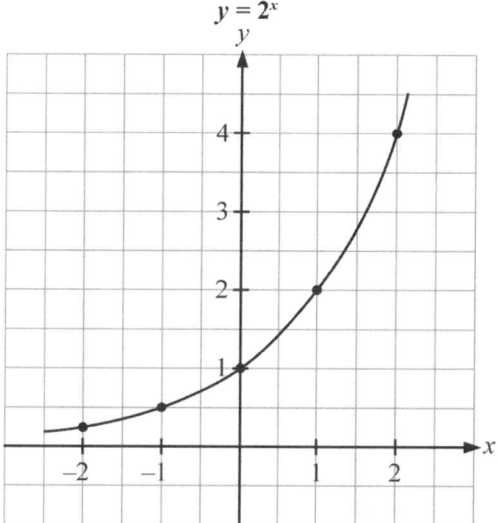

To graph $y = 2^x$ on your graphing calculator, follow these steps:

1. Set your WINDOW as $x:[-3, 3, 1]$, $y:[-2, 6, 1]$.
2. Enter the equation into $\left[Y_1 = \right]$ as follows: $Y_1 = 2^\wedge x$
3. Press GRAPH to see the following screen.

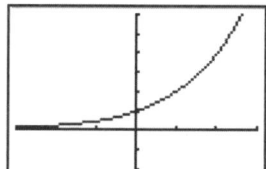

The relation $y = 2^x$ is a function and can be written as $f(x) = 2^x$ based on the following reasons:

- For every x-value in the table or on the graph, there is only one corresponding y-value. **Note:** This can be observed by tracing along your graph on your graphing calculator using the TRACE feature.
- If a vertical line ($x = a$, where $a \in \mathbb{R}$) were to be drawn through any place on the graph, it would only pass through a single point.

Therefore, it can be concluded that the relation $y = a^x$, where $a > 0$ and $a \neq 1$, is also a function and can be written as $f(x) = a^x$.

Practice

Use the following information to answer the next multipart question.

5. Stephanie used her graphing calculator with a WINDOW setting of $x:[-4.7, 4.7, 1]$ and $y:[-3.1, 3.1, 1]$ to graph the exponential relation $y = \left(\frac{3}{2}\right)^x$.

Part A

Which of the following screens represents Stephanie's graph of $y = \left(\frac{3}{2}\right)^x$?

A.

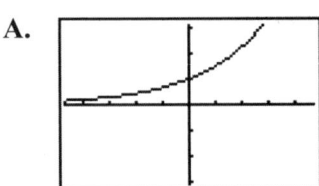

B.

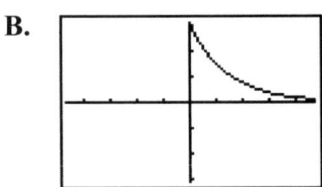

C.

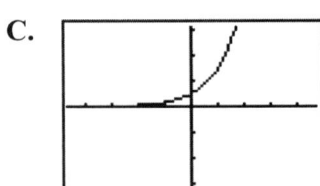

D.

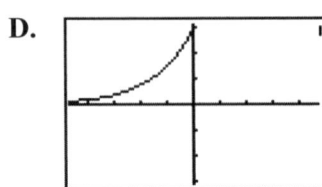

Part B

Stephanie concluded that $y = \left(\frac{3}{2}\right)^x$ could be defined as the function $f(x) = \left(\frac{3}{2}\right)^x$, since

A. for every x-coordinate on the graph, there was only one corresponding y-coordinate

B. every x-coordinate belonged to the set of real numbers

C. the graph never touched the x-axis

D. the graph was a smooth curve

EF1.4 *determine, through investigation, and describe key properties relating to domain and range, intercepts, increasing/ decreasing intervals, and asymptotes for exponential functions represented in a variety of ways*

GATHERING INFORMATION FROM EXPONENTIAL FUNCTIONS

The graphs of exponential functions of the form $f(x) = a^x$, where $a > 0$ and $a \neq 1$, have some unique characteristics.

Four examples of the graphs of the exponential functions $f(x) = \left(\frac{1}{3}\right)^x$, $f(x) = \left(\frac{1}{2}\right)^x$, $f(x) = (1.5)^x$, and $f(x) = 3^x$ are shown in the diagram.

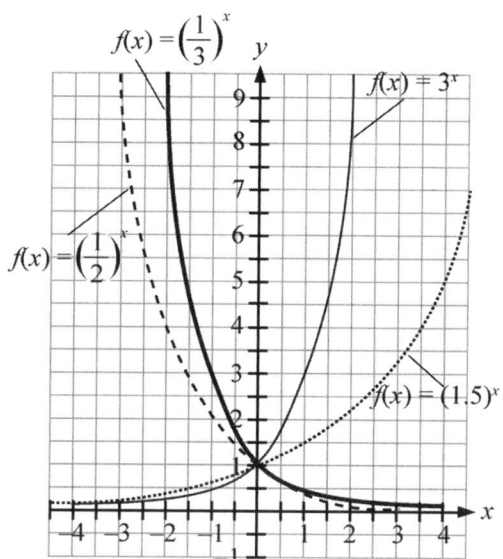

By examining these four graphs, you can make some generalizations about all graphs of exponential functions of the form $f(x) = a^x$.

Domain: $x \in \mathbb{R}$, since all x-values are permissible.

Range: $y > 0$, since each graph has y-values that get closer and closer to the y-axis, but never become 0.

Horizontal asymptote: $y = 0$

Note: An asymptote is the line a curve approaches but never touches, which in this case, is the x-axis defined by the equation $y = 0$.

y-intercept: $(0, 1)$ or 1, since for all exponential functions $f(x) = a^x$, $a^0 = 1$.

x-intercept: None, since the graph never touches the x-axis.

When $a > 1$:

- The graph is an *increasing* function as you move from left to right through the domain, as is shown by the graph of $f(x) = 1.5^x$ and $f(x) = 3^x$.
- The graph is also *flatter* on the left side of the y-axis, and is *steeper* or increases more rapidly on the right side of the y-axis as the value of a *increases*.

When $0 < a < 1$:

- The graph is a *decreasing* function as you move from left to right through the domain, as is shown by the graph of $f(x) = \left(\frac{1}{2}\right)^x$ and $f(x) = \left(\frac{1}{3}\right)^x$.
- The graph is also *flatter* on the right side of the y-axis, and is *steeper* or decreases more rapidly on the left side of the y-axis as the value of a *decreases* or gets closer to 0.

Example

For each representation of an exponential function of the form $f(x) = a^x$ shown below, determine whether it is an increasing or decreasing function, and explain why.

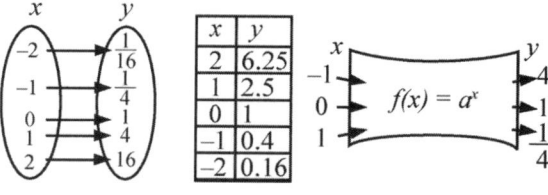

Solution

Mapping: As the x-values move from the top (-2) to the bottom (2), the y-values increase $\left(\frac{1}{16} \rightarrow 16\right)$.

The function is $f(x) = 4^x$, since $f(1) = a^1 = a = 4$.
Therefore, since $a > 1$, this is an increasing function.

Table of values: As the x-values move from the bottom (-2) to the top (2), the y-values increase $(0.16 \rightarrow 6.25)$. The function is $f(x) = 2.5^x$, since $f(1) = a^1 = a = 2.5$.

Therefore, since $a > 1$, this is an increasing function.

Function machine: As the x-values move from the top (-1) to the bottom (1), the y-values decrease $\left(4 \rightarrow \frac{1}{4}\right)$. The function is $f(x) = \left(\frac{1}{4}\right)^x$, since $f(1) = a^1 = a = \frac{1}{4}$.

Therefore, since $0 < a < 1$, this is a decreasing function.

Practice

Use the following information to answer the next question.

A student made the following observations about the graph of $f(x) = 12^x$:

I.   The graph has a range of $y > 0$.

II. The graph has an asymptote of $x = 0$.

III. The graph increases throughout its domain from left to right.

IV. The graph has a y-intercept of 1.

V.   The graph passes through the point $(3, 36)$.

6. Which of the observations are correct?

 A. I, II, III, IV   **B.** I, III, IV, V

 C. I, III, IV   **D.** I, II, IV

7. Which of the following exponential functions would be the **steepest** on the left side of the y-axis?

 A. $y = 16^x$

 B. $y = \left(\dfrac{16}{5}\right)^x$

 C. $y = \left(\dfrac{5}{16}\right)^x$

 D. $y = \left(\dfrac{1}{16}\right)^x$

Use the following information to answer the next multipart question.

8. Two different exponential functions of the form $f(x) = a^x$, $a > 0$ are represented by these tables of values.

Function I

x	-3	-2	-1	0	1	2	3
y	$\dfrac{1}{64}$	$\dfrac{1}{16}$	$\dfrac{1}{4}$	1	4	16	64

Function II

x	-3	-2	-1	0	1	2	3
y	$\dfrac{27}{8}$	$\dfrac{9}{4}$	$\dfrac{3}{2}$	1	$\dfrac{2}{3}$	$\dfrac{4}{9}$	$\dfrac{8}{27}$

Part A

Open Response

Write the equation defining each function.

Part B

Open Response

Explain why the graph of both functions has no x-intercept and the y-intercept is $(0, 1)$.

EF1.5 *determine, through investigation, the exponent rules for multiplying and dividing numeric expressions involving exponents, and the exponent rule for simplifying numerical expressions involving a power of a power, and use the rules to simplify numerical expressions containing integer exponents*

EXPONENT RULES

In previous grades, you learned how to simplify expressions containing powers by using rules called the law of exponents. Let's review some of the terminology and rules pertaining to powers.

DEFINITION OF A POWER

A power is represented through a combination of a base, x, where $x \neq 0$, and an exponent, y.

$$x^y$$

To evaluate a power, factor the base the number of times the exponent indicates, and then do the necessary calculation.

$$4^3 = 4 \times 4 \times 4 = 64$$
$$(-3)^2 = -3 \times -3 = 9$$

PRODUCT OR MULTIPLICATION RULE

When powers with the same base are multiplied together, a rule becomes apparent.

Multiplied Powers	Factored Form
$5^2 \times 5^3$	$(5 \times 5) \times (5 \times 5 \times 5)$

Combined Form	Resulting Power
$5 \times 5 \times 5 \times 5 \times 5$	5^5

In the previous example, the number of factors in the combined form is equal to the sum of the number of factors in the factored form. Since these factors are equal to the exponents of the powers, the exponent of the resulting power is equal to the sum of the exponents of the multiplied powers.

The product rule is as follows:

$$x^m \times x^n = x^{m+n}$$

DIVISION OR QUOTIENT RULE

When powers with the same base are divided, another rule becomes apparent.

Divided Powers	Factored Form
$\dfrac{(-3)^2}{(-3)^4}$	$\dfrac{-3 \times -3}{-3 \times -3 \times -3 \times -3}$

Combined Form	Resulting Power
$\dfrac{\cancel{-3} \times \cancel{-3}}{\cancel{-3} \times \cancel{-3} \times -3 \times -3}$	$\dfrac{1}{(-3)^2}$ or $(-3)^{-2}$

Divided Powers	Factored Form
$\dfrac{\left(\frac{1}{2}\right)^3}{\left(\frac{1}{2}\right)^3}$	$\dfrac{\frac{1}{2} \times \frac{1}{2} \times \frac{1}{2}}{\frac{1}{2} \times \frac{1}{2} \times \frac{1}{2}}$

Combined Form	Resulting Power
$\dfrac{\cancel{\frac{1}{2}} \times \cancel{\frac{1}{2}} \times \cancel{\frac{1}{2}}}{\cancel{\frac{1}{2}} \times \cancel{\frac{1}{2}} \times \cancel{\frac{1}{2}}}$	$\left(\dfrac{1}{2}\right)^0$ or 1

Note:

- $\dfrac{1}{x} = x^{-n}$ or $\left(\dfrac{1}{x}\right)^{-n} = x^n$
- $x^0 = 1$, except when $x = 0$

In these two examples, the number of factors remaining in the combined form is equal to the difference between the number of factors in the numerator and the denominator. Thus, the exponent of the resulting power is equal to the difference of the exponents of the divided powers.

The quotient rule is as follows:

$$\dfrac{x^m}{x^n} = x^{m-n}$$

POWER OF A POWER OR POWER RULE

When a power of a power is simplified, another rule becomes apparent.

Power of a Power	Factored Form
$(5^3)^2$	$5^3 \times 5^3$ $= (5 \times 5 \times 5)$ $\times (5 \times 5 \times 5)$

Combined Form	Resulting Power
$5 \times 5 \times 5 \times 5$ $\times 5 \times 5$	$5^{3+3} = 5^6$

In this example, the exponent of the resulting power is equal to the product of the exponents in the power of a power.

The power rule is as follows:

$$\left(x^m\right)^n = x^{mn}$$

:Example

Use the exponent rules to simplify the numerical expressions $\left(2^3\right)\left(2^6\right)$, $\left(\dfrac{1}{4}\right)^{-2} \div \left(\dfrac{1}{4}\right)^3$, and $\left((-3)^3\right)^2$.

Verify your solutions using your calculator.

Solution
Product Rule (add exponents)
$\left(2^3\right)\left(2^6\right) = 2^{3+6} = 2^9$

Quotient Rule (subtract exponents)
$\left(\dfrac{1}{4}\right)^{-2} \div \left(\dfrac{1}{4}\right)^3 = \left(\dfrac{1}{4}\right)^{-2-3} = \left(\dfrac{1}{4}\right)^{-5}$ or 4^5

Power Rule (multiply exponents)
$\left((-3)^3\right)^2 = (-3)^{3 \times 2} = (-3)^6$

To verify the solutions with the original expressions using your TI-83 Plus Graphing calculator, enter the values and use the ^ button to enter exponents. Also, when the base is a fraction or negative number, use brackets around these values, as shown below.
$2^3 \times 2^6 = 512$ and $2^9 = 512$

```
2^3*2^6
           512
2^9
           512
```

$\left(\dfrac{1}{4}\right)^{-2} \div \left(\dfrac{1}{4}\right)^3 = 1024,$

$\left(\dfrac{1}{4}\right)^{-5} = 1024,$ and $4^5 = 1024$

```
((1/4)^-2)/((1/4
)^3)
            1024
(1/4)^-5
            1024
4^5
            1024
```

$\left((-3)^3\right)^2 = 729$ and $(-3)^6 = 729$

```
((-3)^3)^2
            729
(-3)^6
            729
■
```

:Practice

CHALLENGER QUESTION

Use the following information to answer the next question.

Terri wanted the following three expressions to be equivalent.

$$\dfrac{(-6)^a}{(-6)^4} = (-6)^5(-6)^4 = \left((-6)^b\right)^3$$

9. For the three expressions to be equivalent, the values of a and b are
   A. $a = 13$, $b = 6$
   B. $a = 13$, $b = 3$
   C. $a = -5$, $b = 6$
   D. $a = -5$, $b = 3$

Numerical Response

10. When the exponential expression $\left((0.8)^3\right)^{-2}$ is evaluated, the resulting value, to the nearest hundredth, is ____.

EF1.6 *distinguish exponential functions from linear and quadratic functions by making comparisons in a variety of ways, within the same context when possible*

COMPARING EXPONENTIAL FUNCTIONS TO LINEAR AND QUADRATIC FUNCTIONS

An exponential function, a quadratic function, and a linear function differ in several ways when compared to one another.

Example

Compare the linear function $f(x) = 2x$ to the quadratic function $f(x) = x^2$, and the exponential function $f(x) = 2^x$ by examining their graphs and table of values.

Solution

The graphs of $f(x) = 2x$, $f(x) = x^2$, and $f(x) = 2^x$ are shown below.

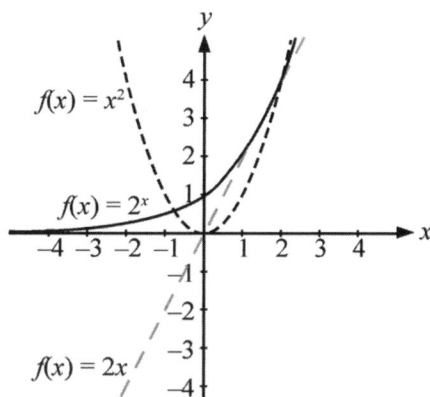

- The graph of $f(x) = 2x$ is a line with a rate of change or slope of 2, a y-intercept of 0, and a range of $f(x) \in \mathbb{R}$.
- The graph of $f(x) = x^2$ is a parabola opening upward, with a vertex or minimum point at $(0, 0)$, a y-intercept of 0, and a range of $y \geq 0$.
- The graph of $f(x) = 2^x$ is a curve that is flat on the left side and rapidly increases or gets steeper on the right side of the y-axis. The graph has a y-intercept of 1 and a range of $y > 0$.

The table of values of $f(x) = 2x$ is as follows:

x	y	D_1	D_2	R
-3	-6			
		} 2		} $\frac{2}{3}$
-2	-4		} 0	
		} 2		} $\frac{1}{2}$
-1	-2		} 0	
		} 2		} 0
0	0		} 0	
		} 2		} undefined
1	2		} 0	
		} 2		} 2
2	4		} 0	
		} 2		} $\frac{3}{2}$
3	6			

First differences (D_1) are differences between successive y-values. Second differences (D_2) are successive differences between the first differences, and ratios (R) are values found by dividing successive y-values.

Since the first differences are constant at 2, defining the value of 2 in $f(x) = 2x$, this is a linear function.

The table of values of $f(x) = x^2$ is as follows:

x	y	D_1	D_2	R
-3	9			
		} -5		} $\frac{4}{9}$
-2	4		} 2	
		} -3		} $\frac{1}{4}$
-1	1		} 2	
		} -1		} 0
0	0		} 2	
		} 1		} undefined
1	1		} 2	
		} 3		} 4
2	4		} 2	
		} 5		} $\frac{9}{4}$
3	9			

Since the second differences are constant at 2 (and not zero), defining the squaring feature in $f(x) = x^2$, this is a quadratic function.

The table of values of $f(x) = 2^x$ is as follows:

x	y	D_1	D_2	R
-3	$\frac{1}{8}$			
		$\}\frac{1}{8}$		
-2	$\frac{1}{4}$		$\}\frac{1}{8}$	$\}2$
		$\}\frac{1}{4}$		
-1	$\frac{1}{2}$		$\}\frac{1}{4}$	$\}2$
		$\}\frac{1}{2}$		
0	1		$\}\frac{1}{2}$	$\}2$
		$\}1$		
1	2		$\}1$	$\}2$
		$\}2$		
2	4		$\}2$	$\}2$
		$\}4$		
3	8			$\}2$

Since the ratios (that define the value of a in $f(x) = 2^x$) are constant at 2, this is an exponential function.

Jake drew diagrams of circles as shown below.

Diagram 1   Diagram 2   Diagram 3   Diagram 4

If x represents the diagram number and y represents the number of circles, then produce a table of values for x = 1, 2, 3, 4, 5, and 6. Also, determine if this pattern is linear, quadratic, or exponential.

Solution

By creating the table of values and then finding the first differences, second differences, and ratios relative to the y-values, you can determine the type of function that the data represents.

x	y	D_1	D_2	R
1	1			
		$\}3$		$\}4$
2	4		$\}2$	
		$\}5$		$\}\frac{9}{4}$
3	9		$\}2$	
		$\}7$		$\}\frac{16}{9}$
4	16		$\}2$	
		$\}9$		$\}\frac{25}{16}$
5	25		$\}2$	
		$\}11$		$\}\frac{36}{25}$
6	36			

Since the second differences are constant, this data or pattern represents a quadratic function.

Practice

Open Response

Use the following information to answer the next question.

The data in the given table shows the speed, v, in kilometres per hour, of an athlete running a 200 m sprint over a time period, t, in seconds.

t	1	2	3	4	5
v	5.00	8.00	12.80	20.48	32.77

11. Cass said that the speed of the athlete increased exponentially. Is he correct? Justify your answer.

12. Four different
storage tanks
were opened at
the bottom to
allow grain to
be removed.
For each tank,
an equation
giving the
height, h, in metres, of the grain in the tank
after t minutes is given:

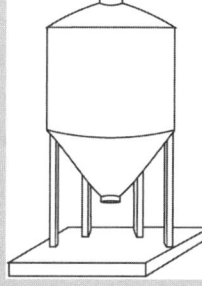

Tank I: $h = 8(0.80)^t$, $0 \leq t \leq 8$
Tank II: $h = 8 - 0.80t$, $0 \leq t \leq 8$
Tank III: $h = 0.016t^2 - 0.8t + 8$,
$0 \leq t \leq 8$
Tank IV: $h = -0.02(t + 2)^2 + 8$, $0 \leq t \leq 8$

Part A

Which tanks allow the height of the grain
in the tank to decrease non-linearly?

A. Tanks I, III

B. Tanks III, IV

C. Tanks I, II, III

D. Tanks I, III, IV

Part B

If the domain was extended to $t \in \mathbb{R}$, which
of the following equations would **not** have
a t-intercept?

A. $h = 8(0.80)^t$

B. $h = 8 - 0.80t$

C. $h = -0.02(t + 2)^2 + 8$

D. $h = 0.016t^2 - 0.8t + 8$

EF2.1 *collect data that can be modelled as an exponential function, through investigation with and without technology, from primary sources, using a variety of tools, or from secondary sources*

MODELLING DATA AS EXPONENTIAL FUNCTIONS

A lot of data from real-life applications can be modelled as an exponential function.

:Example

The data in the table below shows an exponential growing deer population in a particular region over a 10-year period.

Year	Number of Deer
0	4000
1	4800
2	5730
3	6900
4	8295
5	9900
6	11 950
7	14 320
8	17 200
9	20 630
10	25 000

a. Graph the data, and find the approximate rate of growth.
   Solution
   The plotted data is shown on the graph below, where x is the year number and y is the number of deer.

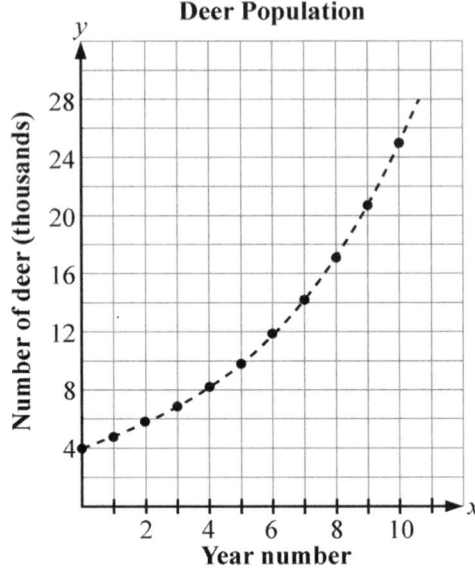

To determine the approximate rate of growth, divide the successive y-values, and round to the nearest thousandth.

$$\frac{4800}{4000} = 1.200, \frac{5730}{4800} = 1.194, \frac{6900}{5730} = 1.204,$$

$$\frac{8295}{6900} = 1.202, \frac{9900}{8295} = 1.193, \frac{11\,950}{9900} = 1.207,$$

$$\frac{14\,320}{11\,950} = 1.198, \frac{17\,200}{14\,320} = 1.201,$$

$$\frac{20\,630}{17\,200} = 1.199, \frac{25\,000}{20\,630} = 1.211$$

Upon examination of the 10 ratios, the approximate rate of growth of the deer population was 1.20.

b. How would the shape of the curve change if there had been wolves in this region?
   Solution
   The curve would increase less rapidly or be flatter, since the wolves would eat a certain amount of deer each year, resulting in annual population values that were less than the original values in the table of values.

   The ratio of growth would be less than 1.20.

Practice

*Use the following information to
answer the next multipart question.*

13. When a golf ball is dropped from the top of
a ladder at a height of 4.00 m, the height to
which it rebounds from the floor, models
an exponential function. The data for the
rebound heights, h, for the first
5 bounces, n, is given in this table.

n	1	2	3	4	5
h	2.80	2.00	1.38	0.97	0.68

Part A

Which of the following graphs correctly
represents the data?

A.
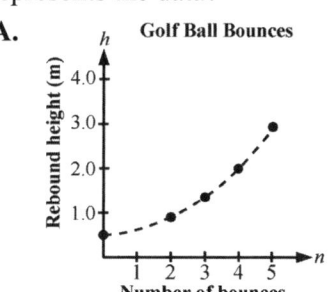

B.
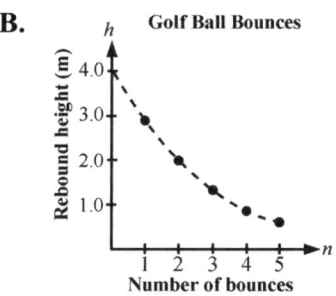

C.
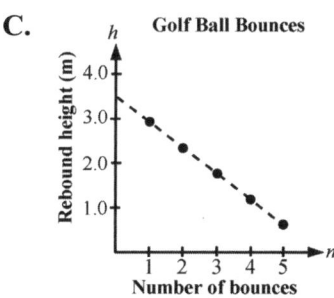

D.
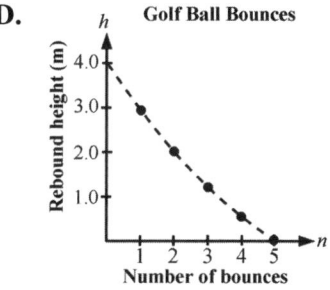

Part B

If a tennis ball is dropped from the same height and its rebound height decreases exponentially, the graph depicting the rebound height of the ball after each bounce would decline

A. at an inconsistent rate, making it impossible to compare to the graph representing the golf ball's data

B. at the same rate as the graph representing the golf ball's data

C. more quickly than the graph representing the golf ball's data

D. less quickly than the graph representing the golf ball's data

EF2.2 *identify exponential functions, including those that arise from real-world applications involving growth and decay, given various representations (i.e., tables of values, graphs, equations), and explain any restrictions that the context places on the domain and range*

IDENTIFYING REAL-WORLD EXPONENTIAL FUNCTIONS

In real-life scenarios that model exponential functions, the patterns of the data either shows exponential **growth** or exponential **decay**.

Exponential growth is a pattern where the ratio between successive y-values is greater than 1. This ratio is often called the **growth factor**.

Exponential decay is a pattern where the ratio is between 0 and 1. This ratio is often called the **decay factor**.

Example

A Petri dish contains 25 bacteria. The number of bacteria, N, doubles every hour.

Construct a table of values, a graph, and an equation to represent the time, t, for the first 4 hours. Highlight the growth factor, r, and explain any restrictions on the domain and range.

Solution

t (h)	0	1	2	3	4
N	25	50	100	200	400
Ratio (r)		$\frac{50}{25}$ $= 2$	$\frac{100}{50}$ $= 2$	$\frac{200}{100}$ $= 2$	$\frac{400}{200}$ $= 2$

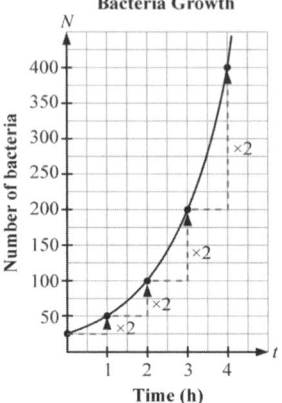

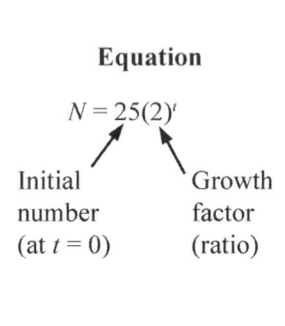

Equation

$$N = 25(2)^t$$

Initial number (at $t = 0$) ← → Growth factor (ratio)

The domain of the scenario is $t \geq 0$ up to a value of t, where the bacteria stop growing in the dish due to a lack of food. The range is $N \geq 25$ up to a value of N, where the number of bacteria reaches its maximum.

Example

A lab technician had an 80 mg sample of a radioactive substance called iodine-131 with a half-life of 8 days. Construct a table of values, a graph, and an equation to represent the amount of mass, m, remaining over time, t, in the first 32 days. Highlight the decay factor, r, and explain any restrictions on the domain and range.

Note: Half-life means the time it takes for a radioactive substance to decay to $\frac{1}{2}$ its original mass.

Solution

t (d)	0	8	16	24	32
m	80	40	20	10	5
Ratio (r)		$\dfrac{40}{80}$ $=\dfrac{1}{2}$	$\dfrac{20}{40}$ $=\dfrac{1}{2}$	$\dfrac{10}{20}$ $=\dfrac{1}{2}$	$\dfrac{5}{10}$ $=\dfrac{1}{2}$

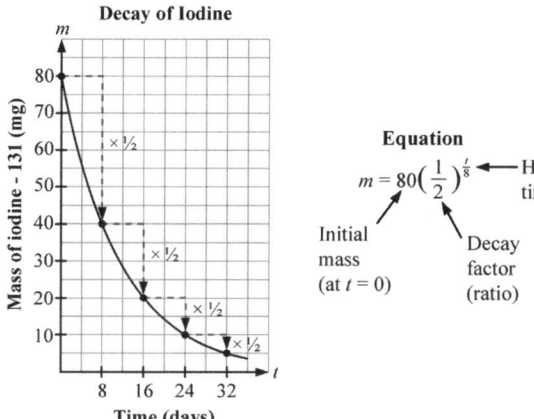

Decay of Iodine

Equation

$$m = 80\left(\frac{1}{2}\right)^{\frac{t}{8}}$$

Half - life time

Initial mass (at $t = 0$)

Decay factor (ratio)

Note: The exponent in the equation is $\dfrac{t}{8}$. A value is placed in the denominator when the growth or decay time is not given as a unit value (e.g., 4 min $\rightarrow \dfrac{t}{4}$, 16.5 years $\rightarrow \dfrac{t}{16.5}$, 175 m $\rightarrow \dfrac{d}{175}$).

The domain of this scenario is $t \geq 0$ up to the time that only one molecule of iodine was left ($t \doteq$ infinity). Therefore, the domain is $t \geq 0$.

The range would be $0 < m \leq 80$, since the mass would realistically never get to 0 mg and also would never become a negative amount.

:Practice

Use the following information to answer the next multipart question.

14. Boon noticed that when he sucked on a large jawbreaker in his mouth, it dissolved slowly at first and then more quickly at the end. He decided to collect some data using his knowledge of geometry. The given table of values shows the volume of the jawbreaker, V, in cubic centimetres, over time, t, in minutes.

Time (min)	Volume (cm³)
0	33.5
1	28.1
2	23.6
3	19.7
4	16.7
5	14.0

Part A

Open Response

State the restrictions on the domain (time) and range (volume). Give reasons for your answer.

Part B

Written as a percentage, the volume of the jawbreaker decays exponentially over time by a factor of

A. 84%   **B.** 80%

C. 8.4%   **D.** 8.0%

EF2.3 *solve problems using given graphs or equations of exponential functions arising from a variety of real-world applications by interpreting the graphs or by substituting values for the exponent into the equations*

SOLVING PROBLEMS USING EXPONENTIAL EQUATIONS AND GRAPHS

Exponential graphs and their corresponding functions, arising from scientific and financial investigations, can be interpreted and analyzed to make accurate predictions.

:Example

The number of cellphone customers of a particular phone company increased by 20% every 6 months from 1996 to 2000. The graph showing this exponential growth, between the number of customers, N, and the time, t, in months from January 1, 1996 is shown below.

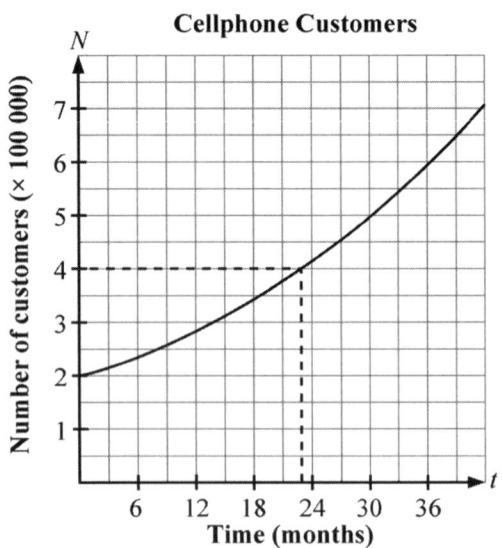

a. How many cellphone customers were there on January 1, 1996?
   Solution
   The y-intercept (value at $t = 0$) describes the number of cellphone customers on January 1, 1996. This value is 200 000.

b. How long does it take for the number of cellphone customers to double?
   Solution
   If the number of cellphone customers at $t = 0$ was 200 000, you need to find the approximate time, t, when there will be 400 000 customers. According to the dotted line on the graph, this occurs at about $t = 23$.

   Therefore, it takes about 23 months for the number of cellphone customers to double.

c. Write the exponential equation that represents the scenario portrayed by the graph.
   Solution
   Since the graph portrays a growth curve, the growth factor has to be larger than 1. Since 100% is a growth ratio of 1 (which means no change), then 120% (100% + 20% increase) is a growth ratio of 1.20, which is the ratio represented by the graph. Whenever a population increases by $i\%$, the growth ratio is $\dfrac{(100\% + i\%)}{100}$.

   This growth ratio occurs every 6 months, and since the original number of customers was 200 000, the equation is

   $$N = 200\ 000(1.20)^{\frac{t}{6}} \longleftarrow \text{Time of growth ratio}$$

   Original amount   Growth ratio

d. Determine the number of cellphone customers there would be on January 1, 2000.
   Solution
   The number of years between the starting time of January 1, 1996 to January 1, 2000 is 4 years or $4 \times 12 = 48$ months. Therefore, you need to find the number of customers, N, at a time, $t = 48$. This can be found by substituting 48 for t and solving for N in the equation:

   $$N = 200\ 000(1.20)^{\frac{t}{6}}$$
   $$= 200\ 000(1.20)^{\frac{48}{6}}$$
   $$= 200\ 000(1.20)^{8}$$
   $$= 859\ 963.392$$
   $$\doteq 859\ 963 \text{ customers}$$

e. Use a graphing calculator to determine the month and year where there would be 650 000 customers.

Solution

To graph the function $N = 200\,000(1.20)^{\frac{t}{6}}$, press the $\left[\,Y_1 = \,\right]$ key, and enter the following:

$Y_1 = 200\,000(1.20)^{\wedge}(t\,/\,6)$

Set your WINDOW to the following settings:

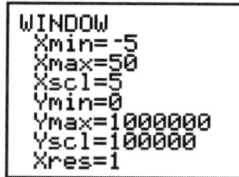

Then, press GRAPH to get the following screen.

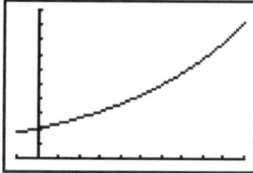

Using the TRACE feature, scroll to the right until the y-value is as close as possible to $y = 650\,000$. The cursor should be at about $x = 38.882\,979$, when $y = 651\,874.18$ as shown below.

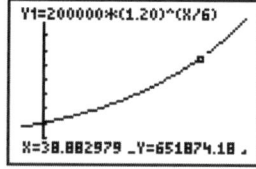

According to the graph, the amount of 650 000 cellphone customers occurs at about 38.88 months after January 1, 1996. Since there are 36 months in 3 years, this value occurs 3 years and 2.88 months after January 1, 1996, which would be at the end of March 1999.

Practice

Numerical Response

Use the following information to answer the next question.

A radioactive isotope technetium-99 is commonly used in various medical diagnoses. Given that a patient is injected with 10 mg of this isotope, the graph shows the amount of the isotope, m, in milligrams, remaining in her body over the next 24 hours, t.

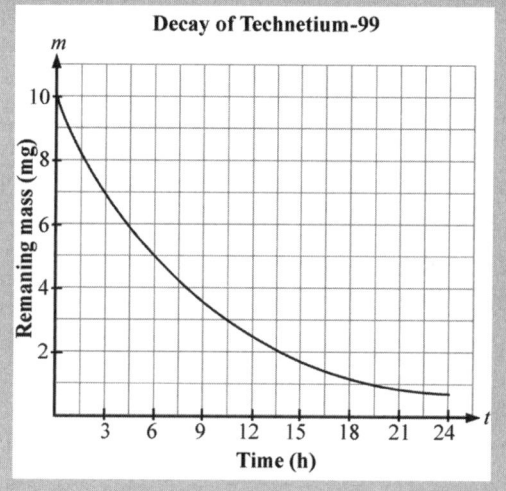

15. To the nearest 0.1 h, the half-life of the radioactive isotope is ____.

Use the following information to answer the next multipart question.

16. A newly married couple invests $20 000 into a variety of stocks in 1989. The exponential function describing the value, $V(t)$, in dollars over time, t, in years since Jan. 1, 1989 is $V(t) = 20\ 000(1.065)^t$.

Part A

Open Response

According to the equation, what is the couple's annual average rate of return as a percentage?

Part B

Open Response

According to the function, what should the value of the stock be in 2000?

Part C

Open Response

Enter the function on a graphing calculator, set an appropriate window, and determine from the graph in what year they should expect their stock to triple in value.

EF3.1 *compare, using a table of values and graphs, the simple and compound interest earned for a given principal (i.e., investment) and a fixed interest rate over time*

COMPARING SIMPLE AND COMPOUND INTEREST

When you invest money in a financial institution such as a bank, you get interest paid to you depending on the interest rate and the terms by which this rate is paid.

The amount that you initially invest is usually referred to as the **principal**, P, or the **present value**, PV, and the **interest rate**, i or r, is usually given as a percentage (%) per year.

The **total interest**, I_T, that you receive depends on the **time**, t or n, that you have the investment in the account, and the resulting total **amount**, A, or **final value**, FV, is the sum of the principal and interest accumulated.

Two forms of interest can be earned on an investment: simple and compound interest.

SIMPLE INTEREST

Simple interest is only earned on the principal, using this formula:

$$I = Prt$$

I is the simple interest, P is the principal, r is the interest rate per year as a decimal, and t is the time in years.

COMPOUND INTEREST

Compound interest is calculated each year using this formula:

$$I = Prt, \text{ where } t = 1$$

This interest is then added to the principal from the previous year before calculating the interest for the following year. Therefore, the principal, P, increases from year to year, as does the interest, I.

Note: Interest can be compounded monthly, quarterly, or semi-annually.

Example

Compare the simple interest and compound interest earned on a $1000 investment that receives 10% interest per year over a 5-year period. To illustrate the interest growth, make a table of values, and graph the problem.

t: time in years
P: principal
I: interest earned
I_T: total interest

Note: The interest rate, r, as a decimal is 0.10.

Solution

Simple Interest Table

t	P	I	I_T
0	$1000	n/a	0
1	$1000	$1000 × 0.10 × 1 = $100	$100
2	$1000	$1000 × 0.10 × 1 = $100	$200
3	$1000	$1000 × 0.10 × 1 = $100	$300
4	$1000	$1000 × 0.10 × 1 = $100	$400
5	$1000	$1000 × 0.10 × 1 = $100	$500

Compound Interest Table

t	P	I	I_T
0	$1000	n/a	0
1	$1000	$1000 × 0.10 × 1 = $100	$100
2	$1100	$1100 × 0.10 × 1 = $110	$210
3	$1210	$1210 × 0.10 × 1 = $121	$331
4	$1331	$1331 × 0.10 × 1 = $133.10	$464.10
5	$1464.10	$1464.10 × 0.10 × 1 = $146.41	$610.51

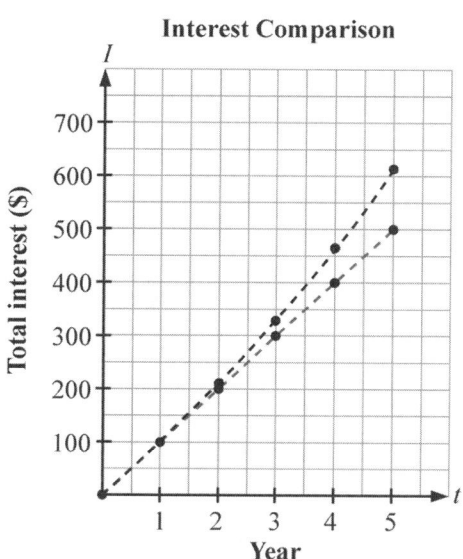

Interest Comparison

The points representing simple interest follow a linear pattern of growth, while the points representing compound interest follow a non-linear pattern of growth. This pattern is also evident in the table of values.

In the first year, the simple and compound interest is the same. However, after the first year, the compound interest is greater than the simple interest, and this difference increases more and more each year. Money invested in a compound interest account grows more rapidly than in a simple interest account.

CHALLENGER QUESTION

Use the following information to answer the next multipart question.

17. Jafar wanted to invest $2000 for four years into an account earning interest at a rate of 10% per year. He used a table of values to compare the total interest, I_T, accumulated if the principal, P, was invested in a simple or compound interest account. His partially completed table is shown.

	Simple Interest		Compound Interest	
Year	P	I_T	P	I_T
0	2000	0	2000	0
1	2000	200	2000	200
2	2000	400	2200	420
3	2000	k	2420	m
4	2000	l	p	n

Part A

If the values k, l, m, n, and p are calculated, then which of the following algebraic statements would be **false**?

A. $l - k = 200$ B. $n - m > 250$

C. $n - l = m - k$ D. $n - l > m - k$

Part B

If Jafar increased the table to include the values for year 5, how much more would the total accumulated amount be in the compound interest account compared to the simple interest account?

A. $120.00   B. $128.20

C. $196.82   D. $221.02

EF3.2 *solve problems, using a scientific calculator, that involve the calculation of the amount, A (also referred to as future value, FV), and the principal, P (also referred to as present value, PV), using the compound interest formula in the form* $A = P(1 + i)^n$ *[or FV = PV (1 + i)^n]*

SOLVING COMPOUND INTEREST PROBLEMS

When solving compound interest problems, the resulting amount, A, or final value, FV, can be found using the compound interest formula.

$$A = P(1 + i)^n \text{ or } FV = PV(1 + i)^n$$

A or FV is the accumulated amount, P is the principal or original investment, i is the interest rate (as a decimal) per compounding period, and n is the number of compounding periods over the total time of the investment.

Compound interest is often added to the principal more than once a year. The time when interest is calculated and added to the principal is called the **compounding period**.

The interest rate, r, is usually quoted as an annual rate but can be compounded more than once a year. To calculate the interest, i, that is added per compounding period, *divide* the annual interest rate by the frequency, f, of the compounding periods in a year.

To calculate the number of compounding periods, n, over the total time of the investment, *multiply* the number of years by the frequency, f, of the compounding periods in a year.

The following chart will illustrate the concept of compounding.

r	f	i	n
5%/a **annually** 3 years	1	$= \dfrac{0.05}{f}$ $= \dfrac{0.05}{1}$ $= 0.05$	$= 3 \times f$ $= 3 \times 1$ $= 3$
6%/a **semi-annually** 4 years	2	$= \dfrac{0.06}{f}$ $= \dfrac{0.06}{2}$ $= 0.03$	$= 4 \times f$ $= 4 \times 2$ $= 8$
12%/a **quarterly** 2 years	4	$= \dfrac{0.12}{f}$ $= \dfrac{0.12}{4}$ $= 0.03$	$= 2 \times f$ $= 2 \times 4$ $= 8$
9%/a **monthly** 6 years	12	$= \dfrac{0.09}{f}$ $= \dfrac{0.09}{12}$ $= 0.0075$	$= 6 \times f$ $= 6 \times 12$ $= 72$
10%/a **daily** 1 year	365	$= \dfrac{0.10}{f}$ $= \dfrac{0.10}{365}$ (leave as a fraction)	$= 1 \times f$ $= 1 \times 365$ $= 365$

Note: The designation "a" in the quoted interest rate stands for *annum*, which means *year*.

:Example

Natacha wanted to invest $60 000 into an account. She has these two options:
Option 1: 10%/a compounded semi-annually for 4 years
Option 2: 10%/a compounded daily for 4 years

Which option is the best choice?
Solution
Use the formula $A = P(1 + i)^n$ to calculate the total amount for each option after 4 years.

Option 1: Compounded semi-annually $\Rightarrow f = 2$
$i = 0.10 \div f = 0.10 \div 2 = 0.05$
$n = 4 \times f = 4 \times 2 = 8$
$$A = P(1 + i)^n$$
$$= 60\ 000(1 + 0.05)^8$$
$$= 60\ 000(1.05)^8$$
$$= \$88\ 647.33$$

Option 2: Compounded daily $\Rightarrow f = 365$
$i = 0.10 \div f$
$$= 0.10 \div 365 = \dfrac{0.10}{365}$$
$n = 4 \times f = 4 \times 365 = 1460$
Use brackets around i when it is a fraction.
$$A = P(1 + i)^n$$
$$= 60\ 000\left(1 + \left(\dfrac{0.10}{365}\right)\right)^{1460}$$
$$= \$89\ 504.58$$

The best choice is to put the $60 000 investment into the daily compounded option, since more accumulates over the 4 years than in the semi-annually compounded option. You should expect a better final amount with the option that gives you interest most often in the year.

:Example

Determine the present value, PV, when the future value, FV, after 15 years in an investment is $40 000, where the interest earned is 8%/a compounded annually.

Solution
Compounded annually $\Rightarrow f = 1$
$$i = 0.08 \div f = 0.08 \div 1 = 0.08$$
$$n = 15 \times f = 15 \times 1 = 15$$
$$FV = PV(1 + i)^n$$
$$40\ 000 = PV(1 + 0.08)^{15}$$
$$40\ 000 = PV(3.172\ 169\ 114)$$
$$\dfrac{40\ 000}{3.172\ 169\ 114} = PV$$
$$12\ 609.67 = PV$$

The present value is $12 609.67

Practice

18. If interest is compounded bi-weekly where interest is 5.2%/a, then which of the following equations correctly represents the future value, FV, for a given present value, PV, over $3\frac{1}{2}$ years?

   A. $FV = PV(1.001)^{182}$

   B. $FV = PV(1.02)^{91}$

   C. $FV = PV(1.002)^{91}$

   D. $FV = PV(1.0052)^{84}$

Numerical Response

19. Sheniel wanted to put $44 000 into a GIC for 8 years where the annual interest rate was 12%/a. What is the difference in the total interest if she put it in a daily compounded account as opposed to a semi-annually compounded account, to the nearest dollar? $____

EF3.3 *determine, through investigation, that compound interest is an example of exponential growth*

COMPOUND INTEREST AS EXPONENTIAL GROWTH

In the previous lesson, you learned how to use the compound interest formula, $FV = PV(1 + i)^n$ or $A = P(1 + i)^n$, to find the future value, FV or A, or the present value, PV or P, as follows:

$$FV = PV(1 + i)^n \Rightarrow \text{Given the value of } PV$$
$$PV = \frac{FV}{(1 + i)^n} \Rightarrow \text{Given the value of } FV$$

Note: Using the exponent law $\frac{1}{x^n} = x^{-n}$, the present value formula can be rewritten in the following ways:

$$PV = \frac{FV}{(1 + i)^n} \text{ or}$$
$$PV = FV\left(\frac{1}{1 + i}\right)^n \text{ or}$$
$$PV = FV(1 + i)^{-n}$$

Each variation of the compound interest formula can be represented as an exponential function of the form $f(x) = a(b)^x$.

Example

Jake invested $2000 into a GIC account that earned 12% interest per year compounded semi-annually. Use a table of values to show that the growth in the final amount, FV, can be represented as an exponential function $f(x) = a(b)^x$, where b reflects the compound interest rates.

Solution

Note: The interest per compounding period is $i = \frac{12\%}{2} = 6\%$, and the number of compounding periods, n, is 2 times per year.

Semi-Annual Periods	Final Amount (FV)	Growth Factor
0	$2000	—
1	$2000(1 + 0.06)^1$ = $2120	$2120 \div 2000$ = 1.06
2	$2000(1 + 0.06)^2$ = $2247.20	$2247.20 \div 2120$ = 1.06
3	$2000(1 + 0.06)^3$ = $2382.03	$2382.03 \div 2247.20$ ≈ 1.06
4	$2000(1 + 0.06)^4$ = $2524.95	$2524.95 \div 2382.03$ ≈ 1.06
5	$2000(1 + 0.06)^5$ = $2676.45	$2676.45 \div 2524.95$ ≈ 1.06
6	$2000(1 + 0.06)^6$ = $2837.04	$2837.04 \div 2676.45$ ≈ 1.06

The table shows that the growth factor is constant at 1.06. This is a characteristic of an exponential function. The exponential function $f(x) = 2000(1.06)^x$ would therefore describe this scenario, where 2000 represents the original present value and 1.06 is the growth factor.

The interest rate per compounding period, i, is represented by the value after the decimal point of the growth factor $(1.06 \Rightarrow 6\%)$.

Example

Stephanie needed to determine the present value, PV, that she needed to put into a bank account now at an interest rate of 10% per annum compounded annually so that she had $1610 spending money for a planned holiday in 5 years. Determine the decreasing present value, PV, each year. Then, graph this data on your graphing calculator, and show that the graph represents an exponential function $f(x) = a(b)^x$, where b reflects the annual interest rate.

Solution

Use the formula $PV = FV(1 + i)^{-n}$ to determine the present values for the years 0 to 5.

Year (x)	Present Value (y)
0	$1610
1	$1610(1 + 0.10)^{-1} = \$1463.63$
2	$1610(1 + 0.10)^{-2} = \$1330.58$
3	$1610(1 + 0.10)^{-3} = \$1209.62$
4	$1610(1 + 0.10)^{-4} = \$1099.65$
5	$1610(1 + 0.10)^{-5} = \$999.68$

Enter this data as lists L₁ and L₂ on your graphing calculator, set the WINDOW to x:$[-2, 6, 1]$, y:$[0, 2000, 100]$, and then graph the data using the $2^{nd}[Y =]$ or STAT PLOT feature, as shown below.

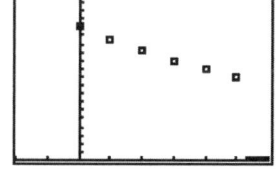

Do an exponential regression on the data by using the STAT CALC 0 or Exp Reg feature to get the following exponential equation on your screen.

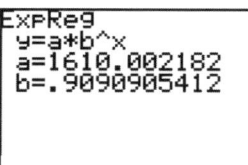

Finally, enter this equation in $[Y_1 =]$ as $Y_1 = 1610 \times 0.909\,091^{\wedge}x$, and graph it to show it passing through the plotted points.

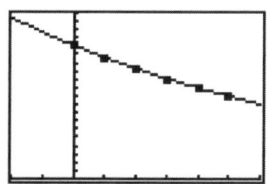

This graph shows that the exponential function $f(x) = 1610(0.909\,091)^x$ represents the decreasing present value, y, over the annual compounding periods, x.

Since $PV = FV(1 + i)^{-n}$ can also be written as $PV = FV\left(\dfrac{1}{1+i}\right)^n$, then the value of $\dfrac{1}{b}$ in the exponential function $f(x) = a(b)^x$ should reflect the interest rate, i. Notice that this holds true in this scenario.

$$\frac{1}{b} = \frac{1}{0.909\,091} = 1.099\,999\,89 \approx 1.10$$

The value after the decimal point in the reciprocal of the decay factor $(1.10 \Rightarrow 10\%)$ represents the interest rate per compounding period, i.

:Practice

Use the following information to answer the next multipart question.

20. Achmed wanted to observe how a $2000 investment would grow in an account where interest was compounded annually. He chose a particular annual interest rate and plotted points that showed how the total interest would accumulate over a four-year period.

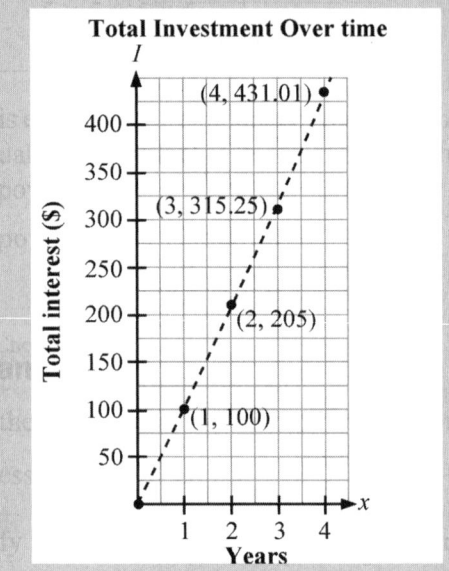

Total Investment Over time

(4, 431.01)

(3, 315.25)

(2, 205)

(1, 100)

Total interest ($)

Years

Part A

The exponential function that correctly reflects the annual interest rate represented by the values of the graph over a period of x years is

A. $f(x) = 2000(1.10)^x$

B. $f(x) = 2000(1.05)^x$

C. $f(x) = 2000(1.36)^x$

D. $f(x) = 2000(1.005)^x$

Part B

How much total interest is accumulated after 5 years?

A. $2552.56   B. $1221.02

C. $552.56   D. $452.56

EF3.4 *solve problems, using a TVM Solver on a graphing calculator or on a website, that involve the calculation of the interest rate per compounding period, i, or the number of compounding periods, n, in the compound interest formula*
$$A = P(1 + i) \text{ or } FV = PV(1 + i)^n$$

SOLVING COMPOUND INTEREST PROBLEMS USING A GRAPHING CALCULATOR

The TVM Solver, which is an application program in your graphing calculator, can be used to solve compound interest problems. The program is found by pressing the APPS key, opening the Finance program, and then opening the TVM Solver feature to get the screen below. An explanation of each variable is also given.

N=0
I%=0
PV=0
PMT=0
FV=0
P/Y=1
C/Y=1
PMT:**END** BEGIN

N = number of years of the investment
I% = annual interest rate for any compounding period
PV = principal or present value, which is entered as a negative value ($-PV$ or $-P$) because you pay money out when you invest
FV = amount or future value, which is entered as a positive value (A or FV) because you receive money when the investment matures
C/Y = number of compounding periods per year
Note: For all compound interest problems, the values or highlights of PMT, P/Y, and PMT are always set as follows:
PMT = 0, P/Y = 1, PMT:END

:Example

A present value of $8000 amounted to a final value of $11 406 after 6 years when placed in an account where interest was compounded semi-annually. What was the annual interest rate?

Solution

Enter the given values for N, PV, FV, and C/Y.

N = 6 (number of years)
PV = −8000 (present value)
FV = 11 406 (future value)
C/Y = 2 (since semi-annually means two compounding periods per year)

Then, move the cursor to the I% position, and press APLHA ENTER to calculate the annual interest rate as shown below.

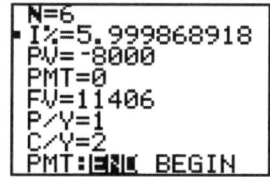

According to the TVM Solver result, the annual interest rate, to the nearest hundredth percent, is 6.00%.

:Example

How long will it take for a $5000 investment to triple in value if interest is 9% per year compounded quarterly?

Solution

Enter the given values for I%, PV, FV, and C/Y.
Note: FV = 15 000, since triple means $3 \times PV = 3 \times 5000$.

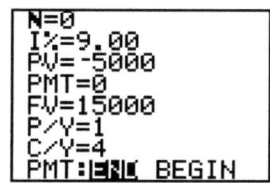

Then, move your cursor to the N position, and press ALPHA ENTER, as shown below.

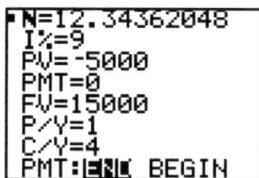

According to the TVM Solver result, it takes a little more than 12 years for the money to triple in value. Since the interest is compounded quarterly, you need to round up to the nearest quarter year (i.e., 0.25, 0.50, 0.75, or 1). Thus, it would take 12.5 years for the invested amount of $5000 to triple in value.

:Practice

21. Charissa used her TVM Solver to determine the annual interest rate compounded monthly that would have a $4800 investment achieve a final value of $8000 over 66 months. The values of N and PV that she should enter are

    A. N = 66, PV = 4800

    B. N = 5.5, PV = 4800

    C. N = 66, PV = −4800

    D. N = 5.5, PV = −4800

Numerical Response

CHALLENGER QUESTION

22. The exponential function $f(x) = a(b)^x$ can be formed to represent the growth of a present value of $10 000 over 10 years collecting interest that compounds annually.

    If the future value is $33 945, then with the aid of the TVM Solver, the resulting value of b in $f(x) = a(b)^x$, to the nearest hundredth, is ____.

EF3.5 *explain the meaning of the term annuity, through investigation of numeric and graphical representations using technology*

ANNUITIES

An **annuity** is a series of payments or investments made at regular intervals of time. A **simple** annuity is an annuity where the payments are made at the same time as the compounding periods of interest. A simple **ordinary** annuity is an annuity where the payments are made at the end of each interval of time.

:Example

Kaitlyn plans to invest $1000 at the end of each 6-month period in an annuity that earns interest at a rate of 6%/a compounded semi-annually for the next 3 years.

Show how you would calculate the future value of the annuity after 3 years.

Solution
Since the number of compounds per year is 2 (semi-annually), the interest per compounding period, i, and number of compounds, n, are

$i = \dfrac{6\%}{2} = 3\%$ or 0.03

$n = 3 \times 2 = 6$

You can use a timeline to represent each regular $1000 deposit and its compounded final value at the end of 3 years.

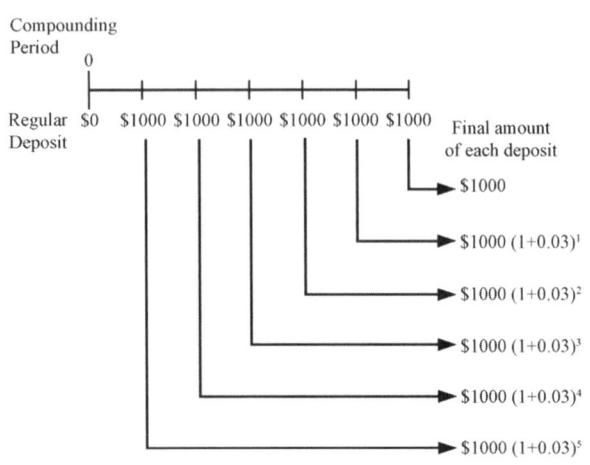

To calculate the future value (FV) of the annuity after 3 years, add up all the final amounts of each regular deposit.

$FV = \$1000 + \$1000(1.03)^1$
$\quad + \$1000(1.03)^2 + \$1000(1.03)^3$
$\quad + \$1000(1.03)^4 + \$1000(1.03)^5$
$\quad = \$1000 + \$1030 + \$1060.90 + \$1092.73$
$\quad + \$1125.51 + \$1159.27$
$\quad = \$6468.41$

The future value of the annuity after 3 years is $6468.41.

:Practice

Use the following information to answer the next question.

Brittany invested $800 at the end of each 6-month period into an annuity over 5 years where interest was 8.8%/a compounded quarterly. To see how this annuity would grow, she used the timeline shown to determine the final value of each invested deposit.

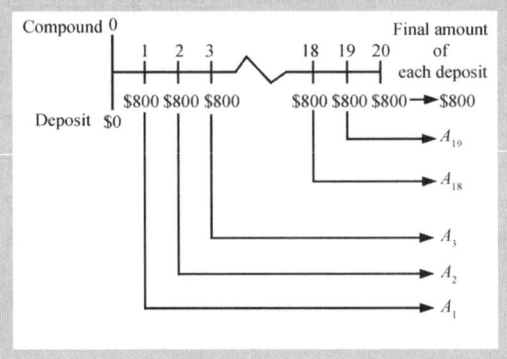

23. Which of the following expressions represents the final amount, A_3?

A. $\$800(1.022)^2$

B. $\$800(1.022)^3$

C. $\$800(1.022)^{17}$

D. $\$800(1.022)^{18}$

EF3.6 *determine, through investigation using technology, the effects of changing the conditions (i.e., the payments, the frequency of the payments, the interest rate, the compounding period) of ordinary simple annuities (i.e., annuities in which payments are made at the end of each period, and the compounding period and the payment period are the same)*

EFFECTS OF CHANGING CONDITIONS OF ANNUITIES

By changing the conditions, such as the interest rate or the frequency of payment, of an ordinary simple annuity, varying outcomes result that are interesting to investigate. You can use the TVM Solver on your graphing calculator to examine these changes by entering values according to the following instructions:

N = number of payments made
I% = annual interest rate
PV = present value (+) if money is coming to you like a loan, and (−) if money is being invested into an account.
PMT = regular payment (−) if they are made into an account, and (+) if they are withdrawn from an account.
FV = future invested amount (+), debt paid off (0), or debt owing (−)
P / Y = total number of payments made in a year
C / Y = number of compounding periods in a year
Note: PMT will always be END, indicating that the payments are made at the end of each compounding period. Also, P / Y = C / Y in all ordinary simple annuity questions.

Example

Use your TVM Solver to compare the future value of an investment annuity when the frequency and amount of the payment change and the annual interest rate changes.

Solution

Choose an annual payment amount of $3600 over a 10 year period, with a present value, $PV = 0$, and investigate the following changes in the frequency and amount of the payment changes and the annual interest rates using the TVM Solver. The results are recorded in the table below.

N	P/Y and C/Y	PMT
10	Annually: 1	$= \dfrac{\$3600}{1}$ $= \$3600$
40	Quarterly: 4	$= \dfrac{\$3600}{4}$ $= \$900$
120	Monthly: 12	$= \dfrac{\$3600}{12}$ $= \$300$
FV at I%		
6%	8%	10%
$47 450.86	$52 151.62	$57 374.73
$48 841.10	$54 361.78	$60 662.30
$49 163.80	$54 883.81	$61 453.49

According to the table of values, the payment amount per compounding period does not change the future value by drastic amounts.

i. Annual→ quarterly change (6%): $1390.24 OR $139.02/year

ii. Annual→ monthly change (6%): $1712.94 OR $171.29/year

However, the future values do change dramatically when the annual interest rates change.

i. 6% → 8% change: Between $4700.76 (annually) to $5720.01 (monthly) or about $470/year to $572/year.

ii. 6% → 10% change: Between $9923.87 (annually) to $12 289.69 (monthly) or about $992/year to $1229/year.

:Example

Use your TVM Solver to compare the future value of an investment annuity when changes are made to the length of times of the investment.

Solution

Now, investigate what happens as the length of time of the investment changes for an annual payment of $3600 at the various annual interest rates.

N	PMT	FV of I%		
		6%	8%	10%
5	$3600	$20 293.53	$21 119.76	$21 978.36
10	$3600	$47 450.86	$52 151.62	$57 374.73
15	$3600	$83 793.49	$97 747.61	$114 380.93
20	$3600	$132 428.13	$164 743.07	$206 190.00
25	$3600	$197 512.24	$263 181.38	$354 049.41

The chart shows that the length of time that the investment is in the account combined with a good interest rate has the greatest effect on the future value (FV). To clarify this effect, you can calculate the interest/year at a 10% annual interest rate.

N	Total PMT	Total Interest	Interest per Year
5	$3600 × 5 = $18 000	$21 978.36 − $18 000 = $3978.36	$795.67
10	$3600 × 10 = $36 000	$57 374.73 − $36 000 = $21 374.73	$2137.47
15	$3600 × 15 = $54 000	$114 380.93 − $54 000 = $50 380.93	$3358.73
20	$3600 × 20 = $72 000	$206 190.00 − $72 000 = $134 190.00	$6709.50
25	$3600 × 25 = $190 000	$354 049.41 − $90 000 = $264 049.41	$10 561.98

It pays to invest over as long a period of time as possible.

Obviously, the reverse effect would occur if you paid off a loan over a period of time at the above interest rates and regular payments. You would want to pay off the loan as quickly as possible.

:Practice

Use the following information to answer the next multipart question.

24. On their 20th birthday, identical twins Dale and Dana discussed the age they would start to make regular, annual deposits into an RRSP plan so that at age 60 they would have a particular accumulated amount, A, due to an accumulated interest, I.

They arranged their decisions in a chart as shown.

Twin	Dale	Dana
Annual interest rate	6%	6%
Starting age	20	30
Annual deposits	$1000	$2000
Number of deposits	40	30
Accumulated amount	A_1	A_2
Accumulated interest	I_1	I_2

Part A

If the values of A_1, A_2, I_1, and I_2 were calculated on a TVM Solver, the correct relationships are

A. $A_1 > A_2, I_1 > I_2$

B. $A_1 > A_2, I_1 < I_2$

C. $A_1 < A_2, I_1 > I_2$

D. $A_1 < A_2, I_1 < I_2$

Part B

Numerical Response

If Dale wanted to end up with an accumulated amount, A_1, of $500 000, then his annual deposits, to the nearest dollar, would need to be $____.

EF3.7 *solve problems, using technology, that involve the amount, the present value, and the regular payment of an ordinary simple annuity*

SOLVING SIMPLE ANNUITY PROBLEMS

To solve problems involving annuities, make sure that you distinguish between the values and terms of a loan and those of a savings or retirement plan.

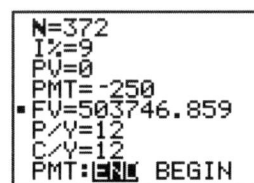 **Example**

Ethan is 24. He wants to put aside $250 at the end of every month into a retirement fund earning 9%/a interest compounded monthly until he is 55. At 55, he wants to withdraw regular monthly amounts until the fund is depleted over the next 20 years (at age 75). How much will his regular monthly withdrawals be when he retires at age 55?

Solution

This problem is a retirement investment. The first step to the problem is to determine the final accumulated amount, *FV*, of the retirement savings plan from age 24 to 55.

Step 1: The total number of years that the monthly deposits are made is 55 − 24 = 31 years.

Since the deposits are made monthly, the total number of compounds over the 31 years is N = 31 × 12 = 372. This value and the other values in the problem can be entered into the TVM Solver of your graphing calculator to enable you to find the final accumulated amount, FV, as shown below.

```
N=372
I%=9
PV=0
PMT=-250
■FV=503746.859
P/Y=12
C/Y=12
PMT:END BEGIN
```

According to the resulting value, FV, on the screen, the total accumulated amount in the retirement fund after 31 years, when Ethan is 55 years old, is $503 746.86.

Step 2: The second step of this problem is to see how the present value or principal of $503 746.86 will deplete to a future value of FV = 0 after the next 20 years. The total number of compounds is N = 20 × 12 = 240.

Now, enter PV = −503 746.86, and determine the monthly withdrawals, PMT, that can be made over the next 240 months. Enter these values into the TVM Solver as shown below to solve for PMT.

```
N=240
I%=9
PV=-503746.86
■PMT=4532.341251
FV=0
P/Y=12
C/Y=12
PMT:END BEGIN
```

According to the resulting value, PMT, on the screen, the regular amount of $4532.34 can be withdrawn monthly from the account over the 20 years until it is completely depleted (at age 75).

 **Practice**

CHALLENGER QUESTION

Use the following information to answer the next question.

Both Stephen and Marie took out a loan of $30 000 from a bank where the rate of interest was 9.60%/a compounded weekly. Both Stephen and Marie make weekly payments, but Marie takes 5 years and Stephen takes 7 years to pay off the loan.

25. How much more interest does Stephen pay compared to Marie to pay off the loan?

   A. $3247.40   B. $3957.72

   C. $4554.00   D. $7801.40

Use the following information to answer the next multipart question.

26. Esther wants to retire at age 55 with enough money in her retirement fund, which earns interest at 10.77%/a compounded monthly, so that she could withdraw regular monthly amounts of $5000 until it is depleted 25 years later.

Part A

Open Response

How much does Esther need to deposit at the end of every month at the age of 25 in order to have the required amount in her retirement fund at age 55?
Show your work.

Part B

Open Response

What is the total interest that would be paid to her retirement fund from age 25 to age 80? Show your work.

Part C

Open Response

How does the total amount withdrawn during her retirement compare to the total amount of deposits she made before retirement? Show your work.

SOLUTIONS–EXPONENTIAL FUNCTIONS

1. C	**8.** Part A- **OR**	Part B- **C**	Part B- **D**	**24.** Part A- **C**
2. OR	Part B- **OR**	**14.** Part A- **OR**	**18. C**	Part B- **3231**
3. D	**9. B**	Part B- **A**	**19. 3121**	**25. A**
4. 1.08	**10. 3.81**	**15. 6.0**	**20.** Part A- **B**	**26.** Part A- **OR**
5. Part A- **A**	**11. OR**	**16.** Part A- **OR**	Part B- **C**	Part B- **OR**
Part B- **A**	**12.** Part A- **D**	Part B- **OR**	**21. D**	Part C- **OR**
6. C	Part B- **A**	Part C- **OR**	**22. 1.13**	
7. D	**13.** Part A- **B**	**17.** Part A- **C**	**23. C**	

1. C

The value $\frac{1}{64}$ written as an expression with a base of 8 is $\frac{1}{8^2}$, since $64 = 8 \times 8 = 8^1 \times 8^1 = 8^{1+1} = 8^2$. The expression $\frac{1}{8^2}$ can also be written in the form 8^{-2} since $\frac{1}{x^n} = x^{-n}$.

Therefore, $8^r \times 8^r \times 8^r = 8^{-2}$.

According to the product rule $\left(x^m\right) \times (x)^n = x^{m+n}$, the expression on the left side of the equal sign can be simplified as follows:

$\left(8^r\right)\left(8^r\right)\left(8^r\right) = 8^{r+r+r} = 8^{3r}$

In the simplified expression $8^{3r} = 8^{-2}$, the exponents must be equal since the bases are equal.

$3r = -2$

$r = -\frac{2}{3}$

The correct value of r is $-\frac{2}{3}$.

2. Open Response

To find the y-value corresponding to $x = \frac{9}{4}$ in the expression $16^{\frac{9}{4}}$, continue the pattern of increasing the x-values (exponent on 16) by $\frac{1}{4}$, and multiply the previous y-value by 2.

Increase of x-value	Increase of y-value
$16^{\frac{4}{4}}$	16
$16^{\frac{4}{4}+\frac{1}{4}} = 16^{\frac{5}{4}}$	$16 \times 2 = 32$
$16^{\frac{5}{4}+\frac{1}{4}} = 16^{\frac{6}{4}}$	$32 \times 2 = 64$
$16^{\frac{6}{4}+\frac{1}{4}} = 16^{\frac{7}{4}}$	$64 \times 2 = 128$
$16^{\frac{7}{4}+\frac{1}{4}} = 16^{\frac{8}{4}}$	$128 \times 2 = 256$
$16^{\frac{8}{4}+\frac{1}{4}} = 16^{\frac{9}{4}}$	$256 \times 2 = 512$

According to this pattern, $16^{\frac{9}{4}} = 512$.

Similarly, to find the y-value corresponding to $x = -\frac{3}{4}$, continue the pattern in the opposite direction by decreasing the x-values (exponent on 16), and divide the previous y-value by 2.

Decrease of x-value	Decrease of y-value
$16^{\frac{1}{4}}$	2
$16^{\frac{1}{4}-\frac{1}{4}} = 16^{\frac{0}{4}}$	$2 \div 2 = 1$
$16^{\frac{0}{4}-\frac{1}{4}} = 16^{-\frac{1}{4}}$	$1 \div 2 = \frac{1}{2}$
$16^{-\frac{1}{4}-\frac{1}{4}} = 16^{-\frac{2}{4}}$	$\frac{1}{2} \div 2 = \frac{1}{4}$
$16^{-\frac{2}{4}-\frac{1}{4}} = 16^{-\frac{3}{4}}$	$\frac{1}{4} \div 2 = \frac{1}{8}$

According to this second pattern, $16^{\frac{-3}{4}} = \frac{1}{8}$.

Note: These two values could be verified by graphing the function $y = 16^x$ on your graphing calculator and finding the corresponding y-values for each value of $x = -\dfrac{3}{4}$ and $\dfrac{9}{4}$.

Enter $y = 16^x$ into your calculator using the $\left[Y_1 = \right]$ key.
$Y_1 = 16^\wedge x$

Then, set an appropriate WINDOW, such as ZOOM 6, and graph the function by pressing GRAPH.

Then, use the 2nd TRACE VALUE feature to find the y-values of $\dfrac{1}{8}$ or 0.125 for $x = -\dfrac{3}{4}$ and 512 for $x = \dfrac{9}{4}$ or 2.25 as shown on the screens below.

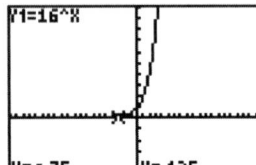 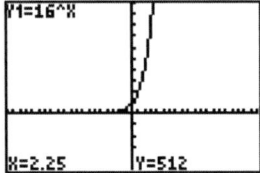

3. D

According to the product rule
$$\left(x^m\right)\left(x^n\right) = x^{m+n}, (2)(2)(2) = \left(2^1\right)\left(2^1\right)\left(2^1\right)$$
$$= 2^{1+1+1} = 2^3$$

Since $\sqrt{4} = 2$ because $2 \times 2 = 4$, rewrite this expression as follows:
$$(2)^3 = \left(\sqrt{4}\right)^3 = (4)^{\frac{3}{2}}, \text{ since } \left(\sqrt[n]{x}\right)^m = x^{\frac{m}{n}}.$$

You also know that $x^n = \left(\dfrac{1}{x}\right)^{-n}$, so $(4)^{\frac{3}{2}} = \left(\dfrac{1}{4}\right)^{-\frac{3}{2}}$.

Therefore, for $\left(\dfrac{1}{4}\right)^k$ to be equivalent to $(2)(2)(2)$, the value of k is $-\dfrac{3}{2}$.

4. 1.08

Use your graphing calculator with the $\wedge$ button to evaluate the exponential expression to the nearest hundredth. Put brackets around the exponent.
$$\left(\dfrac{5}{4}\right)^{\frac{7}{20}} = \left(\dfrac{5}{4}\right)^{\left(\frac{7}{20}\right)} = 1.081\ 231\ 039 = 1.08$$

5. Part A –A

In order to graph the exponential relation $y = \left(\dfrac{3}{2}\right)^x$ in your graphing calculator, it needs to be entered into the $\left[Y_1 = \right]$ feature with brackets around the base as follows.
$$Y_1 = \left(\dfrac{3}{2}\right)^\wedge X$$

Then, set your WINDOW to the given settings of x:[-4.7, 4.7, 1] and y:[-3.1, 3.1, 1], and press GRAPH.

The graph that should appear on your screen is the one shown in choice A. Since $y = \left(\dfrac{3}{2}\right)^0 = 1$, the graph has a y-intercept of 1.

Part B –A

In order for $y = \left(\dfrac{3}{2}\right)^x$ to be a function, every x-value or x-coordinate on the graph can only have one corresponding y-value or y-coordinate.

6. C

The graph of any exponential function, where $a > 1$ has the following features, which correspond to the observation made by the student of $f(x) = 12^x$.

- The domain is $x \in R$.
- The range is $y > 0 \to$ observation I.
- The graph has a horizontal asymptote of $y = 0$.
- The graph increases throughout its domain from left to right $\to$ observation III.
- The graph has a y-intercept of 1 $\to$ observation IV.

The graph does not have an asymptote of $x = 0$ as given in observation II, nor does it pass through the point $(3, 36)$ as given in observation V, since $12^3 \neq 36$. Therefore, the observations that correctly describe the graph of $f(x) = 12^x$ are observations I, III, IV.

7. D

When $0 < a < 1$, the graph of an exponential function $f(x) = a^x$ is a decreasing function from left to right. In other words, it is steep on the left side of the y-axis. As the value of a gets closer to zero, the steepness on the left side of the y-axis increases. Since $\dfrac{1}{16}$ is below 1 and closer to zero than $\dfrac{5}{16}$, the function $y = \left(\dfrac{1}{16}\right)^x$ or $f(x) = \left(\dfrac{1}{16}\right)^x$ decreases most rapidly or is steepest on the left side of the y-axis.

8. Part A – Open Response

To determine the equation of each function, examine the y-value corresponding to an x-value of 1. The y-value is a when $x = 1$, since
$$y = a^x \to y = a^1 \to y = a$$
Function I:
At $x = 1$, $y = 4$, so $a = 4$.

Therefore, the equation is $f(x) = 4^x$.
Function II:
At $x = 1$, $y = \dfrac{2}{3}$, so $a = \dfrac{2}{3}$.

Therefore, the equation is $f(x) = \left(\dfrac{2}{3}\right)^x$.

Part B – Open Response

There is no x-intercept for any exponential function of the form $f(x) = a^x$, $a > 0$, since the graph never touches the x-axis. In the function $f(x) = 4^x$, as you go left on the x-axis to values of $x < 0$, the y-values get smaller and smaller, but never reach 0.

Similarly, for $f(x) = \left(\frac{2}{3}\right)^x$, as you go right on the x-axis to values of $x > 0$, the y-values get smaller and smaller, but never reach 0.

The y-intercept for both $f(x) = 4^x$ and $f(x) = \left(\frac{2}{3}\right)^x$ is $(0, 1)$, since according to the exponent law $a^0 = 1$, where $a \neq 0$. Thus, $f(x) = 4^0$ and $f(x) = \left(\frac{2}{3}\right)^0$ equals 1.

9. B

According to the product rule $x^m \times x^n = x^{m+n}$, the middle expression $(-6)^5(-6)^4$ can be simplified as $(-6)^5(-6)^4 = (-6)^{5+4} = (-6)^9$

The first expression $\dfrac{(-6)^a}{(-6)^4}$ can be simplified according to the quotient rule $\dfrac{x^m}{x^n} = x^{m-n}$ as follows:

$$\frac{(-6)^a}{(-6)^4} = (-6)^{a-4}$$

In order for the first simplified expression $(-6)^{a-4}$ to be equivalent to the second simplified expression $(-6)^9$, the exponents must be equal, since the bases are equal. $(-6)^{a-4} = (-6)^9$, only if $a - 4 = 9$.

Now, solve for a.

$a - 4 = 9$
$\quad a = 4+9$
$\quad a = 13$

For the first expression to be equivalent to the second expression, the value of a must be 13.

The third expression $\left((-6)^b\right)^3$ can be simplified according to the power rule $\left(x^m\right)^n = x^{mn}$ as follows:

$$\left((-6)^b\right)^3 = (-6)^{b \times 3} = (-6)^{3b}$$

In order for the second simplified expression $(-6)^9$ to be equivalent to the third simplified expression $(-6)^{3b}$, the exponents must be equal, since the bases are equal. $(-6)^9 = (-6)^{3b}$, only if $9 = 3b$.

Now, solve for b.

$3b = 9$
$\quad b = \dfrac{9}{3}$
$\quad b = 3$

For the second expression to be equivalent to the third expression, the value of b must be 3.

10. 3.81

The exponential expression $\left((0.8)^3\right)^{-2}$ involves a power of a power and can be simplified using the power rule $\left(x^m\right)^n = x^{mn}$.

$$\left((0.8)^3\right)^{-2} = (0.8)^{3 \times -2} = (0.8)^{-6}$$

Using the graphing calculator with the $\wedge$ button, this expression can be evaluated as follows:

$$(0.8)^{-6} \Rightarrow (0.8)^\wedge(-6) = 3.814\ 697\ 266 \approx 3.81$$

11. Open Response

When given a table of values, a function increases exponentially if the ratios between successive y-values are constant. Given below are the calculations of the ratios between successive y-values (speeds).

Time (s)	Speed (km/h)	Ratios
1	5.00	$\frac{8.00}{5.00} = 1.6$
2	8.00	$\frac{12.80}{8.00} = 1.6$
3	12.80	$\frac{20.48}{12.80} = 1.6$
4	20.48	$\frac{32.77}{20.48} = 1.6$
5	32.77	

Since the ratios between successive y-values (speeds) are constant at 1.6, the speeds increase exponentially. Therefore, Cass is correct in his assessment.

12. Part A –D

Tank I:

The equation representing the flow of grain $h = 8(0.80)^t$ is an exponential function since the variable t is in the exponent position and has the form of $f(x) = a(b)^x$. The graph of this function is a non-linear curve, so the height of the grain, h, would decrease non-linearly in this tank.

Tank II:

The equation representing the flow of grain $h = 8 - 0.80t$ is a linear function of the form $y = mx + b$. The graph of this function is a line, so the height of the grain, h, would not decrease non-linearly, but rather linearly.

Tank III and Tank IV:

The equation representing the flow of grain $h = 0.016t^2 - 0.8t + 8$ and $h = -0.02(t + 2)^2 + 8$ are quadratic functions of the form $y = ax^2 + bx + c$ or $y = a(x - h)^2 + k$. The graphs of both these function are parabolas (U-shaped curves), so the height of grain, h, would decrease non-linearly in these two tanks.

The tanks that allow the height of the grain to decrease non-linearly over time are tanks I, III, and IV.

Part B –A

An exponential function of the form $f(x) = a(b)^x$, $b > 0$ does not have an x-intercept, since it is a curve that approaches the x-axis but never touches it. Therefore, the equation $h = 8(0.80)^t$ would never have a t-intercept in the domain $t \in \mathbb{R}$. This can be verified by entering the function as $Y_1 = 8(0.80)^\wedge x$ in your graphing calculator, and pressing 2nd GRAPH. Scroll down the table. As you scroll down using the ∇ key, you will see that as x gets larger, y never reaches 0, as shown by the screen below.

X	Y1
125	6E -12
126	5E -12
127	4E -12
128	3E -12
129	3E -12
130	2E -12
131	2E -12

X=131

13. Part A –B

The data shows exponential decay, since the rebound heights decrease after each successive bounce.
An exponential decay curve should be steep at first and then flatten out as you move from left to right (remember the graph of $f(x) = a^x$, where $0 < a < 1$). Also, the graph should not touch the x-axis, which makes choice D incorrect. The correct graph depicting the decay of rebound heights, h, over the bounce number, n, is shown in choice B.

Part B –C

A tennis ball is softer (squishier) than a golf ball, so it will not rebound as high after each bounce compared to the golf ball. The data values of rebound heights, h, would be *smaller* for each value of n. Therefore, the rebound heights would decline more quickly than those represented by the graph of the golf ball.

14. Part A – Open Response

The jawbreaker is the largest when the boy puts it in his mouth at $t = 0$ minutes. This value is 33.5 cm³.
The jawbreaker is smallest when it is completely dissolved at 0 cm³. Realistically, this would occur some time after 5 minutes, to say about 15 minutes, which can be called t_f (final time). Therefore, the restrictions of the domain (time) and range (volume) are as follows:
Domain: 0 to t_f minutes or $0 \leq t \leq 15$
Range: 0 to 33.5 cm³ or $0 \leq V \leq 33.5$

Part B –A

To determine the decay factor, find the ratio between successive volume values, V, in the data table, as shown below.

t	0	1	2	3	4	4
V	33.5	28.1	23.6	19.7	16.7	14.0
Ratio (R)		$\dfrac{28.1}{33.5}$ = 0.839	$\dfrac{23.6}{28.1}$ = 0.840	$\dfrac{19.7}{23.6}$ = 0.835	$\dfrac{16.7}{19.7}$ = 0.848	$\dfrac{14.0}{16.7}$ = 0.838

The decay ratio seems consistent at 0.84, to two decimal places. As a percentage, this decay factor is $0.84 \times 100\% = 84\%$.

15. 6.0

If the original mass of the isotope is 10 mg at $t = 0$ h , then the half-life is the time taken for this mass to decay to half its original amount, namely $\dfrac{10}{2} = 5$ mg. According to the graph, the mass of 5 mg occurs at $t = 6.0$ h.

16. Part A – Open Response

The value of 1.065 in the equation describes the growth factor of 1.065 of their stock value. When the growth factor is converted to a percentage, it is $1.065 \times 100\% = 106.5\%$.
Since 100% means no growth (stays the same at 100% of its original amount), the annual average rate of return is $106.5 - 100 = 6.5\%$.

Part B – Open Response

The value of t is the number of years since 1989. Therefore, in 2000, $t = 2000 - 1989 = 11$.
Substitute $t = 11$ into the equation, and solve for $V(t)$, the value of the stock.

$$V(11) = 20\,000(1.065)^{11}$$
$$= 39\,983.028\,01$$

To the nearest cent, the value of the stock in the year 2000 is $39 983.03.

Part C – Open Response

An appropriate WINDOW setting could be $x:[0, 20, 1]$, $y:[0, 70\,000, 10\,000]$.

Then, enter the function as $Y_1 = 20\,000(1.065)^\wedge x$ into your graphing calculator, and press GRAPH.
Then, use your TRACE feature to locate the point that is as close to a y-value = 60 000 (triple the value of 20 000). This value is highlighted in the calculator screen shown below.

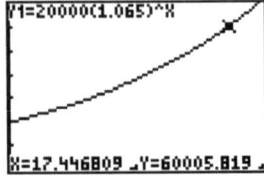

According to this point, the x-value, or time, t, is 17.446 809 years. This means the stock triples 17.446 809 years after Jan. 1, 1989, which is 1989 + 17.446 809 = 2006.446 809.

Therefore, the stock triples about half-way through the year 2006.

17. Part A –C

The interest accumulated with simple interest is linear. In this particular case, 10% of 2000 = $200 is the interest added each year.

Therefore, k = $400 + $200 = $600 and l = $600 + $200 = $800.

In a compound interest account, the interest rate changes, since it is always calculated on the previous accumulated amount.

The interest in year 3 would be 10% × $2420 = 0.10 × 2420 = $242.

If you add this interest to the previous total interest, you get m = 420 + 242 = $662.

The new principal, p, in year 4 would be the principal in year 3 of $2420 added to the new interest in year 3 of $242 to get p = $2420 + $242 = $2662.

Finally, the interest in year 4 would be 10% × $2662 = $266.20.

Then, add this to the previous total interest to get n = $662 + $266.20 = $928.20.

With this information, determine which choice makes a false algebraic statement.

$l - k$ = 800 – 600 = 200 is a true statement.

$n - m$ = 928.20 – 662 = 266.20 > 250, so $n - m > 250$ is a true statement.

$n - l$ = 928.20 – 800 = 128.20
$m - k$ = 662 – 600 = 62
$n - l > m - k (128.20 > 62)$ is a true statement.

Therefore, $n - l = m - k$ is a false statement.

Part B –D

In the simple interest account, the interest made in year 5 would be the same as in every other year, namely $200, to produce a total amount of $1000 in interest. Thus, the total accumulated amount would be $2000 + $1000 = $3000.

In the compound interest account, you need to find the new principal in year 5 by taking the principal in year 4 and adding the interest made in year 4.

$P_5 = P_4 + I_4$
$= 2662 + 266.20$
$= \$2928.20$

Then, find the interest made in year 5 using this new principal, P_5.

$I_5 = P_5 \times 10\%$
$= 2928.20 \times 0.10$
$= \$292.82$

The total accumulated amount after 5 years in this account is

$P_5 + I_5 = \$2928.20 + \$292.82 = \$3221.02.$

Therefore, the difference between the accumulated amounts of the two accounts is $3221.02 – $3000 = $221.02.

18. C

Since this account is compounded bi-weekly, the number of compounds per year is 26 (52 weeks in a year and 26 bi-weeks per year).

Determine the interest rate per compound, i, and the number of total compounds over the $3\frac{1}{2}$ years, n.

$i = \dfrac{5.2\%}{26} = 0.2\% = \dfrac{0.2\%}{100\%} = 0.002$

$n = 3.5 \times 26 = 91$

Therefore, the correct compound interest equation depicting the final value, FV, is

$FV = PV(1 + 0.002)^{91}$ or $PV(1.002)^{91}$

19. 3121

In a daily compounded account, the number of compounds per year is 365.

$i = \dfrac{12\%}{365} = 0.032\ 876\ 7123\%$ or $0.000\ 328\ 7671\ (23)$

$n = 8 \times 365 = 2920$

Using the compound interest equation,

$A_1 = P(1 + i)^n$

$= 44\ 000(1 + 0.000\ 328\ 7671\ (23))^{2920}$
$= \$114\ 896.52$

In a semi-annually compounded account, the number of compounds per year is 2.

$i = \dfrac{12\%}{2} = 6\%$ or 0.06

$n = 8 \times 2 = 16$

Using the compound interest equation,

$A_2 = P(1 + i)^n$

$= 44\ 000(1 + 0.06)^{16}$
$= \$111\ 775.47$

The difference in interest, I, between the accounts would be the same as the difference between their accumulated amounts.

$I = A_1 - A_2$
$= 114\ 896.52 - 111\ 775.47$
$= \$3121.05$

The difference in interest rounded to the nearest dollar is $3121.

20. Part A –B

To find the annual interest rate, take the interest of $100 accumulated in year 1, and divide it by the principal amount of $2000.

$i = \dfrac{\$100}{\$2000} = 0.05$ or 5%

In the function representing this growth $f(x) = a(b)^x$, the value of b equals 100% + 5% = 105% or 1.05. Therefore, the function representing the growth of this account is

$f(x) = 2000(1.05)^x.$

Part B –C

Method I

The function $f(x) = 2000(1.05)^x$ can be used to find the accumulated amount, $f(5)$, after 5 years as follows:

$f(5) = 2000(1.05)^5 = \$2552.56$

The total interest, I, after 5 years is the value of $f(5)$ minus the original principal amount of \$2000.

$I_T = f(5) - 2000$
$= 2552.56 - 2000$
$= \$552.56$

Method II

Use the final point on the graph $(4, 431.01)$ to find the total interest, I_5, in year 5 as follows.

Step 1

Add the total interest \$431.01 to the original principal to get the new principal in year 5.
$P_5 = \$431.01 + \$2000 = \$2431.01$

Step 2

Find the interest, I_5, made in year 5 by multiplying the new principal, P_5, by 5%.
$I_5 = P_5 \times 5\%$
$= \$2431.01 \times 0.05$
$= \$121.55$

Step 3

Add this new interest to the total interest in year 4.
Total interest = \$121.55 + \$431.01 = \$552.56

21. D

The value of N = in the TVM Solver needs to be given in years, so convert 66 months to years.

$$N = \frac{66 \text{ months}}{12 \text{ months}} = 5.5$$

The present value, PV, on the TVM Solver is the negative value of the principal \$4800 (since you are giving it away to the bank); therefore, PV = –4800.

22. 1.13

First, determine the entries going into the TVM Solver of your graphing calculator.

PV = –10 000	P/Y = 1
FV = 33 945	PMT = 0
C/Y = 1	I% = Blank
N = 10	

Now, enter these, move your cursor to I% = , and press APLHA ENTER. The following screen will result.

According to the result, I% = 12.999 775 67 per year.

When entered as a b-value in the function $f(x) = a(b)^x$, you need to add 100 % to get 100% + 12.999 775 67% = 112.999 775 67% or as a decimal 1.129 997 7567, which is 1.13 when rounded to the nearest hundredth.

23. C

The total amount, A_{19}, reflects the total amount of the 19th deposit plus one period of interest $\left(i = \dfrac{8.8\%}{4} = 2.2\%\right)$.

$$A_{19} = \$800(1.022)^1$$

Similarly, the total amount, A_{18}, reflects the total amount of the 18th deposit plus two periods of interest.

$$A_{18} = \$800(1.022)^2$$

If this pattern continued, the total amount, A_3, reflects the total amount of the 3rd deposit plus seventeen periods of interest.

$$A_3 = \$800(1.022)^{17}$$

24. Part A –C

The accumulated amounts, A_1, for Dale and, A_2, for Dana can be determined by making the following entries on the TVM Solver and selections as shown on each screen below.

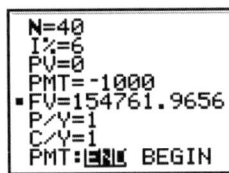 

According to the results, the accumulated amounts at age 60 are $A_1 = \$154\ 761.97$ and $A_2 = \$158\ 116.37$.

Therefore, $A_1 < A_2$.

To find the total accumulated interest, I_T, for each person, find the total amount of all deposits, D, and subtract that from the accumulated amounts, A.

$I_1 = A_1 - D_1$
$= \$154\ 761.97 - (40 \times \$1000)$
$= \$154\ 761.97 - \$40\ 000$
$= \$114\ 761.97$
$I_2 = A_2 - D_2$
$= \$158\ 116.37 - (30 \times \$2000)$
$= \$158\ 116.37 - \$60\ 000$
$= \$98\ 116.37$

Based on the above calculations, $I_1 > I_2$.

Part B – 3231

To determine the annual deposit (payment) that Dale would need to make to accumulate a total of $500 000 by age 60, make the following entries on your TVM Solver, and select PMT.

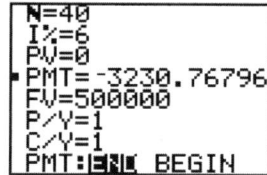

According to the resulting selection, PMT, on the TVM Solver, Dale would need to make annual deposits, to the nearest dollar, of $3231.

25. A

Determine the weekly payments, PMT, made by both Stephen and Marie by using your TVM Solver.

Since the payments are made weekly and there are 52 weeks in a year, the number of compounds for Stephen and Marie are as follows:

Marie: N = 3 years × 52 = 156
Stephen: N = 5 years × 52 = 260

The screens below show the resulting payments, PMT, for each person, based on the appropriate entries.

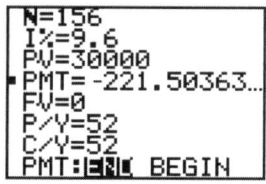 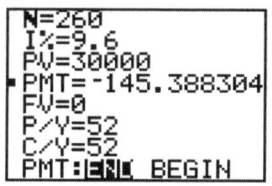

According to these results, Marie's regular weekly payment is $221.50, and Stephen's regular weekly payment is $145.39.

Determine the total interest, I_T, that each person pays over the course of all the weekly payments, A, and subtract the principal of the loan, P.

Marie:
$$I_T = A - P$$
$$= (\$221.50 \times 156) - \$30\ 000$$
$$= \$34\ 554 - \$30\ 000$$
$$= \$4554$$

Stephen:
$$I_T = A - P$$
$$= (\$145.39 \times 260) - \$30\ 000$$
$$= \$37\ 801.40 - \$30\ 000$$
$$= \$7801.40$$

Therefore, Stephen pays $7801.40 – $4554 = $3247.40 more interest to pay off the loan compared to Marie.

26. Part A – Open Response

This problem requires two steps.

Step 1: Find the present value, PV, of the retirement fund at age 55 based on $5000 monthly withdrawals to deplete it to a final value, FV = 0, over a 25 year period.

Since the compounding period is monthly, there are 12 compounds and 12 monthly withdrawals made each year.

Thus, N = 12 × 25 = 300.

Enter this value and the other respective values in your TVM Solver to determine the present value, PV, as shown below.

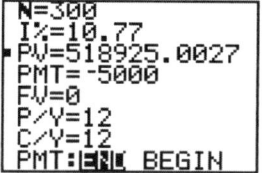

Based upon the resulting value, PV, the present value or principal in the retirement fund at age 55 is $518 925.

Step 2: The present value $518 925 at age 55 is the future value, FV, that Esther needs to accumulate from age 25 to 55. Determine the regular monthly deposit Esther needs to make over the 30 year period.

Since there are 12 compounds and 12 monthly deposits made each year, N = 30 × 12 = 360.

Enter this value and the other respective values in your TVM Solver to determine each monthly deposit, PMT.

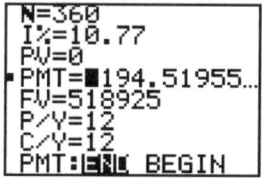

Based upon the resulting value, PMT, Esther needs to make a regular deposit of $194.52 at the end of every month from the age of 25 to 55 to earn enough money in her retirement fund so she will have enough to withdraw regular monthly amounts of $5000 up to the age of 80.

Part B – Open Response

To determine the total interest, I, accumulated in her retirement fund from age 25 to 80, you need to make two calculations, I_1 and I_2.

I_1 represents the interest accumulated from age 25 to 55 when she made regular monthly deposits of $194.52 to acquire a total of $518 925.

$$I_1 = FV - \text{total deposits}$$
$$= \$518\ 925 - (\$194.52 \times 12 \times 30 \text{ years})$$
$$= \$518\ 925 - \$70\ 027.20$$
$$= \$448\ 897.80$$

I_2 represents the interest accumulated from age 55 to 80 when the present value, PV = $518 925 depletes to $0 after the regular monthly withdrawals of $5000 over those 25 years.

I_2 = Total withdrawals – PV
    = ($5000 × 12 × 25) – $518 925
    = $1 500 000 – $518 925
    = $981 075

The total interest earned in Esther's retirement fund over the 55 years (age 25 to 80) is $448 897.80 + $981 075 = $1 429 972.80.

Part C – Open Response

As was calculated earlier in part B, the total withdrawals after age 55 were $1 500 000, and the total deposits from age 25 to 55 were $70 027.20.

Therefore, by making $70 027.20 worth of contributions to her fund, it allowed her to withdraw $1 500 000 ÷ 70 027.20 = 21.4 times the amount in her retirement.

1. For $\left(\dfrac{5}{9}\right)^{\frac{2}{3}} = \sqrt[n]{\left(\dfrac{9}{5}\right)^m}$, the values of m and n are

   A. $m = 2, n = 3$

   B. $m = 3, n = 2$

   C. $m = -2, n = 3$

   D. $m = -3, n = 2$

Open Response

Use the following information to answer the next question.

Raoul wanted to understand the exponential expression $8^{\frac{m}{3}}$. He used the following patterning method:

$$8^0 = 1$$

$$8^{-\frac{1}{3}} = \frac{1}{2} \qquad 8^{\frac{1}{3}} = 2$$

$$8^{-\frac{2}{3}} = \frac{1}{4} \qquad 8^{\frac{2}{3}} = 4$$

$$8^{-\frac{3}{3}} = \frac{1}{8} \qquad 8^{\frac{3}{3}} = 8$$

$$8^{-\frac{4}{3}} = \frac{1}{16} \qquad 8^{\frac{4}{3}} = 16$$

$$\vdots \qquad\qquad \vdots$$

2. Continue this pattern to discover the values of $8^{\frac{m}{3}}$ when $m = -5$ and $m = 7$.
   Show your work.

CHALLENGER QUESTION

Use the following information to answer the next question.

To evaluate $(0.04)^{-\frac{3}{2}}$, Anjuli went through the following steps using paper and pencil:

$$(0.04)^{-\frac{3}{2}} = (k)^{\frac{3}{2}} = l$$

3. Her respective values of k and l are

   A. 0.04, 125   B. 0.04, 0.032

   C. 25, 125   D. 25, 7.8125

Numerical Response

4. To the nearest tenth, the difference between the values of $(2.02)^5$ and $(5)^{2.02}$ is ____.

Use the following information to answer the next multipart question.

5. Kyra graphed an exponential relation of the form $y = a^x$ by hand, as shown.

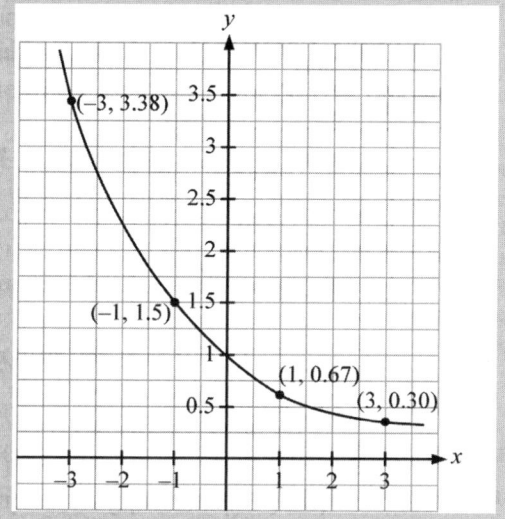

Part A

The equation representing Kyra's graph is

A. $y = \left(\dfrac{1}{3}\right)^x$

B. $y = \left(\dfrac{2}{3}\right)^x$

C. $y = \left(\dfrac{3}{2}\right)^x$

D. $y = (3)^x$

Part B

Which of the following lines could be drawn on the graph to verify that it is a function?

A. $x = a$, where $a = 1$

B. $y = a$, where $a = 1$

C. $x = a$, where $a \in R$

D. $y = a$, where $a \in R$

---

6. Which of the following function machines does **not** represent an exponential function $y = a^x$, where $a > 1$?

A.
x	$f(x) = a^x$	y
-3		$3\sqrt{3}$
-1		$\sqrt{3}$
1		$\dfrac{\sqrt{3}}{3}$

B.
x	$f(x) = a^x$	y
-3		$\dfrac{\sqrt{3}}{9}$
-1		$\dfrac{\sqrt{3}}{3}$
1		$\sqrt{3}$

C.
x	$f(x) = a^x$	y
3		1.331
1		1.100
-1		0.909

D.
x	$f(x) = a^x$	y
3		3.375
1		1.5
-1		$\dfrac{1}{1.5}$

7. Which of the following features does **not** describe the graph of $f(x) = 10^x$?

A. The range is $y > 0$.

B. The horizontal asymptote is $y = 0$.

C. The graph is flatter on the left side of the y-axis than the graph of $f(x) = 8^x$.

D. The graph is steeper on the right side of the y-axis than the graph of $f(x) = 12^x$.

---

8. Which of the following exponential expressions is equivalent to $\left(\left(\frac{1}{2}\right)^3\right)^{-1}$?

A. $\left(\frac{1}{2}\right)^3 \times \left(\frac{1}{2}\right)^{-1}$

B. $\left(\frac{1}{2}\right)^3 \div \left(\frac{1}{2}\right)^{-1}$

C. $\frac{1}{2} \times \frac{1}{2} \times \frac{1}{2}$

D. $2 \times 2 \times 2$

Numerical Response

9. If the expression $(4^3)(4^2)$ is equivalent to the expression $(4^x) \div (4^3)$, then the value of x is ____.

10. Which of the following functions does **not** have a y-intercept of 1?

A. $f(x) = 3^x$

B. $f(x) = 3x^2$

C. $f(x) = 3x + 1$

D. $f(x) = 3(x - 1)^2 - 2$

Use the following information to answer the next multipart question.

11. Katja examined three patterns involving diagrams of blocks.

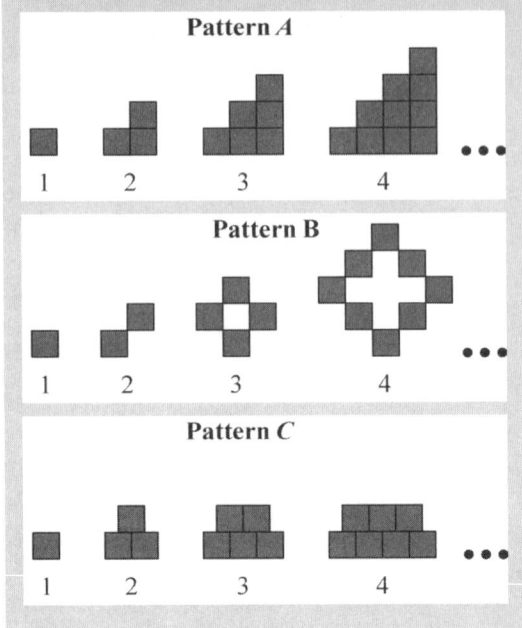

Part A

Open Response

Is Pattern C a linear, quadratic, or exponential pattern? Give reasons for your answer.

Part B

Open Response

On the given grid, graph the pattern shown in Pattern A, where x is the diagram number and y is the number of blocks. Then, state whether the pattern is linear, quadratic, or exponential.

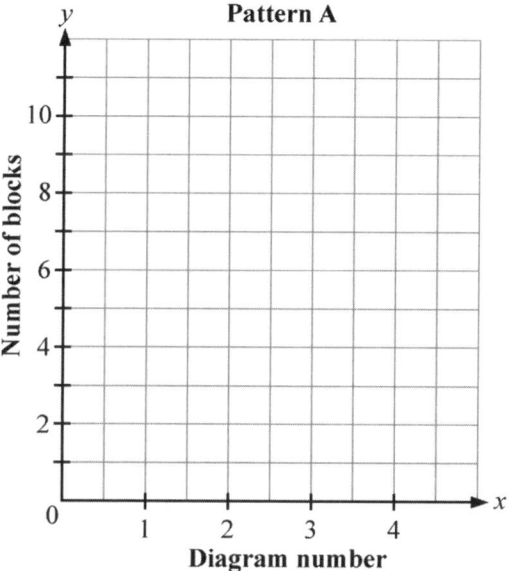

Part C

Open Response

Complete the table of values of the number of blocks in Pattern B, and predict the number of blocks that would occur in diagram number 6. Give reasons for your answer.

Diagram Number	Number of Blocks
1	
2	
3	
4	

Use the following information to answer the next multipart question.

12. A rare coin, A, increased exponentially in its dollar value, V, over time, t, in years, according to this data.

t	0	5	10	15	20
V	100	250	624	1563	3900

Part A

Paul used his graphing calculator to enter the values of time in list L_1 and the dollar values of the coin in list L_2.

If he then entered his WINDOW setting at $x:[-5, 25, 5]$, $y:[-500, 4000, 1000]$, which of the following graphs correctly represents his data entries?

A.

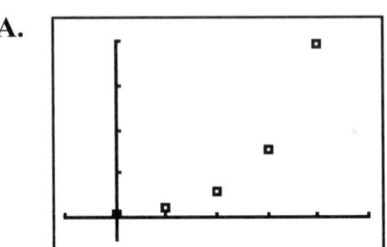

B.

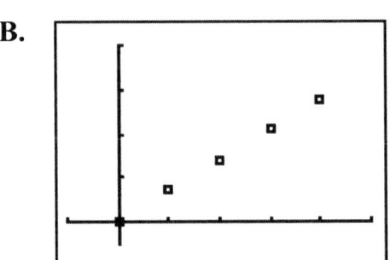

C.

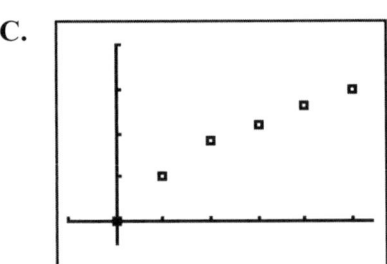

D.

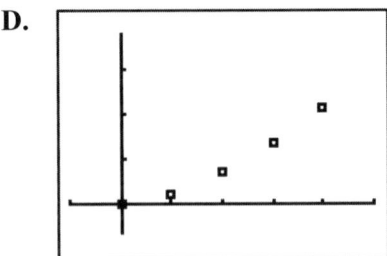

Part B

The dollar value of another rare coin B increased exponentially at $\frac{3}{5}$ the rate of the dollar value of coin A. The rate at which the dollar value of coin B increased is

A. 3 times every year

B. 1.5 times every year

C. 3 times every 5 years

D. 1.5 times every 5 years

Use the following information to answer the next multipart question.

13. A teacher had Cheyenne collect data showing the temperature, T, in degrees Celsius over time, t, in hours of an insulated glass of juice placed in a refrigerator at an initial temperature of 22°C. She put her data in a table of values as shown.

t	0	1	2	3	4	5
T	22	18.5	15.5	13.0	10.9	9.2

Cheyenne recognized that the temperature decayed exponentially over time.

Part A

If t represents the time in hours for the temperature of the juice to be **half** its original temperature, which of the following equations correctly describes the decay process of temperature?

A. $T = 22(0.84)^t$

B. $T = 22(0.50)^t$

C. $T = 22(0.50)^{\frac{t}{4}}$

D. $T = 22(0.50)^{4t}$

Part B

Open Response

If the orange juice is placed in a regular glass, how would the half time change, and what restrictions would there be on the range of the temperatures. Give reasons for your answer.

Use the following information to answer the next multipart question.

14. For every metre that a diver descends below the water, the light intensity or percentage of sunlight is reduced by 2.5%. The function showing this exponential decay is $P = 100(0.975)^d$, where P is the percentage of sunlight and d is the distance below the water surface in metres.

Part A

Numerical Response

To the nearest hundredth, the percentage of sunlight found 100 m below the water surface is____%.

Part B

A student graphed this function on his graphing calculator with the appropriate WINDOW settings. He found that the change in percentage of sunlight for a diver going from 40 to 60 m below the water surface is about

A. 14% **B.** 17% **C.** 22% **D.** 36%

Use the following information to answer the next question.

The measure of the acidity in any aqueous solution is called its pH, and is related exponentially to the concentration of hydrogen ions, H^+, in moles per litre, by the function: $H^+ = 10^{-pH}$.

A student used this function to determine the hydrogen ion concentration of three types of water solution.
Rain water: pH = 5.6
Distilled water: pH = 6.9
Acid rain: pH = 4.0

15. Which of the following statements about these calculated hydrogen ion concentrations is **incorrect**?

A. The concentration of H^+ in acid rain is the highest.

B. The concentration of H^+ in rain water is greater than 10^{-7} mol / L.

C. The difference in the H^+ concentration between acid rain and rain water is 9.75×10^{-5} mol / L

D. The difference in the H^+ concentration between acid rain and rain water is less than the difference in the H^+ concentration between rain water and distilled water.

Use the following information to answer the next multipart question.

16. A student examined a graph comparing the annual increase in the amount of a $200 investment of a simple and compound interest account.

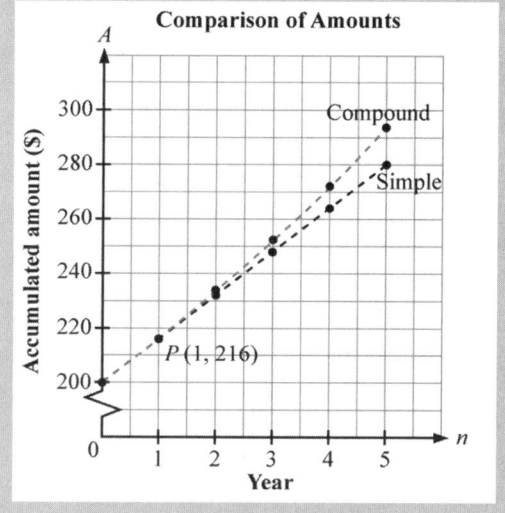

Part A

The point labelled $P(1, 216)$ indicates that after 1 year, the accumulated amounts in both accounts is $216. Based on this value, the annual interest rate in both accounts must be

A. 16.0%   **B.** 10.8%

C. 8.0%   **D.** 7.4%

Part B

The graph describing simple interest is __i__ and after 5 years shows that the account accumulated __ii__ in interest, while the graph describing compound interest accumulated about __iii__ more interest after 5 years.

Which of the following rows correctly completes this statement?

A.

i	ii	iii
linear	$64	$10

B.

i	ii	iii
linear	$80	$14

C.

i	ii	iii
non-linear	$64	$10

D.

i	ii	iii
non-linear	$80	$14

CHALLENGER QUESTION

Use the following information to answer the next question.

Jason was contemplating how much principal, P, he should put into a bank account paying interest at $k\%$/a compounded semi-annually so that in 30 months he would have a final amount, A, of $6000 to be used for a vacation.

17. If Jason used the formula $P = \dfrac{A}{(1+i)^n}$ to determine P, then the expression of i in terms of k and the value of n, respectively, are

   A. $i = \dfrac{k}{2}, n = 15$

   B. $i = \dfrac{k}{20}, n = 15$

   C. $i = \dfrac{k}{100}, n = 5$

   D. $i = \dfrac{k}{200}, n = 5$

Numerical Response

Use the following information to answer the next question.

Ed was considering four investments as shown.

Investment 1:
$10 000 invested at 10%/a compounded monthly for 6 years.

Investment 2:
$8600 invested at 9%/a compounded daily for $9\frac{1}{4}$ years

Investment 3:
$11 000 invested at $11\frac{1}{2}\%$/a compounded semi-annually for $4\frac{1}{2}$ years.

Investment 4:
$9200 invested at $10\frac{1}{4}\%$/a compounded quarterly for 7 years.

Ed calculated the final amounts, FV, of all four investments.

18. From the greatest to the least value of the final amounts, what is the order of the numbered investments?

   ____, ____, ____, ____

19. If the exponential function

   $f(x) = 1000(1.015)^{\frac{x}{4}}$ represents an investment of $1000 in a savings account over a period of x years, then the annual interest rate is

   A. 1.5%/a compounded quarterly

   B. 6.0%/a compounded quarterly

   C. 1.5%/a compounded annually

   D. 6.0%/a compounded annually

Use the following information to answer the next question.

Rebecca wants to earn $8000 in 5 years. She needs to know how much she should put into an account earning interest at 8%/*a* compounded annually. She used the formula $PV = FV(1+i)^{-n}$ to calculate the present values over 5 years. Then she entered her data as lists on her graphing calculator as shown and did an exponential regression on the data.

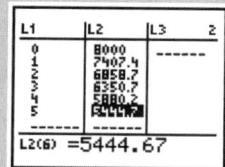

20. According to her exponential regression, the exponential function describing this pattern of decay and present values over *x* years is

   A. $f(x) = 5444.67(0.926)^{-x}$

   B. $f(x) = 5444.67(1.08)^{-x}$

   C. $f(x) = 8000(0.926)^{x}$

   D. $f(x) = 8000(1.08)^{x}$

CHALLENGER QUESTION

Use the following information to answer the next question.

Morgan used the TVM Solver on her calculator to determine the annual interest rate, *I*%, compounded quarterly that would enable a given principal value to mature to a final amount after 6 years. The entries on her screen are shown.

21. If Morgan determined the annual interest rate, then the correct compound interest formula representing this investment growth is

   A. $A = 4100(1.108)^{n}$

   B. $A = 7771(1.108)^{n}$

   C. $A = 4100(1.027)^{n}$

   D. $A = 7771(1.027)^{n}$

Numerical Response

CHALLENGER QUESTION

Use the following information to answer the next question.

The compound interest formula $FV = 200\,000(1.0075)^{n}$ represents the growth of a $200 000 investment over a period of time collecting an annual interest rate compounded monthly.

22. With the aid of the TVM Solver on a graphing calculator, the correct value of *n* in the formula that would produce a final value of $444 888 is ____.

Use the following information to answer the next question.

Aaron invested $400 at the end of each month for 6 years into an annuity, where the interest rate was 6%/a compounded monthly.

23. Which of the following equations represents the total accumulated amount after 6 years?

   A. $FV = \$400 + \$400(1.06)^1 + \$400(1.06)^2 \ldots + \$400(1.06)^5$

   B. $FV = \$400 + \$400(1.06)^1 + \$400(1.06)^2 \ldots + \$400(1.06)^6$

   C. $FV = \$400 + \$400(1.005)^1 + \$400(1.005)^2 \ldots + \$400(1.005)^{71}$

   D. $FV = \$400 + \$400(1.005)^1 + \$400(1.005)^2 \ldots + \$400(1.005)^{72}$

Use the following information to answer the next question.

Cliff took out a loan of $12 000 where the interest rate was 6.4%/a compounded monthly. He was not sure if he wanted to pay off the loan in 3 or 5 years by making payments at the end of each month.

24. How much more would his monthly payment be if he chose to pay off the loan in 3 years as opposed to 5 years?

   A. $367.24   B. $234.23

   C. $136.89   D. $133.01

Numerical Response

Use the following information to answer the next question.

Debbie was going to make regular deposits of $800 every 3 months for 6 years into a savings account where interest was posted at 5.8%/a compounded quarterly. Her friend Albert told her that if she made these deposits in his bank, she would accumulate $1000 more over the 6-year period.

25. The annual interest rate at Albert's bank, to the nearest hundredth of a percent, was ____%.

Use the following information to answer the next multipart question.

26. Both Ted and Bill want to make regular monthly deposits into their savings accounts so that they can make future regular monthly withdrawals until they are depleted.

   Ted deposits $800 at the end of every month for 4 years and then makes regular withdrawals of $905 at the end of every month thereafter until his account is depleted.

   Bill deposits $600 at the end of every month for 5 years and then makes regular $1105 withdrawals at the end of every month thereafter until his account is depleted.

   Both savings accounts earn 7.80%/a interest compounded monthly.

Part A

Which of the following statements is **true**?

   A. Bill's account lasted the longest by 2 months.

   B. Ted's account lasted the longest by 2 months.

   C. Bill's account lasted the longest by 12 months.

   D. Ted's account lasted the longest by 12 months.

Part B

How much should Bill have deposited every month in the first 5 years to make it last 1 year longer after all his withdrawals?

A. $610.54

B. $728.53

C. $800.00

D. $924.90

Use the following information to answer the next multipart question.

27. Daniel is 28 years old and has $2000 in his savings account. He then makes the following investment decisions over the next years of his life.

A. Regular deposits of $800 at the end of each 6-month period over 8 years into the savings account earning interest at 5.25 %/a compounded semi-annually.

B. At the end of 8 years withdraws $5000 for a car down payment.

C. Transfers the remaining amount in his savings account to a GIC account that earns 7.50 %/a compounded monthly.

D. Withdraws $331 at the end of every month to pay off his car loan until the GIC is depleted.

Part A

| Open Response |

How much will be in Daniel's savings account when he is 36? Show your work.

Part B

| Open Response |

How much money does Daniel transfer into his GIC account at age 36? Show your work.

Part C

| Open Response |

How old will Daniel be when his GIC account is depleted? Show your work.

SOLUTIONS

1. C	**8. D**	**13.** Part A- **C**	**18. 2431**	**26.** Part A- **B**
2. OR	**9. 8**	Part B- **OR**	**19. B**	Part B- **B**
3. C	**10. B**	**14.** Part A- **7.95**	**20. C**	**27.** Part A- **OR**
4. 7.8	**11.** Part A- **OR**	Part B- **A**	**21. C**	Part B- **OR**
5. Part A- **B**	Part B- **OR**	**15. D**	**22. 107**	Part C- **OR**
Part B- **C**	Part C- **OR**	**16.** Part A- **C**	**23. C**	
6. B	**12.** Part A- **A**	Part B- **B**	**24. D**	
7. C	Part B- **D**	**17. D**	**25. 7.22**	

1. C

The expression $\left(\frac{5}{9}\right)^{\frac{2}{3}}$ can be written in the form

$\left(\frac{1}{\frac{5}{9}}\right)^{-\frac{2}{3}}$, since $x^n = \left(\frac{1}{x}\right)^{-n}$.

Since dividing a fraction by a second fraction is the same as multiplying by the reciprocal of the second fraction, the result is

$$\left(\frac{1}{\frac{5}{9}}\right)^{-\frac{2}{3}} = \left(\frac{1}{1} \times \frac{9}{5}\right)^{-\frac{2}{3}} = \left(\frac{9}{5}\right)^{-\frac{2}{3}}$$

A power with a rational exponent can be rewritten as a radical expression.

$$x^{\frac{m}{n}} = \sqrt[n]{x^m}$$

Therefore, $\left(\frac{9}{5}\right)^{-\frac{2}{3}} = \sqrt[3]{\left(\frac{9}{5}\right)^{-2}}$

The values of $m = -2$ and $n = 3$ for $\sqrt[n]{\left(\frac{9}{5}\right)^m}$ to be

equivalent to $\left(\frac{5}{9}\right)^{\frac{2}{3}}$.

2. Open Response

The pattern shows that as $\frac{1}{3}$ is added to the exponent of 8, the corresponding resulting values increase by a ratio of $2(\times 2)$.

Therefore, you can find the value for $m = 7$ by the right side of the pattern as follows:

$$8^{\frac{4}{3}} = 16 \rightarrow 8^{\frac{5}{3}} = 16 \times 2 = 32 \rightarrow 8^{\frac{6}{3}}$$

$$= 32 \times 2 = 64 \rightarrow 8^{\frac{7}{3}} = 64 \times 2 = 128$$

Similarly, the pattern shows that as $\frac{1}{3}$ is subtracted from the exponent, the resulting values decrease by a ratio of $2(\div 2)$.

Therefore, you can find the value for $m = -5$ by following the left side of the pattern as follows:

$$8^{-\frac{4}{3}} = \frac{1}{16} \rightarrow 8^{-\frac{5}{3}} = \frac{1}{16} \div 2 = \frac{1}{16} \times \frac{1}{2} = \frac{1}{32}$$

According to the pattern of $8^{\frac{m}{3}}$, the values for $m = 7$ is

128 and for $m = -5$ is $\frac{1}{32}$.

3. C

Before evaluating k in the expression $(k)^{\frac{3}{2}}$, convert 0.04 to a fraction.

$$0.04 = \frac{4}{100} = \frac{4 \div 4}{100 \div 4} = \frac{1}{25}$$

Thus, $(0.04)^{-\frac{3}{2}}$ is equivalent to $\left(\frac{1}{25}\right)^{-\frac{3}{2}}$.

Since $\left(\frac{1}{x}\right)^{-n} = x^n$, you can convert this expression from

$\left(\frac{1}{25}\right)^{-\frac{3}{2}}$ to $(25)^{\frac{3}{2}}$.

Therefore, in $(k)^{\frac{3}{2}}$, the value of k must be 25.

You know that $x^{\frac{m}{n}} = \sqrt[n]{x^m}$, so you can convert the

expression of $(25)^{\frac{3}{2}}$ to the radical form of $\sqrt{25^3}$ or

$(\sqrt{25})^3$.

Since $\sqrt{25} = 5$ $(5 \times 5 = 25)$,

$(\sqrt{25})^3 = 5^3 = 5 \times 5 \times 5 = 125$.

The value of l is 125.

Unit Test – Solutions   140   Castle Rock Research

4. 7.8

Evaluate each expression using the $\wedge$ button on your graphing calculator.

$(2.02)^5 = 33.632\ 3216$

$(5)^{2.02} = 25.817\ 8105$

The difference between these two values to the nearest tenth is

$33.632\ 3216 - 25.817\ 8105 = 7.814\ 511\ 103 \doteq 7.8$

5. Part A – B

Kyra's graph indicates that it passes through the following points: $(-3, 3.38), (-1, 1.5), (1, 0.67), (3, 0.30)$.
To establish the choice of function that represents the points of the graph, you can use your calculator to determine the y-values of each function by substituting the corresponding x-values in as shown below:

$y = \left(\dfrac{1}{3}\right)^x$

$x = -3$	$x = -1$	$x = 1$	$x = 3$
$y = \left(\dfrac{1}{3}\right)^{-3}$	$y = \left(\dfrac{1}{3}\right)^{-1}$	$y = \left(\dfrac{1}{3}\right)^{1}$	$y = \left(\dfrac{1}{3}\right)^{3}$
$= 27$	$= 3.0$	≈ 0.33	≈ 0.04

$y = \left(\dfrac{2}{3}\right)^x$

$x = -3$	$x = -1$	$x = 1$	$x = 3$
$y = \left(\dfrac{2}{3}\right)^{-3}$	$y = \left(\dfrac{2}{3}\right)^{-1}$	$y = \left(\dfrac{2}{3}\right)^{1}$	$y = \left(\dfrac{2}{3}\right)^{3}$
≈ 3.38	$= 1.5$	≈ 0.67	≈ 0.30

$y = \left(\dfrac{3}{2}\right)^x$

$x = -3$	$x = -1$	$x = 1$	$x = 3$
$y = \left(\dfrac{3}{2}\right)^{-3}$	$y = \left(\dfrac{3}{2}\right)^{-1}$	$y = \left(\dfrac{3}{2}\right)^{1}$	$y = \left(\dfrac{3}{2}\right)^{3}$
≈ 0.30	≈ 0.67	$= 1.50$	≈ 3.38

$y = (3)^x$

$x = -3$	$x = -1$	$x = 1$	$x = 3$
$y = (3)^{-3}$	$y = (3)^{-1}$	$y = (3)^{1}$	$y = (3)^{3}$
≈ 0.04	≈ 0.33	$= 3.0$	$= 27$

According to the y-values calculated in the table, the ones that match the y-coordinates of the points of the graph are those for the function $y = \left(\dfrac{2}{3}\right)^x$.

Part B –C

To verify that a graph represents a function, every vertical line drawn throughout its domain must only pass through a single point. A vertical line is defined by $x = a$, and since the domain of an exponential function is $x \in \mathbb{R}$, any line $x = a$, where $a \in \mathbb{R}$, must pass through only one point of the graph of $y = \left(\dfrac{2}{3}\right)^x$.

6. B

To determine which function machine does not represent an exponential function $y = a^x$, where $a > 1$, follow the value of $x = 1$ through the machine, and see if the corresponding y-value is greater than 1, since $a^1 = a$.

	x-value	y-value	a-value
A	1	$\sqrt{3} \doteq 1.732$	$a > 1$
B	1	$\dfrac{\sqrt{3}}{3} \doteq 0.577$	$a < 1$
C	1	1.100	$a > 1$
D	1	1.5	$a > 1$

Choice B has a function $y = a^x$, where a is **not** greater than 1.

7. C

As the value of a increases, the graph gets flatter on the left side of the y-axis and gets steeper on the right side.
Since $a = 8$ in $f(x) = 8^x$ is smaller (not greater) than $a = 10$ in the original function $f(x) = 10^x$, this statement is incorrect.
The range is $y > 0$, and the horizontal asymptote is $y = 0$.
The value of $a = 12$ in $f(x) = 12^x$ is greater than $a = 10$ in the original function $f(x) = 10^x$, so this statement is also correct.

8. D

The original expression $\left(\left(\dfrac{1}{2}\right)^3\right)^{-1}$ can be simplified according to the power rule $(x^m)^n = x^{mn}$ as follows:

$\left(\left(\dfrac{1}{2}\right)^3\right)^{-1} = \left(\dfrac{1}{2}\right)^{3 \times -1} = \left(\dfrac{1}{2}\right)^{-3}$

Since $\left(\dfrac{1}{x}\right)^{-n} = x^n$, the expression $\left(\dfrac{1}{2}\right)^{-3}$ can also be written as 2^3.

The expression $\left(\dfrac{1}{2}\right)^3 \times \left(\dfrac{1}{2}\right)^{-1}$ can be simplified using the product rule $x^m \times x^n = x^{m+n}$ as follows:

$\left(\dfrac{1}{2}\right)^3 \times \left(\dfrac{1}{2}\right)^{-1} = \left(\dfrac{1}{2}\right)^{3+-1} = \left(\dfrac{1}{2}\right)^2$

This expression is not equivalent to either form of the simplified original expression $\left(\frac{1}{2}\right)^{-3}$ or 2^3.

The expression $\left(\frac{1}{2}\right)^3 \div \left(\frac{1}{2}\right)^{-1}$ can be simplified using quotient rule $x^m \div x^n = x^{m-n}$ as follows:

$$\left(\frac{1}{2}\right)^3 \div \left(\frac{1}{2}\right)^{-1} = \left(\frac{1}{2}\right)^{3--1} = \left(\frac{1}{2}\right)^4$$

This expression is not equivalent to either form of the simplified original expression $\left(\frac{1}{2}\right)^{-3}$ or 2^3.

The expression $\frac{1}{2} \times \frac{1}{2} \times \frac{1}{2}$ can also be simplified using the product rule.

$$\frac{1}{2} \times \frac{1}{2} \times \frac{1}{2} = \left(\frac{1}{2}\right)^1 \times \left(\frac{1}{2}\right)^1 \times \left(\frac{1}{2}\right)^1$$
$$= \left(\frac{1}{2}\right)^{1+1+1} = \left(\frac{1}{2}\right)^3$$

This expression is not equivalent to either form of the simplified original expression $\left(\frac{1}{2}\right)^{-3}$ or 2^3.

The expression $2 \times 2 \times 2$ can also be simplified using the product rule.

$$2 \times 2 \times 2 = 2^1 \times 2^1 \times 2^1 = 2^{1+1+1} = 2^3$$

This expression is equivalent to the second form of the simplified original expression 2^3.

9. 8

The expression $(4)^3(4)^2$ can be simplified according to the product rule $x^m \times x^n = x^{m+n}$ as follows:

$$(4)^3(4)^2 = (4)^{3+2} = 4^5$$

The expression $\left(4^x\right) \div \left(4^3\right)$ can be simplified according to the quotient rule $\frac{x^m}{x^n} = x^{m-n}$ as follows:

$$\frac{\left(4^x\right)}{\left(4^3\right)} = 4^{x-3}$$

For the two simplified expressions 4^5 and 4^{x-3} to be equivalent, the exponents must be equal, since the bases are equal.

$4^5 = 4^{x-3}$, only if $5 = x - 3$

Now, solve for x.

$$x - 3 = 5$$
$$x = 5+3$$
$$x = 8$$

Therefore, the expressions $\left(4^3\right)\left(4^2\right)$ and $\left(4^x\right) \div \left(4^3\right)$ are equivalent if $x = 8$.

10. B

Since $f(x) = 3^x$ is an exponential function of the form $f(x) = a^x$, where $a > 0$, it has a y-intercept of 1.

You can also determine which functions have y-intercepts of 1 by substituting the value of $x = 0$ into each function:

$3^x \Rightarrow 3^0 = 1$ is correct.

$3x^2 \Rightarrow 3(0)^2 = 0$ is not correct.

$3x + 1 \Rightarrow 3(0) + 1 = 1$ is correct.

$3(x-1)^2 - 2 \Rightarrow 3(0-1)^2 - 2 = 3 - 2 = 1$ is correct.

The function $f(x) = 3x^2$ does not have a y-intercept of 1.

11. Part A – Open Response

To determine if Pattern C is linear, quadratic, or exponential, make a table of values, where x is the diagram number and y is the number of blocks in each diagram. Then, calculate the first differences, the second differences, and the ratios between successive y-values.

x	y	1st diff	2nd diff	Ratio
1	1			
		} 2		} 3
2	3		} 0	
		} 2		} $\frac{5}{3}$ = 1.67
3	5		} 0	
		} 2		} $\frac{7}{5}$ = 1.4
4	7			

According to these calculations, the first differences are constant at 2, which is the defining feature of a linear pattern.

Thus, Pattern C follows a linear pattern increasing by 2 blocks for every increase in diagram number.

Part B – Open Response

Plot the points as shown, and examine the pattern of vertical increases between the points.

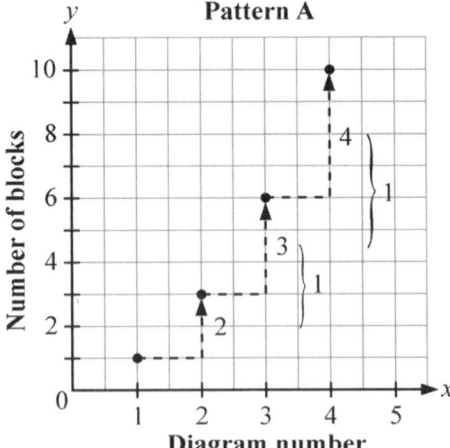

Since the second differences between the vertical increases between points is constant at 1 and the points seem to follow a curved or non-linear pattern, this pattern is quadratic.

Part C – Open Response

The completed table of values for the first four diagrams of Pattern B is shown below.

Diagram No.	No. of Blocks
1	1
2	2
3	4
4	8

×2
×2
×2

The pattern shows that the number of blocks increases by a constant ratio of 2 for each increase in diagram number (an exponential pattern).

Therefore, the predicted number of blocks in diagram 6 would be the result of multiplying 8 by two ratios, namely $8 × 2 × 2 = 32$. There would be 32 blocks in diagram number 6.

12. Part A –A

To get the graph of the data entered as lists, you press 2nd [Y =] ENTER and highlight ON before graphing. The graph of the data should look like the one represented in choice A.

This is because data showing exponential growth should slowly increase vertically and then quickly to the final point.

Part B –D

To find the growth factor of the value of coin A, find the ratio between successive V-values (y-values) as shown.

Time (years)	0	5	10	15	20
Value ($)	100	250	624	1 563	3 900
Ratio		$\frac{250}{100}$ $= 2.5$	$\frac{624}{250}$ $= 2.496$	$\frac{1\ 563}{624}$ $= 2.505$	$\frac{3\ 900}{1\ 563}$ $= 2.495$

According to the calculated ratios, the growth factor, or ratio, is constant at about 2.50 times every 5 years. Since the dollar value of coin B increased exponentially at $\frac{3}{5}$ the rate of the dollar value of coin A, its rate would be $\frac{3}{5} × 2.5 = 1.5$ times every 5 years.

13. Part A –C

The original temperature is 22°C. One half of this is $22°C × \frac{1}{2} = 11°C$. Since 10.9°C is very close to 11°C, the table shows that it takes about 4 hours for the temperature to decay by a factor of $\frac{1}{2}$ or 0.50.

Therefore, the correct equation describing the decay of the temperature of juice, T, over time t, is given by

$$T = 22(0.50)^{\frac{t}{4}}$$

The exponent is $\frac{t}{4}$, since the decay factor of $\frac{1}{2}$ or 0.50 does not occur every 1 hour but every 4 hours.

To confirm that the formula is correct, substitute 4 into t to see if $T = 11$ ($\frac{1}{2}$ the value of 22°C).

$$T = 22(0.50)^{\frac{t}{4}} = 22(0.50)^{\frac{4}{4}} = 22(0.50)^1 = 11.$$

Part B – Open Response

If the orange juice is put in a regular glass, it would cool quicker or take *less* time to cool to half of its original temperature, since there would be less insulating effect on the juice.

The coldest the juice temperature could reach is dictated by the temperature of the air in the refrigerator, which is usually about 4°C. Since the temperature of the juice started at 22°C, the range of its temperatures would be 4°C to 22°C or $4 \leq T \leq 22$.

14. Part A – 7.95

Substitute the value of 100 m into d of the equation, and solve for the percentage, P.

$$P = 100(0.975)^d$$
$$= 100(0.975)^{100}$$
$$= 7.951\ 728\ 986$$

Rounded to the nearest hundredth, this value is 7.95%.

Part B –A

An appropriate WINDOW setting, based on the result of $d = 100$ and $P = 7.95$, could be x:[0, 100, 10], y:[0, 100, 10]. Enter the function $P = 100(0.975)^d$ into [Y =] as $Y_1 = 100(0.975)^\wedge X$, and press GRAPH.

Then, use your VALUE feature by pressing 2nd TRACE 1 to enter x-values of 40 and 60, respectively, and get the corresponding y-values, as shown:

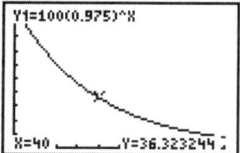 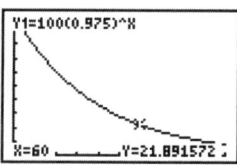

The difference between the two y-values (or P-values) is $36.323\ 244 – 21.891\ 572 = 14.431\ 672$ or 14%.

15. D

Substitute each pH value into the function to solve for the H^+ concentration in each type of water:

Rain water: $H^+ = 10^{-pH} = 10^{-5.6} = 2.51E - 6$
$= 2.51 \times 10^{-6}$ mol / L.

Distilled water: $H^+ = 10^{-pH} = 10^{-6.9} = 1.26E - 7$
$= 1.26 \times 10^{-7}$ mol / L

Acid rain: $H^+ = 10^{-pH} = 10^{-4.0} = 1E - 4$
$= 1 \times 10^{-4}$ mol / L

Based on these results, you can see which choice is incorrect.

The concentration of H^+ in acid rain is 1×10^{-4} mol / L, which is higher than the concentration of H^+ in the other two solutions.

The concentration of H^+ in rain water, namely 2.51×10^{-6} mol / L, is greater than 10^{-7} mol / L.

The difference between the H^+ concentrations of acid rain and rain water is
$(1 \times 10^{-4}) - (2.51 \times 10^{-6}) = 9.75 \times 10^{-5}$ mol / L

The difference between the H^+ concentrations of rain water and distilled water is
$(2.51 \times 10^{-6}) - (1.26 \times 10^{-7}) = 2.384 \times 10^{-6}$ mol / L

The difference between the H^+ concentrations of acid rain and rain water is **greater** than the difference between the H^+ concentrations of rain and water and distilled water. Therefore, choice D is incorrect.

16. Part A –C

Method 1:

Since the total amount after 1 year is $A = \$216$, the interest, I, accumulated is the difference between A and the principal $P = \$200$. $I = A - P = 216 - 200 = \$16$

Then, if you use the simple interest formula $I = Prt$, you can find the annual interest rate, r:

$I = Prt$
$16 = 200(r)(1)$
$\dfrac{16}{200} = r$
$0.08 = r$

The rate 0.08 as a percentage is $0.08 \times 100\% = 8.0\%$.

Method 2:

You can find the growth rate or factor from year 0 to year 1 by dividing the total amount A after 1 year by the principal, P.

$\dfrac{A}{P} = \dfrac{216}{200} = 1.08$

The decimal value 0.08 of this rate represents the annual interest rate, $i = 0.08$ or $0.08 \times 100\% = 8.0\%$.

Part B –B

When a simple interest account is graphed, it produces linear growth since the interest is the same every year. Therefore, i = linear.

The graph shows that after 5 years, the accumulated amount in the simple interest account is \$280. Subtract the original principal, $P = \$200$, to get an accumulated interest, I_T.

$I_T = A - P$
$= 280 - 200$
$= 80$

Therefore, $ii = \$80$.

The graph shows that the total accumulated amount of the compound interest account after 5 years is about \$294. The difference between the total accumulated amounts of both amounts after 5 years is $294 - 280 = \$14$.

Therefore, $iii = \$14$ more interest.

17. D

Since the interest is compounded semi-annually, the number of compounding periods per year is $f = 2$. From this, you can determine the interest per compound, i, and the total number of compounds, n.

$i = \dfrac{k\%}{2} = \dfrac{\frac{k\%}{100\%}}{2} = \dfrac{k}{200}$ (as a decimal)

$n = 2.5 \times 2 = 5$

Note: The value of n is equal to the number of years not months, so you need to convert 30 months to years.

$\dfrac{30 \text{ months}}{12 \text{ months}} = 2.5$ years

Also, the value of i is always written as a decimal, not a percent.

Therefore, $\dfrac{k}{2}$ is not the value of i as a decimal.

18. 2431

This table shows how the number of compounding periods per year, f, interest per compound, i, and total compounds, n, are calculated for each investment, I.

I	f	i	n
1	12 (monthly)	$= \dfrac{0.10}{12}$ $= 0.008\,333\,333$	$= 6 \times 12$ $= 72$
2	365 (daily)	$= \dfrac{0.09}{365}$ $= 2.465\,75E-4$	$= 9.25 \times 365$ $= 3376.25$
3	2 (semi-annually)	$= \dfrac{0.115}{2}$ $= 0.0575$	$= 4.5 \times 2$ $= 9$
4	4 (quarterly)	$= \dfrac{0.1025}{4}$ $= 0.025\,625$	$= 7 \times 4$ $= 28$

Now, calculate the final value, FV, for each investment's present value, PV, using the value in the table and the compound interest equation: $FV = PV(1 + i)^n$

Investment 1: $FV = 10\,000(1 + 0.008\,333\,333)^{72}$
$= \$18\,175.94$

Investment 2:

$FV = 8600(1 + 2.465\ 753\ 425\text{E}{-}4)^{3376.25} = \$19\ 769.88$

Investment 3: $FV = 11\ 000(1 + 0.0575)^9 = \$18\ 193.49$

Investment 4: $FV = 9200(1 + 0.025\ 625)^{28}$
$= \$18\ 683.95$

Note: For investment 2, use your 2nd, or EE feature to enter the value of $i = 2.465\ 753\ 425\text{E}{-}4$.

If you order the investment number from greatest to least final values, FV, the order is 2, 4, 3, 1.

19. B

In the function $f(x) = 1000(1.015)^{\frac{x}{4}}$, the term $\frac{x}{4}$ represents an annual interest rate compounded quarterly, since if x represents years, then $\frac{x}{4}$ represents every $\frac{1}{4}x$ or $\frac{1}{4}$ of a year. If this is the case, then the growth ratio of 1.015 in the function describes a growth rate of every quarter of a year or quarterly.

The value after the decimal of 1.015 represents this quarterly interest rate, $i = 0.015$ or $0.015 \times 100\% = 1.5\%$.

Therefore, to find the annual interest rate, multiply the quarterly rate by 4.

$1.5\% \times 4 = 6\%$

Thus, the function $f(x) = 1000(1.015)^{\frac{x}{4}}$ represents an investment of $1000 put into an account where the interest rate is 6.0 %/a compounded quarterly.

20. C

When the data is entered as lists L_1 and L_2 as shown in the STAT EDIT mode and the exponential regression is done on the data, the following screen on your calculator should appear:

Therefore, the exponential regression function is
$f(x) = 8000(0.926)^x$.

21. C

Use your TVM Solver on your graphing calculator to calculate the value of I% = by entering the given values, scrolling to I% = , and pressing ALPHA ENTER.

The resulting value for I% = should be 10.8 % to one decimal (the annual interest rate).

To find the interest rate per compounding period, i, in the compound interest formula, divide the annual interest rate by the compounding period, which is quarterly.

This quarterly period is shown as the C / Y value of your TVM Solver screen, C / Y = 4.

$i = \dfrac{\text{I}\%}{4} = \dfrac{10.8\%}{4} = 2.7\% \div 100\% = 0.027$

The present value, P, of the investment is 4100 (since PV = −4100).

$A = P(1 + i)^n$
$A = 4100(1 + 0.027)^n$
$A = 4100(1.027)^n$

Therefore, the correct compound interest equation is
$A = 4100(1.027)^n$.

22. 107

From the compound interest equation
$FV = 200\ 000(1.0075)^n$, you know that
$i = 1.0075 - 1 = 0.0075 \times 100\% = 0.75\%$.

However, this interest value $i = 0.75\%$ is the rate per compounding period, which is stated as monthly. Thus, the annual interest rate is 12 times as much.
I% = 0.75% × 12 = 9%

You now have all the information required as entries in your TVM Solver in order to find the value of n, which is the total number of months for 200 000 to grow to $444 888.

Highlight N = and press ALPHAENTER to get the following screen values:

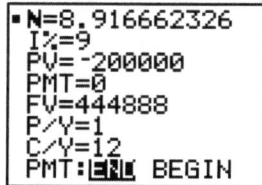

You know that the value N = 8.916 662 326 represents the total number of years to accumulate this amount, so to convert it to the number of compounds, n, in months, multiply it by 12.

$n = (\text{N} =) \times 12$
$= 8.916\ 662\ 326 \times 12$
$= 106.999\ 9479$
$\doteq 107$

The total number of months is 107.

23. C

Since the number of compounds per year is 12 (monthly), the interest per compounding period, i, and number of compounds, n, over 6 years are as follows:

$i = \dfrac{6\%}{12} = 0.5\%$ or 0.005

$n = 6 \times 12 = 72$

The first deposit of $400 would receive 71 compounds of interest, namely, $400(1 + 0.005)^{71}$.

The second deposit would receive 70 compounds of interest, namely, $400(1 + 0.005)^{70}$.

If this pattern continued, the 71st deposit would receive 1 compound of interest, namely, $400(1 + 0.005)^1$, and the last deposit would receive no interest.

The total accumulated amount, *FV*, over 6 years is represented as the total sum of the final amounts of each deposit as shown:

$$FV = \$400 + \$400(1.005)^1 + \$400(1.005)^2 \ldots$$
$$+ \$400(1.005)^{70} + \$400(1.005)^{71}$$

24. D

Since the interest is compounded monthly, there would be 12 compounding periods in a year. Therefore, for 3 and 5 years, the total number of compounds, N, to be entered into the TVM Solver for 3 and 5 years is as follows:

$$N_3 = 3 \times 12 = 36$$
$$N_5 = 5 \times 12 = 60$$

The resulting screens on the TVM Solver that would occur for both of these entries and the others pertaining to the problem are shown.

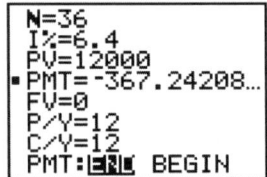 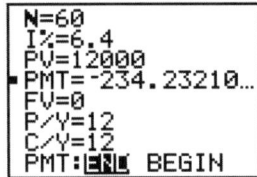

According to the indicated values for PMT on each screen, the regular monthly payments over 3 and 5 years are as follows:

PMT (3 years): $367.24
PMT (5 years): $234.23

The difference between the regular monthly payments is $367.24 − $234.23 = $133.01.

Therefore, Cliff would have to pay $133.01 more per month if he chose to pay off the loan in 3 years as opposed to 5 years.

25. 7.22

First, determine the total accumulated amount, *FV*, if Debbie made her quarterly deposits of $800 in the savings account advertised as 5.8%/a compounded quarterly. The screen on the TVM Solver finding this value, *FV*, is shown below.

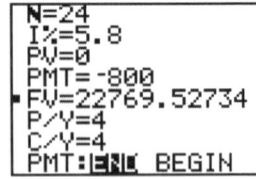

The final accumulated total after 6 years in the 5.8%/a account is *FV* = $22 769.53.

If she could accumulate another $1000 in Albert's bank, then the total accumulated amount in that bank would be $22 769.53 + $1000 = $23 769.53.

Enter this new value of *FV* into your TVM Solver, and solve for I%, as shown below.

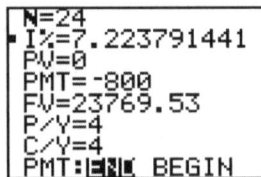

Therefore, the annual interest rate, I%, at Albert's bank would be 7.22 % to the nearest hundredth.

26. Part A –B

First, determine the final accumulated amount, *FV*, in both Ted's and Bill's savings accounts after all their deposits are made.

The total number of compounds and deposits is as follows:

Ted: N = 4 × 12 = 48

Bill: N = 5 × 12 = 60

Then, enter the respective entries into your TVM Solver to determine each person's final amount, *FV*, as shown.

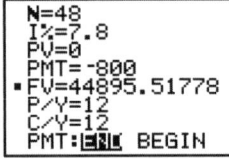 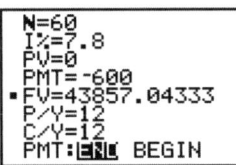

Ted's final accumulated amount after 4 years is *FV* = $44 895.52, and Bill's final accumulated amount after 5 years is *FV* = $43 857.04.

Enter these values as present values, *PV*, for the withdrawals processes in each account. Then, find the time, N, in months that it will take for each savings account to become completely depleted by entering respective entries in your TVM Solver, as shown.

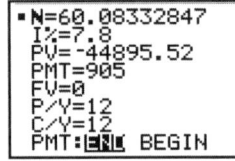 

Ted's savings account is depleted after 60 months of withdrawing regular monthly amounts of $905, and Bill's savings account depletes after 46 months of withdrawing regular monthly amounts of $1105.

Therefore, the total time that each savings account lasted during the deposit and withdrawal processes is as follows:

Ted: 48 + 60 = 108 months

Bill: 60 + 46 = 106 months

Therefore, Ted's account lasted the longest, staying open for 2 months longer than Bill's account.

Part B –B

To make Bill's account last 1 year or 12 months longer, the present value, PV, in his savings account must have a value that enables it to not deplete for N = 46+12 = 58 months. So, entering N = 58, with all respective entries you can determine that present value, PV.

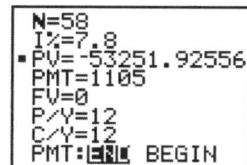

The present value needed in Bill's account at the start of his withdrawal process needs to be $53 251.93, in order to extend his depletion time by 12 months (1 year). Therefore, the final accumulated amount, FV, at the end of his 5 years of making regular monthly deposits of $600 must be $53 251.93. So, entering this value and all respective entries, you can determine the regular monthly deposit, PMT, that Bill would need to make.

According to the resulting value of PMT, Bill should have deposited $728.53 every month over the first 5 years in order to extend the life of his account by 1 year.

27. Part A – Open Response

Since Daniel makes his deposits every 6 months and interest is compounded semi-annually, the number of compounds, N, over 8 years(36 – 28 = 8) is
N = 8 × 2 = 16.

Enter this value and all other entries given in decision A into your TVM Solver to determine the total accumulated amount, FV, in the account after 8 years, as shown below.
Note: Remember that his present value $PV = 2000$, since that was in the account before making any deposits.

According to the resulting value of FV, Daniel will have $18 684.25 in his savings account when he is 36.

Part B – Open Response

At age 36 (after 8 years), Daniel removes $5000 from his savings account to make a car down payment.
Therefore, the amount that he transfers to the GIC account is $18 684.25 – $5000 = $13 684.25.

Part C – Open Response

His present value, at age 36, in the GIC account is PV = $13 684.25. In decision D, he starts to make regular monthly withdrawals of $331. Use the values given in decision C with respect to the GIC account, and enter the regular withdrawals as PMT = 331, to determine the total number of months, N, that it takes for the GIC to deplete to a final amount of $FV = 0$.

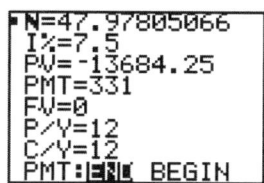

According to the resulting value of N, Daniel's GIC account will be completely depleted after 48 months of regular monthly withdrawals of $331. Since 48 months = 4 years, Daniel will be 36 + 4 = 40 years old when his GIC account is depleted.

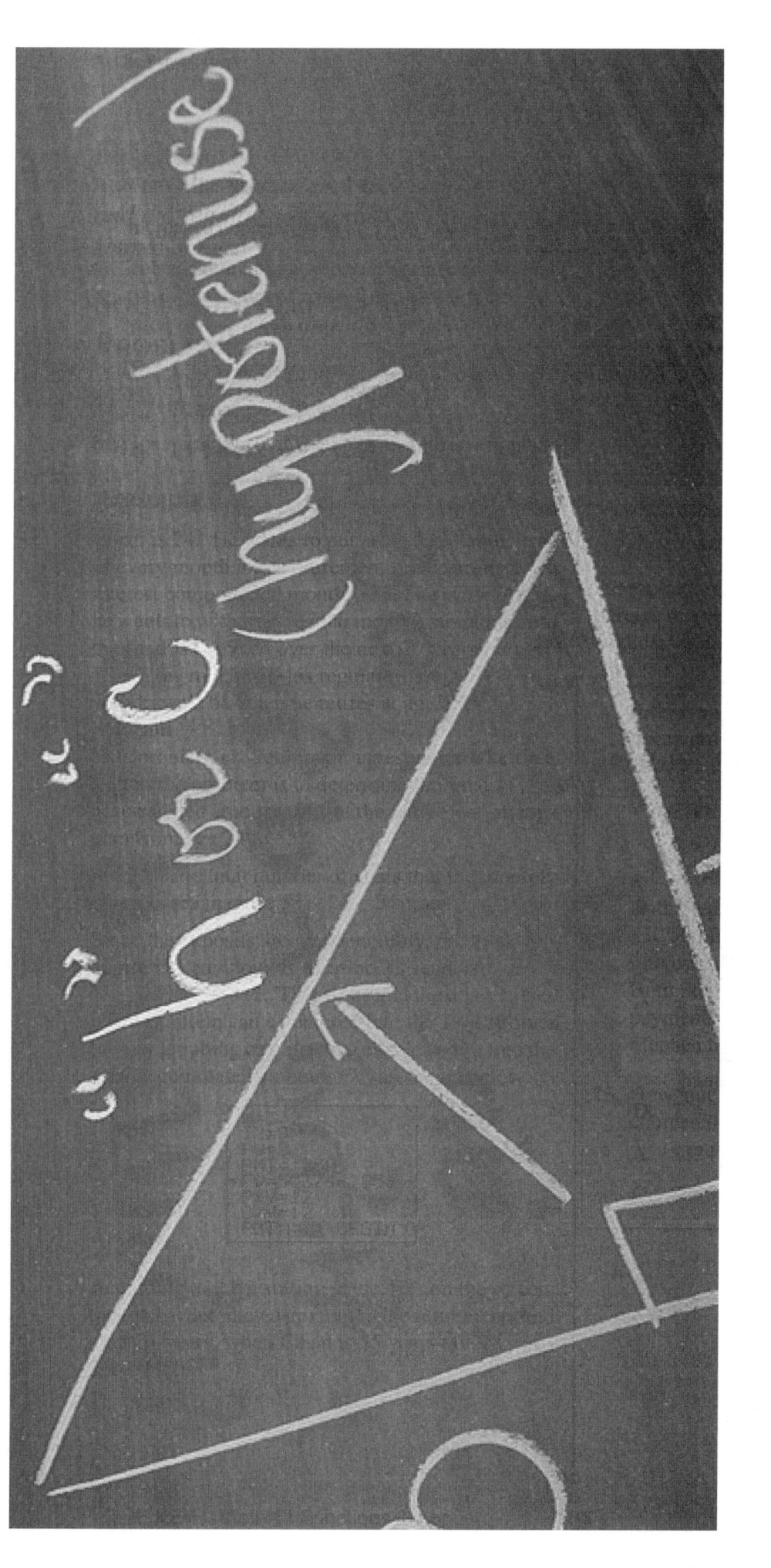

Trigonometric Functions

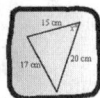

Trigonometric Functions
Table of Correlations

Specific Expectation	Practice Questions	Unit Test Questions
TR1.0 Applying the Sine Law and the Cosine Law in Acute Triangles		
TR1.1 *solve problems, including those that arise from real-world applications, by determining the measures of the sides and angles of right triangles using the primary trigonometric ratios*	1, 2	1, 2
TR1.2 *solve problems involving two right triangles in two dimensions*	3, 4	3a, 3b, 3c, 4
TR1.3 *verify, through investigation using technology, the sine law and the cosine law*		
TR1.4 *describe conditions that guide when it is appropriate to use the sine law or the cosine law, and use these laws to calculate sides and angles in acute triangles*	5, 6	5, 6
TR1.5 *solve problems that require the use of the sine law or the cosine law in acute triangles, including problems arising from real-world applications*	7, 8a, 8b	7, 8
TR2.0 Connecting Graphs and Equations of Sine Functions		
TR2.1 *describe key properties of periodic functions arising from real-world applications, given a numeric or graphical representation*	9a, 9b, 10	9a, 9b, 10
TR2.2 *predict, by extrapolating, the future behaviour of a relationship modelled using a numeric or graphical representation of a periodic function*	11	11
TR2.3 *make connections between the sine ratio and the sine function by graphing the relationship between angles from 0° to 360° and the corresponding sine ratios, with or without technology, defining this relationship as the function $f(x) = \sin x$, and explaining why the relationship is a function*	12, 13	12, 13
TR2.4 *sketch the graph of $f(x) = \sin x$ for angle measures expressed in degrees, and determine and describe its key properties (i.e., cycle, domain, range, intercepts, amplitude, period, maximum and minimum values, increasing/decreasing intervals)*	14, 15	14, 15
TR2.5 *make connections, through investigation with technology, between changes in a real-world situation that can be modelled using a periodic function and transformations of the corresponding graph*	16, 17a, 17b, 17c, 17d	16, 17
TR2.6 *determine, through investigation using technology, the roles of the parameters a, c, and d in functions in the form $f(x) = a\sin x$, $f(x) = \sin x + c$, and $f(x) = \sin(x - d)$, and describe these roles in terms of transformations on the graph of $f(x) = \sin x$ with angles expressed in degrees*	18, 19, 20	18, 19
TR2.7 *sketch graphs of $f(x) = a\sin x$, $f(x) = \sin x + c$, and $f(x) = \sin(x - d)$ by applying transformations to the graph of $f(x) = \sin x$, and state the domain and range of the transformed functions*	21, 22	20, 21
TR3.0 Solving Problems Involving Sine Functions		
TR3.1 *collect data that can be modelled as a sine function, through investigation with and without technology, from primary sources, using a variety of tools, or from secondary sources, and graph the data*	23a, 23b	22
TR3.2 *identify periodic and sinusoidal functions, including those that arise from real-world applications involving periodic phenomena, given various representations (i.e., tables of values, graphs, equations), and explain any restrictions that the context places on the domain and range*		23
TR3.3 *pose problems based on applications involving a sine function, and solve these and other such problems by using a given graph or a graph generated with technology from a table of values or from its equation*	24a, 24b, 25a, 25b	24a, 24b

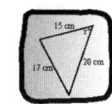

TR1.1 *solve problems, including those that arise from real-world applications, by determining the measures of the sides and angles of right triangles using the primary trigonometric ratios*

Using Primary Trigonometric Ratios

In order to use the primary trigonometric ratios to solve problems involving right triangles, you need to know the measures of two sides, or one side and one acute angle of the right triangle. The measures you are given and the sides or angles that are to be solved determines which ratio to use.

The given right triangle *ABC* has sides with lengths of 3, 4, and 5 units.

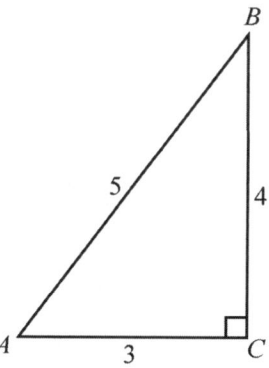

Primary Trigonometric Ratios	
Angle *A*	**Angle *B***
$\sin A = \dfrac{\text{opposite}}{\text{hypotenuse}} = \dfrac{4}{5}$	$\sin B = \dfrac{\text{opposite}}{\text{hypotenuse}} = \dfrac{3}{5}$
$\cos A = \dfrac{\text{adjacent}}{\text{hypotenuse}} = \dfrac{3}{5}$	$\cos B = \dfrac{\text{adjacent}}{\text{hypotenuse}} = \dfrac{4}{5}$
$\tan A = \dfrac{\text{opposite}}{\text{adjacent}} = \dfrac{4}{3}$	$\tan B = \dfrac{\text{opposite}}{\text{adjacent}} = \dfrac{3}{4}$

Note: You may find it helpful to use the acronym SOH CAH TOA to help you remember the primary trigonometric ratios.

When solving a real-world problem, draw and label the right triangle representing the situation. Then use the appropriate primary trigonometric ratio to find the answer.

Example

A 12 m ladder leans against a building, so that its base is 2.5 m away from the building. What is the angle formed, to the nearest tenth degree, where the ladder meets the ground?

Solution
Draw and label a diagram of the right triangle representing the situation as shown below. Use the symbol, θ, to represent the missing angle.

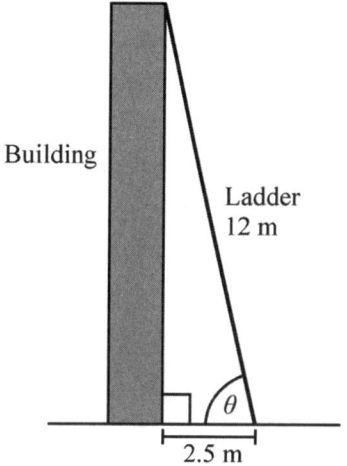

The side labelled 2.5 m is adjacent to the acute angle, θ. The side measuring 12 m is the hypotenuse of the triangle. The ratio that includes the adjacent and hypotenuse sides, is the cosine ratio.

$$\cos \theta = \frac{\text{adjacent}}{\text{hypotenuse}} = \frac{2.5}{12}$$

$$\angle \theta = \cos^{-1}\left(\frac{2.5}{12}\right)$$

$$\approx 78.0°$$

Therefore, the angle formed where the ladder meets the ground is 78.0°.

Some problems use expressions involving an "angle of elevation" or "angle of depression." The angle of elevation is measured above the horizontal; the angle of depression is measured below the horizontal. Both of these angles are equivalent in any problem.

:Example

From a searchlight in a lighthouse 60 m above the surface of the water, the angle of depression to a ship at sea is 25°. How far is the ship from the base of the lighthouse? Round the answer to the nearest metre.

Solution
Draw a labelled diagram to represent the situation.
Note: The angle of depression from the searchlight to the ship is the same as the angle of elevation from the ship to the searchlight.

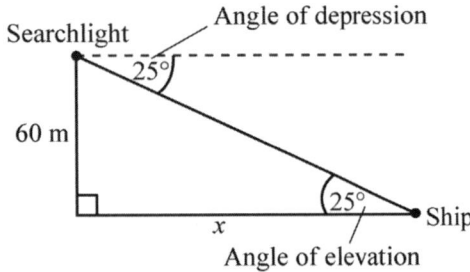

The side labelled x is adjacent to the given acute angle, which measures 25°.
The side measuring 60 m is opposite the angle of 25°.
The ratio that includes the opposite and adjacent sides is the tangent ratio.

$$\tan 25° = \frac{60}{x}$$

Multiply both sides by x
$$x(\tan 25°) = 60$$
Divide both sides by $\tan 25°$
$$x = \frac{60}{\tan 25°}$$
$$x \approx \frac{60}{0.466\ 307\ 6582}$$
$$x \approx 129$$

Therefore, the ship is approximately 129 m from the base of the lighthouse.

:Practice

Use the following information to answer the next question.

A helicopter is involved in an air rescue mission of a stranded person in a dinghy on the ocean during a fierce storm, as illustrated below. The pilot determines that the angle of depression from the helicopter to the stranded person is 15°.
The helicopter is located at a distance of 900 m from the person.

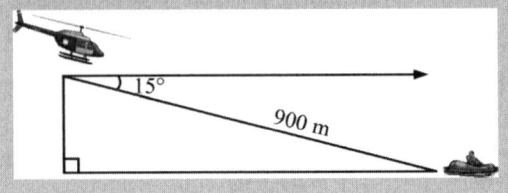

1. The altitude of the helicopter above the water, to the nearest metre, is
    A. 233 m   **B.** 241 m
    C. 869 m   **D.** 932 m

Numerical Response

2. From a position on the ground 40 m away from the foot of a tower, the angle of elevation to the top of the tower is 68°. The height of the tower, to the nearest metre, is ____ m.

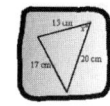

TR1.2 *solve problems involving two right triangles in two dimensions*

PROBLEMS INVOLVING TWO RIGHT TRIANGLES

Some problems involve solving two right triangles or using the solution to one right triangle in order to solve a second right triangle.

Example

Determine the measure of angle D, to the nearest degree, in the diagram shown below.

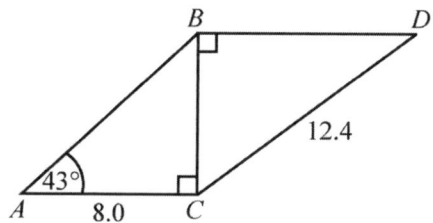

Solution

First, determine the length of line BC using the tangent ratio.

$$\tan 43° = \frac{BC}{8.0}$$
$$8.0(\tan 43°) = BC$$
$$BC = 7.460\ 120\ 689$$

Note: Do not round off answers in intermediary steps. Only round off solutions in the final step.

Now use the length of line BC and 12.4 to determine the measure of $\angle D$.

$$\sin D = \frac{BC}{CD}$$
$$= \frac{7.460\ 120\ 689}{12.4}$$
$$\angle D = \sin^{-1}\left(\frac{7.460\ 120\ 689}{12.4}\right)$$
$$\approx 37°$$

The measure of angle D is 37°.

Example

From a point 100 m from the foot of a building, the angle of elevation to the top corner of a building is 40°, and the angle of elevation to the top of a flagpole attached to the same top corner is 46°. What is the height of the flagpole, to the nearest tenth of a metre?

Solution

First, draw and label a diagram to represent the situation.

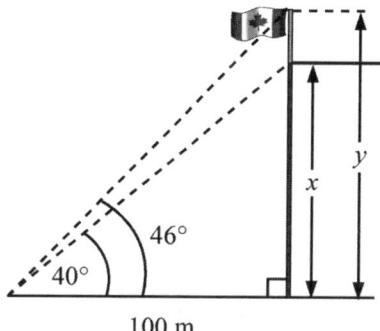

Let x = the height of the building.
Let y = the height from the ground to the top of the flagpole.

Solve for x:

$$\tan 40° = \frac{x}{100}$$
$$100(\tan 40°) = x$$
$$x = 83.909\ 963\ 12$$

Solve for y:

$$\tan 46° = \frac{y}{100}$$
$$100(\tan 46°) = y$$
$$y = 103.553\ 0314$$

Find the height, h, of the flagpole by subtracting x from y.

$$h = y - x$$
$$= 103.553\ 0314 - 83.909\ 963\ 12$$
$$\approx 19.6$$

The height of the flagpole, to the nearest tenth of a metre, is 19.6 m.

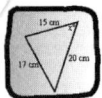

:Practice

Use the following information to answer the next question.

The given diagram shows two right triangles.

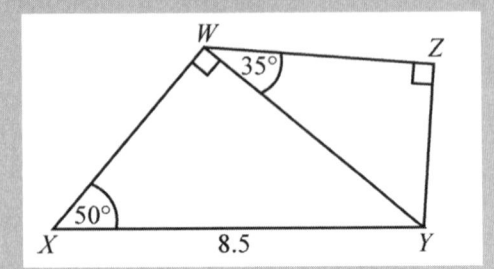

3. What is the length of side *WZ*, to the nearest tenth, in the given diagram?

   A. 4.5   **B.** 5.3   **C.** 7.9   **D.** 8.3

Numerical Response

CHALLENGER QUESTION

Use the following information to answer the next question.

From a 60 m tall fire tower, a park ranger spots one fire at an angle of depression of 28° and another fire at an angle of depression of 42°.

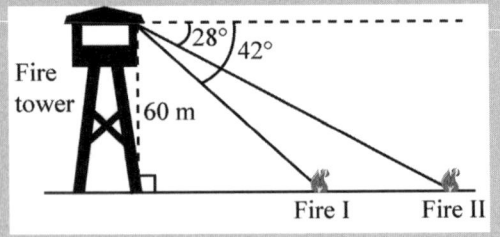

4. The distance between the two fires, to the nearest tenth metre, is _____ m.

TR1.3 *verify, through investigation using technology, the sine law and the cosine law*

THE SINE LAW AND COSINE LAW

Any triangle that is not a right triangle is called an **oblique triangle**. If all the angles in an oblique triangle are smaller than 90°, the triangle is called an **acute triangle**. The primary trigonometric ratios can only be applied to a right triangle, so a new method needs to be used to solve acute triangles. Consider the acute $\triangle ABC$.

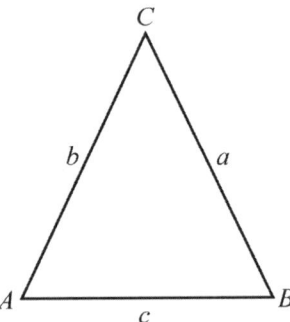

Side *BC* is on the opposite side of angle *A*, which can be denoted by *a*. Similarly, side *AC* is on the opposite side of angle *B*, which can be denoted by *b*, and side *AB* is on the opposite side of angle *C*, which can be denoted by *c*.

The **sine law** states that the sides and angles of an oblique triangle are related in such a way that:

$$\frac{a}{\sin A} = \frac{b}{\sin B} = \frac{c}{\sin C}$$

The ratio of each side of a triangle to the sine value of its opposite angle are the same. The sine law can be used to solve for any side or angle.

The **cosine law** states that the sides and angles of an oblique triangle are related in such a way that:
$$a^2 = b^2 + c^2 - 2bc(\cos A)$$
This form of the equation can be used to solve for any side of the triangle.

The formula can be rearranged to solve for any angle:
$$\cos A = \frac{b^2 + c^2 - a^2}{2bc}$$

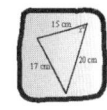

TR1.4 *describe conditions that guide when it is appropriate to use the sine law or the cosine law, and use these laws to calculate sides and angles in acute triangles*

CHOOSING THE SINE LAW OR THE COSINE LAW

Both the sine law or the cosine law can be used to find any measure in an acute triangle, provided that at least any three measures are given.

The sine law should be used when you have a known pair, namely a side with its corresponding opposite angle. The measure that you calculate then depends on what the third known measure is:

- If another side length is known, the angle opposite the known side can be calculated
- If another angle is known, the side opposite the known angle can be calculated

The cosine law should be used when you do not have a known pair, namely a side with its corresponding opposite angle. The measures that you calculate then depends on these known measures:

- If all three sides of the triangle are given, any of the angles can be calculated
- If two sides of the triangle and the angle contained between those sides are known, the unknown side can be calculated

⠶Example

Given $\triangle ABC$, where $\angle A = 24°$, side $a = 14.0$ cm, and side $c = 33.9$ cm, determine the length of side b, to the nearest tenth centimetre.

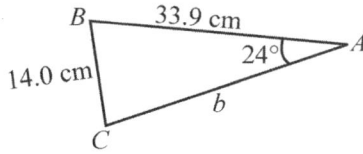

Solution
Since a known pair (a side with its corresponding opposite angle) is given, use the sine law.

First, find $\angle C$ using its corresponding opposite side.

$$\frac{a}{\sin A} = \frac{c}{\sin C}$$
$$\frac{14.0}{\sin 24°} = \frac{33.9}{\sin C}$$
$$14.0(\sin C) = 33.9(\sin 24°)$$
$$\sin C = \frac{33.9(\sin 24°)}{14.0}$$
$$= 0.984\ 883\ 7286$$
$$\angle C = \sin^{-1}(0.984\ 883\ 7286)$$
$$\approx 80.0°$$

Since the sum of the measures of all three angles within a triangle is equal to 180°, you can find the measure of $\angle B$.
$$\angle B = 180° - 80.0° - 24° = 76°$$

Next, find side b by using its corresponding opposite angle B.

$$\frac{a}{\sin A} = \frac{b}{\sin B}$$
$$\frac{14.0}{\sin 24°} = \frac{b}{\sin 76°}$$
$$14.0(\sin 76°) = b(\sin 24°)$$
$$\frac{14.0(\sin 76°)}{\sin 24°} = b$$
$$33.397\ 876\ 49 = b$$
$$b \approx 33.4$$

The length of side b, to the nearest tenth centimetre, is 33.4 cm.

Note: The length of side b could also have been found using the sine law with side c and $\angle C$ or the cosine law.

$$\frac{c}{\sin C} = \frac{b}{\sin B} \text{ or } b^2 = a^2 + c^2 - 2ac(\cos B)$$

⠶Example

Given $\triangle PQR$, where side $p = 13.0$, side $q = 12.0$, and side $r = 6.4$, find the measure of $\angle P$, to the nearest degree.

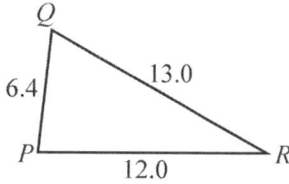

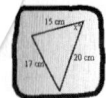

Solution

Since a known pair (a side with its corresponding opposite angle) is not given, use the form of the cosine law arranged to solve for the missing $\angle P$.

$$\cos P = \frac{q^2 + r^2 - p^2}{2qr}$$
$$= \frac{(12.0)^2 + (6.4)^2 - (13.0)^2}{2(12.0)(6.4)}$$
$$= 0.103\ 906\ 25$$
$$\angle P = \cos^{-1}(0.103\ 906\ 25)$$
$$\approx 84.0°$$

The measure of $\angle P$, to the nearest degree, is 84°

Use the following information to answer the next question.

> The given diagram shows $\triangle ABC$ with its labelled sides and angles.
>
>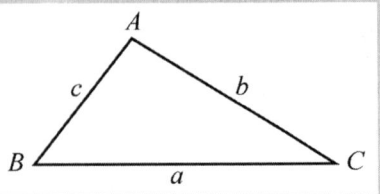

5. Which of the following sets of values would you need, to calculate the measure of an unknown value on $\triangle ABC$, using the cosine law?

   A. $\angle A, \angle B, \angle C$

   B. $a, b, \angle A$

   C. $b, c, \angle A$

   D. $a, \angle B, \angle C$

Open Response

Use the following information to answer the next question.

A surveyor needs to find the length, b, of a bridge across a pond in a park.

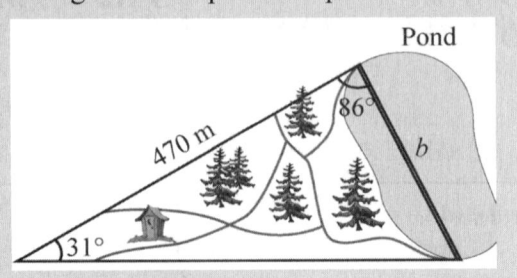

6. Explain which trigonometric law you would use to find the length of the bridge, b. Then, use the trigonometric law to find the length of the bridge, to the nearest whole metre.

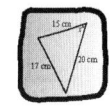

TR1.5 *solve problems that require the use of the sine law or the cosine law in acute triangles, including problems arising from real-world applications*

SOLVING REAL-WORLD PROBLEMS USING THE SINE OR COSINE LAWS

The sine and the cosine laws can be used to solve problems involving acute triangles. To solve real-world problems, follow the strategies outlined below:

1. Read the problem carefully and determine which measure you are asked to solve for and what information you are given.

2. If a diagram is not given, draw a sketch to represent the situation presented in the problem.

3. Examine the diagram in order to decide whether to use the sine law or the cosine law.

4. Make substitutions into the appropriate formula and use the correct algebraic steps to solve for the unknown value.

5. Write a concluding statement.

Example

A sailboat travels 1.2 km on a straight course, turns 140° in a clockwise direction, and then travels on a straight course for a particular distance.
The sailboat then makes a 120° clockwise turn and goes directly back to its starting point. How far, to the nearest hundredth of a kilometre, did the sailboat travel from start to finish?

Solution
Draw and label a diagram that represents this situation.

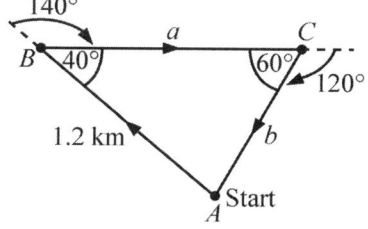

First, find distance b.
Since there is a known pair, namely the length 1.2 km and its corresponding opposite angle of 60°, use the sine law to solve for b.

$$\frac{b}{\sin B} = \frac{c}{\sin C}$$
$$\frac{b}{\sin 40°} = \frac{1.2}{\sin 60°}$$
$$b = \frac{1.2(\sin 40°)}{(\sin 60°)}$$
$$= 0.890\ 672\ 6388$$
$$\approx 0.89\text{ km}$$

Next, find distance a.

Since the sum of the measures of the angles in a triangle are 180°, you can find the measure of angle A.
$$\angle A = 180° - 40° - 60° = 80°$$

Now, you could use the sine law or the cosine law to find the distance, a. Using the cosine law,
$$a^2 = b^2 + c^2 - 2bc(\cos A)$$
$$= (0.89)^2 + (1.2)^2 - 2(0.89)(1.2)(\cos 80°)$$
$$= 1.861\ 187\ 493$$
$$a = 1.364\ 253\ 456$$
$$\approx 1.36\text{ km}$$

Add up all three distances to find the total distance travelled by the boat.
$$1.2 + 0.89 + 1.36 = 3.45$$

Therefore, the total distance travelled by the sailboat, to the nearest hundredth, is 3.45 km.

:Practice

Use the following information to answer the next question.

In an unofficial game of soccer, a shot is made from a particular point of the field. The distance from the shooter to one goal post is 25 m, and the distance from the shooter to the other goal post is 20 m. The angle between these two straight paths is 20°.

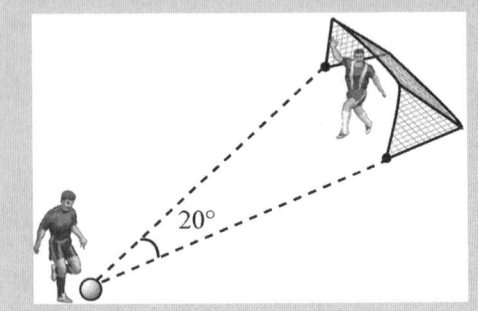

7. The width of the goal, to the nearest tenth of a metre, is

   A. 7.0 m   **B.** 7.3 m

   C. 8.4 m   **D.** 9.2 m

Use the following information to answer the next multipart question.

8. Two pieces of wire are bent to form triangles, as shown.

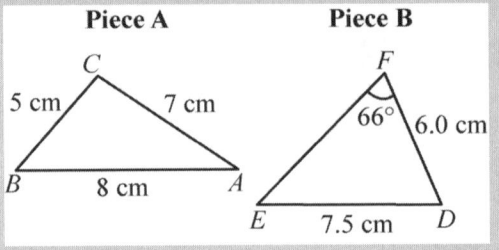

Part A

   Open Response

If you needed to find the measure of the smallest angle in the triangle labelled Piece A, which trigonometric law would you use, and how would you set up the formula to find this angle?

Part B

   Open Response

Which of the two pieces of wire is the shortest, and by how much, to the nearest 0.1 cm? Show your work.

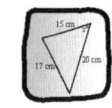

TR2.1 *describe key properties of periodic functions arising from real-world applications, given a numeric or graphical representation*

TR2.2 *predict, by extrapolating, the future behaviour of a relationship modelled using a numeric or graphical representation of a periodic function*

PERIODIC FUNCTIONS

There are many familiar phenomena that repeat themselves over time. For example, the sun comes up every day, the news is reported hourly on the radio, the leaves drop off the trees every fall, your height on a Ferris wheel repeats as the wheel turns, and sound waves rise and fall. When the repetition is consistent and can be described by a function, that function is known as a **periodic function**.

Each repetitive completion of the y-values over a particular x-interval of the domain is called a **cycle**, and the length of this x-interval of a cycle is called the **period** of the function.

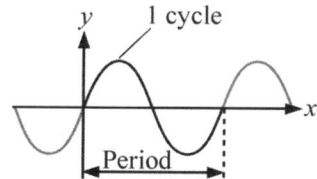

If the graph of the periodic function oscillates regularly between its maximum and minimum y-values, then the equation of the **horizontal midline axis**, d, located halfway between the maximum and minimum points, is given as follows:

$$y = d = \frac{\text{maximum} + \text{minimum}}{2}$$

The **amplitude**, a, of the graph is the vertical distance from the function's horizontal midline axis to any maximum or minimum point. The amplitude can be calculated by two methods:

$$a \begin{cases} (\text{maximum}) - (d\text{-value}) \\ (d\text{-value}) - (\text{minimum}) \end{cases}$$

or $a = \dfrac{\text{maximum} - \text{minimum}}{2}$

The **range** of an oscillating periodic function is the set of all the y-values represented by its graph. If there is a minimum and maximum y-value, then the range is, minimum $\leq y \leq$ maximum.

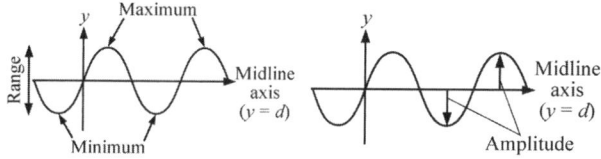

By understanding the repetitive nature of a periodic function you can predict particular x- and y-values beyond the given values. This method is called **extrapolating**.

Example

Determine the period, the equation of the horizontal midline axis, the amplitude, and the range of the graph of the periodic function shown below. Predict what the y-value will be when $x = 16$.

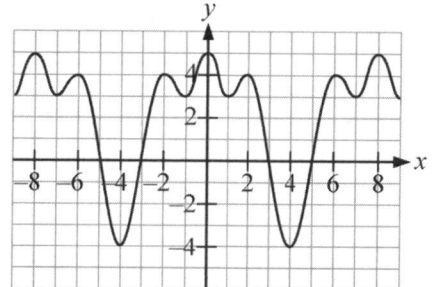

Solution

By examining the repetitive nature of the graph of the periodic function, you can determine the period. For example, the length of the x-interval from one maximum ($y = 5$) to each of the next repeated ones is 8 units.

$$-8 \xrightarrow{\ 8\ } 0 \xrightarrow{\ 8\ } 8$$

Therefore, the period is 8 units.

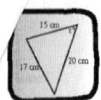

The maximum y-value is 5 and the minimum y-value is -4. Based on these values you can find the equation of the horizontal midline axis $(y = d)$, the amplitude (a), and the range of the graph.

$$y = d = \frac{\text{maximum} + \text{minimum}}{2}$$
$$= \frac{5 + (-4)}{2} = 0.5$$

The equation of the midline axis $y = d = 0.5$.

$a = (\text{maximum}) - (d\text{-value})$
  $= 5 - 0.5 = 4.5$
The amplitude is 4.5 units.

The range is, minimum $\leq y \leq$ maximum, namely $-4 \leq y \leq 5$.

To predict the y-value at $x = 16$, you need to find a y-value from the graph that is located exactly one or more periods away. In this case, since the period is 8 units, you would look for a y-value located 8 (or multiples of 8) units to the left of $x = 16$.

For example,
at $x = 16 - 8 = 8 \rightarrow y = 5$
at $x = 16 - 2(8) = 0 \rightarrow y = 5$
at $x = 16 - 3(8) = -8 \rightarrow y = 5$
Since $y = 5$ at each of these x-positions, you can predict that $y = 5$ when $x = 16$.

:Example

The given table lists the maximum and minimum heights of the tide at St. Andrews, Station 40, in the Bay Of Fundy on September 1, 2008.

2008-09-01 (Monday)

Time (ADT)	Height (m)
01:23	7.3
07:44	0.3
13:47	7.3
20:07	0.4

The height of the tide defines a periodic function with respect to time, starting at 00:00 on September 1, 2008.

a. What is the approximate period of the function?
   Solution
   The first high tide occurs at 01:23 and then again at 13:47. The period would be the length of the time interval between these two values.
   Period $= 13:47 - 01:23 = 12:24$.
   The period is 12 hours and 24 minutes.

b. What is the amplitude of the function, to the nearest tenth of a metre?
   Solution
   The amplitude, a, of the periodic function can be found as follows:
   $$a = \frac{\text{maximum} - \text{minimum}}{2}$$
   $$= \frac{7.3 - 0.3}{2} = 3.5$$
   The amplitude of the function is 3.5 m.

c. At what time do you predict that the tide would be the lowest for the first time on Wednesday, September 3, 2008?
   Solution
   The first low tide on Monday, September 1, 2008, was at 07:44. Since the period is about 12 hours and 24 minutes, add successive periods to 07:44 until the first low tide occurs on Wednesday, September 3, 2008.
   07:44 (Mon) + 12:24 = 20:08 (Mon)
   20:08 (Mon) + 12:24 = 32:32, or 08:32 (Tues)
   08:32 (Tues) + 12:24 = 20:56 (Tues)
   20:56 (Tues) + 12:24 = 33:20, or 09:20 (Wed)
   The first low tide on Wednesday, September 3, 2008, would occur approximately at 09:20.

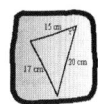

Use the following information to
answer the next multipart question.

9.

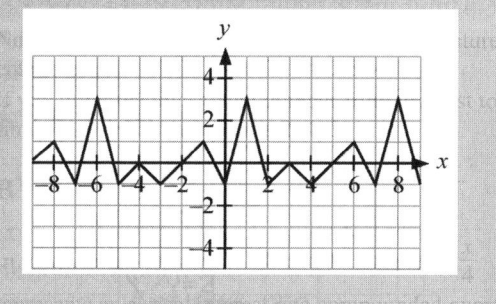

Part A

What is the period of the function for the given graph?

A. 2 units   **B.** 4 units

C. 7 units   **D.** 8 units

Part B

What would be the predicted y-value for the function in the given graph at $x = 22$, if the function existed for values of the domain greater than 9?

A. −1   **B.** 0

C. 1   **D.** 3

Open Response

Use the following information to
answer the next question.

The given table lists the amount of daylight for a city in Ontario, for various dates in 2007, including those with the most and least hours of daylight. The year 2007 was not a leap year.

Date	Amount of Daylight
February 21	10 h 42 min
April 21	13 h 49 min
June 21	15 h 41 min
August 21	13 h 50 min
October 21	10 h 41 min
December 21	8 h 43 min

10. If the number of hours of daylight were a function of the days in a non-leap year, and if that function were periodic, then what would be the period of daylight time, to the nearest day? What would be the amplitude of the daylight time, to the nearest minute? Explain your answer.

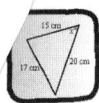

Numerical Response

Use the following information to answer the next question.

Marta has an investment plan in which she makes a deposit into a savings account each month. The given table shows the amounts of the deposits for the first six months of the previous year.

Month	Amount Deposited ($)
January	450
February	425
March	400
April	350
May	350
June	375

11. If the deposit amounts were a model of a periodic function with a period of 6 months, then the predicted amount Marta would deposit in September is $____.

TR2.3 *make connections between the sine ratio and the sine function by graphing the relationship between angles from 0° to 360° and the corresponding sine ratios, with or without technology, defining this relationship as the function f (x) = sin x, and explaining why the relationship is a function*

THE SINE FUNCTION

The sine ratio of an acute angle A, for right-triangle trigonometry, is defined as:

$$\sin A = \frac{\text{opposite side}}{\text{hypotenuse}}$$

This definition is valid for acute angles from 0° to 90° only. To include angles of any measure, θ, it is useful to examine these angles in **standard position** on the Cartesian plane.

An angle, θ, is in standard position on the Cartesian Plane, when the initial arm (defined by the positive x-axis) is rotated about the origin in a clockwise or counterclockwise direction to a final position, defined by the terminal arm. If the rotation is counterclockwise, the angle formed is positive, and if the rotation is clockwise, the angle formed is negative.

The sine ratio for each angle in standard position can be defined as follows:

Given an angle, θ, drawn in standard position on the Cartesian plane with $P(x, y)$ on the terminal arm of angle θ, then:

$$\sin \theta = \frac{y}{r}, \text{ where } r = \sqrt{x^2 + y^2}$$

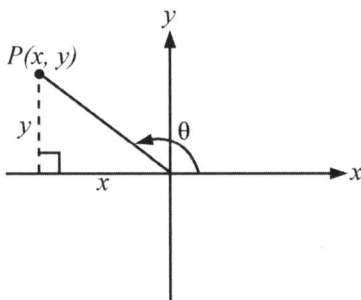

Furthermore, if every point $P(x, y)$ were located 1 unit from the origin, so that $r = 1$, then:

$$\sin \theta = \frac{y}{1} = y$$

Note: These sets of points $P(x, y)$, located 1 unit from the origin, form a **unit circle** that is centered at the origin.

Conclusion: The y-coordinate of any point $P(x, y)$ on the unit circle, is equal to the sine ratio for its corresponding angle θ, in standard position.

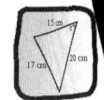

:Example

Given the point $\left(-\frac{1}{2}, -\frac{\sqrt{3}}{2}\right)$, on the unit circle, determine the sine ratio of its corresponding angle in standard position.

Solution

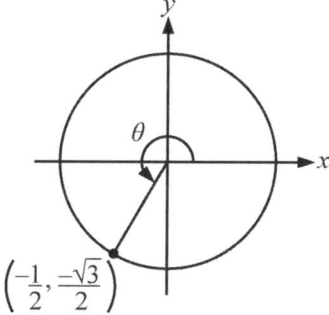

As shown in the diagram above, the sine ratio for angle θ in standard position, that has the point $\left(-\frac{1}{2}, -\frac{\sqrt{3}}{2}\right)$ on its terminal arm, is equal to the y-coordinate $-\frac{\sqrt{3}}{2}$.

:Example

Point P is on both the unit circle and the terminal arm of an angle of $320°$ when it is drawn in standard position. Determine the y-coordinate of point P to the nearest thousandth.

Solution

The y-coordinate of point P is equal to the sine ratio for $320°$. You can calculate $\sin 320°$ on your graphing calculator to get $-0.642\ 787\ 6097$. Thus, the y-coordinate of point P is -0.643, to the nearest thousandth.

:Example

Consider the relation $y = \sin x$ in which x represents an angle of any measure and y is the y-coordinate of a point P on both the terminal arm of the angle and the unit circle. Is the relation $y = \sin x$ a function?

Solution

Use your graphing calculator to determine the sine ratio values, y, for the angles, x, between $0°$ and $360°$ that are multiples of $30°$. These resulting values are in the given table.

Angle Measure (x)	Sine Ratio (y)
0°	0
30°	0.5
60°	0.866
90°	1
120°	0.866
150°	0.5
180°	0
210°	−0.5
240°	−0.866
270°	−1
300°	−0.866
330°	−0.5
360°	0

If these values are placed on the Cartesian plane and connected with a smooth curve, the graph of $y = \sin x$ is formed for all angles between $0°$ to $360°$.

Note: The y-value on the unit circle corresponds to its angle, x, as seen at $210°$.

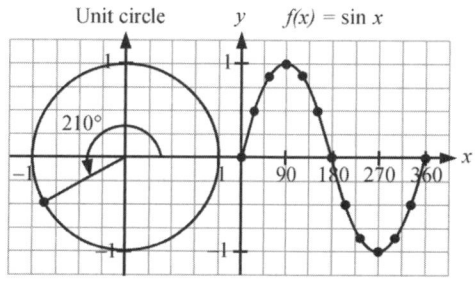

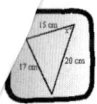

Examining the table of values, the relation $y = \sin x$ seems to be a function, since for every angle measure, x, in degrees, there is a single unique sin ratio value, y.

The graph passes the *vertical line test*, which means that for every vertical line drawn through any x-value of the graph, each line would only pass through one y-value. Therefore, the relation $y = \sin x$ is a function, and can be written as $f(x) = \sin x$.

Practice

12. The expression $f(x) = \sin x$ is a function because every value of

   A. x is paired with exactly one value of sin x

   B. sin x is paired with exactly one value of x

   C. x is paired with at least one value of sin x

   D. sin x is paired with at least one value of x

CHALLENGER QUESTION

13. If $\sin \theta = -1.2$, and $0° \leq \theta \leq 360°$, then how many possible values exist for θ?

   A. 0   B. 1

   C. 2   D. Infinite

TR2.4 *sketch the graph of $f(x) = \sin x$ for angle measures expressed in degrees, and determine and describe its key properties (i.e., cycle, domain, range, intercepts, amplitude, period, maximum and minimum values, increasing/decreasing intervals)*

DESCRIBING THE SINE FUNCTION

The function exists for angles that are negative as well as for angles larger than 360°. The sine ratio repeats as the terminal arm of the unit circle rotates beyond 360° in a counterclockwise direction or beyond 0° in a negative, or clockwise, direction. The result is a periodic function with a period of 360°.

There are two methods for obtaining a sketch of $f(x) = \sin x$.

- Use a table of values and then draw a freehand curve
- Use the graph illustrated on your graphing calculator upon entering sin (x) into $Y_1 =$.

KEY PROPERTIES OF THE SINE FUNCTION

The given graph shows the function $f(x) = \sin x$ for the domain of $-360° \leq x \leq 360°$.

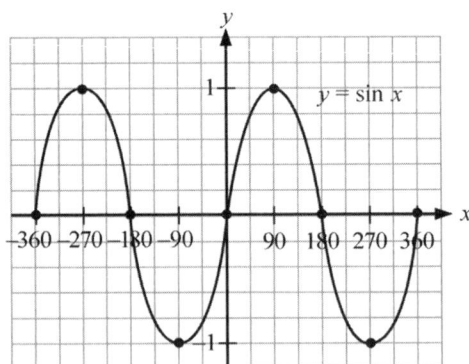

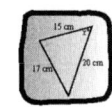

By examining the above graph, the key properties of the graph of $f(x) = \sin x$, where $x \in \mathbb{R}$, can be identified.

- **period**—One cycle of the graph occurs over an interval of 360°. Thus, the period is 360°.
- **domain**—Since the function is defined for all real measures of the angle x, the domain is $x \in \mathbb{R}$.
- **maximum and minimum values**—For the graph of $f(x) = \sin x$, the maximum value is $+1$ and the minimum value is -1.
- **amplitude** (a)—The amplitude, a, can be determined from the maximum and minimum values as follows:

$$a = \frac{\text{maximum} - \text{minimum}}{2}$$
$$= \frac{1 - (-1)}{2} = 1$$

The amplitude is $a = 1$.
- **equation of horizontal midline axis** $(y = d)$—The equation of the midline axis is determined as follows:

$$y = d = \frac{\text{maximum} + \text{minimum}}{2}$$
$$= \frac{1 + (-1)}{2} = 0$$

The equation of the midline axis is $y = d = 0$.
- **range**—For the function $f(x) = \sin x$, the maximum value is $+1$ and the minimum value is -1. Therefore, since the range is defined as minimum $\leq y \leq$ maximum, the range of $f(x) = \sin x$ is $-1 \leq f(x) \leq 1$.
- **intercepts**—The y-intercept is 0. The x-intercepts are $-360°$, $-180°$, $0°$, $180°$, $360°$, etc. These intercepts can be described as multiples of 180°, using the recursive formula $x = 180°n$, $n \in I$.
- **increasing/decreasing intervals**—The function increases for x-values between $-90°$ and $90°$. Similarly, the function decreases between $90°$ and $270°$. Since the function is periodic with a period of 360°, it can be said that the function is increasing for $(-90 + 360n)° < x < (90 + 360n)°$, $n \in I$, and decreasing for $(90 + 360n)° < x < (270 + 360n)°$, $n \in I$.

:**Practice**

14. Which of the following expressions describes the x-intercepts of $f(x) = \sin x$?

    A. $x = 90n°$, $n \in W$

    B. $x = 180n°$, $n \in I$

    C. $x = 180n°$, $n \in W$

    D. $x = 360n°$, $n \in I$

15. Which of the following statements about the function $f(x) = \sin x$ is **incorrect**?

    A. The y-intercept is 0.

    B. An x-intercept of the graph is $-900°$.

    C. The equation of the horizontal midline axis is $y = d = 1$

    D. The vertical distance between the minimum and maximum values is 2.

TR2.5 *make connections, through investigation with technology, between changes in a real-world situation that can be modelled using a periodic function and transformations of the corresponding graph*

SOLVING PROBLEMS USING PERIODIC FUNCTION TRANSFORMATIONS

Recall that the properties and behaviours of periodic functions can describe real-world situations. Transformations to graphs of periodic functions can also be used to describe and model other real-world phenomena.

Example

Some football players run wind sprints before practice. Ryan repeatedly runs from the goal line to the 20-yard line and back to the goal line. Matt runs the same 20-yard sprints as Ryan, but he started 6 seconds later than Ryan. Matt completes one cycle of his run in the same time as Ryan completes one cycle of his. Sam also runs a 20-yard sprint, but he runs from the 10-yardline to the 30-yard line and back. He completes one cycle of his run in the same time as Ryan completes one cycle of his, and he starts at the same time as Ryan.

The following graph represents the position, *s* in yards, that Ryan is from the goal line *t* seconds after he starts his run.

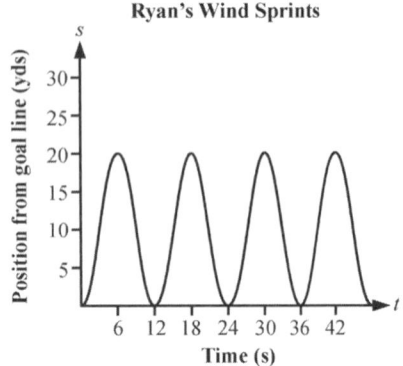

a. Sketch the graphs for both Matt's run and Sam's run on the same set of axes as for the graph of Ryan's run.
Solution

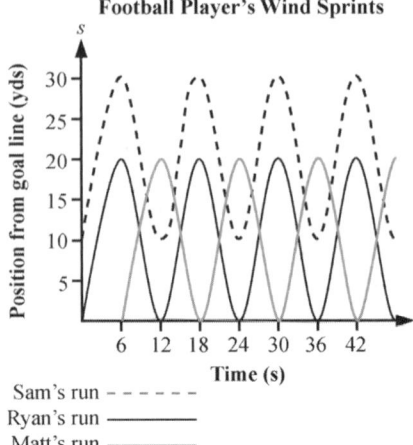

Sam's run - - - - - -
Ryan's run ————
Matt's run ————

b. If another player, Larry, runs the same sprints as Ryan, but runs only half as quickly, how would the graph of his run compare to the graph of Ryan's run?
Solution
To graph Larry's run, you would have to stretch the graph of Ryan's graph horizontally, since it takes Larry 24 s to complete one cycle, rather than 12 s.

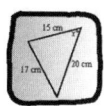

Practice

CHALLENGER QUESTION

16. Margot swam laps in a pool so that her position, s, from the starting end of the pool, t seconds after starting, was given by the periodic function, $s = f(t)$.
Margot returned the next day and swam the same laps but she swam more quickly. What would you have to do to the graph of the first swim, $s = f(t)$, to produce the graph of the second swim?

A. Stretch the graph, $s = f(t)$, vertically.

B. Stretch the graph, $s = f(t)$, horizontally.

C. Compress the graph, $s = f(t)$, vertically.

D. Compress the graph, $s = f(t)$, horizontally.

Use the following information to answer the next multipart question.

17. Kyle rides his motorcycle at a constant speed over a series of hills that are all the same size. He started his ride at the top of the first hill. The given graph shows his height, h, in metres, above the ground, t seconds after he starts the ride.

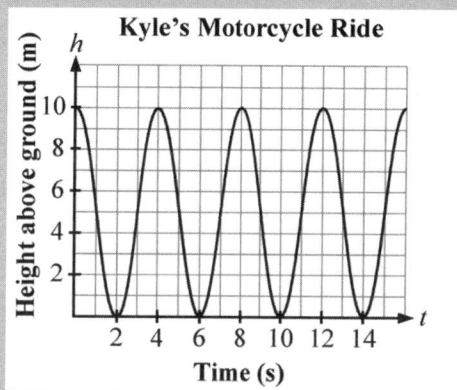

Explain how the following changes would affect the graph:

Part A

Open Response

Kyle started his ride at the bottom of the first hill.

Part B

Open Response

The hills are made wider.

Part C

Open Response

The hills are made taller.

Part D

Open Response

Kyle travelled twice as fast.

TR2.6 *determine, through investigation using technology, the roles of the parameters a, c, and d in functions in the form* $f(x) = a\sin x$, $f(x) = \sin x + c$, *and* $f(x) = \sin(x - d)$, *and describe these roles in terms of transformations on the graph of* $f(x) = \sin x$ *with angles expressed in degrees*

SOLVING TRANSFORMATION PROBLEMS

When the graph of $f(x) = \sin x$ is transformed to the graph of $f(x) = a\sin x$, $f(x) = \sin x + c$, or $f(x) = \sin(x - d)$, each parameter a, c, and d has a unique effect on the features of the resulting graph. To investigate the effects to each parameter, use your graphing calculator in Degree MODE and with a WINDOW setting ZOOM ZTrig.

⁞Example

What are the changes to the graph of $f(x) = \sin x$ when it is transformed to $f(x) = -3\sin x$ and $f(x) = 0.5\sin x$?

Solution

Enter all three functions into $[Y =]$ as follows: $Y_1 = \sin(x)$, $Y_2 = -3\sin(x)$, and $Y_3 = 0.5\sin(x)$.

To make the graphs of $Y_2 = -3\sin(x)$ and $Y_3 = 0.5\sin x$ look different from $Y_1 = \sin(x)$ you can highlight the line left of $Y_2 =$ to make it dotted and left of $Y_3 =$ to make it thick, using the arrow key $\triangleleft$ ENTER. Then press GRAPH to produce the following graphs on your calculator screen.

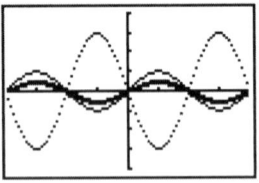

The graph of $f(x) = -3\sin x$ undergoes a vertical stretch by a factor of 3 about the x-axis, giving it an amplitude of 3 units. Therefore, the maximum is 3 and the minimum is -3. The function is also reflected in the x-axis.

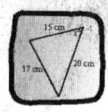

The graph $f(x) = 0.5 \sin x$ undergoes a vertical compression by a factor of 0.5 about the x-axis, giving it an amplitude of 0.5. The maximum is 0.5 and the minimum is -0.5.

When the graph of $f(x) = \sin x$ is transformed to the graph of $f(x) = a \sin x$, the parameter a has the following effects.

- If $|a| > 1$, the graph is stretched vertically by a factor of $|a|$ about the x-axis. If $|a| < 1$, the graph is compressed vertically by a factor of $|a|$ about the x-axis. If $a < 0$, the graph is also reflected about the x-axis.
- The amplitude of the graph is $|a|$.
- The maximum is $|a|$ units and the minimum is $-|a|$ units.

:Example

What are the changes to the graph of $f(x) = \sin x$ when it is transformed into $f(x) = \sin x + 3$ and $f(x) = \sin x - 2$?

Solution

Enter all three functions into $[Y =]$ as follows: $Y_1 = \sin(x)$, $Y_2 = \sin(x) + 3$, and $Y_3 = \sin(x) - 2$. Then highlight the lines left of $Y_2 =$ and $Y_3 =$ to produce thick and dotted lines.

Press GRAPH to produce the following graphs on your calculator screen.

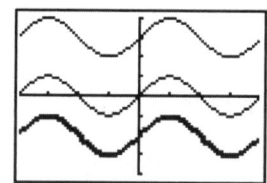

The graph of $f(x) = \sin x + 3$ undergoes a vertical translation of 3 units up. The equation of the horizontal midline axis is $y = 3$. The maximum is 4 and the minimum is 2.

The graph of $f(x) = \sin x - 2$ undergoes a vertical translation of 2 units down. The equation of the horizontal midline axis is $y = -2$. The maximum is -1 and the minimum is -3.

When the graph of $f(x) = \sin x$ transforms into the graph of $f(x) = \sin x + c$, the parameter c has the following effects:

- When $c > 0$, the graph is vertically translated up c units, and when $c < 0$, the graph is vertically translated down c units.
- The equation of the horizontal midline axis is $y = c$.
- The maximum is $c + 1$ and the minimum is $c - 1$.

:Example

What are the changes to the graph of $f(x) = \sin x$ when it is transformed into $f(x) = \sin(x + 45°)$ and $f(x) = \sin(x - 90°)$?

Solution

Enter all three functions into $[Y =]$ as follows: $Y_1 = \sin(x)$, $Y_2 = \sin(x + 45)$, and $Y_3 = \sin(x - 90)$. Then highlight the lines left of $Y_2 =$ and $Y_3 =$ to produce thick and dotted lines.

Press GRAPH to produce the following graphs on your calculator screen.

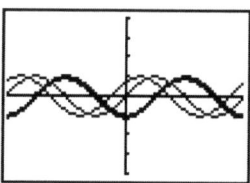

The graph of $f(x) = \sin(x + 45°)$ undergoes a horizontal translation of 45° to the left, so every point of $f(x) = \sin x$, slides 45° to the left.

The graph of $f(x) = \sin(x - 90°)$ undergoes a horizontal translation of 90° to the right, so every point of $f(x) = \sin x$, slides 90° to the right.

When the graph of $f(x) = \sin x$ is transformed into the graph of $f(x) = \sin(x - d)$, the parameter d has the following effects:

- When $d > 0°$, the graph is horizontally translated to the right d units.
- When $d < 0°$, the graph is horizontally translated to the left d units.

:Practice

18. Which of the following transformations describes the change to the graph of $f(x) = \sin x$ when it changed into $f(x) = -4\sin x$?

   A. The graph is translated 4 units down.

   B. The graph is stretched horizontally by a factor of -4.

   C. The graph is reflected in the x-axis and translated 4 units down.

   D. The graph is stretched vertically about the x-axis by a factor of 4 and is reflected about the x-axis.

   Use the following information to answer the next question.

   The given functions represent three different transformations to the basic sine function:

   $f(x) = a\sin x,$
   $f(x) = \sin x + c,$
   $f(x) = \sin (x - d)$

19. Which of the following parameters and values would cause the graph of $f(x) = \sin x$ to be translated $50°$ to the right?

   A. $a = 50°$ B. $c = 50°$

   C. $d = 50°$ D. $d = -50°$

Numerical Response

20. The graph of $f(x) = \sin x + 11$ can be obtained by translating the graph of $f(x) = \sin x - 46$____ units up.

TR2.7 *sketch graphs of $f(x) = a\sin x$, $f(x) = \sin x + c$, and $f(x) = \sin (x - d)$ by applying transformations to the graph of $f(x) = \sin x$, and state the domain and range of the transformed functions*

SKETCHING TRANSFORMATIONS

You should be able to sketch the graphs of transformed forms of $f(x) = \sin x$ when the transformations are vertical or horizontal translations, vertical stretches and compressions about the x-axis, or reflections about the x-axis. To sketch a reasonable graph by hand for the transformed functions $f(x) = a\sin x$ or $f(x) = \sin x + c$, substitute enough angle values of $x = 0° + 90°n, n \in I$, to draw one or two cycles of the graph. To sketch a reasonable graph for $f(x) = \sin (x - d)$, substitute angles of $x - d = 0° + 90°n$ or $x = d + 90°n, n \in I$. Once the graph is drawn as a smooth graph through the points, you can determine the domain and range of the transformed function.

:Example

Sketch the graph of $f(x) = \sin x + 2$, from $0°$ to $360°$ inclusive, and state its domain and range.

Solution
Substitute the angle values of $x = 0°, 90°, 180°, 270°,$ and $360°$ into the function $f(x) = \sin x + 2$ to calculate the value of $f(x)$. The corresponding values are shown in the given table:

x	$f(x) = \sin x + 2$
$0°$	$f(0°) = \sin 0° + 2 = 0 + 2 = 2$
$90°$	$f(90°) = \sin 90° + 2 = 1 + 2 = 3$
$180°$	$f(180°) = \sin 180° + 2 = 0 + 2 = 2$
$270°$	$f(270°) = \sin 270° + 2 = -1 + 2 = 1$
$360°$	$f(360°) = \sin 360° + 2 = 0 + 2 = 2$

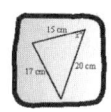

Plot these points on a grid and draw a smooth curve through these points.

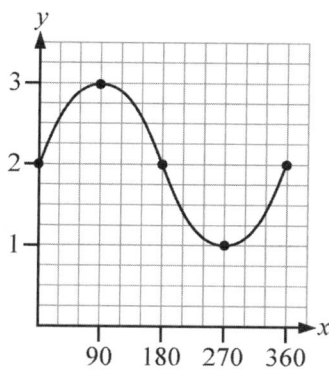

According to the graph, the domain is $0° \leq x \leq 360°$, since the graph is restricted to values between $0°$ and $360°$ inclusive. The minimum value of the graph is 1 and the maximum value is 3. Therefore, the range is $1 \leq f(x) \leq 3$ or $1 \leq y \leq 3$.

:Example

Sketch the graph of $f(x) = \sin(x - 45°)$ and state its domain and range.

Solution

Since the function is in the form of $f(x) = \sin(x - d)$, and there are no restrictions on the angle values, find enough sine values of the angles $x = d + 90°n$, $n \in I$, to draw two cycles of the graph. Since $d = 45°$ in the function $f(x) = \sin(x - 45°)$, suitable angle values can be found when $x = 45° + 90°n$, $n \in I$.

When $n = -4, -3, -2, -1, 0, 1, 2, 3$, the corresponding angle values are $-315°$, $-225°$, $-135°$, $-45°$, $45°$, $135°$, $225°$, $315°$. Substitute these angle values into $f(x) = \sin(x - 45°)$. The given table shows the corresponding values of $f(x)$.

x	$f(x) = \sin(x - 45°)$
$-315°$	$f(-315) = \sin(-315° - 45°) = 0$
$-225°$	$f(-225) = \sin(-225° - 45°) = 1$
$-135°$	$f(-135) = \sin(-135° - 45°) = 0$
$-45°$	$f(-45) = \sin(-45° - 45°) = -1$
$45°$	$f(45) = \sin(45° - 45°) = 0$
$135°$	$f(135) = \sin(135° - 45°) = 1$
$225°$	$f(225) = \sin(225° - 45°) = 0$
$315°$	$f(315) = \sin(315° - 45°) = -1$

Plot these points on a grid and draw a smooth curve through these points.

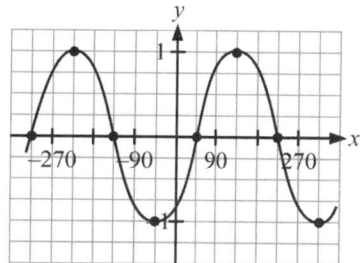

According to the graph, the domain is $x \in \mathbb{R}$, since there are no restrictions on angle values. The minimum value of the graph is -1 and the maximum value is 1. Therefore, the range is $-1 \leq f(x) \leq 1$ or $-1 \leq y \leq 1$.

:Practice

CHALLENGER QUESTION

21. Hannah used several key points to draw the partial graph of $f(x) = \sin(x + 90°)$. Which of the following graphs **best** represents this function?

A.

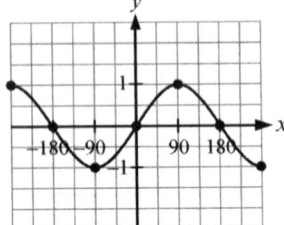

B.

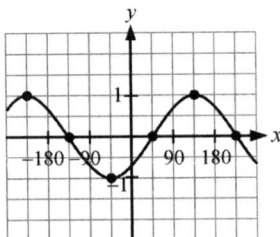

C.

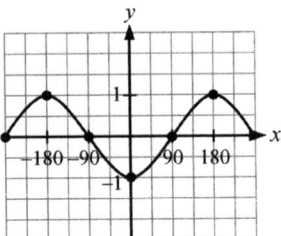

D.

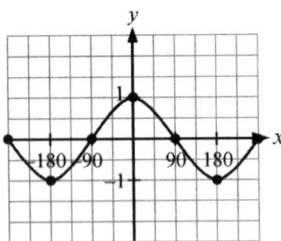

22. For the function $f(x) = \sin x - 17$, the correct domain and range, respectively, are

   A. $x \in \mathbb{R}$ and $f(x) \geq -18$

   B. $x \in \mathbb{R}$ and $-18 \leq f(x) \leq -16$

   C. $-360° \leq x \leq 360°$ and $f(x) \geq -18$

   D. $-360° \leq x \leq 360°$ and $-18 \leq f(x) \leq -16$

TR3.1 *collect data that can be modelled as a sine function, through investigation with and without technology, from primary sources, using a variety of tools, or from secondary sources, and graph the data*

TR3.2 *identify periodic and sinusoidal functions, including those that arise from real-world applications involving periodic phenomena, given various representations (i.e., tables of values, graphs, equations), and explain any restrictions that the context places on the domain and range*

ANALYZING PERIODIC FUNCTIONS

Real-life data can be collected and analyzed that model periodic functions. The data can be represented in a table of values, a graph, an equation or in other ways. Features of the periodic pattern can be identified. Restrictions on the domain and range can also be defined, by recognizing the limitations of values set out by the context of the scenario.

Note: A special type of periodic function whose graph is a transformation of the sine function $y = \sin x$ is called a **sinusoidal** function.

:Example

In a physics lab, the centre of a bicycle pedal mechanism is 30 cm above the ground. Each pedal is 22 cm from this centre point.

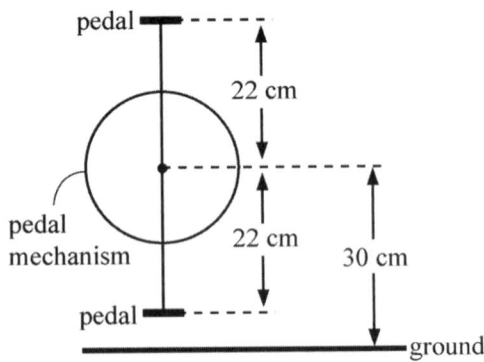

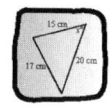

The pedal is rotated at a constant speed, using a small motor. A student then uses a motion sensor to record the vertical height, h, in centimetres, of one pedal above the ground over a time of 2.0 seconds. The sensor records the heights every 0.1 seconds. The given table lists the heights, h, in centimetres, of the pedal above the ground, over time, t, in seconds.

t (s)	h (cm)	t (s)	h (cm)	t (s)	h (cm)	t (s)	h (cm)
0	52.0	0.5	10.8	1.0	41.8	1.5	29.0
0.1	49.0	0.6	8.0	1.1	48.8	1.6	18.8
0.2	40.2	0.7	10.0	1.2	51.8	1.7	10.1
0.3	30.0	0.8	19.0	1.3	49.2	1.8	8.2
0.4	18.6	0.9	30.6	1.4	40.0	1.9	10.5
						2.0	19.9

a. Graph the data and draw a smooth curve of best fit through the data points. Then analyze some of the features of the periodic sinusoidal motion.

Solution

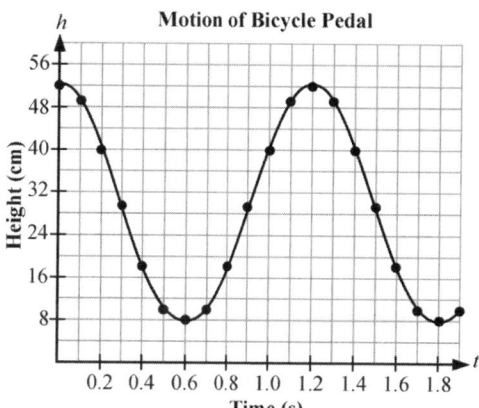

From the shape of the graph, the following observations could be made:

- The maximum height of the pedal is about 52 cm and the minimum height is about 8 cm above the ground.
- The horizontal midline axis runs through a y-value of $\frac{52 + 8}{2} = 30$ cm, and the amplitude is the length of each pedal arm, 22 cm.
- Since the first maximum starts at $t = 0$ s, and occurs again for the first time at $t = 1.2$ s, the period of the graph is 1.2 s. This means that the pedal rotates once every 1.2 s.

b. What restrictions, if any, are there on the domain and range of the graph within the context of this investigation?

Solution

Domain: The experiment started at $t = 0$ s and was over at $t = 2$ s, since that is the extent of the motion sensor's detection period. Therefore, the domain in this context is $0 \le t \le 2$. However, if the sensor was set for a longer time period, T, then the domain would be $0 \le t \le T$.

Range: For this experiment the range is $8 \le h \le 52$, since those are the h-values between the maximum and minimum values of the graph. However, if the bicycle was set closer or further from the ground, the range would change relative to the new position.

:Practice

Use the following information to answer the next multipart question.

23. The blades on a wind turbine are mounted on top of a 5 m tall shaft. Each blade is 2 m long when measured from the shaft to the tip of the blade.

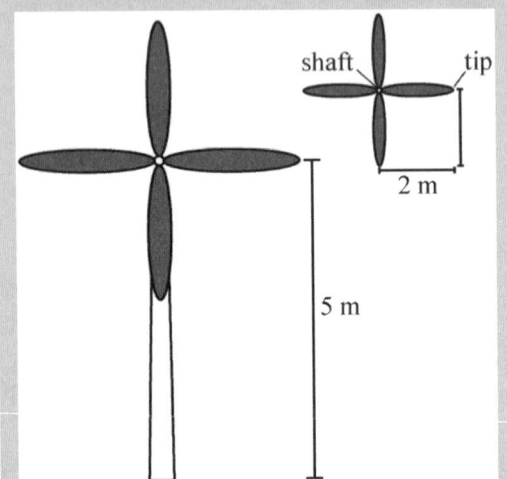

A student observed the motion of the blades and realized that they rotated in a periodic pattern of 30 revolutions per minute.

Part A

The student graphed the height, *h* in metres, for one of the blades above the ground with respect to time, *t*, in seconds. If the blade was at its maximum height when *t* = 0, which of the following graphs shows the motion that the student observed?

A.

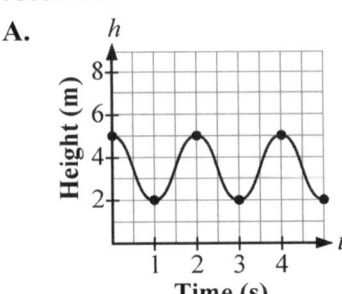

B.

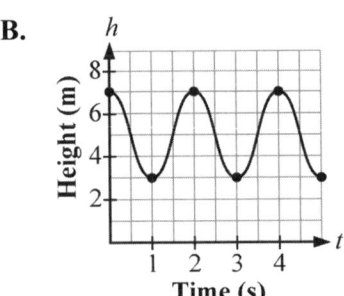

C.

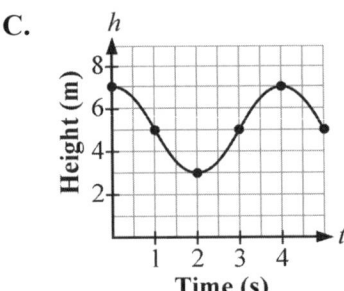

D.

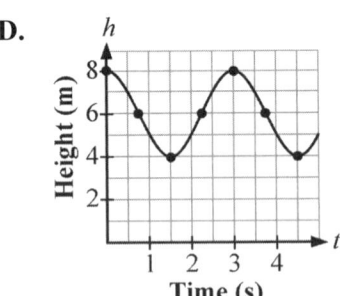

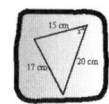

Part B

If a new 2.8 m long blade were to replace the original blade, and it rotated 30 revolutions per minute over a total time of 40 minutes, what would the new restrictions be on the domain and range of the graph of the height, h, in metres, of one of these blades with respect to time, t, in seconds?

A. Domain: $0 \le t \le 40$
   Range: $2.8 \le h \le 7.8$

B. Domain: $0 \le t \le 40$
   Range: $2.2 \le h \le 7.8$

C. Domain: $0 \le t \le 2400$
   Range: $2.8 \le h \le 7.8$

D. Domain: $0 \le t \le 2400$
   Range: $2.2 \le h \le 7.8$

TR3.3 *pose problems based on applications involving a sine function, and solve these and other such problems by using a given graph or a graph generated with technology from a table of values or from its equation*

SINUSOIDAL MOTION

When a description of an event involving sinusoidal behaviour is modelled by a graph, table of values or an equation, you can solve problems relevant to the context of the event. Technology, such as a graphing calculator, is often useful for solving these problems.

Example

A piston in the engine of a car moves up and down in its cylinder in a sinusoidal fashion. The motion of the piston can be described by the equation: $h = 5\sin(157.08t) + 15$, where h is the height in centimetres and t is the time in seconds.

a. According to the equation, what are the minimum and maximum heights of the piston while moving up and down in the cylinder?

Solution

According to the equation, the number 15 describes the middle (horizontal midline axis of the graph of the sine function). The number 5 in the equation describes the amplitude of the sinusoidal motion. The maximum and minimum values can then be determined as follows:

Maximum = Midline + amplitude
   $= 15 + 5 = 20$ cm
Minimum = Midline – amplitude
   $= 15 - 5 = 10$ cm

The maximum height of the piston is 20 cm and the minimum height is 10 cm.

b. Determine the graph represented by the equation, using your graphing calculator in radian mode.

Solution

For many real-life problems involving sinusoidal motion, the equation is usually defined with respect to angles measured in **radians**. A radian is simply another unit used to define the change in angle of the periodic (circular) motion of the event. Therefore, the graphing calculator needs to be changed from degree to radian, by pressing MODE. Then, use the down arrow ∇ to highlight Radian and press ENTER. Now you can enter the given equation in $[Y =]$ as follows:

$Y_1 = 5\sin(157.08x) + 15$

Set a suitable WINDOW setting, such as $x:[0, 0.10, 0.01]$, $y:[0, 25, 5]$ and press GRAPH. The following graph should appear on the screen of your calculator.

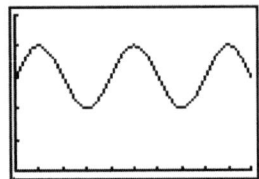

c. Use the calculator to find the period of the function. Then explain the meaning of this value in terms of the context of this problem.

Solution

Use the 2nd TRACE maximum feature on your calculator to find the times at which the first two maximum values of the graph occur. These two values are highlighted in the two following screens.

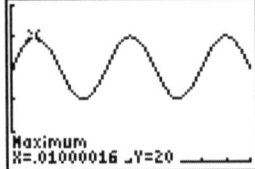 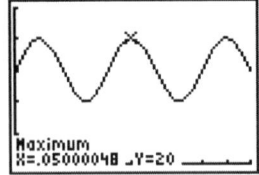

The two values that represent the times at which these two maximums occurred are

$x = 0.010\ 000\ 16$ and $x = 0.050\ 000\ 48$

Remember that the period of a graph is the length of the x-interval of one cycle of the graph, which in this case occurs between the two repeated maximum values. Thus, if the values of x are rounded to the nearest hundredth, the period is $0.05 - 0.01 = 0.04$ seconds. This period describes the time needed for the piston to go up and then down through one cycle within the cylinder.

d. Suppose the piston operates for 1 hour. How many complete cycles does it make?

Solution

Since one cycle takes 0.04 s, then the number of cycles made in 1 hour (or $60 \times 60 = 3600$ s) can be found as follows:

$$\text{Number of cycles} = \frac{3600 \text{ s}}{0.04 \text{ s/cycle}}$$
$$= 90\ 000$$

The piston goes through 90 000 cycles in one hour.

Other features of the piston's motion could also be determined (e.g., heights at different times, changes to the graph for pistons moving in other engines, etc.)

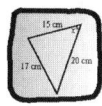

:Practice

Use the following information to answer the next multipart question.

24. Pierre lives on a small farm that gets its water supply from a well with a pump. Pierre notices that the water pressure in his farm house is not consistent. He decides to test the pressure, P, in psi (pressure per square inch), of the water over time, t, in hours. The given table shows the data Pierre recorded.

t (h)	P (psi)
0	22.2
1	19.0
2	18.3
3	16.8
4	16.0
5	17.5
6	18.1
7	20.2
8	23.0
9	23.5
10	21.4
11	19.5
12	17.0

Part A

Open Response

Enter the given data into your graphing calculator as lists, L_1 and L_2, and then find the sinusoidal regression equation representing the data. Write the equation in the form $y = a\sin(bx + c) + d$, where the values of a, b, c, and d are rounded to the nearest hundredth.

Note: Remember to have your calculator in **Radian** mode.

Part B

Open Response

Pierre does not want the water pressure to drop below 17.0 psi. Using your graphing calculator, determine the number of hours, to the nearest tenth, that the water pressure is below 17.0 psi over the 12 hour period.

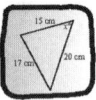

Use the following information to answer the next multipart question.

25. The height, h, in metres, above the ground of a person on a ferris wheel ride is a sinusoidal function with respect to the time, t, in seconds. The given graph illustrates a particular person's height above the ground from the time the ferris wheel is loaded until the end of the ride.

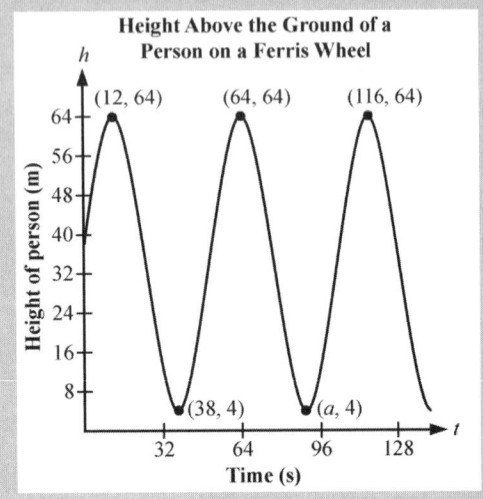

Part A

The height, h, above the ground, when the rider is halfway to the top of the ferris wheel, is

A. $h = 30$ m   **B.** $h = 32$ m

C. $h = 34$ m   **D.** $h = 38$ m

Part B

Numerical Response

The time a, defined by the point $(a, 4)$ on the graph is _____ s.

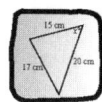

Solutions–Trigonometric Functions

1. A	**8.** Part A- **OR**	**13. A**	Part D- **OR**	Part B- **D**
2. 99	Part B- **OR**	**14. B**	**18. D**	**24.** Part A- **OR**
3. B	**9.** Part A- **C**	**15. C**	**19. C**	Part B- **OR**
4. 46.2	Part B- **D**	**16. D**	**20. 57**	**25.** Part A- **C**
5. C	**10. OR**	**17.** Part A- **OR**	**21. D**	Part B- **90**
6. OR	**11. 400**	Part B- **OR**	**22. B**	
7. D	**12. A**	Part C- **OR**	**23.** Part A- **B**	

1. A

Draw a labelled diagram of the situation, where x is the altitude of the helicopter, H, above the water. Label the angle of elevation of the person, P, to the helicopter as 15°, since it is equivalent to the angle of depression.

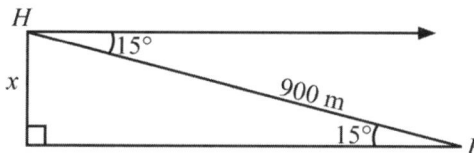

The ratio that includes the opposite and hypotenuse sides is the sine ratio.

$$\sin 15° = \frac{x}{900}$$

Multiply both sides by 900

$$900(\sin 15°) = x$$
$$900(0.258\ 819\ 0451) \approx x$$
$$233 \approx x$$
$$x \approx 233$$

Therefore, the altitude of the helicopter above the water, to the nearest metre, is 233 m.

2. 99

Draw a labelled diagram to represent the situation. Let x = height of the tower.

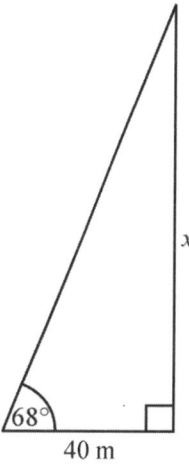

The ratio that includes the opposite and adjacent sides is the tangent ratio.

$$\tan 68° = \frac{x}{40}$$

Multiply both sides by 40

$$40(\tan 68°) = x$$
$$40(2.475\ 086\ 853) \approx x$$
$$99 \approx x$$

The height of the tower, to the nearest metre, is 99 m.

3. B

First, determine the length of side WY.

$$\sin 50° = \frac{WY}{8.5}$$
$$8.5(\sin 50°) = WY$$
$$WY = 6.511\ 377\ 767$$

Now use the value of side WY to find the length of side WZ.

$$\cos 35° = \frac{WZ}{WY}$$

$$\cos 35° = \frac{WZ}{6.511\ 377\ 767}$$
$$6.511\ 377\ 767(\cos 35°) = WZ$$
$$WZ \approx 5.3$$

The length of side WZ, to the nearest tenth, is 5.3 units.

4. 46.2

Sketch and label a diagram to represent this situation. Remember that the angles of depression from the tower to the fires are equal to the angles of elevation from the fires to the tower.

Let x = horizontal distance from the tower to Fire I.

Let y = horizontal distance from the tower to Fire II.

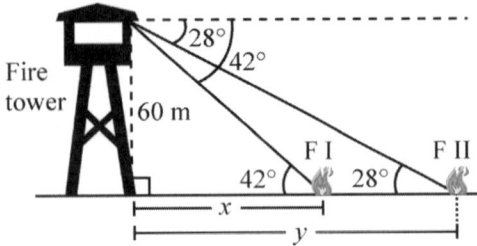

Solve for x:

$$\tan 42° = \frac{60}{x}$$

$$x(\tan 42°) = 60$$

$$x = \frac{60}{\tan 42°}$$

$$x = 66.636\ 750\ 89$$

Solve for y:

$$\tan 28° = \frac{60}{y}$$

$$y(\tan 28°) = 60$$

$$y = \frac{60}{\tan 28°}$$

$$y = 112.843\ 5879$$

Therefore, the distance, d, to the nearest tenth metre, between the two fires is:

$$d = y - x$$
$$= 112.843\ 5879 - 66.636\ 750\ 89$$
$$\approx 46.2 \text{ m}$$

5. C

To use the cosine law, you can determine the measure of an angle given all three sides of the triangle, or you can determine the measure of a side given the other two sides and the angle contained between the two sides.

Since the sides b and c contain $\angle A$, these measures can be used with the cosine law to calculate the measure of the third side. Therefore, alternative C is the correct answer.

6. Open Response

The missing angle in the triangle can be easily determined, since the sum of the measures of the angles must be equal to 180°. This will provide a known pair with the side 470 m. Therefore, the sine law would be the correct formula to use to find the length of the bridge, b.

First, find the missing angle, A.

$$\angle A = 180° - 86° - 31° = 63°$$

Next, let side a = 470 m and $\angle B = 31°$ in the given triangle. Then, use the sine law to find the value of b.

$$\frac{a}{\sin A} = \frac{b}{\sin B}$$

$$\frac{470}{\sin 63°} = \frac{b}{\sin 31°}$$

$$\frac{470(\sin 31°)}{\sin 63°} = b$$

$$b = 271.679\ 1501$$

The length of the bridge, b, to the nearest whole metre, is 272 m.

7. D

Draw and label a diagram that represents this situation. Let d = distance between the goal posts B and C.

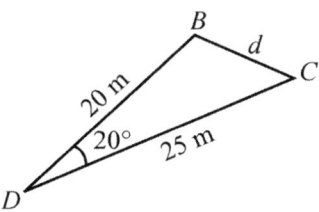

Since you have no known pair (a given side with its corresponding opposite angle) use the cosine law to solve for the width of the goal, d.

$$d^2 = b^2 + c^2 - 2bc(\cos D)$$
$$= (25)^2 + (20)^2 - 2(25)(20)(\cos 20°)$$
$$= 85.307\ 379\ 21$$
$$d = 9.236\ 199\ 392$$

The width of the goal, to the nearest tenth of a metre, is 9.2 m.

8. Part A – Open Response

According to the sine law, all ratios between the sides and the sine value of their corresponding opposite angles are equivalent.

$$\frac{a}{\sin A} = \frac{b}{\sin B} = \frac{c}{\sin C}$$

Therefore, the sine law for Piece A gives the following ratios:

$$\frac{5}{\sin A} = \frac{7}{\sin B} = \frac{8}{\sin C}$$

For these ratios to be equal, $\angle A$ would be less than $\angle B$, and $\angle B$ would be less than $\angle C$, since $5 < 7 < 8$. Therefore, the smallest angle formed is $\angle A$.

To solve for $\angle A$, you should use the cosine law, since there is no known pair (a known side with its corresponding opposite angle). The rearranged formula for the cosine law to solve for $\angle A$ is as follows:

$$\cos A = \frac{b^2 + c^2 - a^2}{2bc} = \frac{(7)^2 + (8)^2 - (5)^2}{2(7)(8)}$$

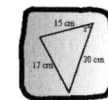

Part B – Open Response

To determine which piece of wire is the shortest, you need to calculate the measure of side EF, or side d, opposite of $\angle D$. To do this, you first need to find $\angle E$ using the sine law.

$$\frac{f}{\sin F} = \frac{e}{\sin E}$$
$$\frac{7.5}{\sin 66°} = \frac{6.0}{\sin E}$$
$$7.5(\sin E) = 6.0(\sin 66°)$$
$$\sin E = \frac{6.0(\sin 66°)}{7.5}$$
$$= 0.730\ 836\ 366$$
$$\angle E = \sin^{-1}(0.730\ 836\ 366)$$
$$= 46.956\ 555\ 47°$$
$$\approx 47.0°$$

Now, find $\angle D$. Since the sum of all the measures of the angles of a triangle is 180°, $\angle D$ is the difference between the sum and the two known angles.
$$\angle D = 180° - 66° - 47.0° = 67°$$

Finally, find the length of side d (opposite to $\angle D$) using the sine law again.

$$\frac{d}{\sin D} = \frac{f}{\sin F}$$
$$\frac{d}{\sin 67°} = \frac{7.5}{\sin 66°}$$
$$d(\sin 66°) = 7.5(\sin 67°)$$
$$d = \frac{7.5(\sin 67°)}{\sin 66°}$$
$$= 7.557\ 135\ 053$$
$$\approx 7.6 \text{ cm}$$

Note: The cosine law could also have been used with sides e and f and the included angle D.

You can now determine which wire piece is the shortest.
Piece A: $5 + 7 + 8 = 20$ cm
Piece B. $6.0 + 7.5 + 7.6 = 21.1$ cm

The difference in the sizes of the pieces of wire can be calculated as follows:
$21.1 - 20 = 1.1$ cm

Therefore, the shortest piece of wire is piece A, by 1.1 cm.

9. Part A –C

The y-values on the graph repeat across an x-interval of 7 units. For example, the maximum y-value of 3 occur at x-values of -6, 1, and 8. The difference between these values is always 7. Therefore, the period of the graph is 7 units.

Part B –D

Since the function has a period of 7, you can predict the y-value at $x = 22$ by determining the y-values for the graph located exactly one or more periods to the left of $x = 22$.
At $x = 22 - 7 = 15 \rightarrow y = ?$
At $x = 22 - 2(7) = 8 \rightarrow y = 3$
At $x = 22 - 3(7) = 1 \rightarrow y = 3$
At $x = 22 - 4(7) = -6 \rightarrow y = 3$
Since $y = 3$ at each of the x-positions shown on the graph, you can predict that $y = 3$, when $x = 22$.

10. Open Response

Since Earth travels around the sun once (1 cycle) every 365 days, the period would be equal to this repeated cycle. Therefore, the period would be 365 days.

To find the amplitude, a, you need to know the minimum and maximum amounts of daylight time in the year. The minimum amount of daylight is 8 h and 43 min, which occurs on December 21. The maximum amount of daylight is 15 h and 41 min, which occurs on June 21. Determine the amplitude, a, as follows:

$$a = \frac{\text{maximum} - \text{minimum}}{2}$$
$$= \frac{15 \text{ h } 41 \text{ min} - 8 \text{ h } 43 \text{ min}}{2}$$
$$= \frac{6 \text{ h } 58 \text{ min}}{2}$$
$$= 3 \text{ h } 29 \text{ min}$$

The amplitude of the function is 3 h 29 min of daylight time.

11. 400

Since the period of the function is 6 months, she would deposit the same amount as she did 6 months previous to September, which is the amount in March of $400.

12. A

One definition of a function is that every element of the domain is paired with exactly one element of the range. For $f(x) = \sin x$, the domain consists of all angles, x, which is uniquely paired with the corresponding sine values, y, of the range.

13. A

The definition of the sine ratio is $\sin \theta = \frac{y}{r}$, in which r is the radius of the unit circle (1), and y is the y-value of any point on the unit circle. Since the range of $y = \sin \theta$ is $-1 \le y \le 1$, the values of $\sin \theta$ must fit these limitations, for any angle, θ. Therefore, since -1.2 is a value less than -1, which is outside the range, there would be zero (0) solutions for θ.

14. B

The x-intercepts of $f(x) = \sin x$ are multiples of 180°. This means that n must be an integer ($n \in I$) so that $x = 180n°$ includes both negative and positive multiples, as well as zero.

The expression given in alternative C, $x = 180n°, n \in W$, is incorrect because $n \in W$ means that n is only a whole number, which excludes negative multiples of 180°.

15. C

The equation of the horizontal midline axis is not $y = d = 1$, but instead is $y = d = 0$, since

$$y = d = \frac{\text{maximum} + \text{minimum}}{2}$$
$$= \frac{1 + (-1)}{2} = 0$$

Therefore alternative C is incorrect.
Since $f(0) = \sin(0°) = 0$, the y-intercept is 0.
Alternative A is correct
Any x-intercept of $f(x) = \sin x$, is $x = n180°$, $n \in I$.
When $n = -5$, $x = -5(180°) = -900°$. Therefore, $-900°$
is an x-intercept of the graph of $f(x) = \sin x$.
Alternative B is correct.
The maximum value is 1 and the minimum value is -1 for
the graph of $f(x) = \sin x$. Therefore, the vertical distance
between these value is $1 - (-1) = 2$. Alternative D is
correct.

16. D

Because Margot swam more quickly on the second day,
she would have completed each cycle in a shorter time
period. Therefore, you would have to compress the graph
of $s = f(t)$ horizontally, to produce the graph of her
second swim.

17. Part A – Open Response

The bottom of the first hill is reached two seconds after the
start in the original graph. However, if Kyle started at the
bottom of the hill, then his height of 0 m would occur at
0 seconds. To portray this change graphically, the original
graph would be translated 2 units horizontally to the left,
namely, $(2, 0) \to (0, 0)$.

Part B – Open Response

If the hills are made wider, the original graph would be
stretched horizontally. The period would then be larger,
since it would take the rider longer to go from one hill to
the next wider hill.

Part C – Open Response

If the hills are taller, the maximum values would be higher.
The original graph would be stretched vertically about
the t-axis, resulting in a greater amplitude and an equation
of the horizontal midline axis at a higher position.

Part D – Open Response

If Kyle travelled faster, he would have driven over each
hill in a shorter time, namely in $\frac{1}{2}$ the time. The original
graph would be compressed horizontally, since the period
of the new graph would be $\frac{1}{2}$ of the period of the original
graph. The period would be 2 seconds instead of
4 seconds.

18. D

The 4 in $f(x) = -4\sin x$ will cause the graph of
$f(x) = \sin x$ to stretch vertically about the x-axis by a
factor of 4, and the negative sign in front of the number 4
causes the graph of $f(x) = \sin x$ to also reflect about
the x-axis.

19. C

Changing the parameter d causes a horizontal translation.
The translation is to the right when $d > 0$ and to the left
when $d < 0$. Therefore, since the graph is translated $50°$
to the right, the value of parameter $d = 50°$.

20. 57

The graph of $f(x) = \sin x - 46$ is produced by vertically
translating the graph of $f(x) = \sin x$, 46 units down.
The graph of $f(x) = \sin x + 11$ is produced by vertically
translating the graph of $f(x) = \sin x$, 11 units up.
Thus, the graph of $f(x) = \sin x + 11$ can be obtained by
vertically translating the graph of $f(x) = \sin x - 46$ a total
of $11 - (-46) = 57$ units up.

21. D

Since $f(x) = \sin(x + 90°)$ is in the form
$f(x) = \sin(x - d)$, Hannah should have used angle values
of $x = d + 90°n$, $n \in I$ to sketch her graph. These values
could be generated using the recursive formula
$x = -90° + 90°n$, $n \in I$. Then if Hannah substituted
$n = -2, 1, 0, 1, 2, 3, 4$, she would generate angle values
of $-270°, -180°, -90°, 0°, 90°, 180°$, and $270°$.
The given table of values shows the angles, x, and their
corresponding $f(x)$ values.

x	$f(x) = \sin(x + 90°)$
$-270°$	$f(-270°) = \sin(-270° + 90°) = 0$
$-180°$	$f(-180°) = \sin(-180° + 90°) = 1$
$-90°$	$f(-90°) = \sin(-90° + 90°) = 0$
$0°$	$f(0°) = \sin(0° + 90°) = 1$
$90°$	$f(90°) = \sin(90° + 90°) = 0$
$180°$	$f(180°) = \sin(180° + 90°) = -1$
$270°$	$f(270°) = \sin(270° + 90°) = 0$

Therefore, graph D best represents $f(x) = \sin(x + 90°)$
because it passes through all the points represented in the
table above.

22. B

There is no restriction on the domain, so the domain is the
set of real numbers $x \in \mathbb{R}$.
Since the graph of $f(x) = \sin x - 17$ is the graph of
$f(x) = \sin x$ translated 17 units down, and the maximum
value of the graph would be $-17 + 1 = -16$ and the
minimum would be $-17 - 1 = -18$, the range of the graph
is $-18 \leq f(x) \leq -16$.

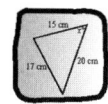

23. Part A –B

The maximum height of each blade above the ground would be 2 m above the top of the shaft (located 5 m above the ground), which is $2 + 5 = 7$ m. The minimum height of each blade above the ground would be 2 m below the top of the shaft (located 5 m above the ground), which is $5 - 2 = 3$ m. If the blade rotates 30 times each minute, or 30 times every 60 s, it means that the blade rotates once every $\frac{60}{30} = 2$ seconds. Therefore, 1 cycle takes 2 s, which would be the period of the graph.

Therefore, graph B shows the correct plotted points and curve of best fit.

Part B –D

Since the total time is 40 minutes = 40×60 s = 2400 s, the domain restriction, in seconds, would be $0 \le t \le 2400$. The maximum height of the new blade would be 2.8 m higher than the shaft (5 m), namely $5 + 2.8 = 7.8$ m. The minimum height of the new blade would be 2.8 m lower than the shaft (5 m), namely $5 - 2.8 = 2.2$ m. Therefore, the restricted range would be $2.2 \le h \le 7.8$.

24. Part A – Open Response

Enter the data values for time, t, in list L_1, and enter the data values of pressure, P, in list L_2 in the STAT feature of your graphing calculator. Then, to find the sinusoidal regression equation press STAT CALC SinReg (C) L_1, L_2 ENTER to get the following screen:

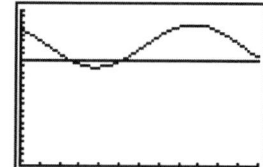

Now you round off the values of a, b, c, and d to the nearest hundredth, and write the sinusoidal regression equation as $y = 3.44\sin(0.64x + 2.28) + 19.32$.

Part B – Open Response

Enter the regression equation into $\left[Y_1 = \right]$ as follows:

$Y_1 = 3.44\sin(0.64x + 2.28) + 19.32$

Enter 17.0 into $\left[Y_2 = \right]$ as follows:

$Y_1 = 17.0$

Set your WINDOW at x:[0, 12, 1], y:[0, 25, 1] and then press GRAPH.

The following screen shows the resulting graph.

Find the two intersection points between the line and the curve using the 2nd TRACE Intersect feature. The screens below show these two intersection values.

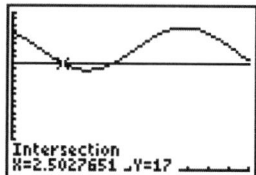 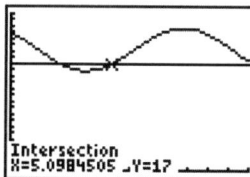

The two times when the pressure is 17.0 psi is at 2.5 hours and 5.1 hours. Therefore, the amount of time, to the nearest tenth, that the water pressure would be less than 17.0 psi is $t = 5.1 - 2.5 = 2.6$ h.

25. Part A –C

Since the maximum height of the ride is 64 m above the ground, and the minimum height is 4 m above the ground, the height of the rider halfway to the top would be located at the horizontal midline axis, d,(halfway between the maximum and minimum).

$$d = h = \frac{\text{max} + \text{min}}{2} = \frac{64 + 4}{2} = \frac{68}{2} = 34 \text{ m.}$$

Part B – 90

To determine the time a defined by the point $(a, 4)$, you need to find the period of the graph. Examine two successive maximum points on the graph to determine that the period, P, is the difference between these two points.

$P = 64 - 12 = 52$ s

If the period is 52 s, then the rider would be at the minimum point $(a, 4)$, 52 s after reaching the first minimum point of $(38, 4)$. Therefore, $a = 38 + 52 = 90$ s.

CHALLENGER QUESTION

Use the following information to answer the next question.

Chico drew two right triangles and labelled them as shown.

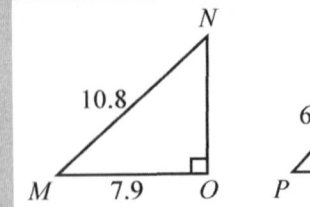

1. Which angle is the **smallest**?

    A. ∠M

    B. ∠N

    C. ∠P

    D. ∠Q

Numerical Response

Use the following information to answer the next question.

A surveyor wants to calculate the width of a river. He locates a point *A*, and then moves his transit 75 m along the shore to point *B*. From there, he determines that the angle to point *C* on the other side of the river is 37°.

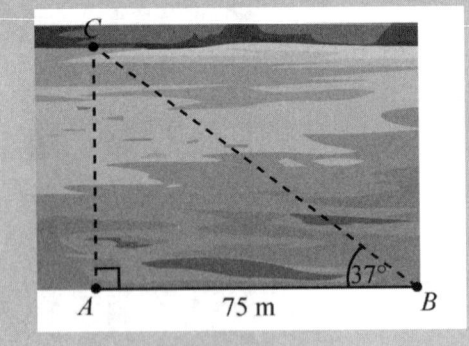

2. The width of the river, line *AC*, to the nearest tenth of a metre, is ____ m.

Use the following information to answer the next multipart question.

3. A sheet metal worker designs a piece of metal to be used for a special 3-D structure. Some of the dimensions are illustrated in the given diagram.

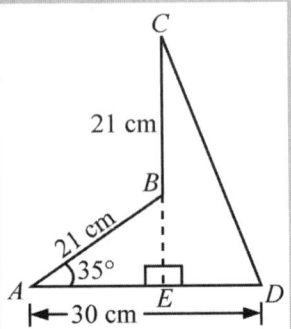

To complete the design, the worker needs to find the measure of angle *D*.

Part A

Open Response

To find the measure of ∠*D*, the measures of two sides of △*CDE* need to be determined. What two sides of △*CDE* could be determined if all the dimensions of △*ABE* were given? Explain your answer.

Part B

Open Response

Determine the lengths of the two sides of △*CDE*, to the nearest tenth of a metre.

Part C

Open Response

Find the measure of angle D, to the nearest degree.

Use the following information to answer the next question.

Jeremy makes the following measurements as a surveyor so he can determine the distance, x, between the two caves.

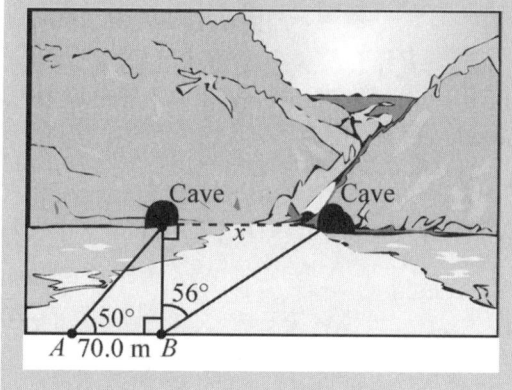

4. The distance, x, to the nearest tenth metre, between the two caves is

   A. 56.3 m   **B.** 69.2 m

   C. 100.6 m   **D.** 123.7 m

Use the following information to answer the next question.

Triangle ABC has sides measuring 17 m, 23 m, and 24 m.

5. What is the measure of the angle opposite to the side with a length of 24 m, to the nearest degree?

   A. 35°   **B.** 42°   **C.** 66°   **D.** 72°

Open Response

Use the following information to answer the next question.

The given triangle is $\triangle ABC$ with its labelled sides and angles.

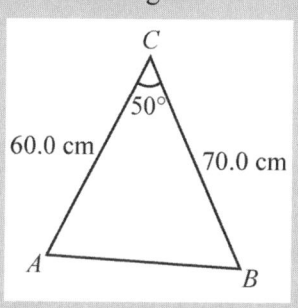

6. Shelby suggested that she could find the length of side AB using the sine law. Is she correct? Explain why or why not. Then find the perimeter of the triangle, to the nearest tenth.

CHALLENGER QUESTION

Use the following information to answer the next question.

Derek is asked to determine the length of side c in the labelled diagram below.

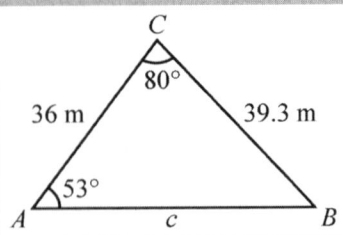

7. Which of the following equations could Derek **not** use to solve for the length of side c?

A. $\dfrac{c}{\sin 80°} = \dfrac{39.3}{\sin 53°}$

B. $\dfrac{c}{\sin 80°} = \dfrac{36}{\sin 47°}$

C. $c^2 = 36^2 + 39.3^2 - 2(36)(39.3)(\cos 80°)$

D. $c^2 = 36^2 + 39.3^2 - 2(36)(39.3)(\cos 47°)$

Use the following information to answer the next question.

Using its radar, ship A receives signals indicating that two other ships B and C are 4.8 km and 6.2 km away from ship A, respectively. The angle between the two radar signals is 74°.

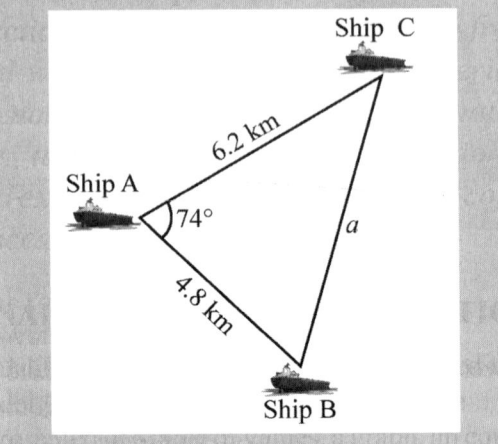

8. The distance, a, between ships B and C, to the nearest tenth, is

A. 0.5 km   **B.** 5.0 km

C. 6.7 km   **D.** 7.1 km

Use the following information to answer the next multipart question.

9. At a home in Ontario, the water usage over a 12-month time period is shown in the given table.

Month	Usage (m^3)
Jan	12
Feb	11.5
Mar	10.5
Apr	10.2
May	11.2
Jun	12.4
Jul	13.2
Aug	13.0
Sep	12.4
Oct	11.2
Nov	9.8
Dec	11.4

Part A

Open Response

Explain how this data represents a periodic function, and state the range of the function.

Part B

Which of the following statements about the periodic function of the water usage over a 12-month time period is **incorrect**?
- The expected amount of water used for the following August would be ____ m^3.
- The average amount of water usage throughout the year is about ____ m^3.
- The amplitude of the function is about ____ m^3.

A. The expected amount of water used for the following August would be 13.0 m^3.

B. The average amount of water usage throughout the year is about 11.5 m^3.

C. The amplitude of the function is about 1.7 m^3.

D. The period of the function is 12 months.

Numerical Response

10. Blake has been monitoring the amount of electricity he has been using at his business and has determined that the hourly usage during any business day can be modelled by a periodic function with a period of 24 hours, amplitude of 14 kW, and a maximum hourly usage of 31 kW. The minimum hourly usage is ____ kW.

CHALLENGER QUESTION

Use the following information to answer the next question.

The following table gives the amount of daylight in a particular city in Ontario, at various dates of 2007, including those with most and least hours of daylight. The year 2007 was not a leap year.

Date	Amount of Daylight
February 21	10 h 34 min
April 21	14 h 00 min
June 21	16 h 07 min
August 21	14 h 02 min
October 21	10 h 32 min
December 21	8 h 18 min

11. Based on the information in the table, which of the following times would **most likely** be the number of hours of daylight on September 1, 2008?

    A. 13 h 50 min   B. 13 h 25 min

    C. 13 h 0 min   D. 12 h 45 min

12. If $\sin \theta = 0.5$ and $0° \leq \theta \leq 360°$, then the number of possible values for θ is

    A. 1   B. 2   C. 4   D. 30

13. Point P is on both the unit circle and the terminal arm of an angle of $214°$ drawn in standard position. The y-coordinate of point P, to the nearest thousandth, is

    A. -0.829 B. -0.559

    C. 0.363 D. 0.932

14. The amplitude of $f(x) = \sin x$ is

    A. 0   B. $\dfrac{1}{2}$

    C. 1   D. 2

CHALLENGER QUESTION

Use the following information to answer the next question.

Four students examined the graph of $f(x) = \sin x$ and made the following observations.

Jeremy: The function increases between $-450°$ and $-270°$.

Emily: The minimum and maximum values occur every $180°$.

Derek: One of the minimum points of the graph occurs at an angle of $990°$.

Ralyn: An angle where the graph passes through its horizontal midline axis is at $-530°$

15. Which of the student's observations about the graph of $f(x) = \sin x$ is **incorrect**?

    A. Jeremy   B. Emily

    C. Derek   D. Ralyn

*Use the following information to
answer the next question.*

A go-cart travels around a circular track
with a radius of 40 m. A student used a
motion sensor to record the distances, d,
from the go-cart to a straight wall that runs
beside the track, over a period of t seconds
after the go-cart started moving. The given
diagram shows the track, the wall, and the
distance being recorded.

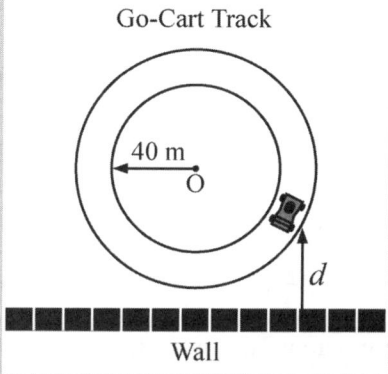

After collecting the data, the student
graphed this periodic motion as the
function $d = f(t)$.

16. If the radius of the track were increased to
50 m, and the go-cart were to travel at the
same speed as on the original track, then
what change to the student's graph of
$d = f(t)$, would produce the graph of the
go-cart's motion through this new course?

   A. The graph of $d = f(t)$ would have to
be stretched vertically.

   B. The graph of $d = f(t)$ would have to
be stretched horizontally.

   C. The graph of $d = f(t)$ would have to
be translated vertically.

   D. The graph of $d = f(t)$ would have to
be translated horizontally.

CHALLENGER QUESTION

17. Lisa is jumping at a consistent height on a
large trampoline. If a graph were drawn of
Lisa's height, h, above the ground, t
seconds after she starts jumping, then how
would the graph change if she were to
jump higher?

   A. It would stretch vertically only

   B. It would stretch horizontally only.

   C. It would stretch vertically and
horizontally.

   D. It would stretch vertically and
horizontally, and translate vertically.

*Use the following information to
answer the next question.*

The graph of $f(x) = \sin x$ is transformed
to the graph of $f(x) = \sin x - 7$.

18. Which of the following statements does
not describe the transformed graph?

   A. The graph has been vertically
translated down 7 units.

   B. The graph passes through the
point $(90°, -6)$.

   C. The graph has a minimum value
of -7.

   D. The graph has a maximum value
of -6.

Use the following information to answer the next question.

Tim used a computer program to obtain the following graph of a transformed sine function.

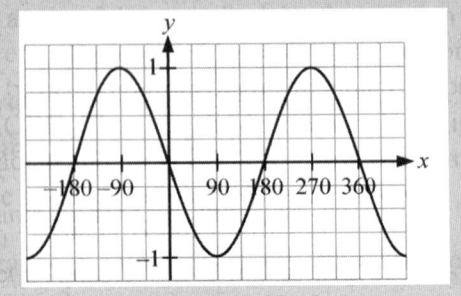

19. Tim realized that the equation describing the graph above, can be written in **two** of the forms of $f(x) = a\sin x$, $f(x) = \sin x + c$, or $f(x) = \sin(x - d)$. Write these two equations and explain the transformations to $f(x) = \sin x$ that would produce the resulting equations.

20. Which of the following procedures describes a correct method for sketching the graph of $f(x) = -\frac{1}{3}\sin x$?

   A. Compress the graph of $f(x) = \sin x$ by a factor of $\frac{1}{3}$ about the x-axis and reflect the graph about the x-axis.

   B. Stretch the graph of $f(x) = \sin x$ by a factor of 3 about the x-axis and reflect the graph about the x-axis.

   C. Compress the graph of $f(x) = \sin x$ by a factor of $\frac{1}{3}$ about the x-axis and reflect the graph about the y-axis.

   D. Stretch the graph of $f(x) = \sin x$ by a factor of 3 about the x-axis and reflect the graph about the y-axis.

21. The domain and range of the function $f(x) = -12\sin x$, $0° \le x \le 720°$ are, respectively,

   A. $-360° \le x \le 360°$ and $f(x) \ge -12$

   B. $0° \le x \le 720°$ and $13 \le f(x) \le -13$

   C. $-360° \le x \le 360°$ and $f(x) \ge -13$

   D. $0° \le x \le 720°$ and $-12 \le f(x) \le 12$

Use the following information to answer the next question.

Michelle used the E-STAT website to search for statistical data that modelled a sine function. She found an example, and recorded the data as a graph.

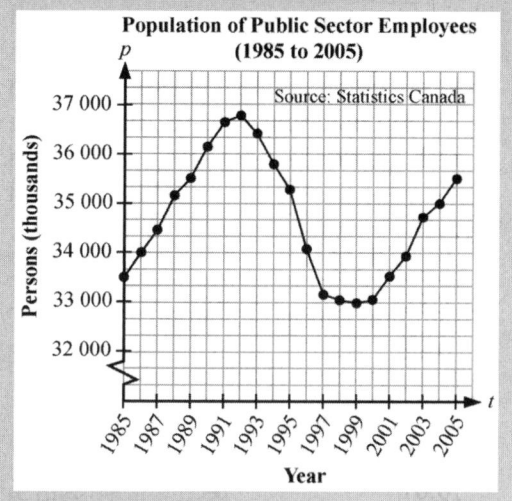

Population of Public Sector Employees (1985 to 2005)

Source: Statistics Canada

22. According to the approximate sinusoidal graph, the period, or time for one cycle, is about

A. 21 years   **B.** 16 years

C. 10 years   **D.** 7 years

23. Which of the following graphs **best** represents a periodic function?

A.

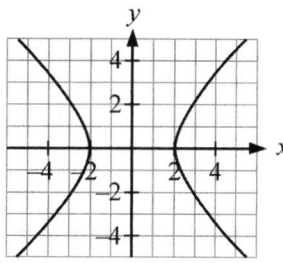

B.

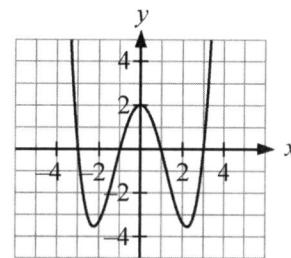

C.

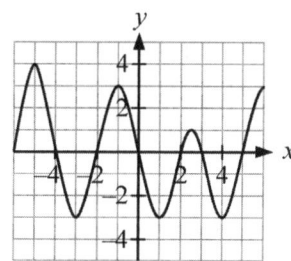

D.

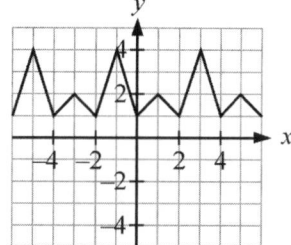

Use the following information to answer the next multipart question.

24. A stone is stuck in the tread of the back tire of a bicycle wheel. The height, h, in centimetres, of the stone relative to the ground with respect to the angle, x, in degrees that the tire rotates through is represented by the given graph.

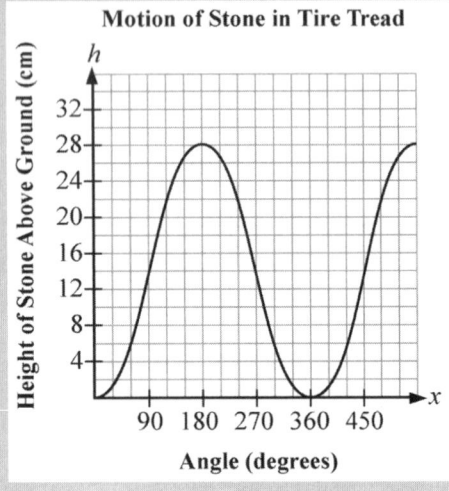

Motion of Stone in Tire Tread

Part A

Numerical Response

The sine equation that describes the graph of the height, h, of the stone, in terms of the angle of rotation, x is
$h = 14\sin(x - c) + 14$. The value of c, to the nearest whole degree, is ____°.

Part B

If the rock dislodged from the tire tread after making $3\frac{1}{3}$ revolutions, what is the height, h, that it fell out of the tire?

A. 7 cm   **B.** 14 cm

C. 21 cm   **D.** 28 cm

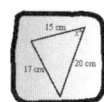

SOLUTIONS

1. D	**5. D**	**10.** 3	**16.** A	**22.** B
2. 56.5	**6.** OR	**11.** B	**17.** D	**23.** D
3. Part A- **OR**	**7.** D	**12.** B	**18.** C	**24.** Part A- **90**
Part B- **OR**	**8.** C	**13.** B	**19.** OR	Part B- **C**
Part C- **OR**	**9.** Part A- **OR**	**14.** C	**20.** A	
4. D	Part B- **D**	**15.** D	**21.** D	

1. D

In $\triangle MNO$, use the cosine ratio to determine the value of $\angle M$.

$$\cos M = \frac{7.9}{10.8}$$
$$\angle M = \cos^{-1}\left(\frac{7.9}{10.8}\right)$$
$$\approx 43°$$

Since the sum of the measures of all angles in a triangle is 180°,
$$\angle N = 180° - 90° - \angle M$$
$$= 180° - 90° - 43°$$
$$= 47°$$

In $\triangle PQR$, use the sine ratio to determine the value of $\angle P$
$$\sin P = \frac{4.9}{6.6}$$
$$\angle P = \sin^{-1}\left(\frac{4.9}{6.6}\right)$$
$$\approx 48°$$
$$\angle Q = 180° - 90° - \angle P$$
$$= 180° - 90° - 48°$$
$$= 42°$$

Therefore, $\angle Q = 42°$ is the smallest angle in the two triangles.

2. 56.5

Draw a labelled diagram of the situation, letting x = the distance across the river from A to C.

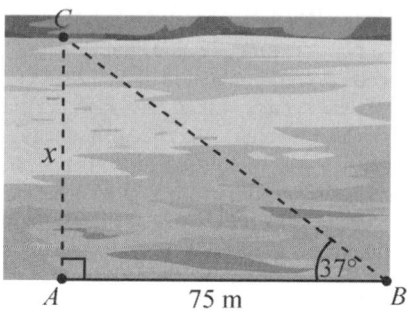

The ratio that includes the opposite and adjacent sides is the tangent ratio.

$$\tan 37° = \frac{x}{75}$$

Multiply both sides by 75
$$75(\tan 37°) = x$$
$$75(0.753\,554\,0501) \approx x$$
$$56.5 \approx x$$
$$x \approx 56.5$$

The width of the river, to the nearest tenth of a metre, is 56.5 m.

3. Part A – Open Response

If the length of side AE of $\triangle ABE$ was known, you could find the missing length of DE of $\triangle CDE$ as follows:
$$DE = 30\text{ cm} - AE$$

If the length of side BE of $\triangle ABE$ was known, you could find the missing length of CE of $\triangle CDE$ as follows:
$$CE = 21\text{ cm} + BE$$

Part B – Open Response

To find the length of DE, find the length of AE in $\triangle ABE$.

$$\cos 35° = \frac{AE}{21}$$
$$21(\cos 35°) = AE$$
$$AE = 17.202\,192\,93$$

Therefore, the length of DE, to the nearest tenth of a metre, is $30 - 17.202\,192\,93 \approx 12.8$ cm.

To find the length of CE, find the length of BE in $\triangle ABE$.

$$\sin 35° = \frac{BE}{21}$$
$$21(\sin 35°) = BE$$
$$BE = 12.045\,105\,16$$

Therefore, the length of CE, to the nearest tenth of a metre, is $21 + 12.045\,105\,16 \approx 33.0$ cm.

Part C – Open Response

To find the measure of angle D use the tangent ratio.
$$\tan D = \frac{CE}{DE} = \frac{33.0}{12.8}$$
$$\angle D = \tan^{-1}\left(\frac{33.0}{12.8}\right)$$
$$\angle D = 68.799\,783\,34°$$

The measure of angle D, to the nearest degree, is 69°.

4. D

Draw and label a diagram that represents this situation. Let C_1 and C_2 be the points that represent the cave.

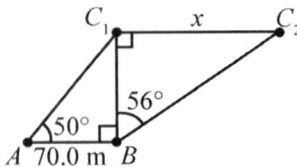

First, find the distance of BC_1.

$$\tan 50° = \frac{BC_1}{70.0}$$

$$70.0(\tan 50°) = BC_1$$

$$BC_1 = 83.422\ 751\ 48$$

Next, find the distance between the caves, x.

$$\tan 56° = \frac{x}{83.422\ 751\ 48}$$

$$83.422\ 751\ 48(\tan 56°) = x$$

$$x \approx 123.7$$

The distance between the caves, to the nearest tenth metre, is 123.7 m.

5. D

Draw a labelled triangle representing this situation, where the angle opposite side 24 m is $\angle B$.

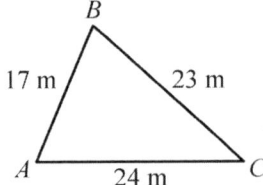

Since you have no known pair (a side with the corresponding opposite angle), use the cosine law rearranged to solve for the missing $\angle B$.

$$\cos B = \frac{a^2 + c^2 - b^2}{2ac}$$

$$= \frac{(23)^2 + (17)^2 - (24)^2}{2(23)(17)}$$

$$= 0.309\ 462\ 9156$$

$$\angle B = \cos^{-1}(0.309\ 462\ 9156)$$

$$= 71.973\ 133\ 72°$$

The measure of the angle opposite the side of a length of 24 m, to the nearest degree, is 72°.

6. Open Response

Shelby is wrong. She cannot use the sine law because she has no known pair (a side and its corresponding opposite angle). Therefore, she should use the cosine law to find the length of side AB, or side c.

$$c^2 = a^2 + b^2 - 2ab(\cos C)$$

$$= (70.0)^2 + (60.0)^2 - 2(70.0)(60.0)(\cos 50°)$$

$$= 3100.584\ 079$$

$$c = 55.682\ 888\ 56$$

The length of side AB, or side c, to the nearest tenth of a centimetre, is 55.7 cm. Therefore, the perimeter, P, of the triangle, to the nearest tenth of a centimetre, is $P = 55.7 + 60.0 + 70.0 = 185.7$ cm

7. D

The angle 47° is not located between sides $a = 39.3$ m and $b = 36$ m, so the equation $c^2 = 36^2 + 39.3^2 - 2(36)(39.3)(\cos 47°)$ could not be used to solve for side c. Therefore choice D is incorrect. The missing $\angle B$ can be found by remembering that the sum of the measures of all angles of a triangle is 180°.

$$\angle B = 180° - 53° - 80° = 47°$$

Since there is a known pair, namely $\angle A = 53°$ with its corresponding opposite side $a = 39.3$, you can use the following sine law ratios to solve for the length of side c.

$$\frac{c}{\sin 80°} = \frac{39.3}{\sin 53°} \text{ and } \frac{c}{\sin 80°} = \frac{36}{\sin 47°}$$

You can also use the cosine law, since you have two sides, $a = 39.3$ m and $b = 36$ m, with the included angle of $\angle C = 80°$. The setup would be:

$$c^2 = a^2 + b^2 - 2ab(\cos C)$$

$$= 39.3^2 + 36^2 - 2(39.3)(36)(\cos 80°) \text{ or}$$

$$= 36^2 + 39.3^2 - 2(36)(39.3)(\cos 80°)$$

8. C

Since there is no known pair given (a known side with its corresponding opposite angle), use the cosine law to solve for a.

$$a^2 = b^2 + c^2 - 2bc(\cos A)$$

$$= (6.2)^2 + (4.8)^2 - 2(6.2)(4.8)(\cos 74°)$$

$$= 45.074\ 064\ 58$$

$$a = 6.713\ 722\ 111$$

$$\approx 6.7$$

The distance between ships B and C, to the nearest tenth of a kilometre, is 6.7 km.

9. Part A – Open Response

This is a periodic function since the y-values go through a repeated cycle throughout the given x-intervals. This is evident because the y-value starts high (12) in January, drops to a low y-value (10.2) in April, and then goes back up to a high y-value (13.2) in July. This pattern then repeats itself from July to December. Therefore, the data cycles through its y-values about every 6 to 7 months. The range of the function is defined as

minimum $\leq y \leq$ maximum. The minimum is 9.8 m^3 and the maximum is 13.2 m^3. Thus, the range is $9.8 \text{ m}^3 \leq y \leq 13.2 \text{ m}^3$.

Part B –D

As mentioned in the previous question, the data cycles through its y-values about 6 to 7 months, not 12. Therefore, choice D is incorrect.

Since the given data represents a periodic function, and the period is about 6 months, the expected water usage for the following August would be the same as it was for the August in the given data (6 months + 6 months). Therefore, the expected water usage for the next August would be 13.0 m^3.

The average amount of water usage throughout the year is defined by the equation of the midline axis, $y = d$.

$$y = d = \frac{\text{maximum} + \text{minimum}}{2}$$
$$= \frac{13.2 + 9.8}{2}$$
$$= 11.5$$

The average amount of water usage is about 11.5 m^3.

To find the amplitude, a, you need to know the minimum and maximum y-values, which are 9.8 m^3 and 13.2 m^3, respectively.

Thus, $a = \dfrac{\text{maximum} - \text{minimum}}{2} = \dfrac{13.2 - 9.8}{2} = 1.7$

The amplitude is about 1.7 m^3.

10. 3

The amplitude, a, is determined by knowing the maximum and minimum values of usage. Let x = minimum usage. Then substitute the amplitude $a = 14$ kW and maximum = 31 kW into the following equation, to solve for x.

$$a = \frac{\text{maximum} - \text{minimum}}{2}$$
$$14 = \frac{31 - x}{2}$$
$$28 = 31 - x$$
$$-3 = -x$$
$$x = 3$$

The minimum hourly usage is 3 kW.

11. B

Since the amount of daylight reduces by 3 hours and 30 minutes from August 21 to October 21, it would be expected that the daylight would reduce by a portion of this amount by September 1. The difference between August 21 to October 31 is 61 days, and the difference between August 21 to September 1 is 11 days. Thus, the portion of daylight lost is likely to be about $\dfrac{11}{61}$ or $\dfrac{1}{6}$. One sixth of 3 hours and 30 minutes is 35 minutes. Subtracting 35 minutes from the August 21 daylight amount of 14 h 02 minutes gives 13 h 27 minutes. The closest value to this is 13 h 25 min.

12. B

Since the domain for the graph is from 0° and 360°, the number of possible angles, θ, with a sine ratio of 0.5 is 2. The two angles are 30° and 150°, since sin 30° = 0.5 and sin 150° = 0.5.

13. B

The y-coordinate of point P is equal to the sine ratio for 214°. According to your graphing calculator, $\sin 214° \approx -0.559$. Thus, the y-coordinate of point P is −0.559, to the nearest thousandth.

14. C

The maximum value of the function is 1, and the minimum value is −1. The amplitude, a, is found as follows:

$$a = \frac{\text{maximum} - \text{minimum}}{2} = \frac{1 - (-1)}{2} = 1.$$

15. D

Ralyn's observation is incorrect. The angles occurring on the horizontal midline axis, $y = d = 0$, are the x-intercepts. The x-intercepts occur when $x = 180n°$, $n \in I$. Thus, solve for "n" when $x = -530°$.

$$-530° = 180n°$$
$$\frac{-530°}{180°} = n$$
$$n = -2.9444…$$

Since n does not equal an integer, −530° does not lie on the horizontal midline axis of the graph of $f(x) = \sin x$.

Jeremy's observation is correct. The sine function increases for intervals $(-90 + 360n)° < x < (90 + 360n)°$, $n \in I$, and when $n = -1$, you get $(-90 - 360)° < x < (90 - 360)°$, or $-450° < x < -270°$.

Emily's observation is correct. The period is 360° for $f(x) = \sin x$, which indicates the interval between successive maximum values or successive minimum values. Thus, the interval between minimum and maximum values would be $\dfrac{360°}{2} = 180°$.

Derek's observation is correct. Minimum points occur at angles of −90°, 270°, 630°, … or $(-90 + n360)°$, $n \in I$. When $n = 3$, $\theta = -90 + 3(360)° = 990°$. Thus, there is a minimum point at 990°.

16. A

To graph the motion of the go-cart through the increased track size, you would have to stretch the graph of $d = f(t)$ vertically, with respect to the horizontal midline axis (which includes the point representing the centre of the circular track). The amplitude of the new graph would be 10 m more than the amplitude of the graph of $d = f(t)$, to reflect the vertical stretch.

17. D

The graph would stretch vertically about the t-axis because Lisa is jumping higher. The graph would also stretch horizontally, because the time for each jump would be longer. In other words, the period to complete one jump would be longer. There would also be a vertical translation, creating a horizontal midline axis that would be further up from the t-axis. This would be determined by the amount of rebound from the trampoline.

18. C

The minimum value of $f(x) = \sin x - 7$ is $-7 - 1 = -8$, not -7. Therefore choice C is incorrect.
When $f(x) = \sin x$ is transformed to $f(x) = \sin x - 7$, the new graph is the result of being vertically translated down 7 units. When $90°$ is substituted for x in $f(x) = \sin x - 7$, you get $f(90°) = \sin (90°) - 7 = 1 - 7 = -6$. Therefore, the point $(90°, -6)$ exists on transformed graph. The maximum value of $f(x) = \sin x - 7$ is $-7 + 1 = -6$.

19. Open Response

One of the equations can be written in the form $f(x) = -\sin x$, since the graph is a reflection of $f(x) = \sin x$ in the x-axis. The other equation that could be written is in the form $f(x) = \sin (x + 180°)$ or $f(x) = \sin (x - 180°)$, since they could be obtained by horizontally translating the graph of $f(x) = \sin x$ to the left $180°$, or to the right $180°$.

20. A

The value $\frac{1}{3}$ in the function $f(x) = -\frac{1}{3}\sin x$ is a compression factor of $\frac{1}{3}$ about the x-axis and the negative sign causes a reflection about the x-axis.

21. D

The domain is restricted to angles between $0°$ to $720°$ inclusive. Therefore, the domain is $0° \leq x \leq 720°$. The graph of $f(x) = -12\sin x$ is the graph of $f(x) = \sin x$ stretched by a factor of 12 about the x-axis, and reflected about the x-axis. Thus, the graph of the function has a minimum of -12 and a maximum of $+12$. Therefore, the range is $-12 \leq f(x) \leq 12$. The reflection about the x-axis does not affect the range.

22. B

If you select a point, like the one for 1986, and follow the curve for one cycle, this point reoccurs in 2002, which makes the period for one cycle $2002 - 1986 = 16$ years. If you select a point, like the one for 1989 and follow the curve for one cycle, this point reoccurs in the year 2005, which makes the period for one cycle $2005 - 1989 = 16$ years. Therefore, the period of one cycle of the graph is about 16 years.

23. D

To be a periodic function, the vertical and horizontal changes must be consistent throughout the domain of the graph. In graph D, each tall V is 3 units high and 2 units wide, and each neighbouring small v is 1 unit high and 2 units wide. Each cycle of the graph (every 4 horizontal units) is the same. Therefore, graph D represents a periodic function.

24. Part A – 90

In the transformed function $f(x) = a\sin (x - d) + c$, the value d describes the horizontal translation that the graph of $f(x) = \sin x$ has undergone. This translation is observed with respect to the horizontal midline axis, which in this graph is at $d = h = 14$. The graph of $f(x) = \sin x$ would be moved right $90°$, namely to $f(x) = \sin (x - 90°)$, since that is how far the point is from the y-axis. Therefore, the value c, in $h = 14\sin (x - c) + 14$, is $90°$.

Part B –C

The period of the graph is $360°$. After 3 revolutions, the graph would rotate 3 full times, or $3 \times 360° = 1080°$. At that point the rock would be at a height of $h = 0$ cm. After that point, its $360°$ rotation would follow the same pattern as the first cycle (i.e., go up to the maximum of 28 m and then came down to its minimum height of 0 m).

The angle that the tire passes through in $\frac{1}{3}$ of a cycle is

$\frac{1}{3} \times 360° = 120°$. The height of the rock is $h = 21$ cm when $x = 120°$ on the graph. Therefore, since this pattern is the same after each revolution, the height of the rock after $3\frac{1}{3}$ revolutions (which is $120°$ more than $1080°$) would be $h = 21$ cm.

KEY Strategies for Success on Tests

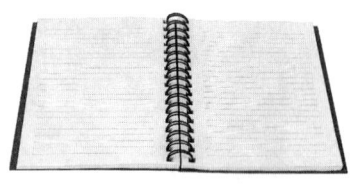

TEST PREPARATION AND TEST-TAKING SKILLS

Things to Consider When Taking a Test

- It is normal to feel anxious before you write a test. You can manage this anxiety by:
    - o thinking positive thoughts. Visual imagery is a helpful technique to try.
    - o making a conscious effort to relax by taking several slow, controlled, deep breaths. Concentrate on the air going in and out of your body.
- Before you begin the test, ask questions if you are unsure of anything.
- Jot down key words or phrases from any oral directions.
- Look over the entire test to assess the number and kinds of questions on the test.
- Read each question closely and reread if necessary.
- Pay close attention to key vocabulary words. Sometimes these are bolded or italicized, and they are usually important words in the question.
- Mark your answers on your answer sheet carefully. If you wish to change an answer, erase the mark completely and then ensure your final answer is darker than the one you have erased.
- On the test booklet, use highlighting to note directions, key words, and vocabulary that you find confusing or that are important to answering the question.
- Double-check to make sure you have answered everything before handing in your test.

When taking tests, the easy words are often overlooked. Failure to pay close attention to these words can result in an incorrect answer. One way to avoid this is to be aware of these words and to underline, circle, or highlight these words while you are taking the test.

Even though some words are easy to understand, they can change the meaning of the entire question, so it is important that you pay attention to them. Here are some examples.

all	always	most likely	probably	best	not
difference	usually	except	most	unlikely	likely

Example

1. Which of the following equations is **not** correct?
    A. $3 + 2 = 5$
    B. $4 - 3 = 1$
    C. $5 \times 4 = 15$
    D. $6 \times 3 = 18$

Helpful Strategies for Answering Multiple-Choice Questions

A multiple-choice question provides some information for you to consider and then asks you to select a response from four choices. Each question has one correct answer. The other answers are distractors, which are incorrect.

Below are some strategies to help you when answering multiple-choice questions.

- Quickly skim through the entire test. Find out how many questions there are and plan your time accordingly.

- Read and reread questions carefully. Underline key words and try to think of an answer before looking at the choices.

- If there is a graphic, look at the graphic, read the question, and go back to the graphic. Then, you may want to underline the important information from the question.

- Carefully read the choices. Read the question first and then each answer that goes with it.

- When choosing an answer, try to eliminate those choices that are clearly wrong or do not make sense.

- Some questions may ask you to select the best answer. These questions will always include words like **best**, **most appropriate**, or **most likely**. All of the answers will be correct to some degree, but one of the choices will be better than the others in some way. Carefully read all four choices before choosing the answer you think is the best.

- If you do not know the answer or if the question does not make sense to you, it is better to guess than to leave it blank.

- Do not spend too much time on any one question. Make a mark (*) beside a difficult question and come back to it. If you are leaving a question to come back to later, make sure you also leave the space on the answer sheet.

- Remember to go back to the difficult questions at the end of the test; sometimes clues are given throughout the test that will provide you with answers.

- Note any negative words like **no** or **not** and be sure your choice fits the question.

- Before changing an answer, *be sure* you have a very good reason to do so.

- Do not look for patterns on your answer sheet.

Helpful Strategies for Answering Open-Response Questions

A written response requires you to respond to a question or directive such as **explain**, **predict**, **list**, **describe**, **show your work**, **solve**, or **calculate**. In preparing for open-response tasks you may wish to:

- Read and reread the question carefully.

- Recognize and pay close attention to **directing words** such as **explain**, **show your work, and describe**.

- Underline key words and phrases that indicate what is required in your answer, such as explain, estimate, answer, calculate, or show your work.

- Write down rough, point-form notes regarding the information you want to include in your answer.

- Think about what you want to say and organize information and ideas in a coherent and concise manner within the time limit you have for the question.

- Be sure to answer every part of the question that is asked.

- Include as much information as you can when you are asked to explain your thinking.

- Include a picture or diagram if it will help to explain your thinking.

- Try to put your final answer to a problem in a complete sentence to be sure it is reasonable.

- Reread your response to ensure you have answered the question.

- **Think**: does your answer make sense

- **Listen**: does it sound right?

- Use appropriate subject vocabulary and terms in your response.

About Mathematics Tests

What You Need to Know about Mathematics Tests

To do well on a mathematics test, you need to understand and apply your knowledge of mathematical concepts. Reading skills can also make a difference in how well you perform. Reading skills can help you follow instructions and find key words, as well as read graphs, diagrams, and tables. They can also help you solve mathematics problems.

Mathematics tests usually have two types of questions: questions that ask for understanding of mathematics ideas and questions that test how well you can solve mathematics problems.

How You Can Prepare for the Mathematics Test

Below are some strategies that are particular to preparing for and writing mathematics tests.

- Know how to use your calculator and, if it is allowed, use your own for the test.

- Note-taking is a good way to review and study important information from your class notes and textbook.

- Sketch a picture of the problem, procedure, or term. Drawing is helpful for learning and remembering concepts.

- Check your answer to practice questions by working backward to the beginning. You can find the beginning by going step-by-step in reverse order.

- When answering questions with graphics (pictures, diagrams, tables, or graphs), read the test question carefully.

    o   Read the title of the graphic and any key words.

    o   Read the test question carefully to figure out what information you need to find in the graphic.

    o   Go back to the graphic to find the information you need.

- Decide which operation is needed.

- Always pay close attention when pressing the keys on your calculator. Repeat the procedure a second time to be sure you pressed the correct keys.

TEST PREPARATION COUNTDOWN

There is little doubt that if you develop a plan for studying and test preparation, you *will* perform well on tests.

Below is a general plan to follow seven days before you write a test.

Countdown: 7 Days before the Test

1. Use "Finding Out About the Test" to help you make your own personal test preparation plan.

2. Review the following information:
   - areas to be included on the test
   - types of test items
   - general and specific test tips

3. Start preparing for the test at least 7 days before the test. Develop your test preparation plan and set time aside to prepare and study.

Countdown: 6, 5, 4, 3, 2 Days before the Test

1. Review old homework assignments, quizzes, and tests.

2. Rework problems on quizzes and tests to make sure you still know how to solve them.

3. Correct any errors made on quizzes and tests.

4. Review key concepts, processes, formulas, and vocabulary.

5. Create practice test questions for yourself and then answer them. Work out many sample problems.

Countdown: The Night before the Test

1. The night before the test is for final preparation, which includes reviewing and gathering material needed for the test before going to bed.

2. Most important is getting a good night's rest and knowing you have done everything possible to do well on the test.

Test Day

1. Eat a healthy and nutritious breakfast.

2. Ensure you have all the necessary materials.

3. Think positive thoughts: "I can do this." "I am ready." "I know I can do well."

4. Arrive at your school early so you are not rushing, which can cause you anxiety and stress.

SUMMARY OF HOW TO BE SUCCESSFUL DURING THE TEST

The following are some strategies you may find useful for writing your test.

- Take two or three deep breaths to help you relax.

- Read the directions carefully and underline, circle, or highlight any important words.

- Survey the entire test to understand what you will need to do.

- Budget your time.

- Begin with an easy question or a question you know you can answer correctly rather than following the numerical question order of the test.

- If you cannot remember how to answer a question, try repeating the deep breathing and physical relaxation activities first. Then, move to visualization and positive self-talk to get you going.

- Write down anything you remember about the subject on the reverse side of your test paper. This activity sometimes helps you to remind yourself that you *do* know something and you *are* capable of writing the test.

- Look over your test when you have finished and double-check your answers to be sure you did not forget anything.

Practice Test

Table of Correlations

Specific Expectation		Practice Test
QF1.0	Solving Quadratic Equations	
QF1.1	*pose problems involving quadratic relations arising from real-world applications and represented by tables of values and graphs, and solve these and other such problems*	1
QF1.2	*represent situations using quadratic expressions in one variable, and expand and simplify quadratic expressions in one variable*	2
QF1.3	*factor quadratic expressions in one variable, including those for which $a \neq 1$, differences of squares, and perfect square trinomials, by selecting and applying an appropriate strategy*	3
QF1.6	*explore the algebraic development of the quadratic formula and apply the formula to solve quadratic equations, using technology*	4
QF1.8	*determine the real roots of a variety of quadratic equations and describe the advantages and disadvantages of each strategy (i.e., graphing; factoring; using the quadratic formula)*	5
QF2.0	Connecting Graphs and Equations of Quadratic Functions	
QF2.2	*substitute into and evaluate linear and quadratic functions represented using function notation, including functions arising from real-world applications*	6
QF2.3	*explain the meanings of the terms domain and range, through investigation using numeric, graphical, and algebraic representations of linear and quadratic functions, and describe the domain and range of a function appropriately*	7
QF2.4	*explain any restrictions on the domain and the range of a quadratic function in contexts arising from real-world applications*	8
QF2.5	*determine, through investigation using technology, the roles of a, h, and k in quadratic functions of the form $f(x) = a(x - h)^2 + k$, and describe these roles in terms of transformations on the graph of $f(x) = x^2$ (i.e., translations; reflections in the x-axis; vertical stretches and compressions to and from the x-axis)*	9
QF2.6	*sketch graphs of $g(x) = a(x - h)^2 + k$, by applying one or more transformations to the graph of $f(x) = x^2$*	10
QF2.9	*sketch graphs of quadratic functions in the factored form $f(x) = a(x - r)(x - s)$ by using the x-intercepts to determine the vertex*	11
QF2.10	*describe the information that can be obtained by inspecting the standard form $f(x) = ax^2 + bx + c$, the vertex form $f(x) = a(x - h)^2 + k$, and the factored form $f(x) = a(x - r)(x - s)$ of a quadratic function*	12
QF2.11	*sketch the graph of a quadratic function whose equation is given in the standard form $f(x) = ax^2 + bx + c$ by using a suitable strategy, and identify the key features of the graph*	13a, 13b, 13c
QF3.0	Solving Problems Involving Quadratic Functions	
EF1.0	Connecting Graphs and Equations of Exponential Functions	
EF1.2	*evaluate, with and without technology, numerical expressions containing integer and rational exponents and rational bases*	14
EF1.3	*graph, with and without technology, an exponential relation, given its equation in the form $a^x (a > 0, a \neq 1)$, define this relation as the function $f(x) = a^x$, and explain why it is a function*	15
EF1.4	*determine, through investigation, and describe key properties relating to domain and range, intercepts, increasing/decreasing intervals, and asymptotes for exponential functions represented in a variety of ways*	16a, 16b, 16c
EF1.6	*distinguish exponential functions from linear and quadratic functions by making comparisons in a variety of ways, within the same context when possible*	17

Specific Expectation		Practice Test
EF2.0	Solving Problems Involving Exponential Functions	
EF2.1	collect data that can be modelled as an exponential function, through investigation with and without technology, from primary sources, using a variety of tools, or from secondary sources	18
EF2.3	solve problems using given graphs or equations of exponential functions arising from a variety of real-world applications by interpreting the graphs or by substituting values for the exponent into the equations	19
EF3.0	Solving Financial Problems Involving Exponential Functions	
EF3.1	compare, using a table of values and graphs, the simple and compound interest earned for a given principal (i.e., investment) and a fixed interest rate over time	21
EF3.2	solve problems, using a scientific calculator, that involve the calculation of the amount, A (also referred to as future value, FV), and the principal, P (also referred to as present value, PV), using the compound interest formula in the form $A = P(1 + i)^n$ [or $FV = PV(1 + i)^n$]	20
EF3.3	determine, through investigation, that compound interest is an example of exponential growth	22
EF3.5	explain the meaning of the term annuity, through investigation of numeric and graphical representations using technology	23
EF3.6	determine, through investigation using technology, the effects of changing the conditions (i.e., the payments, the frequency of the payments, the interest rate, the compounding period) of ordinary simple annuities (i.e., annuities in which payments are made at the end of each period, and the compounding period and the payment period are the same)	24
EF3.7	solve problems, using technology, that involve the amount, the present value, and the regular payment of an ordinary simple annuity	25
TR1.0	Applying the Sine Law and the Cosine Law in Acute Triangles	
TR1.1	solve problems, including those that arise from real-world applications, by determining the measures of the sides and angles of right triangles using the primary trigonometric ratios	26
TR1.2	solve problems involving two right triangles in two dimensions	27
TR1.5	solve problems that require the use of the sine law or the cosine law in acute triangles, including problems arising from real-world applications	28a, 28b
TR2.0	Connecting Graphs and Equations of Sine Functions	
TR2.1	describe key properties of periodic functions arising from real-world applications, given a numeric or graphical representation	29a, 29b
TR2.3	make connections between the sine ratio and the sine function by graphing the relationship between angles from 0° to 360° and the corresponding sine ratios, with or without technology, defining this relationship as the function $f(x) = \sin x$, and explaining why the relationship is a function	30
TR2.4	sketch the graph of $f(x) = \sin x$ for angle measures expressed in degrees, and determine and describe its key properties (i.e., cycle, domain, range, intercepts, amplitude, period, maximum and minimum values, increasing/decreasing intervals)	31
TR2.5	make connections, through investigation with technology, between changes in a real-world situation that can be modelled using a periodic function and transformations of the corresponding graph	32
TR2.6	determine, through investigation using technology, the roles of the parameters a, c, and d in functions in the form $f(x) = a\sin x$, $f(x) = \sin x + c$, and $f(x) = \sin(x - d)$, and describe these roles in terms of transformations on the graph of $f(x) = \sin x$ with angles expressed in degrees	33
TR2.7	sketch graphs of $f(x) = a\sin x$, $f(x) = \sin x + c$, and $f(x) = \sin(x - d)$ by applying transformations to the graph of $f(x) = \sin x$, and state the domain and range of the transformed functions	34

Specific Expectation		Practice Test
TR3.0	Solving Problems Involving Sine Functions	
TR3.2	*identify periodic and sinusoidal functions, including those that arise from real-world applications involving periodic phenomena, given various representations (i.e., tables of values, graphs, equations), and explain any restrictions that the context places on the domain and range*	35
TR3.3	*pose problems based on applications involving a sine function, and solve these and other such problems by using a given graph or a graph generated with technology from a table of values or from its equation*	36

Practice Test

Numerical Response

1. The unit value of a particular stock, in Japanese yen (JPY), followed a quadratic pattern over a period of 20 consecutive days. Part of this trend is portrayed in the bar graph shown below.

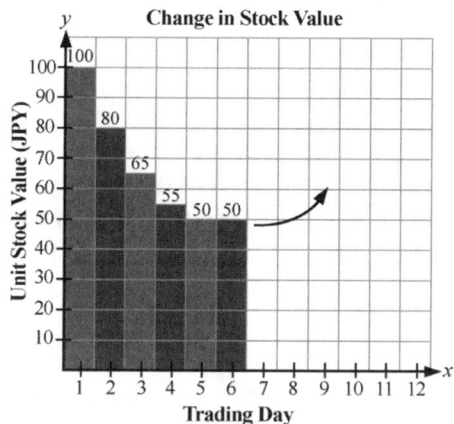

Based on the trend, the stock would recover to its original value of 100 JPY on day ____.

2. In order for the quadratic expression
$(3x+2)(2x-3) - 2(x-2)^2$
$+ Ax^2 + Bx + C$ to equal 0, the values of A, B, and C are
F. $A = 4$, $B = 3$, $C = 14$

G. $A = -4$, $B = -3$, $C = 14$

H. $A = 4$, $B = -3$, $C = 2$

J. $A = -4$, $B = 3$, $C = 2$

3. The expression $x + 3$ is **not** a factor of
A. $x^2 - 2x - 15$ **B.** $-2x^2 + 18$

C. $-3x^2 - 9x$ **D.** $x^2 + 7x + 15$

4. Dawn was solving the quadratic equation $6x^2 = 3x + 5$ by using the quadratic formula:
$$x = \frac{-b \pm \sqrt{b^2 - 4ac}}{2a}$$

After putting her values of a, b, and c into the formula and simplifying some terms she wrote the expression
$$x = \frac{m \pm \sqrt{n}}{12}.$$

The values of m and n in her expression were
F. $m = 3$, $n = 129$

G. $m = 3$, $n = 111$

H. $m = -3$, $n = 129$

J. $m = -3$, $n = 111$

Go On

5. The flight path of a flare fired from the top of a cliff to the ground can be described by the graph of the quadratic function $h(t) = -4.9t^2 + 29.4t + 352.8$, where $h(t)$ is the height, in metres, of the flare above the ground at a time, t, in seconds. Yosef wanted to use his graphing calculator to find the time, in seconds, when the flare hit the ground at $h(t) = 0$, namely the t-intercept.

The window Yosef used to display the whole flight of the flare to the ground ($h(t) = 0$) was __i__, and the t-intercept was __ii__.

Which of the following rows correctly completes this statement?

A.

i	ii
x:$[-10, 10, 1]$ y:$[-10, 10, 1]$	6.0 seconds

B.

i	ii
x:$[-10, 20, 1]$ y:$[-10, 500, 1]$	6.0 seconds

C.

i	ii
x:$[-10, 10, 1]$ y:$[-10, 500, 1]$	12.0 seconds

D.

i	ii
x:$[-10, 20, 1]$ y:$[-10, 500, 1]$	12.0 seconds

Numerical Response

6. For the function $f(x) = 5x^2 - 6x + 25$, the sum of $f(-4)$ and $f(1)$ is ____.

7. What values of the parameters a and b in a quadratic function written as $y = ax^2 + b$ produce a range of $y \leq 0$?
   A. $a > 0$, $b = 0$ B. $a > 0$, $b \in \mathbb{R}$
   C. $a < 0$, $b = 0$ D. $a < 0$, $b \in \mathbb{R}$

Numerical Response

8. The path of a seal jumping up out of water can be represented by the quadratic function $h = -x^2 + 10x - 21$, where h is the height of the seal while in the air above the water and x is the horizontal distance from the edge of the tank, in metres.

The domain restrictions for the flight of the seal while in the air can be found by setting $h = 0$ to get the equation $0 = -x^2 + 10x - 21$. When this equation is solved, the lower limit of the domain is $x = 3$ m, and the upper limit is $x = $ ____ m.

9. The graph of $f(x) = x^2$ is transformed so the graph of the new transformed function $g(x) = a(x - h)^2 + k$ has a vertex of $(1, -4)$ and a positive y-intercept. Which of the following observations is true about the transformations the graph of $f(x) = x^2$ underwent?
   A. It was stretched vertically by a factor of a about the x-axis, translated right 1 unit, and down 4 units.
   B. It was compressed vertically by a factor of $\frac{1}{a}$ about the x-axis, translated right 1 unit, and down 4 units.
   C. It was stretched vertically by a factor of a about the x-axis, translated left 1 unit, and down 4 units.
   D. It was compressed vertically by a factor of $\frac{1}{a}$ about the x-axis, translated left 1 unit, and down 4 units.

10. Which of the following graphs is an accurate sketch of the transformed function $h(x) = \frac{2}{3}(x+4)^2 + 1$?

F.

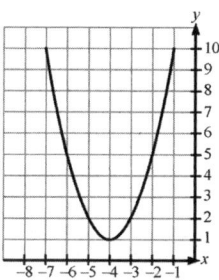

G.

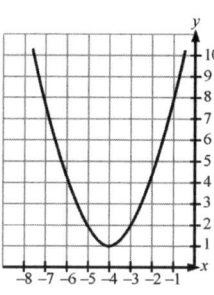

H.

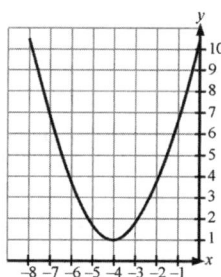

J.

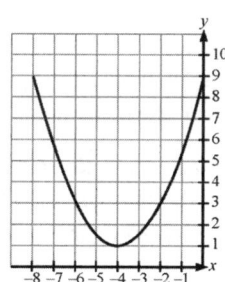

11. For the first question on a test, Samantha knew that the vertex was (3, 8) and that the x-intercepts were 8 units apart. Which of the following functions correctly represents her observations?

A. $f(x) = -\frac{1}{2}(x-7)(x+1)$

B. $f(x) = -\frac{1}{2}(x-1)(x+7)$

C. $f(x) = -\frac{1}{2}(x-4)(x+4)$

D. $f(x) = -\frac{1}{2}(x-0)(x+8)$

12. Michaela wrote a quadratic function in vertex form, as given below.

$$f(x) = 4(x-3)^2 + 8$$

She made the following observations about the features of the graph of this function.

I.   The graph opens upward.

II. The equation of the axis of symmetry is $x = 3$.

III. There are no x-intercepts.

IV. A point on the graph is (3, 8).

How many of her observations could be made based on inspection only?

F. only 1   **G.** 2

H. 3   **J.** all 4

Go On

13. A quadratic function is given as

$$g(x) = -\frac{1}{2}x^2 + 2x + 1.$$

Part A

| Open Response |

Use an appropriate algebraic method to find the vertex of this function.

Part B

| Open Response |

Describe how you would find the x-intercepts.

Part C

| Open Response |

Determine the x-interval where the graph of this function is decreasing. Give reasons for your answer.

Numerical Response

14. To the nearest hundredth, the value of

$(-4.5)^{\frac{4}{3}}$ is ___.

15. Which of the following statements correctly explains why $y = (15)^x$ can be written as the function $f(x) = (15)^x$?

A. When the line $y = x$ is drawn through any place on the graph, it passes through a single point.

B. When the line $y = -x$ is drawn through any place on the graph, it passes through a single point.

C. When the line $x = a$, $x \in \mathbb{R}$ is drawn through any place on the graph, it passes through a single point.

D. When the line $y = a$, $x \in \mathbb{R}$ is drawn through any place on the graph, it passes through a single point.

16. Part A

| Open Response |

Draw a sketch of the graph of
$y = \left(\dfrac{1}{2}\right)^x$ on the grid given below,

passing through the points
with x-values of −3, −2, −1, 0, 1, 2,
and 3.

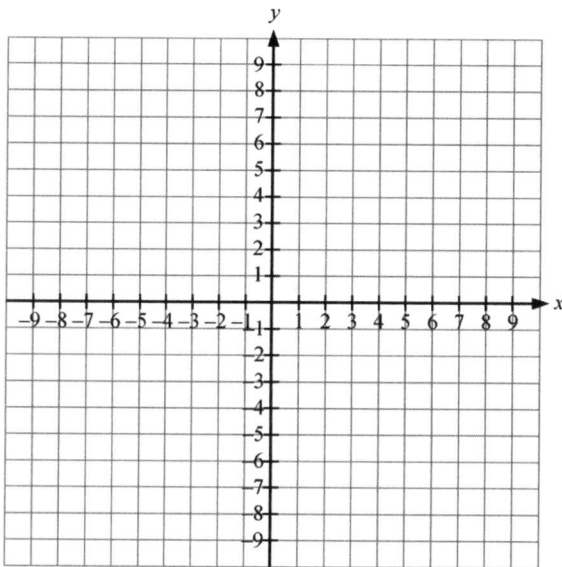

Part B

| Open Response |

State the following features of the
graph:

Domain: ____ y-intercept: ____

Range: ____ x-intercept: ____

Asymptote: ____

Part C

| Open Response |

How is the graph of $y = \left(\dfrac{1}{2}\right)^x$ different

from the graph of $y = \left(\dfrac{2}{3}\right)^x$? Explain.

17. Which of the following tables of values
does **not** represent an exponential
function?

A.
x	1	2	3	4	5
y	2	8	32	128	512

B.
x	1	2	3	4	5
y	729	486	324	216	144

C.
x	1	2	3	4	5
y	0.8	1.2	1.8	2.7	4.05

D.
x	1	2	3	4	5
y	0.5	2.0	4.5	8.0	12.5

Go On

18. Jennifer knew that the population of humans grows exponentially.
She found population figures for the Hawaiian county of Maui from the Internet, some of which are recorded in the given table.

To graph the data, she let 1980 represent a time of 0 years.

Year	Population
1980	70 991
1984	79 385
1987	80 877
1990	100 504
1993	106 280
1996	117 013
2000	128 241
2004	138 347

Including the curve of best fit, which of the following graphs correctly represents the given data?

F.

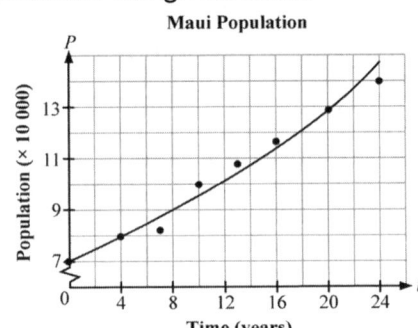

G.

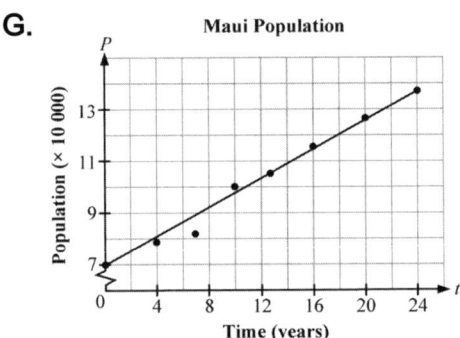

H.

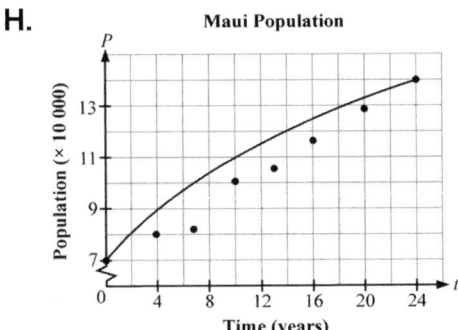

J.

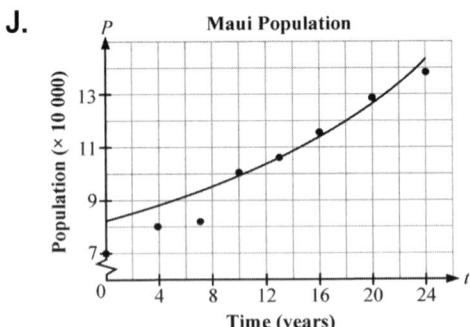

19. A diamond ring was worth $12 000 and increased in value by 15% per year. Jasmine wrote the corresponding exponential equation as:

$V = 12\ 000(a)^t$, where V is the value of the ring after t years.

The value of a in Jasmine's equation and the value, V, of the ring after 40 months, are

A. $a = 1.15$, $V = \$20\ 988$

B. $a = 1.50$, $V = \$46\ 361$

C. $a = 1.15$, $V = \$19\ 121$

D. $a = 1.50$, $V = \$60\ 750$

Numerical Response

20. The principal, P, required to accumulate a final amount of $6958 after 7 years compounded semi-annually at 6% per annum, to the nearest dollar, is $_____.

21. Achmed wanted to compare the growth of the following two interest options over 4 years.
Simple Interest: $2000 at 9% per annum
Compound Interest: $2000 at 8% per annum compounded annually.

To compare these two options, he calculated the annual interest, I, and the total amount, A, in the partially completed tables shown below.

Simple Interest (9%)

Year	0	1	2	3	4
I	0	180	180	180	p
A	2000	2180	2360	2540	q

Compound Interest (8%)

Year	0	1	2	3	4
I	0	160	172.80	186.62	r
A	2000	2160	2332.80	2519.42	s

If the values for p, q, r and s were calculated correctly then the relationship between these values would be.

A. $r > p$ and $q = s$

B. $r < p$ and $q > s$

C. $r > p$ and $q < s$

D. $r < p$ and $q < s$

Go On

Math 11 Functions and Applications

22. Hamid recorded the growth of a $6000 investment in an RRSP account over a $2\frac{1}{2}$ year period where the annual interest rate was compounded semi-annually.

Year	Total Amount
0	$6000.00
0.5	$6210.00
1.0	$6427.35
1.5	$6652.31
2.0	$6885.14
2.5	$7126.12

If x represents the number of compounding periods, then the correct exponential function representing the growth of the $6000 investment is

F. $f(x) = 6000(1.035)^x$

G. $f(x) = 6000(1.070)^x$

H. $f(x) = 6000(1.305)^x$

J. $f(x) = 6000(0.035)^x$

23. Emily deposited $300 at the end of each 6 month period into an annuity that paid interest compounded semi-annually. The given timeline shows the growth of the annuity over time.

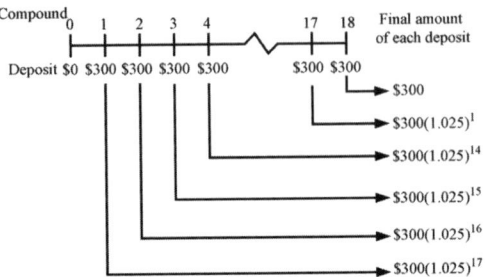

According to Emily's timeline, the annual interest rate, I, and the total number of years, t, of the annuity are

A. $I = 2.5\%$, $t = 9$ years

B. $I = 5.0\%$, $t = 9$ years

C. $I = 5.0\%$, $t = 18$ months

D. $I = 2.5\%$, $t = 18$ months

24. Robbie realized that if he made regular deposits of $3901 at the end of every year into an RRSP account where interest was 7.96%/a compounded annually, he would be a millionaire in 40 years. Jennifer suggested that instead, he should put $\frac{1}{12}$ of the $3901 at the end of every month into an RRSP account, where the 7.96 %/a interest was compounded monthly.

If he followed her advice, how much sooner would he become a millionaire?

F. 16 months   **G.** 14 months

H. 10 months   **J.** 8 months

Numerical Response

25. Both Maureen and Anita take out a $10 000 loan to buy some furniture. Both loans are 7.42%/a compounded monthly. Maureen makes regular monthly payments of $200 until her loan is paid off, and Anita also pays off her loan in $5\frac{1}{2}$ years by making regular monthly payments.

The difference in total interest between Maureen's and Anita's plans, to the nearest dollar, is $____.

26. From an altitude of 2000 metres, the pilot of a fighter jet spots a target on the ground at an angle of depression of 41°. Which of the following equations could be used to determine the distance, *x*, from the fighter jet to the target?

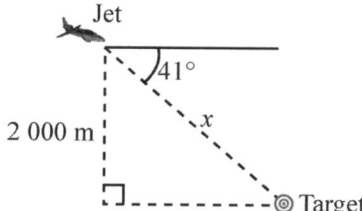

F. $\cos 41° = \dfrac{x}{2000}$

G. $\cos 41° = \dfrac{2000}{x}$

H. $\sin 41° = \dfrac{x}{2000}$

J. $\sin 41° = \dfrac{2000}{x}$

Numerical Response

27. Jordan is building a roof truss as shown in the following diagram.

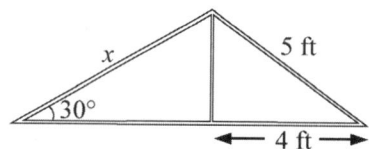

The length of the side labelled *x*, to the nearest foot, is ____ ft.

Go On

28. A golf course engineer designs a golf hole that curves slightly to the left, called a "dog-leg left". The designer places four reference points on his sketch of the hole. One reference point is the tee location (T), one is at each side of the dog leg (A and B), and the last point is where the hole is (H), as shown in the diagram below.

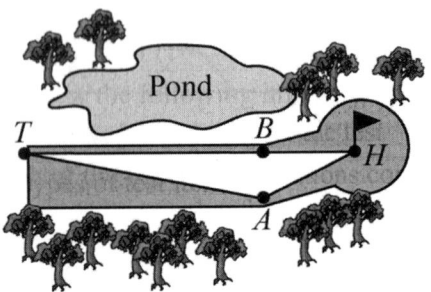

In the designer's sketch, distance $TA = 240.0$ m, distance $TB = 238.5$ m, $\angle ATB = 10°$, $\angle HBA = 89°$, and $\angle HAB = 63°$.

Part A

| Open Response |

Explain how you would find the distance between the two points A and B, to the nearest hundredth metre.

Part B

| Open Response |

Determine the total distance around the dog-leg from the tee to the hole ($T \rightarrow A \rightarrow H$), to the nearest tenth metre.

29. The graph below is a model of the average high temperature for the days of the year at a town in Northern Ontario. The numbers on the horizontal axis are the days of the year, with January 1 being day 1 and December 31 being day 365.

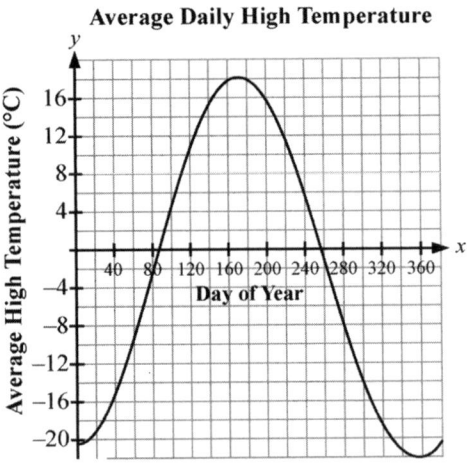

Part A

If the graph is used to estimate the average high temperature on March 1 of the next year, then that temperature is approximately

F. −14°C   **G.** −9°C

H. 0°C   **J.** 9°C

Part B

Open Response

Determine the equation of the horizontal midline axis for the graph of the periodic function, and explain its meaning in the context of this scenario.

30. The point $\left(300°, -\dfrac{\sqrt{3}}{2}\right)$ is on the graph of $f(x) = \sin x$.

If an angle of 300° is drawn in standard position in the unit circle, then the corresponding point on the terminal arm is

F. $\left(\dfrac{\sqrt{2}}{2}, -\dfrac{\sqrt{3}}{2}\right)$

G. $\left(-\dfrac{\sqrt{2}}{2}, -\dfrac{\sqrt{3}}{2}\right)$

H. $\left(\dfrac{1}{2}, -\dfrac{\sqrt{3}}{2}\right)$

J. $\left(-\dfrac{1}{2}, -\dfrac{\sqrt{3}}{2}\right)$

31. Which of the following intervals describes where $y = \sin x$ is decreasing?

A. $(-90 + 180n)° < x < (90 + 180n)°$, $n \in I$

B. $(-90 + 360n)° < x < (90 + 360n)°$, $n \in I$

C. $(90 + 180n)° < x < (270 + 180n)°$, $n \in I$

D. $(90 + 360n)° < x < (270 + 360n)°$, $n \in I$

32. Logan went to the doctor and has his blood pressure measured. The graph of his blood pressure measurements is shown below.

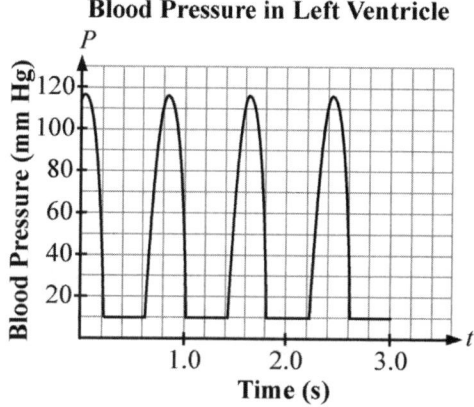

Blood Pressure in Left Ventricle

Logan revisited the doctor a week later and had his blood pressure measured and graphed. The only change to the graph was that the graph was stretched horizontally when compared to the graph above. This indicates that, compared to the first visit to the doctor,

F. Logan had an irregular heartbeat during the second visit.

G. Logan's blood pressure had increased.

H. Logan's heart was beating more quickly.

J. Logan's heart was beating more slowly.

Go On

33. Which of the following statements regarding the functions $f(x) = a\sin x$, $f(x) = \sin x + c$, and $f(x) = \sin(x - d)$ contains an error?

A. If $|a| > 1$, the graph is stretched about the x-axis by a factor of $|a|$; if $|a| < 1$, the graph is compressed about the x-axis by a factor of $|a|$.

B. If $a < 0$, the graph is reflected in the y-axis.

C. Parameter c is a vertical translation parameter. The translation is c units up when c is positive, and $|c|$ units down when c is negative.

D. Parameter d is a horizontal translation parameter. The translation is d units right when d is positive, and $|d|$ units left when d is negative.

34. Jason wanted to draw a sketch of $1\frac{1}{2}$ cycles of the graph of a function in the form $f(x) = \sin(x - d)$. He used the following points, represented in the table below to draw his graph.

x	$-150°$	$-60°$	$30°$	$120°$	$210°$	$300°$	$390°$
$f(x)$	1	0	-1	0	1	0	-1

The graph of the function $f(x) = \sin(x - d)$ that he was trying to sketch could have had a d-value of

F. $-120°$ **G.** $60°$

H. $-30°$ **J.** $120°$

35. September 21 and 22 were two nice sunny days in Laura's city. Starting at 8:00 A.M., when it was sunrise, she measured the length of the shadow of an 80 m tall building at various times until sunset, which occurred at 8:00 P.M. (or 20 hours on Day 1). Next morning at 8:00 A.M. (or 32 hours after Day 1), she did the same, until the sunset at 8:00 P.M. (or 44 hours after Day 1). The graph below shows the relationship between the shadow length, l, in metres, and the time, t, in hours from Day 1. This graph portrays a periodic function.

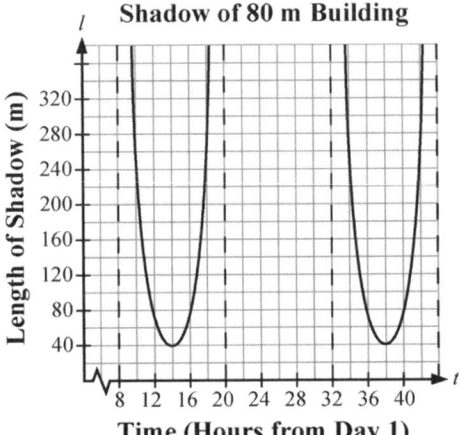

Shadow of 80 m Building

What is the period and range of the above graph representing a periodic function?

A. 10 hours, $40 \le l \le 360$

B. 10 hours, $l \ge 40$

C. 12 hours, $40 \le l \le 360$

D. 12 hours, $l \ge 40$

Numerical Response

36. While breathing, the volume in your lungs is a periodic function of time. The graph below shows how the volume, V, in litres, changes over time, t, in seconds, for a particular person.

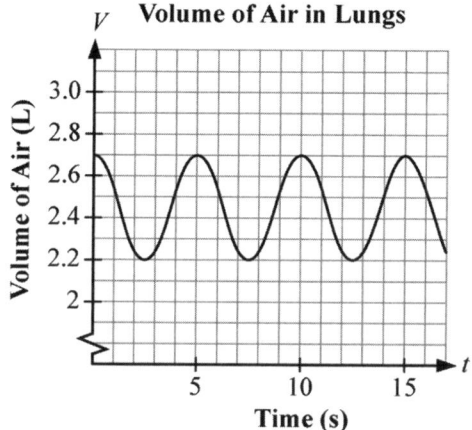

If the length of time (period) for the person to inhale and exhale once is P seconds and the total volume exhaled each time a breath is taken is V litres, then the sum of the values $P + V$, to the nearest tenth, is ____.

Go On

SOLUTIONS–PRACTICE TEST

1. 10	**10.** H	Part B- **OR**	**24.** F	**31.** D
2. G	**11.** A	Part C- **OR**	**25.** 209	**32.** J
3. D	**12.** J	**17.** D	**26.** J	**33.** B
4. F	**13.** Part A- **OR**	**18.** F	**27.** 6	**34.** J
5. D	Part B- **OR**	**19.** C	**28.** Part A- **OR**	**35.** D
6. 153	Part C- **OR**	**20.** 4600	Part B- **OR**	**36.** 5.5
7. C	**14.** 7.43	**21.** C	**29.** Part A- G	
8. 7	**15.** C	**22.** F	Part B- **OR**	
9. A	**16.** Part A- **OR**	**23.** B	**30.** H	

1. 10

A quadratic pattern is symmetrical in that it decreases and increases from its minimum point in equivalent steps. The drops on the left side of the minimum over the first

$$\overset{-20}{\quad}\overset{-15}{\quad}\overset{-10}{\quad}\overset{-5}{\quad}$$

5 days are $100 \rightarrow 80 \rightarrow 65 \rightarrow 55 \rightarrow 50$. Therefore, the increases on the right side of the graph from day 6 onward will follow the same pattern of

$$\overset{+5}{\quad}\overset{+10}{\quad}\overset{+15}{\quad}\overset{+20}{\quad}$$

$$50 \rightarrow 55 \rightarrow 65 \rightarrow 80 \rightarrow 100.$$

This increased pattern of the stock can be represented in the completed graph below.

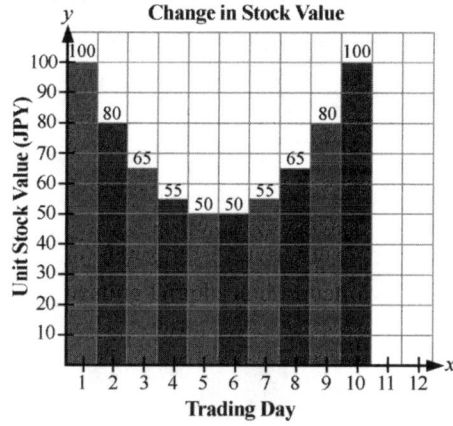

Change in Stock Value

According to the completed pattern shown in the graph, the stock recovers to its original value of 100 JPY on day 10.

2. G

Use the FOIL method and the distributive property to simplify the expressions given below.

$$(3x + 2)(2x - 3) - 2(x - 2)^2$$

$$= (3x + 2)(2x - 3) - 2(x - 2)(x - 2)$$

$$= (3x)(2x) + (-3)(3x) + 2(2x) + (2)(-3) - 2$$
$$[(x)(x) + (-2)(x) + (-2)(x) + (-2)(-2)]$$

$$= 6x^2 - 9x + 4x - 6 - 2(x^2 - 2x - 2x + 4)$$

$$= 6x^2 - 9x + 4x - 6 - 2x^2 + 4x + 4x - 8$$

$$= (6x^2 - 2x^2) + (-9x + 4x + 4x + 4x) + (-6 - 8)$$

$$= 4x^2 + 3x - 14$$

Now, for $Ax^2 + Bx + C + (4x^2 + 3x - 14)$ to equal 0, $Ax^2 + Bx + C$ must be the additive inverse of $4x^2 + 3x - 14$. This means that $Ax^2 = -4x^2$, $Bx = -3x$, and $C = -(-14)$.

Therefore, $A = -4$, $B = -3$, and $C = 14$.

3. D

To determine the expression that does not have $x + 3$ as a factor, you need to factor each given choice.

Alternative A: Trinomial, where $a = 1$, $(x^2 - 2x - 15)$. Find two numbers that have a product of -15 and a sum of -2. These numbers are -5 and 3. Factor the trinomial to two binomials containing -5 and 3.

$x^2 - 2x - 15 = (x - 5)(x + 3)$. This trinomial does have a factor of $x + 3$.

Alternative B: Binomial, with a difference of squares $(-2x^2 + 18)$.

Factor out the GCF of -2.

$-2x^2 + 18 = -2(x^2 - 9)$

Since 1 and 9 are perfect squares, the expression factors to

$-2(\sqrt{x^2} - \sqrt{9})(\sqrt{x^2} + \sqrt{9}) = -2(x - 3)(x + 3)$

This binomial also has a factor of $x + 3$.

Alternative C: Binomial, with a common GCF $(-3x^2 - 9x)$C.

Factor out the common GCF.

$-3x^2 - 9x = -3x(x + 3)$

This alternative also has a factor of $x + 3$.

Alternative D: Trinomial, where $a = 1$, $(x^2 + 7x + 15)$. Find two numbers that have a product of 15 and a sum of 7. There are no two numbers that produce this result. This expression cannot be factored, therefore, $x + 3$ is not one of its factors.

4. F

To find the values of m and n, solve the quadratic equation $6x^2 = 3x + 5$ by rewriting the equation equal to zero and then identifying the values a, b, and c.

$$6x^2 - 3x - 5 = 0$$
$$\downarrow \qquad \downarrow \qquad \downarrow$$
$$a = 6 \quad b = -3 \quad c = -5$$

Now, substitute these values into the quadratic formula, and carry out the steps needed to find m and n.

$$x = \frac{-b \pm \sqrt{b^2 - 4ac}}{2a}$$

$$x = \frac{-(-3) \pm \sqrt{(-3)^2 - 4(6)(-5)}}{2(6)}$$

$$= \frac{3 \pm \sqrt{9 + 120}}{12}$$

$$= \frac{3 \pm \sqrt{129}}{12}$$

After this stage of solving the quadratic equation, it is easy to identify $m = 3$ and $n = 129$.

5. D

Enter the function $h(t) = -4.9t^2 + 29.4t + 352.8$ into your $\left[Y_1 = \right]$ button on your graphing calculator. Then, press GRAPH and use WINDOW (ZOOM 6).

$$Y_1 = -4.9x^2 + 29.4x + 352.8$$

The graph only shows the negative x-intercept which does not apply to this question. Also, the top (maximum) of the graph is not visible. Therefore, the WINDOW needs to be made larger to the right (x_{max}) and moved up (y_{max}) a lot. The window that seems appropriate is given in alternatives B or D as: $\begin{array}{l} x:[-10, 20, 1] \\ y:[-10, 500, 1] \end{array}$

When this WINDOW setting is used, the whole graph is shown with its maximum and the positive x-intercept, namely the point representing when the flare hits the ground. Then, carry out the 2nd TRACE ZERO feature to determine that this x-intercept is 12.0, as shown below:

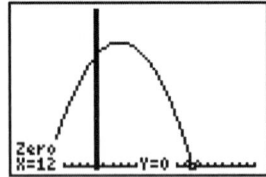

6. 153

To determine $f(-4)$ and $f(1)$, substitute these values in for x in $f(x) = 5x^2 - 6x + 25$, and then evaluate each result.

$$f(-4) = 5(-4)^2 - 6(-4) + 25$$
$$= 80 + 24 + 25$$
$$= 129$$

$$f(1) = 5(1)^2 - 6(1) + 25$$
$$= 5 - 6 + 25$$
$$= 24$$

Therefore, the sum of $f(-4)$ and $f(1)$ is:
$$f(-4) + f(1) = 129 + 24 = 153$$

7. C

In order for a quadratic function to have a range of $y \leq 0$, it must open downward and have a maximum y-value of 0. To portray this, an example of a function where $a < 0$ and $b = 0$ is shown below.

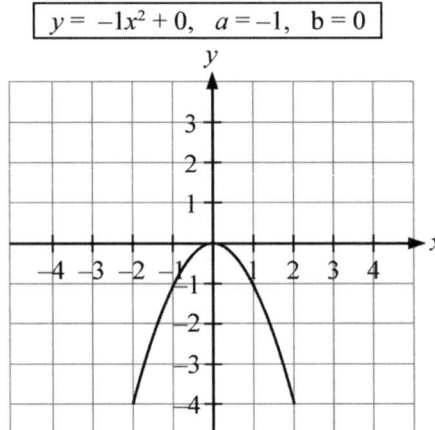

8. 7

To find the limits on the domain (when $h = 0$), you could factor or use the quadratic formula to solve the equation $0 = -x^2 + 10x - 21$

Method 1: Factoring

$0 = -x^2 + 10x - 21$

Factor out GCF of -1.

$= -1\left(x^2 - 10x + 21\right)$

Factor trinomial, $a = 1$.

$= -1(x - 3)(x - 7)$

Solve for x for each factor.

$$\begin{array}{ccc} x - 3 = 0 & & x - 7 = 0 \\ x = 3 & \text{and} & x = 7 \end{array}$$

The lower limit is $x = 3$ m, and the upper limit is $x = 7$ m.

Method 2: Quadratic formula

$x = \dfrac{-b \pm \sqrt{b^2 - 4ac}}{2a}$, where $a = -1$, $b = 10$, $c = -21$

$= \dfrac{-10 \pm \sqrt{10^2 - 4(-1)(-21)}}{2(-1)}$

$= \dfrac{-10 \pm \sqrt{16}}{-2}$

$= \dfrac{-10 \pm 4}{-2}$

$= 3$ and 7

The lower limit is $x = 3$ m, and the upper limit is $x = 7$ m.

9. A

Since the vertex $(0, 0)$ of the graph of $f(x) = x^2$ has been transformed to the new vertex of $(1, -4)$ of the graph of the function $g(x) = a(x - h)^2 + k$, there would be a horizontal translation to the right 1 unit and a vertical translation down 4 units.

To have a positive y-intercept, the transformed function $g(x) = a(x - h)^2 + k$ must open upward from the vertex $(1, -4)$, which means that $a > 0$.

To move from the vertex $(1, -4)$ to a y-intercept of $(0, +c)$, the graph of $f(x) = x^2$ would have to also undergo a vertical stretch by a factor of a about the x-axis.

10. H

The graph of $h(x) = \dfrac{2}{3}(x + 4)^2 + 1$ has a vertex of $(-4, 1)$, since $h = -4$ and $k = 1$. To understand the effect of the vertical stretch factor $a = \dfrac{2}{3}$ about the x-axis, evaluate the vertical upward shifts from the vertex as you move horizontally one unit left and one unit right of the vertex. You know that the vertical changes for $f(x) = x^2$, where $a = 1$, are as follows:

$x \to 1 \Rightarrow y \to 1$

$x \to 1 \to 1 \Rightarrow y \to 4$

$x \to 1 \to 1 \to 1 \Rightarrow y = 9$

$x \to 1 \to 1 \to 1 \to 1 \Rightarrow y = 16$

When $a = \dfrac{2}{3}$, the vertical shifts will change as follows:

$x \to 1 \Rightarrow y \to 1\left(\dfrac{2}{3}\right) = \dfrac{2}{3}$

$x \to 1 \to 1 \Rightarrow y \to 4\left(\dfrac{2}{3}\right) = \dfrac{8}{3}$

$x \to 1 \to 1 \to 1 \Rightarrow y = 9\left(\dfrac{2}{3}\right) = 6$

$x \to 1 \to 1 \to 1 \to 1 \Rightarrow y = 16\left(\dfrac{2}{3}\right) = \dfrac{32}{3}$

Based on these shifts from the vertex, there should be two points that have a vertical shift of 6 units from the vertex, when shifted left/right 3 units. These points would be $(-4 + 3, 1 + 6) = (-1, 7)$ and $(-4 - 3, 1 + 6) = (-7, 7)$. The graph portraying these points is shown in alternative H.

11. A

The vertex of a quadratic function lies on a vertical line (the axis of symmetry) located halfway between the x-intercepts of the function. The vertex $(3, 8)$ lies on the vertical line, the axis of symmetry, defined by $x = 3$. If the two x-intercepts are 8 units apart and $x = 3$ is halfway between them, then each x-intercept can be determined as follows:

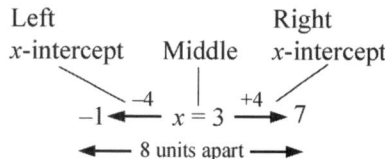

If the x-intercepts are -1 and 7, then you can write the function in factored form, where the one x-intercept is $r = -1$ and the second x-intercept is $s = 7$.

$f(x) = a(x - r)(x - s)$
$\quad = a(x - (-1))(x - 7)$
$\quad = a(x + 1)(x - 7)$

To find the coefficient of a, substitute the x- and y-values of the vertex $(3, 8)$ for x and $f(x)$, and solve for a.

$$f(x) = a(x + 1)(x - 7)$$
$$8 = a(3 + 1)(3 - 7)$$
$$8 = a(4)(-4)$$
$$8 = -16a$$
$$8 = -\frac{1}{2}$$

The final correct factored form of Samantha's quadratic function is $f(x) = -\frac{1}{2}(x - 7)(x + 1)$.

12. J

When a quadratic function is written in the vertex form $f(x) = 4(x - 3)^2 + 8$, the following features of the graph can be identified by inspection only:

- Vertex $(3, 8)$
- Range: $y \geq 8$ (since $a > 0$)
- Axis of symmetry: $x = 3$
- Minimum: 8
- Opens upward (since $a > 0$)
- There are no x-intercepts since the graph goes upward from the vertex $(3, 8)$.

Michaela could make all statements from inspection, therefore, all 4 observations could be made.

13. Part A – Open Response

To find the vertex, convert $g(x) = -\frac{1}{2}x^2 + 2x + 1$ into the vertex form $g(x) = a(x - h)^2 + k$.

$$g(x) = -\frac{1}{2}x^2 + 2x + 1$$

Factor $-\frac{1}{2}$ out of the first two terms.

$$= -\frac{1}{2}\left(x^2 - 4x\right) + 1$$

Find the perfect square, and put the $-/+$ values in the brackets.

$$= -\frac{1}{2}\left(x^2 - 4x + 4 - 4\right) + 1$$

Take -4 out of the brackets by multiplying by $-\frac{1}{2}$.

$$= -\frac{1}{2}\left(x^2 - 4x + 4\right) + 2 + 1$$

Factor the trinomial.

$$= -\frac{1}{2}(x - 2)^2 + 3$$

The function in vertex form is

$$g(x) = -\frac{1}{2}(x - 2)^2 + 3$$

The vertex of the function is $(2, 3)$.

Part B – Open Response

Since $g(x) = -\frac{1}{2}x^2 + 2x + 1$ cannot be factored, find the x-intercepts by using the quadratic formula.

$$x = \frac{-b \pm \sqrt{b^2 - 4ac}}{2a}$$
$$= \frac{-2 \pm \sqrt{(2)^2 - 4\left(-\frac{1}{2}\right)(1)}}{2\left(-\frac{1}{2}\right)}$$
$$= \frac{-2 \pm \sqrt{6}}{-1}$$
$$= 2 \pm \sqrt{6}$$

The x-intercepts are $2 + \sqrt{6}$ and $2 - \sqrt{6}$.

Part C – Open Response

The graph of the function decreases on the right side of the vertex $(2, 3)$, since the vertex has a maximum of 3 and opens downward. Therefore, the x-interval where the graph of the function is decreasing is $x \geq 2$.

14. 7.43

Use your calculator with the $\wedge$ button to evaluate the expression $(-4.5)^{\frac{4}{3}}$ as follows:

$$(-4.5)^{\frac{4}{3}} = (-4.5)^{\left(\frac{4}{3}\right)} = 7.429\,336\,31 \doteq 7.43$$

15. C

To be a function, any vertical line, defined by $x = a$, that is drawn through any part of the graph, can only pass through a single point. Since the domain of the exponential relation $y = (15)^x$ is $x \in \mathbb{R}$, then $y = 15^x$ can be written as the function $f(x) = 15^x$, since every vertical line defined by $x = a$, $x \in \mathbb{R}$, will only pass through a single point.

16. Part A – Open Response

Use a table of values to determine the corresponding y-values for x-values of $-3, -2, -1, 0, 1, 2,$ and 3 of the function $y = \left(\frac{1}{2}\right)^x$.

x	-3	-2	-1	0	1	2	3
y	$\left(\frac{1}{2}\right)^{-3}$ $= 8$	$\left(\frac{1}{2}\right)^{-2}$ $= 4$	$\left(\frac{1}{2}\right)^{-1}$ $= 2$	$\left(\frac{1}{2}\right)^{0}$ $= 1$	$\left(\frac{1}{2}\right)^{1}$ $= \frac{1}{2}$	$\left(\frac{1}{2}\right)^{2}$ $= \frac{1}{4}$	$\left(\frac{1}{2}\right)^{3}$ $= \frac{1}{8}$

Then, plot these points, and join them with a smooth curve to get the graph shown.

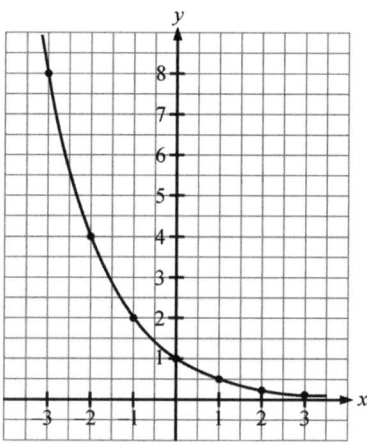

Part B – Open Response

The following features characterize the graph of $y = \left(\frac{1}{2}\right)^x$.

Domain: $x \in \mathbb{R}$ y-intercept: $(0, 1)$

Range: $y > 0$ x-intercept: None

Asymptote: $y = 0$

Part C – Open Response

Since the a value in $y = \left(\frac{1}{2}\right)^x$ is smaller and closer to the value of $a = 0$ than the a value in $y = \left(\frac{2}{3}\right)^x$, the graph of $y = \left(\frac{1}{2}\right)^x$ would be steeper on the left side of the y-axis and flatter on the right side of the y-axis.

17. D

A function is an exponential function if successive y-values in a table have ratios that are constant. R stands for ratio.

Alternative A: This is an exponential function with a constant ratio of 4.

x	1	2	3	4	5
y	2	8	32	128	512
R		$\frac{8}{2}$ $= 4$	$\frac{32}{8}$ $= 4$	$\frac{128}{32}$ $= 4$	$\frac{512}{128}$ $= 4$

Alternative B: This is an exponential function with a constant ratio of 0.67.

x	1	2	3	4	5
y	729	486	324	216	144
R		$\frac{486}{729}$ $= 0.67$	$\frac{324}{486}$ $= 0.67$	$\frac{216}{324}$ $= 0.67$	$\frac{144}{216}$ $= 0.67$

Alternative C: This is an exponential function with a constant ratio of 1.5.

x	1	2	3	4	5
y	0.8	1.2	1.8	2.7	4.05
R		$\frac{1.2}{0.8}$ $= 1.5$	$\frac{1.8}{1.2}$ $= 1.5$	$\frac{2.7}{1.8}$ $= 1.5$	$\frac{4.05}{2.7}$ $= 1.5$

Alternative D: This is not an exponential function since the ratio is not constant.

x	1	2	3	4	5
y	0.5	2.0	4.5	8.0	12.5
R		$\frac{2.0}{0.5}$ $= 4$	$\frac{4.5}{2.0}$ $= 2.25$	$\frac{8.0}{4.5}$ $= 1.78$	$\frac{12.5}{8.0}$ $= 1.56$

18. F

The points on all four graphs are the same.

However, in order to show exponential growth, the graph should start at about the original population of 70 991 and curve upwards slightly, to about 140 000, and pass through the middle of all data points. The graph with the curve of best fit is shown in alternative F.

In alternative G, it is a line not a curve that represents the points incorrectly.

In alternative H, the curve of best fit is curving the wrong way, and does not represent the exponential growth of the data.

In alternative J, the curve of best fit starts too high on the y-axis, not representing the data values for 1980, 1984, and 1987 appropriately

19. C

The value a reflects the growth factor of the value of the ring each year. Since it increases 15% per year, $a = 115\%$ (to show how much above 100% the growth is), or as a decimal, $\dfrac{115\%}{100\%} = 1.15$

To find the value, V, of the ring after 40 months, you need to convert it to t years.

$\dfrac{40 \text{ months}}{12 \text{ months}} = 3.333\,33 \text{ or } \dfrac{10}{3}$

Now, substitute $t = \dfrac{10}{3}$ into the equation to solve for value, V.

$V = 12\,000(1.15)^{\frac{10}{3}}$
$ = 19\,120.858\,19$

The value of the ring, V, after 40 months, to the nearest dollar, is $19\,121.

20. 4600

The compounding period is semi-annually, which means the frequency of compounds per year $f = 2$. From this, you can determine the interest per compound, i, and the total number of compounds, n.

$i = \dfrac{6\%}{2} = \dfrac{0.06}{2} = 0.03$
$n = 7 \times 2 = 14$

Then, substitute these values and the final amount $6958 into the compound interest equation to solve for the principal, P (or present value, PV).

$FV = PV(1+i)^n$
$6958 = PV(1 + 0.03)^{14}$
$6958 = PV(1.512\,589\,725)$
$\dfrac{6958}{1.512\,589\,725} = \dfrac{PV(1.512\,589\,725)}{1.512\,589\,725}$
$4600.057\,693 = PV$

The principal is equal to $4600.

21. C

In a simple interest account, the interest, I, is the same per year, namely, $180. Therefore, $p = 180$, and the amount after 4 years is $q = 2540 + 180 = 2720$.

To find the compound interest, r, take the previous amount $A = 2519.42$, and multiply by the annual interest rate of 8 % or 0.08. Therefore, $r = 2519.42 \times 0.08 = 201.55$. The total amount is $s = 2519.42 + 201.55 = 2720.97$.

When you examine the values of p, q, r, and s, the following relationships hold true:
$r > p$, since $201.55 > 180$
$q < s$, since $2720 < 2720.97$

22. F

The compounding period is semi-annually. To determine the function $f(x) = a(b)^x$, determine the growth factor per compounding period, b, by finding the ratio between successive total amounts.

$b = \dfrac{6210.00}{6000.00} = \dfrac{6427.35}{6210.00} = \cdots$
$b = 1.035$

If a reflects the initial principal at year 0, then $a = 6000$ and the exponential function, representing the growth of the investment, is

$f(x) = 6000(1.035)^x$

23. B

Since the interest is compounded semi-annually, the number of compounds per year is 2. The timeline shows 18 compounds over the total time of the annuity. This means that Emily made regular deposits at the end of each 6-month period over a total time of $t = 18$ semi-annual periods = 9 years.

The final amounts of each deposit show the interest per compounding periods, i, to be 2.5% since $(1 + i) = 1.025$. Since the 2.5% is the interest compounded semi-annually, the annual interest rate is $I = 2 \times 2.5\% = 5.0\%$.

24. F

For the plan suggested by Jennifer, the monthly payments at the end of each month would be

$\dfrac{1}{12} \times \$3901 = \$325.08$. Enter this amount and the other necessary entries into the TVM Solver to determine the number of months (compounding periods), N, it would take to accumulate a final amount of FV = $1\,000\,000.

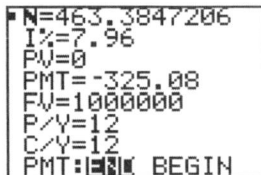

According to the resulting value of N = 463.384 7206, it would take 464 months for Robbie to become a millionaire by making regular monthly payments. Since 40 years in terms of months is $40 \times 12 = 480$, subtract $480 - 464 = 16$. Therefore, if Robbie followed Jennifer's advice he would accumulate $1\,000\,000, 16 months sooner.

25. 209

Determine how long it takes for Maureen to pay off her $10 000 loan at regular monthly payments of $200. Enter the respective values into the TVM solver associated to her payout plan, and find the value, N, the total months needed.

According to the resulting value of N, Maureen takes 60 months to pay off the $10 000 loan.

Now, determine Anita's regular monthly payments, PMT, over a period of $5\frac{1}{2}$ years. Since the interest is compounded monthly and payments are monthly, the number of compounds is N = 5.5 years × 12 = 66. Enter the respective values into the TVM Solver to find her regular monthly payments, PMT.

According to the resulting value of PMT, Anita would need to make regular monthly payments of $184.99 to pay off the $10 000 loan.

To determine the total interest, I_T, that each pays, you need to find the total monthly payments, PMTs, and subtract the principal, P, of the loan.

Maureen: I_T = PMTs − P
= ($200 × 60) − $10 000
= $12 000 − $10 000
= $2000

Anita: I_T = PMTs − P
= ($184.99 × 66) − $10 000
= $12 209.34 − $10 000
= $2209.34

The difference in total interest between the two payout plans, to the nearest dollar, is $2209.34 − $2000 = $209.

26. J

Draw a labelled diagram to represent the situation. Remember that the angle of depression from the jet to the target is the same as the angle of elevation from the target to the jet.

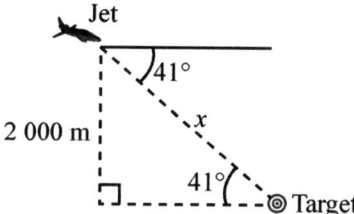

Since the opposite side of the angle (41 °) is 2000 and x is the hypotenuse, the correct ratio to use is the sine ratio.

$$\sin 41° = \frac{\text{opposite}}{\text{hypotenuse}} = \frac{2000}{x}$$

This ratio is given in choice J.

27. 6

First use the Pythagorean Theorem to obtain the length of the vertical beam, h.

$$h^2 + 4^2 = 5^2$$
$$h^2 = 25 - 16$$
$$h^2 = 9$$
$$h = 3$$

Next, use the sine ratio to find the length x.

$$\sin 30° = \frac{3}{x}$$
$$x(\sin 30°) = 3$$
$$x = \frac{3}{\sin 30°}$$
$$x = 6$$

Therefore, the length of side x, to the nearest foot is 6 ft.

28. Part A – Open Response

Draw a labelled diagram of the triangles in this scenario.

To find the distance between points A and B, use the cosine law in ΔABT. The cosine law needs to be used, since you have no known pair (a known side with its corresponding opposite angle) in that triangle.

Also, you cannot use ΔABH to find AB, since there is not enough information (only two known angles are given).

$$(AB)^2 = 240.0^2 + 238.5^2 - 2(240.0)(238.5)(\cos 10°)$$
$$= 1741.458 \, 435$$
$$AB = 41.730 \, 785 \, 22$$
$$\approx 41.73 \, m$$

The distance between points A and B, to the nearest hundredth metre, is 41.73 m.

Part B – Open Response

To find the total distance from T to A to H, you need to first find the distance from A to H in $\triangle ABH$.

To find AH, use the sine law, since you have a known pair (once you find $\angle H$).

$\angle H = 180° - 89° - 63° = 28°$

The known pair is $\angle H = 28°$ and its corresponding opposite side, h, or $AB = 41.73$ m. Therefore,

$$\frac{AH}{\sin B} = \frac{h}{\sin H}$$
$$\frac{AH}{\sin 89°} = \frac{41.73}{\sin 28°}$$
$$AH(\sin 28°) = 41.73(\sin 89°)$$
$$AH = \frac{41.73(\sin 89°)}{\sin 28°}$$
$$= 88.873\,635\,01$$
$$\approx 88.87 \text{ m}$$

Since distance $TA = 240.0$ m and $AH = 88.87$ m, the total distance around the dog-leg from the tee to the hole $(T \to A \to H)$ is $240.0 + 88.87 = 328.87$ or 328.9 m.

29. G

March 1 is day 60. This can be found by counting the days from January 1 to March 1 as follows.
January 1 (Day 1) + 30 = January 31 (Day 31)
January 31 (Day 31) + 28 = February 28 (Day 59)
February 28 (Day 59) + 1 = March 1 (Day 60)

According to the graph the average high temperature on March 1 (Day 60) next year would be about $-9°C$.

Part B – Open Response

The equation of the horizontal midline axis, $y = d$, is found by knowing the maximum and minimum y-values of the graph. The maximum value of about $18\,°C$ occurs at about day 168, and one of the minimum values of about $-22°C$ occurs at about day 350. Now, find the equation of the horizontal midline axis.

$$y = d = \frac{\text{maximum} - \text{minimum}}{2}$$
$$= \frac{18 + (-22)}{2}$$
$$= -2$$

The equation of the horizontal midline axis is $y = d = -2$. This value of $-2°C$ reflects the **average** high temperature of all high temperatures throughout any year.

30. H

Since the point is on the unit circle, then $x^2 + y^2 = 1$ for any ordered pair (x, y). Since the y-value on the graph is the same as the y-value on the unit circle, then $y = -\frac{\sqrt{3}}{2}$.

Thus,
$$x^2 + \left(-\frac{\sqrt{3}}{2}\right)^2 = 1$$
$$x^2 + \frac{3}{4} = 1$$
$$x^2 = \frac{1}{4}$$
$$x = \pm\frac{1}{2}$$

Because an angle of $300°$ in standard position has its terminal arm in quadrant IV, the x-value is positive and therefore, equal to $+\frac{1}{2}$.

Thus, the point on the terminal arm is $\left(\frac{1}{2}, -\frac{\sqrt{3}}{2}\right)$.

31. D

The graph of the function of $y = \sin x$, $0° \le x \le 360°$, decreases in the interval $90° < x < 270°$. Since the function has a period of $360°$, the intervals where $y = \sin x$, $x \in \mathbb{R}$ decreases, are $(90 + 360n)°$ $< x < (270 + 360n)°$, $n \in I$.

32. J

A horizontal stretch of the graph indicates that the period of the graph would be longer. This means that Logan's heart was beating more slowly, to accommodate this increase in period (time).

33. B

When $a < 0$, the graph is reflected in the x-axis, not in the y-axis. All other statements given alternatives A, C and D are correct.

34. J

To determine the function Jason was trying to sketch, you simply pick a point that has a y-value of 1 or -1, substitute the corresponding angle into the function $f(x) = \sin(x - d)$, for all 4 given d-values, and see which one works.

For example $x = -150°$ has a y-value of 1.

Thus, for
$d = -120° \to f(-150°) = \sin(-150° - (-120°)) = -0.5$
$d = -30° \to f(-150°) = \sin(-150° - (-30°)) = -0.866$
$d = 60° \to f(-150°) = \sin(-150° - 60°) = 0.5$
$d = 120° \to f(-150°) = \sin(-150° - 120°) = 1$

The correct d-value is $120°$

35. D

Shadows start to appear at sunrise and disappear at sunset. Since the sunrise is at 8:00 A.M. and the sunset is at 8:00 P.M., the total time there are shadows is 12 hours. Therefore, the period of the graph of the function is 12 hours. At sunrise, shadows would be infinitely long. At hour 14 (2:00 P.M. on Day 1) or at hour 38 (2:00 P.M. on Day 2) the sun would be at its highest point in the sky, producing the smallest shadow defined as 40 m on the graph. At sunset, the shadows would again become infinitely long. Thus, during each day shadows are 40 m or longer, which means the range of the graph is $l \geq 40$.

36. 5.5

Upon examination of the graph, the length of time between the first two successive maximum values is 5 seconds. This is the time required for the person to inhale and exhale once. Therefore, the value of $P = 5$. To find the total volume exhaled each time you need to find the maximum and minimum volumes of air in the lungs during a breath. According to the graph, the maximum volume is 2.7 litres and the minimum volume is 2.2 litres. Therefore, the total volume exhaled in a breath is $2.7 - 2.2 = 0.5$ litres. Therefore, the sum of the values $P + V$ is $5 + 0.5 = 5.5$.

Appendices

Math 11 – Functions and Applications – Formula sheet

Functions and Equations

Linear Relations

Linear Function: $f(x) = mx + b$

Quadratic Relations

Quadratic Function:

Standard form: $f(x) = ax^2 + bx + c, \quad a \neq 0$

Vertex form: $f(x) = a(x - h)^2 + k, \; a \neq 0$

Factored form: $f(x) = a(x - r)(x - s), \; a \neq 0$

Quadratic Equation: $0 = ax^2 + bx + c, \; a \neq 0$

Quadratic Formula: $x = \dfrac{-b \pm \sqrt{b^2 - 4ac}}{2a}$

Discriminant: $D = b^2 - 4ac$

Exponential Relations

Exponential Function: $f(x) = a^x, \; a > 0 \text{ and } a \neq 1$

Exponential Growth / Decay: $y = ab^x$, where b is the growth/decay factor

Sine Relations

Sine Function: $f(x) = \sin x$

Transformed forms: $f(x) = a \sin x$

$f(x) = \sin(x - d)$

$f(x) = \sin x + c$

Exponent Rules

Multiplication: $x^m \times x^n = x^{m+n}$

Division: $\dfrac{x^m}{x^n} = x^{m-n}$

Power: $(x^m)^n = x^{mn}$

Definitions: $x^0 = 1, \; x \neq 0$

$x^{-m} = \dfrac{1}{x^m}$

$x^{\frac{m}{n}} = \sqrt[n]{(x)^m}$

$x^{-\frac{m}{n}} = \dfrac{1}{\sqrt[n]{(x)^m}}$

Finance

Simple Interest: $\qquad I = P\,r\,t$

Compound Interest: $\qquad A = P(1+i)^n \ \text{ or } \ FV = PV(1+i)^n$

Total Interest: $\qquad I_T = A - P \ \text{ or } \ I_T = FV - PV$

Trigonometry

Right Triangles

Pythagorean Theorem: $\qquad a^2 + b^2 = c^2$

Primary trigonometric ratios:

Sine ratio: $\sin A = \dfrac{\text{opposite}}{\text{hypotenuse}}$

Cosine ratio: $\cos A = \dfrac{\text{adjacent}}{\text{hypotenuse}}$

Tangent ratio: $\tan A = \dfrac{\text{opposite}}{\text{adjacent}}$

Acute Triangles

Sine Law: $\qquad \dfrac{a}{\sin A} = \dfrac{b}{\sin B} = \dfrac{c}{\sin C}$

Cosine Law: $\qquad a^2 = b^2 + c^2 - 2bc(\cos A)$

$\qquad\qquad\qquad \cos A = \dfrac{b^2 + c^2 - a^2}{2bc}$

GLOSSARY

acute angle An angle measuring more than 0° but less than 90°.

acute triangle A triangle with all three angles each measuring less than 90°.

adjacent angle Two angles that share a common vertex and a common side. The sum of their measures is 180°. In the diagram below, angles *a* and *b* are adjacent angles as well as angles *a* and *d*.

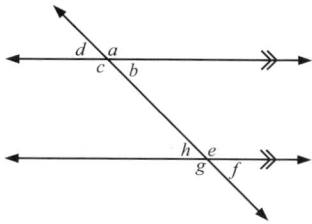

algebra tiles Manipulatives used to assist understanding of algebraic expressions and equations.

algebraic expression A mathematical phrase made up of numbers and variables that are connected by addition, subtraction, or both (3*x*, 5*x* + 6).

altitude A perpendicular line segment from the base of a figure to the opposite side or vertex.

Altitude

amount (*A*) The resulting value of an invested or borrowed amount at the end of a specified time, calculated by adding the principal and total accumulated interest (I_T).

amplitude (*a*) The vertical distance from the horizontal midline axis to any maximum or minimum *y*-value of an oscillating or sinusoidal periodic function.

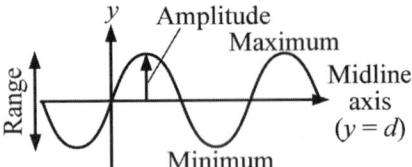

Amplitude (*a*), can be calculated using the following formulas:

$$a = \frac{\text{maximum} - \text{minimum}}{2}$$

$$a \begin{cases} (\text{maximum}) - (d\text{-value}) \\ (d\text{-value}) - (\text{minimum}) \end{cases}$$

angle of depression The angle formed between two rays in which one of the rays is below the horizontal ray.

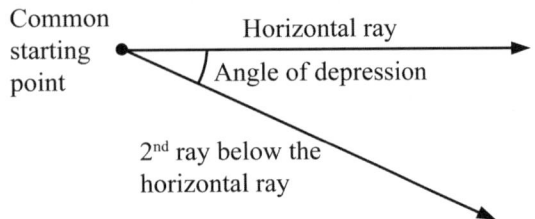

angle of elevation The angle formed between two rays in which one of the rays is above the horizontal ray.

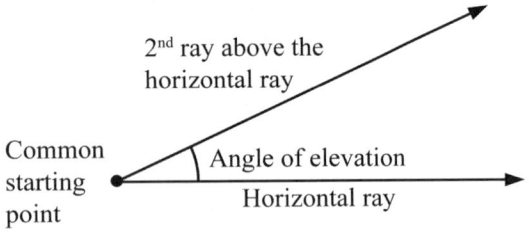

annuity A series of payments or investments made at regular intervals of time.

annum (a) A word used in exponential or compound interest problems which means 'year.'

area The number of square units contained in a defined two-dimensional region.

asymptote A straight line that a curve approaches but never touches.

axis of symmetry A vertical line that passes through the vertex of the parabola and divides the parabola into two equal halves, each of which is a mirror image of the other.

bar graphs Display discrete or categorical data.

base The number or symbol having an exponent ($2^3 \rightarrow 2$ is the base, $(0.4)^{1.5} \rightarrow 0.4$ is the base, $a^x \rightarrow a$ is the base).

binomial A two-termed polynomial ($2x + 3y$).

cartesian (coordinate) plane A two-dimensional surface across which a number line extends horizontally (the x-axis) and is intersected by a number line extending vertically (the y-axis).

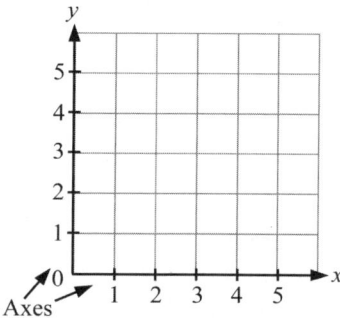

Axes

circle A collection of points in a plane that are an equal distance from a fixed point (the centre).

coefficient (numerical) The number immediately in front of a variable; it determines the factor by which the variable is multiplied. In $13x$, the numerical coefficient is 13.

common factor A number that can be evenly divided into each number within a set of given numbers.

completing the square A mathematical process used to change a quadratic function from the standard form $f(x) = ax^2 + bx + c$, to the vertex form $f(x) = a(x-h)^2 + k$.

compound interest Interest earned on the original loan or investment (principal or present value) plus any interest earned there after. The formula for calculating compound interest is $A = P(1 + i)^n$ or $FV = PV(1+i)^n$.

compounding period The time when interest is calculated and added to the principal throughout each year (daily, weekly, monthly, quarterly, etc.).

constant A term in a polynomial that contains no variables, only a single number.

constant rate of change The constant amount that the y-variable changes with respect to a change in the x-variable of the relation.

corresponding angles/sides Angles and sides that have the same relative positions in two or more geometric figures.

cosine law States that the sides and angles of a non-right triangle are related in a way such that $a^2 = b^2 + c^2 - 2b(\cos A)$.

coterminal angles Angles in standard position which have the same terminal arm.

curve of best fit A curve that passes as close as possible to points plotted on a non-linear graph.

cycle Each repetitive completion of y-values over a particular x-interval of the domain of a periodic function.

data Facts, statistics, or pieces of information.

decay factor The constant ratio of successive y-values with evenly spaced x-values (usually 1) of a function describing exponential decay; the ratio is always greater than 0 and less than 1.

decomposition A commonly used procedure for factoring trinomials of the form $y = ax^2 + bx + c$, $a \neq 0$, in which the middle term (bx) of the trinomial is split into two separate monomials so that the resulting expression can be factored by grouping.

decreasing interval The interval of x-values of the domain of a function, where the y-values of the range decrease in value as you go from the lower to higher x-values of this interval; if the x-interval is the same as the domain, the function is called a decreasing function.

diagonal A line connecting two non-adjacent vertices of a figure.

diameter The longest distance connecting two points on a circle and passing through the origin (see radius).

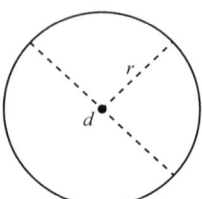

difference of squares A polynomial that can be expressed in the form $a^2 - b^2$, which can then be factored into two monomials $(a + b)(a - b)$.

direction of opening The direction in which the graph of a quadratic function opens; either up or down.

discriminant (D) The value found by evaluating $b^2 - 4ac$ in the quadratic formula, for a particular quadratic equation $ax^2 + bx + c = 0$. It predicts the type and number of roots of the quadratic equation.

distributive property To multiply out the parts of an expression; $a(x + y) = ax + ay$.

domain The set of all input (x-values) for which a particular relation is defined.

down payment A portion of the amount of a purchased item paid, at the time of purchase.

equilateral triangle A triangle that has equal-length sides.

expand To multiply through polynomials using real number properties.

exponent A number or symbol shown in smaller size that is raised to a base. A rational exponent is an exponent that is a fraction or decimal number.

exponential decay A pattern of data modeling an exponential function, where the ratio (often referred to as the decay factor) between consecutive y-values with evenly spaced x-values, is between 0 and 1.

exponential equation An equation where the variable is the exponent.

exponential growth A pattern of data modeling an exponential function, where the ratio (often referred to as the growth factor) between consecutive y-values with evenly spaced x-values, is above 1.

exponential regression The process of determining the equation of the curve of best fit, for a given set of data that appears to be exponential.

exponential relation (function) A relation of the form $y = a^x$, where $a > 0$, and $a \neq 1$, which can also be represented as a function $f(x) = a^x$.

expression An individual term or terms separated by operators ($+, -, \times, \div$) with no equal sign ($2x + 3$).

extrapolation A process of predicting or estimating values beyond a given set of data based on the pattern portrayed.

factor Numbers or expressions that are multiplied to form another number or expression (2 and 4 are factors of 8).

factor by grouping A factor method in which a polynomial is rewritten with an even number of terms, into smaller groups that contain a common factor.

factored form (quadratic function) The equation of a quadratic function in the form $f(x) = a(x - r)(x - s)$, where $a \neq 0$ and $a, b, c \in \mathbb{R}$. The x-intercepts of the graph are r and s, and the axis of symmetry is $x = \dfrac{r + s}{2}$.

factoring The process of breaking down a number or polynomial into its factors.

final value (*FV*) The same as the amount (*A*).

first-degree equation Is a polynomial equation in which the variable has a degree of 1.

first differences The difference between consecutive y-values with evenly spaced x-values.

FOIL Mnemonic device used to help remember the order to multiply binomials.

fractional coefficient Means that the number in front of the variable is a fraction.

frequency (f) The number of times per year that interest is compounded (daily = 365, monthly = 12, quarterly = 4, etc.).

function A special relation, (x, y), where for every x-value, there is exactly one corresponding y-value.

function machine A visual way of displaying the input x-values into a defined relation to produce the corresponding output y-values; a useful method in determining whether or not a relation is a function.

function notation Describes the output $f(x)$ as a result of an input of x into a function f. Function notation is also a way of describing the relationship between one variable as a function of another variable; for example, $h(t) = -2t^2 + t - 1$ describes the relationship between the height, $h(t)$, as a function of time, t.

GIC'S Guaranteed Investment Certificate; investing a sum of money for a specific amount of time in return for the principal plus interest. Often this money is locked in, long-term, and there are penalties for early withdrawals.

greatest common factor (GCF) The largest factor common for two or more numbers.

growth factor The constant ratio of successive y-values with evenly spaced x-values (usually 1) of a function describing exponential growth; the ratio is always greater than 1.

half-life The time it takes for a quantity (usually radioactive) to decay exponentially to half of its original value.

histograms Graphs that visually display continuous data.

horizontal line A line parallel to the x-axis in the Cartesian coordinate plane. Its equation is $y = b$.

horizontal midline axis (d) The horizontal line located halfway between the maximum and minimum points of an oscillating or sinusoidal periodic function, which is defined by the equation: $y = d = \dfrac{\text{maximum} + \text{minimum}}{2}$.

horizontal translation A transformation that moves the graph of a relation horizontally on a coordinate plane.

hypotenuse The longest side of a right triangle; the side that is directly opposite the right angle.

increasing interval The interval of x-values of the domain of a function, where the y-values of the range increase in value as you go from the lower to higher x-values of this interval; if the x-interval is the same as the domain, the function is called an increasing function.

initial arm The final position of an angle, θ, in standard position.

integers The set of all positive and negative whole numbers and zero.

interest rate The rate, usually stated as a percentage per year (annum), that determines the total interest (I_T) made on a principal.

interest rate per compounding period (i) The interest rate (as a decimal number) calculated by dividing the annual interest rate (given as a decimal number) by the frequency.

interior angle The angle on the inside of a closed two-dimensional geometric figure.

interpolation A process of predicting or estimating values between a given set of data based on the pattern portrayed.

intersecting lines Lines with one point in common (see point of intersection).

inverse The operation that cancels its opposite operation (addition and subtraction are inverses; multiplication and division are inverses).

isosceles triangle A triangle that has only two sides of equal length.

like terms Terms that have the same variables with identical exponents ($2y^2$ and $5y^2$).

line segment All the points including and between two given points.

linear function An equation of the form $f(x) = mx + b$.

linear relation A relation of the form $Ax + By + C = 0$, where both A and $B \neq 0$. The graph of this relation forms a straight line.

lower (minimum) limit The minimum x-value of the domain, or y-value of the range, due to restrictions pertaining to the context of a real-world application.

lowest common denominator (LCD) The lowest of all multiples shared by two or more numbers $\left(\text{LCD of } \dfrac{1}{2} \text{ and } \dfrac{1}{3} \text{ is } 6 \right)$.

mapping diagram A visual way of displaying the x-values of a relation with its corresponding y-value(s) using arrows; a useful method in determining whether or not a relation is a function.

maximum value The y-coordinate of the highest point of a parabola representing a quadratic function or a graph representing a sine function.

minimum value The y-coordinate of the lowest point of a parabola representing a quadratic function or a graph representing a sine function.

monomial A polynomial with only one term.

negative angles Angles in standard position that are formed by rotating clockwise.

negative interval The interval of x-values of the domain of a function, where the y-values of the range are less than zero.

net A two-dimensional representation of a three-dimensional object.

number of compounding periods (n) The total number of compounds of interest made on an invested or borrowed principal; it is usually calculated by multiplying the number of years by the frequency.

numerical expression An expression where all terms are numbers.

oblique triangle A triangle that does not contain an angle of 90°.

ordered pair A pair of numbers, (x, y), on a coordinate plane that signify the values of x and y for a given point on the plane.

origin The point of intersection of the horizontal and vertical axes on a graph, defined as $(0, 0)$.

parabola A U-shaped graph representing a quadratic relation.

parallel lines Lines in the same plane that are an equal distance apart and never meet. Parallel lines have the same slope but different y-intercepts.

parameters Variables that have transformational effects on a function; for example, a, c, and d are parameters of the transformed sine function $f(x) = a\sin(x - d) + c$.

payment period The time when a regular payment is made or withdrawn in an annuity; in an ordinary simple annuity, it coincides with the compounding period and occurs at the end of each period.

perfect square trinomial A trinomial of the form $ax^2 + bx + c$, where a and c are perfect squares; its two factored binomials are the same.

perimeter The measure of the distance around a closed figure.

period The length of the x-interval of each cycle of a periodic function.

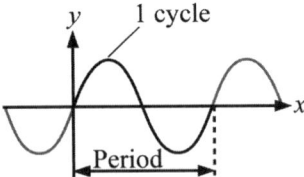

periodic function A function that has a consistent repeating pattern; the y-values repeat over regular x-intervals of the domain. If the y-values repeat between a maximum and minimum value, it is an oscillating or sinusoidal function.

point of intersection The point where two lines intersect and the x-values and the y-values for both lines are equal.

polynomial An algebraic expression that consists of one or more terms that are connected with addition or subtraction signs.

positive angles Angles in standard position that are formed by rotating counterclockwise.

positive interval The interval of x-values of the domain of a function, where the y-values of the range are greater than zero.

power An expression having a base and an exponent $\left(3^2, a^x, 8^{\frac{2}{3}}, 0.8^0 \right)$.

power rule for exponents An exponent law that states that when simplifying a power of a power, multiply the exponents.

present value (PV) The same as the principal (P).

primary data Data collected first-hand; original data collected through investigation.

principal (P) The original invested or borrowed amount.

product The value that results from multiplying numbers.

product rule for exponents An exponent law that states that when multiplying two powers of the same base, add the exponents.

Pythagorean theorem For any right triangle, the area of the square formed on the longest side is equal to the sum of the areas of the squares formed on the other two sides ($a^2 + b^2 = c^2$).

quadratic equation An equation in which the variable is squared and is of the form $ax^2 + bx + c = 0$, where $a \neq 0$.

quadratic formula A formula that can be used to find the exact roots of a quadratic equation, $ax^2 + bx + x = 0$, $a \neq 0$. This formula is given as: $x = \dfrac{-b \pm \sqrt{b^2 - 4ac}}{2a}$.

quadratic regression The process of determining the equation of the curve of best fit for a given set of data that appears to be quadratic.

quadratic relation A relation of the form $0 = Ax^2 + Bxy + Cy^2 + Dx + Ey + F$, in which $B = 0$ and A or $C = 0$ for the purpose of this course; for example, $y = Ax^2 + Dx + F$ or $x = Cy^2 + Ey + F$. The graph of this relation forms a parabola.

quadrilateral Any polygon with four sides (parallelogram, trapezoid, rhombus, rectangle, and square).

quotient rule for exponents An exponent law that states that when dividing two powers of the same base, subtract the exponents.

radian A unit to measure angles, that is useful in many problems involving sinusoidal motion; an angle setting on the graphing calculator.

radical An expression with a radical symbol $\sqrt{}$; for example $\sqrt{4}$, $\sqrt[3]{8^2}$, $\sqrt[n]{x}$.

radius (plural: radii) The distance from the centre of a circle to any point lying on the circumference of the circle (see diameter).

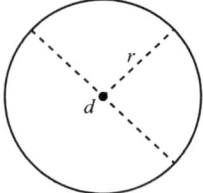

range The set of output (*y*-values) for which a particular relation is definded.

rate of change (linear relations) The ratio of $\dfrac{\text{change in } y\text{-values}}{\text{change in } x\text{-values}}$, which can also be represented as $\dfrac{\Delta y}{\Delta x}$.

rate of return The average annual rate of return would be the average percentage gained or lost per year.

ratio (of *y*-values) The quotient between consecutive *y*-values with evenly spaced *x*-values.

real numbers Numbers that are either rational (integers, fractions, decimal numbers) or irrational (radicals, trigonometric ratios, π) numbers.

reciprocal The multiplicative inverse of a number that has a product of 1 (the multiplicative inverse or reciprocal of $\dfrac{1}{3}$ is $\dfrac{3}{1}$).

rectangle A quadrilateral in which opposite sides are parallel to one another and equal in length, and adjacent sides are perpendicular to one another.

reflection in the *x*-axis A transformation in which all points on a relation that are above the *x*-axis are reflected below the *x*-axis and all points below the *x*-axis are reflected above the *x*-axis. This creates a mirror image, using the *x*-axis as a reflection line.

relation Any set of ordered pairs (x, y), where *x* is the input element and *y* is the corresponding output element.

retirement fund An annuity (like an RRSP) or investment, where the final accumulated amount is usually used by a retired person to provide a regular income during the retirement period.

revolution One complete rotation through an angle of 360°.

right triangle A triangle that has an interior angle of 90° (a right angle).

rise The vertical (*y*-value) change between two points.

roots of an equation The values for the variable that satisfy the equation.

RRSP (Registered Retirement Savings Plan) An investment where the final accumulated amount is usually used by a retired person to provide himself a regular income during the retirement period.

run The horizontal (*x*-value) change between two points.

sample A subgroup representative of the population.

scalene triangle A triangle where with three sides of different lengths.

scatter plot A graph used in statistics to display the relationship of the data of two variables. The points are plotted as ordered pairs on a coordinate plane.

second differences The differences between consecutive first differences with evenly spaced *x*-values.

secondary data Data that already exists or was created by someone else.

simple annuity An annuity where the payments or investments are made at the same time as the compounding period of interest. A simple ordinary annuity is an annuity where the payments or investments are made at the end of each interval of time.

simple interest Interest only earned on the original loan or investment (principal or present value). The formula for calculating simple interest is $I = \text{Pr}\,t$.

simplify To find an equivalent expression that is simpler (more reduced) than the original.

sine function A function defined by $f(x) = \sin x$. The graph of this function is a smooth, wavy curve.

sine law The sides and angles of a non-right triangle are related in a way, such that $\dfrac{a}{\sin A} = \dfrac{b}{\sin B} = \dfrac{c}{\sin C}$.

sinusoidal motion A function that models periodic motion, whose graph is a smooth, wavy curve (like that of a sine function).

sinusoidal regression The process of determining the equation of the sinusoidal curve of best fit, for a given set of data that appears to have a sinusoidal pattern.

slope The rate at which the *y*-values for a line on a coordinate plane change with respect to the change in the *x*-values. It is the measure of the steepness of a line.

slope formula The equation $m = \dfrac{y_2 - y_1}{x_2 - x_1}$ used to find the slope of a line; *m* is the slope. The numerator represents the rise, and the denominator represents the run of the line.

slope *y*-intercept form The equation of a line in the form $y = mx + b$, in which m is the slope and b is the *y*-intercept of the line.

sphere A three-dimensional geometric figure with points that are all equidistant from a given point. Any cross section of a sphere is a circle.

square A quadrilateral in which all four sides are equal in length, the opposite sides are parallel, and the adjacent sides are perpendicular.

standard form (quadratic function) The equation of a quadratic function in the form $f(x) = ax^2 + bx + c$, where $a \neq 0$ and $a, b, c \in \mathbb{R}$. The *y*-intercept of the graph is c.

standard position An angle, θ, is in standard position on the Cartesian plane, when the initial arm (positive *x*-axis) is rotated about the origin in a clockwise or counterclockwise direction, to a final position defined by the terminal arm.

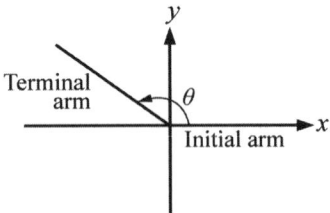

stocks Having a percentage share in the ownership of a company.

substitution When a specific value is used in place of a variable in an algebraic expression or equation.

sum The value that results from adding numbers.

supplementary angles Two angles that have a sum of exactly 180°.

table of values A table where the ordered pairs of a relation are recorded. Typically, the *x*-values are in the left column, and the *y*-values are in the right column.

term A value or algebraic expression separated by plus or minus signs.

terminal arm The initial position (positive *x*-axis) of an angle, θ, in standard position.

time The length of time that a principal earns interest.

time line A linear representation of regular deposits or withdrawals, and their compounded final or present values of an annuity.

transformations Any mapping of a figure that results in a change in position, shape, size, or appearance of the figure; for example, translations, reflections, stretches, and compressions are transformations.

transversal A line that intersects two or more parallel lines.

triangle A three-sided polygon; the sum of the measures of its interior angles is equal to $180°$.

trinomial Any polynomial with exactly three terms; for example, $x^2 + 2x + 1$ is a trinomial.

TVM Solver A program feature of graphing calculators that can be used to solve financial problems.

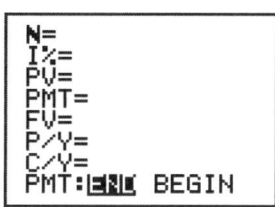

unit circle A circle centered at the origin on the Cartesian plane, so that every point $P(x, y)$ on the circle, is one unit from the origin.

upper (maximum) limit The maximum x-value of the domain, or y-value of the range, due to restrictions pertaining to the context of a real-world application.

variable A letter or symbol used to represent a value.

vertex form (quadratic function) The equation of a quadratic function in the form $f(x) = a(x - h)^2 + k$, where $a \neq 0$ and $h, k \in \mathbb{R}$. The vertex of the graph is (h, k).

vertex of a parabola The ordered pair where the maximum or minimum value of y occurs on the graph of a quadratic function.

vertical compression A transformation in which the graph of a relation vertically flattens.

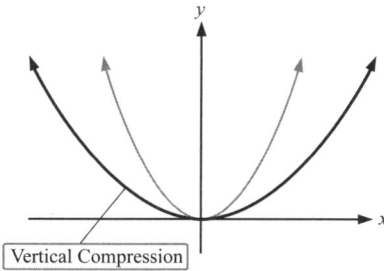

vertical line A line parallel to the y-axis in the Cartesian coordinate plane. Its equation is $x = a$.

vertical line test A test to determine if a relation is a function and can be stated as: "If any vertical line drawn through a relation intersects the graph at more than one point, the relation is not a function."

vertical stretch A transformation in which the graph of a relation becomes elongated vertically.

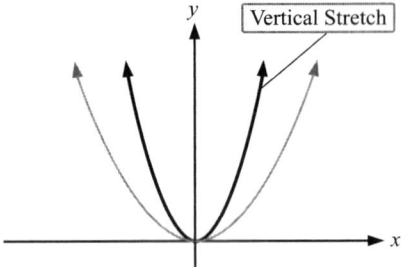

vertical translation A transformation that moves the graph of a relation vertically on a coordinate plane.

vertically-opposite angles Angles across two intersecting lines. These angles have the same measure.

volume The amount of space occupied by a three-dimensional figure measured in cubic units.

x-axis The horizontal number line on a coordinate plane.

x-coordinate The first number or symbol of an ordered pair.

x-intercept The value of x when y is equal to zero or the point where a line or curve crosses the x-axis.

y-axis The vertical number line on a coordinate plane.

y-coordinate The second number or symbol of an ordered pair.

y-intercept The value of y when x is equal to zero or the point where a line or curve crosses the y-axis.

zeros Values that make a function equal to 0. These are also known as the x-intercepts of the graph of a function.

CREDITS

Many photographs and clipart images in this study guide are reproduced under a licence agreement with www.clipart.com.

Statistics Canada information is used with the permission of Statistics Canada. Users are forbidden to copy this material and/or redisseminate the data, in an original or modified form, for commercial purposes, without the expressed permission of Statistics Canada. Information on the availability of the wide range of data from Statistics Canada can be obtained from Statistics Canada's Regional Offices, its World Wide Web site at http://www.statcan.gc.ca, and its toll-free access number 1-800-263-1136

RESOURCE INFORMATION   *Order online at www.castlerockresearch.com*

SCHOOL ORDERS

Schools are eligible for an education discount. Contact Castle Rock Research Ontario for more information.

THE KEY Study Guides assist in preparing students for course assignments, unit tests, and final or provincial assessments.

THE KEY **Study Guides** – $29.95 each plus G.S.T.

SECONDARY	ELEMENTARY
Biology 12, University Prep (SBI4U)	Science 8
Canadian and World Politics 12, University Prep (CPW4U)	Math 7
Chemistry 12, University Prep (SCH4U)	Science 7
English 12, University Prep (ENG4U)	Language 6 Reading & Writing
English 12, College Prep (ENG4C)	Math 6
Math 12 Advanced Functions, University Prep (MHF4U)	Science 6
Math 12 Calculus and Vectors, University Prep (MCV4U)	Math 5
Math 12 Data Management, University Prep (MDM4U)	Science 5
Physics 12, University Prep (SPH4U)	Math 4
World History 12, University Prep (CHY4U)	Science 4
Biology 11, University Prep (SBI3U)	Language 3 Reading & Writing
Chemistry 11, University Prep (SCH3U)	Math 3
English 11, University Prep (ENG3U)	Science 3
Math 11, Foundations for College Mathematics (MBF3C)	
Math 11, Functions and Applications, U/C Prep (MCF3M)	
Math 11, Functions, University Prep (MCR3U)	
World History 11, University/College Prep (CHW3M)	
Canadian History 10, Academic (CHC2D)	
Canadian History 10, Applied (CHC2P)	
Civics 10, (CHV2O)	
English 10, Academic (ENG2D)	
Math 10, Academic, Principles of Mathematics (MPM2D)	
Math 10, Applied, Foundations of Mathematics (MFM2P)	
OSSLT, Ontario Secondary School Literacy Test	
Science 10, Academic (SNC2D)	
English 9, Academic (ENG1D)	
Geography of Canada 9, Academic (CGC1D)	
Math 9, Academic, Principles of Mathematics (MPM1D)	
Math 9, Applied, Foundations of Mathematics (MFM1P)	
Science 9, Academic (SNC1D)	

The **Student Notes and Problems (SNAP)** workbooks provide complete lessons for course expectations, detailed explanations of concepts, and exercises with complete solutions.

SNAP Workbooks – $29.95 each plus G.S.T.

SECONDARY
Physics 12, University Preparation (SPH4U)
Physics 11, University Preparation (SPH3U)
Math 10, Academic, Principles of Mathematics (MPM2D)
Math 9, Academic, Principles of Mathematics (MPM1D)
Math 9, Applied, Foundations of Mathematics (MFM1P)

Visit our website for a tour of resource content and features or order online at
www.castlerockresearch.com

5250 Satellite Drive, Unit 11
Mississauga, ON L4W 5G5
E-mail: Ontario@castlerockresearch.com

Phone: 905.625.3332
Fax: 905.625.3390

CASTLE ROCK
RESEARCH CORP